Counseling in the Elementary School

A Comprehensive Approach

Robert L. Gibson
Indiana University

Marianne H. Mitchell
Indiana University

Sherry K. Basile
Indiana University

Allyn and Bacon
Boston • London • Toronto • Sydney • Tokyo • Singapore

Series Editor: Ray Short
Production Editorial Assistant: Christine Shaw
Production Administrator: Marjorie Payne
Editorial-Production Service: Chestnut Hill Enterprises, Inc.
Cover Administrator: Linda Dickinson
Composition Buyer: Linda Cox
Manufacturing Buyer: Louise Richardson

A Division of Simon & Schuster, Inc.
160 Gould Street
Needham Heights, Massachusetts 02194

Library of Congress Cataloging-in-Publication Data

Gibson, Robert L. (Robert Lewis)
Counseling in the elementary school: a comprehensive approach/ Robert L. Gibson, Marianne H. Mitchell, Sherry K. Basile.
p. cm.
Includes bibliographical references and index.
ISBN 0-205-14706-2
1. Counseling in elementary education—United States.
I. Mitchell, Marianne H II. Basile, Sherry K. III. Title.
LB1027. 5. C4565 1993
372. 14' 0973—dc20 92-29659
CIP

Printed in the United States of America

10 9 8 7 6 5 4 3 2 1 98 97 96 95 94 93

Contents

Preface

Counseling in the Elementary School: A Comprehensive Approach is primarily designed to introduce readers to the role and practice of counseling services in the elementary school. It is appropriate for use in introductory counseling courses and in related fields for those who seek a comprehensive overview of counseling services in the elementary school.

The objectives of this book are to provide the reader with an overview and general understanding of: (1) foundations and a rationale for counseling activities in the elementary school; (2) techniques utilized by counselors; (3) the organization of counseling programs; and (4) legal and ethical guidelines.

The initial chapters lead the reader from the appropriate historical background to the development of a rationale for counseling programs in the elementary school. This rationale is then translated into the elementary school counselor's role and function beginning in Chapters 3, 4, and 5, with the distinguishing activity of counselors—individual and group counseling. Chapter 6 discusses the important activity of classroom guidance at length. Chapters 7 through 10 discuss other basic activities of elementary school counseling and guidance programs including career development, the current and vitally important areas of prevention, consultation, and pupil assessment. Chapter 11 deals with the developing and managing of counseling and guidance programs and their improvement through accountability, evaluation, and research. The final chapter presents legal and ethical considerations and invites readers to anticipate their own personal as well as professional development.

As an introductory text, this book is relatively informal in style in the hope that it may be readable and enjoyable as well as informative.

Finally, we would like to acknowledge all those who have contributed directly and indirectly to the undertaking and completion of this book. These include, of course, the helpful staff of Allyn and Bacon, particularly Mr. Ray Short, editor. We would like to acknowledge the valuable comments of our reviewers, Eileen R. Matthay, Southern Connecticut State University; Reece

Chaney, Indiana State University; Kenneth Matzner, Eastern Illinois State University; Roger L. Hutchinson, Ball State University; Mary Farnum, Northern Illinois University; and Dorlesa Barmettler-Ewing, California State University, Hayward, and we are extremely grateful to the many considerate authors and publishers who granted us permission to quote from their publications. We appreciate the useful suggestions from our departmental colleagues at Indiana University, our fellow counselor-educators who volunteered their time and comments for guidance. We personally acknowledge Jodi Peterson, who, while in third grade, expressed in a poem, "Counselors for Kids," her interpretation of the function of elementary school counselors. We recognize the late Mary Joe Hannaford, whose poem, "A Counselor's Task", captures the spirit and encompasses the levels of human helping provided by counselors. We also acknowledge East Park (West Virginia) Elementary School, Nathan Hale (Toledo, Ohio), and Berkeley (South Carolina) Elementary School whose teachers, administrators, and children contributed to our personal and professional growth and development. We especially acknowledge the thousands of children whose eagerness to learn about themselves, others, and life, perpetuated our understanding of the importance of creating an environment conducive to the discovery of their human potential. We appreciate as well the critical comments of our graduate students (who undoubtedly had in mind the well-being of their counterparts of the future). We are particularly thankful for the patience and persistence of our graduate assistants, Victoria Manion, Brenda Dodds, and Michael C. Altekruse. We also want to give a special vote of thanks to Ms. Camille Sexton-Villalta, an advanced doctoral student at Indiana University who has given extraordinary effort and sacrificed a great deal of personal time in order to ensure the timely production of this text. Her contribution exceeded our capacity to acknowledge in this preface! In conclusion, we acknowledge our close friends and families who have patiently endured our absences and preoccupations while maintaining faith in this project and in us.

R. L. G.
M. H. M.
S. K. B.

Chapter 1

Introduction to Counseling and Guidance in the Elementary School

"I do not know
what your destiny will be,
but this I do know—
the only ones among you
who will be truly happy
are those who
will have sought for
and found a way to serve."
—ALBERT EINSTEIN

Introduction

This introductory chapter is designed to establish a context within which interested readers can visualize the development of counseling programs in elementary schools over the years leading to a rationale and role and function for today's elementary schools. We also invite you, our readers, to examine our "roots," noting with us that while psychology provides a major base for much of what we do, sociology and anthropology are also important contributors to our rationale as well as to our role and function. The last sections of this chapter will discuss this rationale and then translate these "reasons for" into roles and functions; what elementary counselors do, and hence need to know about a basis for the chapters which follow.

Historical and Educational Foundations

Elementary schools have been, since colonial days in America, the most powerful and influential force in developing an educated and socially competent citizenry in this country. Of all the basic institutions of our society, the home and the school are the most influential in determining what the individual and this country of individuals shall be.

> *After the first grade, an increasingly large proportion of the child's life will be dominated by the school. Even outside of school hours, the demands of school through homework assignments, the social obligations and ties of school clubs and activities, and the ways in which school structures children's social networks, make the school a salient force in the child's daily existence. (Hetherington & Parke, 1986, p. 579)*

Although the family as well as the school contribute most extensively to the ongoing development of the child, as a socialization institution, the school differs from the family in that

> *it is more impersonal; the contacts and relationships between adults and children are short-term; the child has contact with a range of adults who offer views different from one another and different in some ways from those of the parents; and evaluation of performance is comparative, public and recurring. (Hetherington and Parke, 1986, p. 579)*

Within the educational hierarchy, the elementary school has been and remains, the most influential of all schools for both the individual and the nation. This importance is highlighted because: (a) the elementary school serves everyone—everyone is required to go; and (b) the elementary school provides the individual with the educational and psychological foundations of one's life.

Thus, the professionals who staff our nation's elementary schools—the teachers, administrators, counselors, and others—are critically important and significant in determining our future as a nation and the future of the millions of individuals who populate our nation.

And what does this most important institution, the elementary school seek to achieve? Traditionally, its basic objectives would appear to be:

1. Providing a basic education in the fundamental literacy skills of reading, writing and mathematics.
2. Transmission of our cultural and historical foundations and preparation for citizenship.

In addition to these traditional objectives, in the last half of the present century, personal/social development has also taken on major significance as a goal of elementary education. As noted by Jarolimek and Foster (Reprinted with permission of Macmillan Publishing Company from *Teaching and Learning in the Elementary School* by John Jarolimek and Clifford D. Foster, Sr. Copyright © 1989 by Macmillan Publishing Company.),

> *Today, the personal growth of individual children, concern about each individual's potential for development, and the broadening of school goals to include emotional, social, and physical growth as well as intellectual development are seen as major purposes of elementary education. The nation expects its elementary schools to be concerned about individual children, to help them develop a sense of self-identity, to help them get to feel good about themselves, to help them know what their individual talents are, and to help them set realistic goals for themselves. (p. 6)*

Thus, while curriculum programs in elementary schools are based on the teaching and learning of the basic knowledge which provide foundations for lifelong learning and earning, counseling programs in elementary schools are based on developing the basic social-personal foundations for lifelong living. These two dimensions represent the knowledge of a culture and the behavior of a culture. They are obviously interrelated. The neglect of one handicaps and lessens the potential of others.

Within this educational context, the broad goal of the elementary school counseling and guidance program is to help each individual pupil prepare to become the best person he or she can become, both academically and personally! As such, the elementary school counseling and guidance programs represent the ultimate effort of a school system to enhance its instructional program and the development of its individual pupils. Even so, elementary school counseling programs are relative newcomers to the U.S. educational scene.

In fact, as we examine the historical framework of the development of education in this country with special attention given to the development of counseling and guidance programs in our elementary schools, it is only in this century that we have noted increased attention to the social-psychological development of the child in the elementary school. The further accenting of this attention through elementary school programs of counseling and guidance is of even more recent vintage. In examining the origins of the elementary school counseling movement, it appears that it probably had its beginning in the mid 1920's and early 1930's, stimulated by the writings and efforts of William Burnham. Faust (1968) indicated that Burnham emphasized the important role of the teacher in the mental health of children in the elementary school. Efforts to develop guidance in elementary schools during this period were scarcely noticeable, but a few notable programs were undertaken. One of these, in Winnetka, Illinois, established a department of elementary counseling with resource personnel for guidance. These personnel included (although not all on a full-time basis) psychiatrists, psychometrists, psychologists, an educational counselor, a psychiatric social worker, and supporting clerical services. Their basic responsibilities were counseling, child study, psychotherapy, pupil analysis, parental assistance, and referrals.

Despite the efforts of Burnham and a handful of others such as Ruth Strang, Harry Smallenberg and Ruth Masterson, it was not until the 1950s that textbooks and journal articles addressing counseling and guidance in elementary schools began to appear in appreciable numbers.

Perhaps, as with other segments of the school counseling movement, it was the National Defense Education Act of 1958 that provided the first significant stimulus for the development of elementary school programs of counseling and guidance. Title V-A of the NDEA provided funding for school counseling programs and Title V-B established funds to support the training of counselors. In 1964, NDEA expanded its focus to include elementary schools, junior colleges, and technical schools. This amendment provided an impetus for the legitimization of elementary school counseling.

A number of training institutes focused on the preparation of counselors for elementary school settings, including a two-year (1964-1965) training institute at Arizona State University directed by an early leader in this field, Verne Faust. However, despite the opportunities to train elementary counselors under the National Defense Education Act in the 1960s, there did not appear to be a commensurate interest on the part of school systems to employ them. Even in the 1970s the growth of counseling in our nation's elementary schools appears to have been slow and uncertain. This sparse attention to elementary counseling prior to the 1980s resulted in generations of today's adults and parents passing through our nation's elementary schools untouched and unaware of the role and contributions which counseling programs can offer to elementary schools and their pupils. Counseling and guidance programs were viewed—and are still viewed by many—as a secondary school phenomena, often focused on college and/or career placement. This public lack of awareness and understanding has handicapped the growth of elementary counseling programs even in current times when the needs appear to be so overwhelming and obvious to the counseling profession.

However, in the 1980s, stimulated by a number of social concerns affecting children (for example, child abuse, substance abuse, sexual abuse, latchkey children, and so on) and the prevention movement, elementary school counseling programs began to rapidly increase in numbers and scope. As we entered the 1990s, twelve states had mandated elementary school counselors, with more moving in this direction (see Table 1–1), and the influential regional associations accrediting elementary and secondary schools had added criteria requiring guidance programs and personnel in elementary schools. (See Appendix B.)

As the need for elementary counselors is increasingly recognized, it should also be increasingly clear that the elementary school counselor faces a most challenging task as she or he seeks to understand and effectively assist that most complicated, ever-changing and difficult to understand human organism, the elementary school child. When we place these complicated and changing human beings in their complex and changing environments, we recognize the enormity of the task of those who seek to understand, predict, assist, and stimulate the development of the elementary school pupil. Because of these complexities, elementary school counselors may be assisted by examining the learnings of other interested disciplines. The next section will identify some of these possibilities.

TABLE 1–1 States Mandating Elementary School Counseling (1990-1991 Academic Year)

Alabama	New Hampshire
Arkansas	North Carolina
Hawaii	South Carolina
Iowa	Vermont
Maine	Virginia
Montana	West Virginia

Interdisciplinary Foundations

In undertaking this challenging responsibility, we may appropriately pause to recognize that many disciplines are concerned with the contributors to our study of human beings and their behavior. In medicine alone, an array of specialists, especially psychiatrists, investigate the human body and mind. Our physiological functioning is also researched by biologists and physiologists. Other disciplines, such as anthropology, examine our cultural background and behavior while sociologists and social psychologists examine human behavior in the context of social situations or social groupings.

To this end, then, we may hope to broaden our understanding of the development and behavior of elementary school children by insights gained through the study of behavior in this context of other disciplines. The paragraphs which follow are not intended to substitute for such study. Rather, they are intended to examine each discipline briefly, and hopefully, to stimulate the readers' further understanding of the perspectives of anthropologists, sociologists, and psychologists. Furthermore, they serve to highlight the implications that each field offers in assisting elementary school children effectively, while also reminding us of our interdisciplinary "roots".

Anthropology

In recent generations, attention has been increasingly given to our multicultural diversity as a nation and its implications for such institutions as education. We have been called upon to become more sensitive and responsive to the traditions and rights of our various ethnic-cultural populations as a nation, and also, as a helping profession. As a profession, we may look to the field of anthropology for knowledge and insights that will increase our helpfulness to all the populations which we have the opportunity to serve.

Anthropology may be viewed as a discipline which studies human beings from a holistic science viewpoint. Within the discipline, two major categories, cultural and physical, are illustrative of the breadth of study in the field. Cultural anthropology is concerned with the cultures of peoples, past and present. It is the study of what the human species has learned to do and is doing in order to adapt and exist. This study includes the examination of socially learned traditions and other causes of contemporary life-styles. Physical anthropology, on the other hand, focuses on the study of human evolution and the relative contributions to human life made by heredity, environment, and culture.

Anthropologists view culture as reflecting the way of life of a society. This way of life is represented by a consensus of behaviors and opinions which are often referred to as *patterns*. These patterns comprise the culture as a whole which in turn provides the society's members with guidelines for living in the society. From such guidelines come concepts of acceptable or *normal* behavior versus behavior which the society deems as unacceptable or abnormal. The accepted or normal behaviors are taught to members of the society, first by the home and later by the school, and implemented by the other basic institutions of the society (government, religions, economic structures, and so on). The individual is motivated to assume or learn these normal behaviors because they quickly prove to be more satisfying for meeting needs and developing social relationships.

Here we note that cultures set priorities for behavioral development by guiding parents in their child-rearing practices and developmental emphasis.

Thus, from an early age, culture influences the early personality development of the child as she or he adapts behaviors that have satisfying results. The anthropological viewpoint is that much, perhaps most, human behavior is taught. For the counselor, it is important to know what the imposed behavioral norms are of the culture and the subcultures as represented by the family and the school. This is obviously important when, for example, the counselor has need to penetrate the facade of social conformity to reach the authentic and "real self" of the client. In addition, other anthropological insights can assist counselors in: (a) recognizing the importance of and differences in the ethnic and cultural backgrounds, including cultural expectancies and conditions influencing both the client and the counselor; (b) differing cultural traditions and their relative influence on schools, pupils/clients, and the development of counseling programs in such settings as elementary schools; and (c) identifying the various cultures and subcultures within the larger societal context and their similarities and differences.

The United States is a country of cultural diversity. In fact, the United States has become more ethnically, culturally, and racially diverse during the last twenty years . . . . and current predictions indicate this trend will continue as well as grow . . . . Further, it is predicted that minorities will constitute majorities in fifty major cities in the United States by the year 2000 (Heid, 1988, p.v.). It has been predicted that by the year 2000, one in three Americans will be white (Clabaugh, 1989).

The recognition of this diversity among the United States population in recent generations has had an impact on the counseling profession, including the development of multicultural counseling. Further, learning to recognize, understand, and accept cultural differences will require ongoing alertness by elementary school counselors and teachers as growing numbers of immigrant children from third-world and other countries enter our elementary schools. The multiculturally aware counselor in the elementary school must, therefore, be an "agent of awareness" to insure that these children's initial school experiences are not diminished by prejudice, tradition, ignorance, or other restrictive forces operating in the school. Additional attention to counseling multicultural populations will be given in Chapter Four.

Sociology

Sociology is concerned with such topics as social interaction, culture, stratification, bureaucracy, population, age and gender roles, collective behavior, ecology, power and politics, norms and values, urban development, and crime and deviance. (Eshleman, Cashion, & Basirico, 1988, p. 6)

Sociologists investigate other areas including: racial and ethnic relationships, prejudice and discrimination, power and politics, jobs and income, families and family life, school systems and the educational process, social control, organizations, bureaucracies, groups and group dynamics, leisure, health, military systems, women's movements, and labor movements. The stratification of people by wealth, education, power, and differences due to sex or age may also be examined. As you can see, sociology is an extremely broad field. (Eshleman, Cashion & Basirico, 1988, p. 8)

Sociology as a discipline, engages in the study of human groups and their influence on human behavior. These human groups are emergent social phenomena with qualities, properties, or characteristics of their own that can be different and unpredictable from the characteristics of the individuals who comprise the group. For example,

If you knew nothing about the kind of group we call a school "class," you would be unable to predict the classroom behavior of other people even if you knew everything about them personally. But if you know that a given number of anonymous strangers are to be members of your class, you will be able to predict much of their classroom behavior with high accuracy from your acquired experience in previous classes. Further, similar groups have similar properties. All lecture classes, like all football teams, are more alike than they are different, phenomena again unknowable from information about the personal characteristics of their members. The human social group, thus, is a subject matter with properties of its own and worthy of study in its own right. (McGee, 1980, p. 8)

The sociologist studies the values of a culture and their relationship to social structures from which a pattern of norms or expectancies emerge. Thus, families, play groups, teachers, and schools have norm patterns that the developing child is expected to adopt. This process of adapting shapes the personality of the developing child and will sooner or later influence the various roles the individual chooses to play. Sociologists then, like counselors, are interested in the study of human groupings and their influences on individual behaviors.

Sociologists are not only interested in the consistencies of patterns, as reflective of social norms, but they are also interested in social change and seek to explain how societies are changing. It is therefore helpful for counselors to understand "the sociological perspective." Eshleman, Cashion and Basirico (1988) describe this perspective as "a way of looking at society and social behavior" (p. 8).

The sociological perspective can provide insights for counselors in, for example, such understandings as: (a) patterns of normal versus abnormal behaviors; (b) the impact of socialization agencies (for example, school, family) and social networks on the individual; (c) groups and structures within society; and (d) the development of the individual's self-concept as well as the influence of significant others and reference groups on these developments. These perspectives will be given additional attention, as appropriate, in the chapters which follow.

Psychology

Of the various scientific disciplines, psychology has been the one most intimately associated with the profession of counseling. Over the years, psychological contributions to the practice of counseling have included counseling theory and process, individual and group techniques, standardized assessment instruments and procedures, and career development and decision-making theories. Traditionally, psychology has also been one of the disciplines most closely related to the study of children and their education. Psychology, along with its first cousins—measurement, educational psychology, and human development studies—is of special importance to counselors due to the nature of their concern for children and the educative process.

For a clear understanding of the development of psychological influences on practices in the elementary school, it is helpful for the counselor to understand how psychology was weaned from its mother, metaphysics, in the 19th century, and then started on its way to becoming a methodical study of behavior by persons like William James, G. Stanley Hall, Wilhelm Wundt, and Joseph M. Rice. Later, Freud, Jung, and Adler had important roles in probing the inner being. The understanding of learning was advanced by the Gestaltists such as Kohler, Koffka, and Wertheimer, while behaviorists like Lashley and Watson proposed the connectionist theory, or stimulus leads to response interpretations of learning. Currently, we recognize that many present-day practices stemmed from, and are still influenced by, these early insights. They include certain basic teaching methods, certain approaches to therapy, and certain forms of programmed learning.

Related work by such giants in the early era of testing or assessment as Binet, Terman, Thorndike, and Pintner is also important. In recent generations, however, corporate development of scales and tests, such as those by the Educational Testing Service of Princeton and Science Research Associates of Chicago, has largely replaced major test development by individuals in the Binet tradition and has led to large-scale, systemwide testing programs, often deemed excessive, across the country. However viewed, testing remains an important, if controversial, field that is closely tied to elementary education and counseling programs in elementary schools.

Elementary counseling has also been influenced by a number of ideas and concepts in the blurred borderland between psychology and human development research. Examples are such widely known contributions as Gesell's longitudinal studies of infants' and children's growth, Olson's idea of *organismic age*, Havighurst's *developmental tasks*, and Erikson's *eight ages of man.*

Learning theory and our knowledge of human development and its evaluation have been extended through work in the field of psychology. It is important to recognize that learning is an ongoing process as insights regarding both the learner and learning continue to accumulate.

To further underscore the relationship between psychology and counseling, we would note that the practice of psychology, as defined in the statement below by the American Psychological Association (1967), stresses developmental as well as remedial activities. This statement refers to the practice of psychology (including counseling psychology) as:

> *rendering to individuals, groups, organizations, or the public a psychological service involving the application of principles, methods and procedures of understanding, predicting and influencing behavior, such as the principles pertaining to learning, perception, motivation, thinking, emotions, and interpersonal relationships; the methods and procedures of interviewing, counseling, and psychotherapy; of constructing, administering, and interpreting tests of mental abilities, aptitudes, interests, attitudes, personality characteristics, emotions, and motivation; and of assessing public opinion.*
>
> *The application of said principles and methods includes but is not restricted to: diagnoses, prevention, and amelioration of individuals and groups; hypnosis; educational and vocational counseling; personnel selection and management; the evaluation and planning for effective work and learning situations; advertising and market research; and the resolution of interpersonal and social conflicts. (pp. 1098-1099)*

Within the general field of psychology are specialty areas of particular interest to counselors and teachers who are working with elementary school children. These include in addition to counseling psychology, educational psychology, school psychology, developmental psychology, social psychology, and ecological psychology.

Developmental psychologists are interested in why and how the human organism grows and changes from conception through birth and over the life span. In this context Mussen, Conger, Kagan and Huston (1984) defined development as:

> *changes in a person's physical and neurological structures, behavior, and traits that emerge in orderly ways and are reasonably enduring. In the first 20 years of*

life, these changes usually result in new, improved ways of reacting—that is, in behavior that is healthier, more organized, more complex, more stable, more competent, or more efficient. We speak of the advances from creeping to walking, from babbling to talking, from concrete to abstract thinking as development. In each instance, we judge the later appearing state to be a more adequate way of functioning than the earlier one. (p. 7)

Developmental psychology helps us understand the universal changes that take place in children as they grow older. It also helps us further understand individual differences in behavior and situational influences on behavior.

Social psychologists study in a scientific way how individuals are affected by social situations. This includes examining, for example, the socialization process and social influences, attitudes and attitude changes, attribution, interpersonal interactions, group dynamics, and influences of environment on behavior, etcetera. The term *social situations* refers:

to any event that occurs in a person's environment. Such an event may, and usually does, involve other people. Therefore, social psychology encompasses such matters as the ways in which people come together to form groups and the ways in which people influence and are influenced by others. It even studies how people are influenced by their own actions and behaviors. (Worchel & Cooper, 1983, p. 9)

Educational psychology involves the combination of the fields of psychology and education whereby scientific study focuses on the principles by which learning for the human can be increased and directed. (From Janice T. Gibson and Louis A. Chandler, *Educational Psychology: Mastering Principles and Applications*, copyright © 1988 by Allyn and Bacon. Reprinted with permission.)

Educational psychologists study the growth and development processes. The purposes are to isolate the principles responsible for both the differences and the similarities in students and to develop teaching techniques suitable for diverse situations and for various students . . . . they study human development . . . . Many developmental changes occur simply as a result of biological aging . . . . Many differences in behavior and ways students learn in school also occur as a result of environmental conditions . . . . The educational psychologist also studies the individual differences caused by these factors and their effects on the ways students learn . . . . The educational psychologist studies classroom learning in order to increase the effectiveness of teaching. Principles shown to be effective are tested, revised, and retested to be certain of their use in the classroom. Behavioral approaches to learning, shown to be critical to classroom learning, are included here . . . . Classroom learning also involves cognitive approaches to learning, including the examination of problem-solving strategies, learning styles, and methods to process and store learned material. The educational psychologist finally studies social learning, including the learning provided by teachers who model behaviors that students imitate and identify with. Today, with increased use of computers in school, educational psychologists are also studying the effects on learning of computer-assisted instruction. . . . The educational psychologist develops methods of evaluating teaching and learning accomplishments so that he or she can discriminate between students who have learned and students who have not learned, as well as between teaching methods that have been successful and those that have not. (Gibson and Chandler, 1988, pp. 4-8)

The role of school psychology, according to the American Psychological Association (APA), is the protection and promotion of mental health and the facilitation of learning in educational settings (Reynolds, Gutkin, Elliott, & Witt, 1984).

APA (1977) refers to the following services as being provided by school psychology:

A. *Psychological and psychoeducational evaluation and assessment of school functioning of children and young persons. Procedures include screening, psychological and educational tests (particularly individual psychological tests of intellectual functioning, cognitive development, affective behavior, and neuropsychological status), interviews, observation, and behavioral evaluations, with explicit regard for the context and setting in which the professional judgments based on assessment, diagnosis, and evaluation will be used.*
B. *Interventions to facilitate the functioning of individuals or groups, with concern for how schooling influences and is influenced by their cognitive, conative, affective and social development . . .*
C. *Interventions to facilitate the educational services and child care functions of school personnel, parents, and community agencies . . .*
D. *Consultation and collaboration with school personnel and/or parents concerning specific school-related problems of students and the professional problems of staff.*
E. *Program development services to individual schools, to school administrative systems, and to community agencies in such areas as needs assessment and evaluation of regular and special education programs; liaison with community, state, and federal agencies concerning the mental health and educational needs of children; coordination, administration, and planning of specialized educational programs; the generation, collection, organization, and dissemination of information from psychological research and theory to educate staff and parents (as seen in Reynolds, et al., 1984, pp. 393-394).*

Ecological psychologists are concerned with how individuals perceive, are shaped by, value and influence their environments. Kurt Lewin (1936) forecast most of this ecological concept with his formula of behavior as a function of persons interacting with their environment . That is, behavior is a function of the person times the environment, which is expressed algebraically as:

$$(E) \cdot B = f(P, E)$$

While Roger Barker and his colleagues at the University of Kansas were studying the ecological psychology of naturally occurring environments in the 1950s, it is only in recent years that increased interest in the application of this viewpoint to the practice of counseling has been noted by Conyne (1987) and others. Within this framework, it is suggested that counselors can, for example, improve their understanding of clients by recognizing the following concepts:

1. Behavior is influenced extensively by environment. In order to predict, control, modify, or prevent behaviors in children we must understand this concept.

2. The individual student's self-concept development and adjustment are affected by significant social environments which include the home, school, and neighborhood.

3. Expectations for behavior, values, and attitudes are generated and passed on through stable, long-term settings. The acceptable limits of deviant behavior, styles of coping, and adjusting are determined in these settings also.

4. A basis for prevention can be provided by understanding that specific environmental settings stimulate certain behaviors.

5. Children strive for optimal environments which will fulfill their needs, maximize their potential, provide opportunities for supporting relationships, and encourage hope for an enjoyable life.

Schools and children cannot be understood on the basis of data alone (for example, test scores, retention rates, reading levels, and so on). Children perform on the stage of life. To understand what they're playing, we must understand the setting. Ecological psychology, then, helps us to better understand children by understanding their psychological interplay with their environment.

Counseling Foundations

Counseling: A Helping Profession

As we broaden our background for examining the potential for counselors and counseling programs in the elementary school, it is important to recognize that in the occupational hierarchy of our society, counseling is viewed as a helping profession. This label "helping profession" has obvious implications for those who aspire to and practice under the title. As a "professional," we are a qualified member or worker in a profession. A true profession is distinguished by the following characteristics:

1. *The members perform a unique and definite social service;*
2. *Performance of the specified social service rests primarily upon intellectual techniques;*

3. *Society has delegated to qualified members of the occupational group exclusive authority to provide the specified social service;*
4. *The members possess a common body of knowledge which can be identified and can be communicated through intellectual processes of higher education;*
5. *Entry into qualified membership requires an extensive period of specialized training;*
6. *The members as a corporate group assure minimum competence for entry into the occupation by setting and enforcing standards for selection, training, and licensure or certification;*
7. *The members possess a broad range of autonomy in performing the specified social service;*
8. *The members accept broad personal responsibility for judgments made and acts performed in providing the specified social service;*
9. *Emphasis is placed upon service to society rather than upon economic gain in the behavior of the corporate group as well as in the performance on the specified social service by individual members;*
10. *Standards of professional conduct for members are made explicit by a functional code of ethics; and*
11. *Throughout his career the member constantly takes positive steps to update his competency by keeping abreast of relevant technical literature, research, and participation in meetings of the corporate group of members. (McCully, 1969, p. 18)*

The helping professions, including medicine, psychology, social work, and education, are distinguished by the unique and needed professional services they provide for their fellow human beings. Helping professionals serve. They seek to enhance the lives and living of the populations that they as professionals are prepared to serve.

Counselors, as professionals, usually function within some sort of organizational context; for example, counseling department, agency, institution, private practice, and so on. These may be viewed as human service organizations that are designed to provide direct professional services to a specified population. Such organizations represent a professional effort to merge resources, knowledge, and practices in order to meet recognized societal needs.

Counseling is also a discipline, a discipline which engages in the ongoing pursuit of knowledge with the purpose of advancing itself as a human service profession. While, as a discipline, we have our roots in the field of psychology, we also benefit from our liaisons with other related scientific disciplines such as anthropology and sociology. As a discipline, we also pursue our own uniqueness. We value our responsibility to serve "the many"—to serve whole populations through such organizational settings as schools, even while attending to the needs of individual clients as well. While we recognize the importance of remediation, we also emphasize, especially in the elementary school, the critical importance of development, enrichment, and prevention.

A Rationale for Counseling Programs in the Elementary School

Elementary schools are a powerful force in shaping human development. For better or worse, virtually all members of modern society carry important impressions from their elementary school experience throughout their lives. The school places two broad sets of adaptive demands on the child. The individual child must learn to master and assimilate increasingly complex bodies of knowledge, as well as meet the school environment's behavioral and interpersonal requirements. These two sets of demands often interlock; thus, failing to adapt to the school's ecological and sociological expectations restricts the child's ability to learn, just as deficits in educational mastery generate psychological or personal adaptive problems (Cowen, Trost, Lorion, Dorr, Izzo, & Isaacson 1975).

It is precisely around the intercept of these two sets of requirements that specialized school mental health and psychological services first came into being and are still its prime justification. School adjustment and development problems of young children—whether educational or behavioral—are rampant, and the specialized school mental health services available for dealing with them in most locales, are limited and spread thin. Therefore, past services have necessarily been limited to a tiny fraction of school children—those with the most serious and evident, non-postponable problems. This has left many others who are in desperate, but less obvious, need of help to find their own way, as best they can, or flounder.

These facts raise several obvious questions. How can the school experience be optimized for all children? How can effective helping services for the great masses of young children who urgently need such help be provided to not only remediate ongoing ills, but better yet, to prevent them in the first place? And how can such services enhance the childrens' special talents so that they can develop to their fullest potential?

This consideration takes on increased urgency as we become familiar with the growing body of evidence (Allen, Chinsky Larcen, Lochman, & Selinger, 1976; Cowen, Pederson, Babigian, Izzo, & Trost, 1973; Dodge, 1983, and others) which indicates that individuals who have problems early in their developmental history tend to have more serious problems in later years as well. Elementary school counseling and guidance programs seek, through prevention and development, not only a reduction in the incidence of detrimental behaviors among their pupils at that educational level, but also to enhance the later functioning of all individuals in their schools as they become adult members of our society. Statewide studies of elementary school counseling programs such as those in North Carolina and Indiana indicate this potential.

Counseling programs are intended to reinforce, enhance, and stimulate the total educational effort in the elementary school. They represent the ultimate effort of a school system to foster the human potential fulfillment of the elementary school pupils and assure their positive future.

Role and Function of Counselors in the Elementary School

We have very briefly examined the role of elementary education and the elementary school in U. S. society as one responsible for providing the basic foundations for lifelong learning and living. We have also noted the historical development of counseling and guidance programs in our nation's elementary schools. Additionally, we have briefly examined interdisciplinary perspectives for not only our "roots," but also for broadening our understandings of human behavior.

We noted that anthropology can provide us with vital knowledge regarding the various cultures of our societies and the problems of youth from differing cultural backgrounds in our multicultural society. These understandings will help us recognize what the elementary counselor needs to know in order to be equally helpful to all elementary school pupils. Sociology can enrich our understandings of human groupings and how they affect behavior. These groupings include the family and those common to the elementary school. Sociology also examines social and ethnic relationships and the problems of prejudice which the elementary school counselor may be called upon to address in their role and function. We have noted the close relationships between psychology and counseling, especially in terms of child development, learning theory, measurement, and the impact of environments. An overview of counseling as a profession and as a discipline has also been provided.

The previous paragraphs proposed a rationale for counseling and guidance programs in the elementary school: a rationale based on both individual need and societal need.

It is within these contexts that we now proceed to examine an old question: "What should a counselor do in an elementary school?" How should you spend your time as a counselor in an elementary school? What is your appropriate role and function? Certainly a number of role and function studies have been reported over the past twelve years. Similar results from these studies may serve as guidelines for beginning elementary school counselors to use from the standpoint of looking at what most of the currently practicing elementary school counselors are doing. For example, in a survey of 54 California elementary school counselors (Furlong, Atkinson & Janoff, 1979), individual counseling, consulting, and parent-help were ranked, in order, as the activities which were most time-consuming in their roles as elementary school counselors. Bonebrake and Borgers (1984) surveyed elementary and middle school counselors and principals and reported the counselors' indications that individual counseling was their highest priority activity, followed by consultation with teachers, student assessment, and parent consultation. Morse and Russell (1988) discussed a study based on responses of 130 Pacific Northwest elementary school counselors which compared how they actually spent their time with how they would ideally like to spend their time. The highest items in these comparative categories may be noted in Table 1–2.

TABLE 1–2 Counselors' Highest and Lowest Rated Items on the Actual and Ideal Scales

Five highest actual items	M	SD	Five highest ideal items	M	SD
Help students with special needs by making appropriate educational referrals within the district	2.43	.78	Help the teacher better understand individual students' behaviors, attitudes and progress	2.80	.44
Work with school psychologists and educational specialists to meet needs of individual students	2.34	.74	Work with students in groups to help them learn appropriate social skills.	2.74	.56
Work with students individually to help them understand their feelings	2.33	.81	Work with students in groups to enhance self-concepts	2.72	.57
Help the teacher better understand individual students' needs by discussing students' behaviors, attitudes, and progress	2.32	.73	Work with students in groups to help them understand their feelings	2.70	.58
Work with students individually to enhance self-concepts	2.27	.78	Work with students in groups to develop problem-solving skills	2.65	.61
Five lowest actual items			**Five lowest ideal items**		
Help manage student behavior by serving as school disciplinarian	.60	.84	Assist school administrators in the evaluation of classroom teachers	.76	1.02
Serve as substitutes in the absence of classroom teachers	.52	.81	Ensure student safety by serving as playground supervisor	.39	.68
Evaluate the effectiveness of the guidance and counseling pro-gram by following the progress of students through the higher grade levels and new schools	.51	.66	Ensure student safety by serving as lunchroom supervisor	.25	.57
Ensure student safety by serving as lunchroom supervisor	.46	.84	Help manage student behavior by serving as school disciplinarian	.24	.48
Assist school administrators in the evaluation of classroom teachers	.46	.69	Serve as substitutes in the absence of classroom teachers	.21	.55

From "How elementary counselors see their role: An empirical study" by C. L. Morse and T. Russell. *Elementary School Guidance and Counseling*, 23, p. 58. Copyright 1988 by the American Counseling Association. Reprinted by permission.

A recent comprehensive study (Gibson, 1989) regarding the roles of counselors, which represented 96 elementary school counseling programs in 42 states, reported the major functions of elementary-school counselors as noted in Table 1–3.

This study also noted that while most programs had at least a dual emphasis, prevention was viewed as a major emphasis by 85 percent of the programs reporting, followed by developmental (78 percent) and remedial (64 percent). Other frequently noted emphases were enhancement and crisis intervention.

A review of a series of documents from state departments of education (24) and local school systems (6) in 1984-1990 led the authors of this text to conclude that elementary school counselors could anticipate responsibilities for counseling

TABLE 1–3 Major Functions of Elementary School Counselors

Order	Function	Percentage Engaged In
1	Individual counseling	98.8
2	Group guidance and counseling	81.0
3	Working with parents	79.2
4	Consultation with teachers and administrators	78.9
5	Classroom guidance instruction	65.5
6	Assessment activity	39.3
7	Coordination with community agencies	39.1

From "Prevention and the elementary school counselor," by Robert L. Gibson, 1989, *Elementary School Guidance and Counseling, 24,* p. 34. Copyright 1989 by the American Counseling Association. Reprinted by permission.

students individually and in groups, classroom group guidance and instruction activities, information services, consultation, coordination, assessment, and public relations.

While role and function studies may provide indicators and guidelines for prospective and beginning elementary school counselors, it is important to recognize that role and function will be shaped, at least to a degree, by the uniqueness of the local elementary school, their pupils, parents, teachers, and the local area environment. For example, the multicultural make-up of a school and community must be reflected in program planning. Certainly, the emphasis on development, prevention, and enhancement also distinguishes the elementary counselor in role and function from his or her secondary school counterpart. Additionally, the elementary school counselor spends much more time working with classroom groups and families. We have included "A Day in the Life of an Elementary School Counselor" (Basile, 1990), a passage written by a practicing school counselor, to assist you in assimilating what you have read about the counselor's role and function in this chapter. Perhaps this context will permit you to apply the remainder of this text to the real-life perspective of elementary school counseling.

> *Children are scattered on the sidewalks, laughing, playing, crying, some hugging poles. It's early morning and as I walk through the safety of the gate, I am welcomed with a deluge of hugs from what seems like a thousand arms. In the distance there are faces with eyes eagerly waiting their turn for mine to acknowledge theirs.*
>
> *The elementary school is a gloriously fulfilling environment for a school counselor. In my opinion the elementary school counselor is the ultimate human resource for hundreds of children. We are perceived by them as an adult who never judges or belittles them. We are their friend. Children depend on us to be*

loving, understanding, happy, always willing to help, incredibly flexible, and genuine. In essence we are our positions.

Truly, our jobs are energizing and rewarding. In the lives of many children, we are possibly the only positive force. Our presence in schools allows all children to experience feeling warm and fuzzy and accepted.

The multifarious position of an elementary school counselor begins as I enter the gate of the school yard. Following my regal entrance into the building, most often I am greeted by teachers who need consultation on discipline problems or to refer a child. They follow me inside. Once in my office, I can find paper and pencil to take necessary notes.

With all their needs met, I get ready for the parent conference that is scheduled next. Many parents work and are unable to come in after school, so they prefer early morning appointments. Teachers may or may not be included depending on the issue.

This type of conference is intervention. When a problem or concern exists, the counselor intervenes, e.g., by suggesting ways of modifying behavior or some other form of problem-solving.

In addition to intervention, another major thrust is toward prevention. The purpose and underlying hope is to help children, early in their lives, to become problem-solvers, to develop self confidence, to become more responsible and thoroughly practice being the best they can be.

We incorporate prevention strategies primarily through classroom guidance activities. In my school, teachers are allowed to choose either the first period of the day or their period before lunch for classroom guidance.

It is now time to gather audio-visual equipment and scurry off to a classroom. Sometimes I pack a cassette player, puppets, posters, handout sheets, books, stickers, but always high energy and a smile. Also, the rule at my school is that, as the counselor walks by, it is not acceptable to get out of line to give hugs. They all raise their hand for a high-five as I walk by their line. This saves the teacher frustration from lining up again, and I am not late for my scheduled activity.

As I open the door and enter the classroom, there's clapping and happy glowing faces. The children are thrilled that I have come to be with them. The teachers sit in the back of the room or at their desks. I invite the children to enter the world of affective education—feelings, thoughts, decision-making, understanding who they are and how to be the best they can be. Through clever and outwardly unacademic techniques of teaching, whether it is musical or magical, the children gain understanding of themselves and life skills that will forever be useful to them. In addition, they are uplifted, excited, and eager to learn.

On my way back to the office, I am inevitably stopped by a teacher or two for a quick suggestion or a follow-up comment on a child they referred. Since I am often stopped on my way to or from a classroom, it is necessary to invite them to come to my office at their activity period or after school.

With a few minutes before my next scheduled activity, I stop in the attendance office to welcome any new students who have registered.

Next is a small group counseling session consisting of children who have been referred for similar reasons. My group size is limited to six children. Guidelines for conducting group counseling are followed.

After group, there are phone calls to return to parents, district office personnel, the school psychologist, doctors, or other counselors.

Now it's time to administer a series of screening tests and counsel with individuals before leaving for the next classroom guidance presentation. If time permits I will join a class for lunch. It's always a treat for children when the counselor shares extra time.

After lunch, again there are phone calls to return and messages that need attention. It may be necessary to visit a classroom to do an observation or go to the rescue in an emergency situation. This time is also used for paperwork. On days when I make an abuse or neglect report to the Department of Social Services, three copies of the report must be made and sent to appropriate agencies. Afternoons are scheduled for individual and small group counseling also.

After children leave for the day, typically there is a constant flow of teachers in the guidance office. This time is also used for parent/teacher conferences and staffing of children into handicapped programs.

On days when the school psychologist is working in my school, I work closely with her as a liaison for teachers who have referred children for psychological testing. Teachers depend on the counselor to make accurate reports to the school psychologist related to the special needs of their children. It is often advisable to set up times for her to observe in these classrooms.

After testing and proper discussion of test results, we set up staffing dates and parent conferences to explain test scores and recommendations. I send letters of invitation to parents and teachers a week in advance of the meetings. Administrators are also included in these staffing meeting dates.

By now, the school day has come to an end. I pack my school bag, exchange hugs and say my goodbyes. It could be an evening when I'm conducting a parenting class at school. If so, things at home are put into fast forward so I can leave again for school. There are parents who are a little nervous, yet eager to learn how to better care for their children and relieved that other parents share their woes. Parenting groups are very supportive and encouraging ways to reach the children. Our jobs are made easier because of them.

Elementary school counselors are special, caring people who are dedicated to educating children in the affective domain. We help them become more self-confident, productive, and successful adults. Our day is ended with a feeling of accomplishment because of the constant feedback we get from children, parents, and teachers about the difference we make in the lives of people they care about. Elementary school counselors: every child deserves one! (cited in Gibson & Mitchell, 1990)

Summary

In America, the elementary school has traditionally been expected to provide a sound foundation for the individual's future learning, for their responsibilities as productive citizens of the society, and for their socialization into that society. Within this traditional framework, the instructional programs in the elementary school have been planned around the teaching and learning of those basic skills which provide a foundation for lifelong learning. More recently, counseling and guidance programs have been recognized as providing an important and needed dimension in the child's development, the acquiring of basic social/personal foundations for lifelong living. These two dimensions represent the knowledge of a culture and the behavior of a culture. Within this educational context, the broad and ideal goals of the elementary school counseling and guidance program are to help both individual pupils and the school itself become the best they can be.

In undertaking these challenges, we should capitalize on the understandings and knowledge base of other disciplines who study human behavior. As examples, we have briefly focused on anthropology and its studies of the impact of culture on the individual; sociology and its study of human groups and their influence on behavior, including the impact of such socializing agents as the school and family; and psychology, for understanding of learning, human development, individual assessment, behavior patterns, and environmental influences.

TABLE 1–4 Benefits of Counseling Programs in Elementary Schools

The Elementary School exists to provide:	The Counseling Program in the Elementary School can contribute by:	This implies the following:
1. Foundations for learning and living	1. Providing classroom (c/r) guidance to enhance learning and relate learning to preparation	1.1 Classroom guidance 1.2 Consultation with teachers and administrators
2. Transmission of our culture and historical heritage	2. Developing multicultural awareness: pride in our cultural diversity; and respect for the uniqueness of all cultural/ethnic groups	2.1 Classroom guidance activities 2.2 Consultation with teachers and administrators 2.3 Group guidance and counseling
3. Development as a social-psychological being	3. Providing for the socialization (social development) of all children, including respect for self and others	3.1 Group guidance and group counseling focusing on prevention, development, and remediation 3.2 Individual counseling 3.3 Consultation with parent
4. Preparation for citizenship	4. Providing for the development of each individual's human potential	4.1 Career development 4.2 Individual assessment 4.3 Talent and skill enhancement

To meet their important responsibilities, it is imperative that the elementary school counselor be trained and recognized as a "professional." This responsibility—to staff counseling programs and positions—with well-prepared professionals must not be lost sight of as state after state are increasing the demand by mandating elementary school counseling and guidance programs. It can also be assumed that the training of professionals in every profession presumes their preparedness to assume certain tasks—to be prepared for an expected role and function. The previous section of this chapter discussed expected roles and functions of elementary school counselors, including data from current studies. Table 1–4 shows, in summary form, how the fundamental goals of an elementary school education are advanced by counseling programs in elementary schools and function as activities for advancing these goals.

Chapter two will now establish some developmental frameworks for planning counseling and guidance programs to serve elementary school pupils.

Chapter 2

Essentials of Child Development

All the flowers of all
the tomorrows are in the
seeds of today.
—CHINESE PROVERB

Introduction

Elementary school counselors are human development specialists. Fulfillment of this role requires an in-depth understanding of the developmental characteristics of children. Although this chapter provides only an overview of child development, future development courses will cover this fundamental topic in its entirety.

The term *human development* generally refers to the changes that occur over time that produce greater adaptability to our environments. We can consider four categories of development in human beings. Naturally, *physical development* involves bodily changes as we grow. *Personal development* occurs in one's personality and involves internal changes in attitudes, values, and beliefs. *Social Development* involves changes that occur as a result of one's interactions with others. *Cognitive development* refers to changes in mental processes that, as we grow, enable us to think more complexly.

Understanding the behavior of children, developmental antecedents, and their implications, is the sine qua non for elementary school counselors. Before a counselor can effectively facilitate the development of human potential in children and intervene in crises, he or she must understand the four concurrent developmental processes involved in becoming a person.

There are varying opinions among theorists regarding specifics of development. The nature versus nurture dispute continues among behavioral, cognitive, psychoanalytic, and humanistic psychologists. However, there are three principles of development on which there is general agreement among theorists.

The first principle stipulates that development occurs at different rates. For example, in a third grade class that contains twelve girls, the physical development of only two girls necessitates wearing a training bra. The second principle maintains that there is an orderly progression to development. That is, infants learn to crawl before they walk; counselors learn the core conditions of counseling before they learn the models of existentialism and cognitive-behaviorism. The third general principle of development is that it occurs gradually over time. Children do not miraculously wake up on their eighteenth birthday as adults. Changes occur and accumulate gradually in all four areas of development and continue to do so as long as we live.

Relationships exist between the child's physiological and psychological development and his or her behavior. Understanding these dynamics is essential for the counselor's role in counseling students and in consulting with parents, teachers, and others who value the counselor's expertise.

Elementary schools provide a rich cognitive environment for children. This chapter will emphasize Jean Piaget's theory of cognitive development in order to provide a framework for understanding his view of how children think and make sense of their worlds.

While schools are also rich social environments where children learn about themselves and others through their social interactions, it is impossible to separate children from the social influences of parents and their home environments. Thus, the work of Erik Erikson will be examined as one comprehensive way of understanding the personal and social development of children in the school and home environments.

The development of friendships and self-concept in children are included in personal and social development because of the significant impact they have on psychosocial development and school achievement. Self-concept is a major force whose energy permeates all experiences of children (and adults) in both positive and negative ways. One role of the elementary school counselor involves creating a school environment conducive to the development of positive self-concepts in all children. This task is accomplished through your own counseling, through your consultation with teachers and parents, and through all your interactions with others that explicitly and implicitly communicate your philosophy of education.

Moral development is not included in this chapter. However, you may refer to the work of Lawrence Kohlberg (1963, 1975, 1981). Kohlberg's stages of moral reasoning parallel Piaget's stages of cognitive development. The work of both Kohlberg and Piaget reflects their interest in the reasoning that precedes decisions rather than the decisions themselves. Another source of reference, which utilizes Kohlberg's theory, is Parr and Ostrovsky (1991) who describe how to tailor and refine counseling techniques to match the client's stage of moral development in a typical school setting (p. 15).

The point of interest is that school counselors are responsible for advancing positive growth in all dimensions of human development. Counselors activate and teach children to regulate internal systems which increase the healthy development of the whole child.

Developmental changes occur in children and influence their behaviors both at home and in school. By gaining an understanding of the antecedents of these behaviors from both a physiological and psychological perspective, counselors will be more equipped to function effectively as human development specialists.

While this chapter only briefly examines some important factors in development, you will become acquainted with the broad scope of topics that complete courses cover. Should this information intrigue you and leave you hungry for more, it is likely that you will prosper as an elementary school counselor. Indubitably, you marvel at the accomplishments of children, yearn for their high energy levels, and secretly wish to be as open, honest, and in love with life as they are. Fortunately, it is through observing and working with children that we can learn from them as well. Inadvertently, we capture some of their wonder and exhilaration and enthusiastically extend it to other adults who behave as though they have lost that childlike passion for life. Isn't it amazing and gratifying that working with children can be reciprocally lifegiving and enlightening?

As you gain a professional understanding of child growth and development, your understanding of development throughout the lifespan will be enhanced as well. By acquiring self-knowledge about your own development and how it has affected your behavior, you will increase the effective application of knowledge to the population of children, parents, and teachers that you serve.

The Physiological Development of the Elementary School Child

The wonder of childhood begins with physiological change. The child's physical growth makes new experiences possible, and influences the range of responses available to individuals. One's physical growth affects the child's self-concept and self-esteem. It influences how others view them, and it expands or limits the experiences in which individuals may participate and how they may participate. Their growth can make new behaviors possible and can also lead to the discarding of old behaviors. These physical transformations include observable changes in height and weight, body shape, and muscles. Not so observable changes occur in the nervous system, in glandular or hormonal systems, and in sexual maturation. Let us briefly review some of the major characteristics of these changes as they may affect the elementary school child.

Physical Development

Because of physical development, as the elementary school child grows older she or he gets taller and weighs more. However, this growth is neither smooth nor

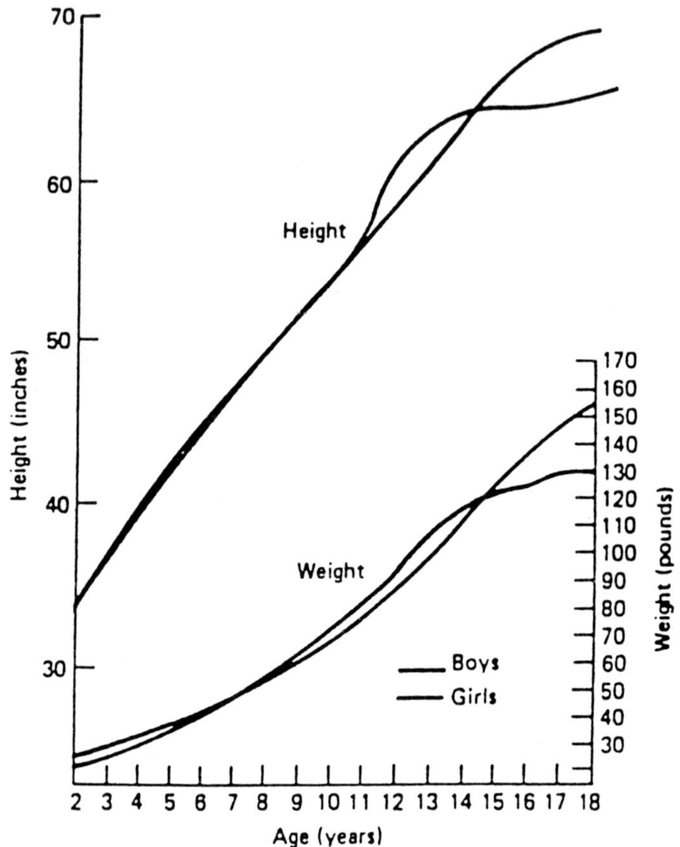

FIGURE 2–1 Growth In Height And Weight From 2 to 18 Years

From National Center for Health Statistics: NCHS Growth Charts, 1976) Washington, D.C.: Copyright 1976 by the National Center for Health Statistics.

continuous. While there will be variations in the rate of growth, as mentioned earlier, across any segment of this population, generally, the rate of growth slows down and becomes relatively steady after early childhood (first two years) until adolescence. This steady growth adds an average of two to three inches in height and six pounds in weight per year until the so-called "growth spurt" signaling the onset of adolescence (refer to Figure 2–1.).

As the child grows, other physical changes are also taking place. One notable change takes place in the size and shape of the child's jaw as (during these "tooth fairy" years) the permanent teeth come in. Muscle tissues also develop steadily over the grade school years, but the difference in muscle strength between boys and girls is not nearly as noticeable until the adolescent years.

TABLE 2–1 Sequence of Changes in Sexual Development with Approximate Ages of Onset

Age of onset	Girls	Boys
10	Onset of breast development (breast bud)	
11	Pubic hair-sparse, slightly pigmented	Onset of growth of testes and scrotum
12	Between 12 and 13, underarm hair begins to appear	Appearance of pubic hair-lightly pigmented
13	Breast enlargement continues; areola and papilla project above the contour of the breast Onset of menarche	First ejaculation of semen
14	Increase in pubic hair, but area covered is smaller than in adult	Underarm and facial hair Voice deepens
15	Breasts and pubic hair are fully mature	Penis, testes, and pubic hair are fully developed Onset of growth of mustache and beard hair

From *Child Psychology* (p. 218) by E. M. Heatherington and R. D. Parke (New York: McGraw Hill). Copyright 1986 by McGraw Hill as adapted from "The Biological approach to Adolescence" by A. C. Petersen and B. Taylor, 1980, New York: Wiley and "Foetus into man" by J. M. Tanner, 1978 (Cambridge, MA: Harvard University Press). Reprinted by permission.

Girls generally have more fat tissue than boys (and this too will dramatically increase during the adolescent years). Secondary sexual characteristics—those not necessary for reproduction—begin in both boys and girls at about age 10 or 11 (See Table 2–1).

Of course, the child's normal physical development can be influenced significantly by diet and nutrition, illness, heredity, and environmental factors that affect healthy living.

Motor Development

During the early elementary school years, small muscle coordination is developing rapidly and large muscle skills are improving. In younger elementary school children, large muscle control is noticeably ahead of refined coordination (for example, many young children have difficulty in manipulating a pencil). By six to eight years of age, motor coordination is well developed and the development of play and athletic skills can progress with practice through the remaining elementary years. From ages 9 to 11,

> *Children continue to refine and develop their coordination and motor skills. They experience a gradual, steady gain in body measurements and proportion. Manual dexterity, posture, strength and balance improve. This period of late*

childhood becomes a transitional period into the major changes experienced during adolescence (Zastrow & Kirst-Ashman, 1987, pp. 45-46).

As a general rule, children are also fairly consistent in their motor development. Those who are slow to develop their motor skills in the early grades will probably also be slow in mastering motor skills in later grades. Children who run the fastest in the earlier years will continue to be the "speedsters" in their groups later on. More specifically, children are in the process of developing and improving such motor skills as running, jumping, throwing, balancing themselves, and developing agility and coordination. By age twelve, they will have developed most of their mobility and speed of action. Boys will perform, on the average, only slightly better than girls in the various motor skills during the elementary school years as the marked differences do not begin to assert themselves until early adolescence.

During this period it is important for the elementary school child to actively engage in motor activities that contribute to motor skill development and, at the same time, support one's self-concept, and contribute to peer relationships. While some of this activity takes place out of the school setting, it is important that provisions be made by the school to ensure the positive development of these motor skills. Unless these foundational motor skills are developed and refined reasonably in the elementary school, their later development and progression in middle or junior high schools will be very difficult.

The promotion of physical fitness promotes health in other areas of development as well. Physical exercise has positive effects on energy level, emotions, relationships, problem-solving ability, health, level of satisfaction and tension (Carlson, 1990, p. 298).

This information is valuable for the school counselor in the roles of both counselor and consultant. At times, it may be appropriate to recommend physical exercise as an intervention strategy to parents and teachers for implementation with children.

Gerler incorporates physical exercise in many of the activities in *Counseling the Young Learner* (1982). "Exercises I Can Do," "Running Across the United States," and "Physical Exercise Accidents" are examples. Scherman's (1989) study (cited in Carlson, 1990) stresses the importance of school counselors using physical activities as therapeutic intervention techniques. He states that

because physical activity is fun and often involves students in groups, it provides students the opportunity to develop social skills within a pleasant environment. In this capacity, participating in physical activity can strengthen and expand a student's social support network (cited in Carlson, 1990, p. 299).

While encouraging physical fitness through exercise, the counselor can emphasize its development through proper nutrition. Helpful activities that can be implemented in the classroom with students are contained in Gerler's (1982) book.

The current emphasis on wellness in our society and on prevention in counseling focuses our attention on the value of physical fitness. Encouraging physical activities is suggested to integrate and facilitate mind/body connections that promote healthy psychological and physical development in children.

To summarize, understanding children's physical development is relevant to school counselors because of its influence on other areas of development. How children develop and perform in comparison to their peers affects the physical and emotional well-being of children. Development occurs in people simultaneously in four areas: physical, personal, social, and cognitive. Children have thoughts and feelings about all these changes. Counselors are in schools to listen to concerns regarding all of these areas.

The Psychological Development of the Elementary School Child

Though not as observable as the child's physical development, the psychological development is of equal importance and likewise impacts behaviors. As noted earlier, the elementary school years are characterized by rapid development, constant change, and the establishment of foundations for future learning and personality development.

You will notice that some theorists categorize psychological development in stages which is indicative of orderly development. We have chosen to briefly describe the work of two influential thinkers here. Note that these are overviews of complex theories and serve as no substitute for subsequent development coursework in your counselor training. Their purpose is to familiarize and prepare you for deeper thinking.

Cognitive Development

Changes in understanding and thinking pertains to cognitive development. Jean Piaget (1896-1980), a Swiss psychologist, derived perhaps the most influential theory of cognitive development. His ideas are important to elementary school counselors because they provide a description of the thought processes of children.

Understanding how children think enables counselors to choose developmentally appropriate activities for individual and group counseling and for classroom guidance. For example, it is unlikely that a counselor would expect a kindergartner to discuss his or her communication style in terms of transactional analysis or use certain forms of psychoanalysis with an elementary school population. Higher level thinking skills that are required to process such concepts are generally not developed in children.

Knowledge of cognitive development is also useful for consulting with teachers and parents, for example, in determining possible reasons for frustration in classrooms, lack of task completion skills, and low motivation.

Communicating with children is also easier when adults understand that children do not perceive the world in adult terms, nor are they equipped with as elaborate mental tools. Speaking in concrete terms with children is usually effective. In listening to children talk, you will become aware of their level of cognitive functioning and will be able to match it.

Piaget's theory is only one approach to cognitive development. Some psychologists have criticized as vague his method of gathering data, thus making replication of research impossible. Many of his conclusions have been questioned. Subsequent research has supported some and not others.

Although there is disagreement regarding some aspects of Piaget's theory, there is agreement on the accuracy of important issues. He has accurately described children's thinking and reasoning, and apparently the ways of thinking do change during child development.

Within Piaget's theory there exists a functional framework for understanding cognitive development. This will serve as a basis for understanding cognitive development as you continue your education in elementary school counseling.

The Work of Piaget

Piaget believed that nature and nurture work together in development. Human beings are genetically programmed for biological changes that will occur during development. As stated in the section above, physical maturation provides more abilities for children to act on their environments. Children explore and observe objects in their environments and progressively organize more information and become more adaptive. Simultaneously, thinking processes are changing that allow organization and adaptation.

Piaget began his career as a biologist. He concluded from his biological research that all species inherit two basic tendencies: to organize (combine and arrange thoughts and behaviors), and to adapt (to adjust to their environments). In human beings, organization allows us to form psychological structures, or systems, for making sense of our worlds. These mental systems become more complex as we get older and are exposed to more experiences.

While organizing psychological structures, we are also adapting to our environments. Assimilation and accommodation are the two processes involved in adaptation. Assimilation occurs when people understand something new by fitting in into an already existing system or category. For example, children may say they see a bus when they actually see a truck. That is their way of making the new object fit into a system that is already in place.

However, when new information cannot fit appropriately into an existing system, a new system must be created, or an old one altered. This mental process is called accommodation. A child has accommodated new information when he or she creates a new category of identification into which "truck" will fit.

These changes in thinking which result from organization, assimilation, and accommodation require a complex mental balancing process. Piaget calls this search for balance equilibration. That is, when new information comes in and it fits into an existing system, a balance is achieved. If it does not fit, disequilibrium exists which causes discomfort. To alleviate this discomfort, the person continues to search for a solution through assimilation and accommodation. It is through these processes that thinking changes and moves toward understanding information at increasingly higher levels of difficulty.

According to Piaget, drastic changes occur in sequential stages in our thinking processes. Piaget's stages of cognitive development are sensorimotor, preoperational, concrete operational, and formal operational. These stages are associated with approximate ages, however knowing the age of the child does not guarantee that she or he is using the thinking abilities associated with that stage. These are, rather, general descriptions of the ways children think. In fact, some children may think at the preoperational stage for some tasks and in the concrete operational stage for others. Refer to Table 2–2 for a summary of these stages, ages, and characteristics.

In the sensorimotor stage, 0–2 years of age, children process information taken in through their senses (sensori-) and from physical movements (motor). The major goal of this stage is to master the concept of object permanence. That is, to realize that objects exist even though they are not in view; for example, a child sees a ball roll under a sofa, if he or she realizes that the ball has not disappeared, that it is simply out of sight, under the sofa, then object permanence is achieved.

Two other accomplishments of the sensorimotor stage are goal-directed actions, deliberately reaching for an object, and reversing actions, taking things out of a container and putting them back in again.

The preoperational stage is characterized by the development of language and one-way thinking, that is, thinking in one direction, but not backwards. Egocentricity is another characteristic of children in this stage. They assume that everyone perceives the world as they do. It is puzzling to a child who is looking out the window that an adult in the same room, who is not looking out the window, cannot answer questions about the dog next door. The child assumes that everyone sees what the child sees.

Piaget calls another phenomenon of the preoperational stage collective monologue. This too is an example of egocentrism. A mother may say to you that she has heard her young son, Trevor, alone in his room, conversing with proper inflection as if someone were present. This occurs among groups of children, as well. Each child talks, but not to each other, nor do they expect an answer from anyone. Thus, collective monologue is not social interaction. It is an example of a child living in her or his own world.

As an elementary school counselor, a clear understanding of how a child's mind makes sense of the world will enable you to enter that world and communicate at appropriate levels. You will prepare individual, group, and classroom guidance activities dependent upon the children's cognitive stage of development.

Using actions and concrete objects, such as puppets, along with words, is most effective for all elementary school children. Even when elaborate props are used however, sometimes they may not be enough to capture every child's interest for the duration of your presentation. Elkind (1991) put it this way, "we should treat young children as we might treat a visitor from another country—with good manners, but without the expectation that they will understand everything we have to say" (p. 20).

An example is: a parent reports to you, the counselor, that her 5-year old daughter responded to, "What did you learn in classroom guidance today?" with, "My counselor has the smallest feet I have ever seen!" This is not necessarily indicative that your presentation was uninteresting, or that your discussion included various foot sizes. Instead, the child was perceiving the world from her own perspective. Since the kindergartner sat on the floor, and you sat on a small child's chair, crossing your legs places your foot at a child's eye level. Observing and thinking about the foot in view is, for this particular child, more memorable than the puppets you displayed or the story you read. Transition from the stage of preoperational to concrete operational generally occurs between the ages of five and seven years. Children learn to mentally do what they previously did only physically.

The concrete operational stage acknowledges mastery of conservation, reversible thinking, and the ability to solve concrete problems logically. Conservation involves the realization that objects or liquids maintain their original characteristics although the form has been changed. For example, a child thinks concretely when she or he understands that when there are two identical glasses of water, you may pour the contents of one in a taller thinner glass, but the amount of water remains unchanged.

Reversible thinking is the ability to think forward and backward. Children can take things apart, or rearrange the pieces, and put them back together. Solving concrete problems includes classifying objects according to color and shape. Seriation is the ability to arrange objects in order, as from smallest to largest. Children in the concrete operational stage are still tied to the physical world. "In dealing with young children, it is well to keep in mind their tendency to think about the world in concrete ways and to remember that their language ability often far exceeds their cognitive understanding" (Elkind, 1991, p. 20).

The fourth and final stage is formal operational in which a child's thinking abilities are extended internally and abstractly. This stage is characterized by the ability to hypothesize, analyze one's thinking, and the ability to reason scientifically.

In this stage, a child can think hypothetically and systematically. It is best for elementary school counselors to continue the use of props and visual aids. However, when counseling children in this stage and in classroom guidance situations, children may be asked to discuss at more sophisticated levels, for example, to make comparisons or discuss alternative responses in crisis situations or to resolve conflicts.

Table 2–2 outlines Piaget's theory of cognitive development.

TABLE 2–2 Piaget's Stages of Cognitive Development

Stage	Approximate Age	Characteristics
Sensorimotor	0-2 years	Begins to make use of imitation, memory, and thought. Begins to recognize that objects do not cease to exist when they are hidden. Moves from reflex action, to goal-directed activity.
Preoperational	2-7 years	Gradual language development and ability to think in symbolic form. Able to think operations through logically in one direction. Has difficulties seeing another person's point of view.
Concrete operational	7-11 years	Able to solve concrete (hands on) problems in logical fashion. Understands laws of conversation and is able to classify and seriate. Understands reversibility.
Formal operational	11-15 years	Able to solve abstract problems in logical fashion. Thinking becomes more scientific. Develops concerns about social issues, identity.

From *Educational Psychology* (p. 47) by A. E. Woolfolk, Copyright © 1990, Englewood Cliffs, NJ: Prentice-Hall as reprinted from *Piaget's Theory of Cognitive and Affective Development* (4th ed.), by B. J. Wadsworth, 1984, New York: Longman. Copyright © 1989 by Longman. Reprinted by Permission.

Thus, we must strive to enter into their cognitive worlds to effectively communicate at their level of understanding.

Learning Theories

Two types of learning theories have been developed by psychologists to explain how learning occurs in individuals. Cognitive learning theories provide accounts of unobservable mental processes that occur in human learning. The human mind is emphasized as an active processor of information which enables people to not only react to the environment, but to seek, initiate, and reorganize information as part of the learning process. Cognitive theorists believe that learning is the result of one's attempts to make sense out of one's world. Mental components such as feelings, beliefs, and expectations interact to process information and achieve new learning. These mental processes allow for the acquisition of knowledge and changes in knowledge which make changes in behavior possible.

Jean Piaget is a cognitive psychologist. His theory reflects the interest in discovering how learning takes place, how people solve problems, and how they perform complex mental operations. He believed that learning is an internal process and that learners are active in their environments.

In contrast, behavioral learning theories emphasize observable behavior that can be demonstrated, observed, and measured. These theorists believe that the behavior of individuals is determined by the consequences of behavior, that is, rewards or punishment.

Behavioral psychologists believe that learners are passive and react to their environments. Thus, behaviors and learners are products of the environment. Behaviorists do not acknowledge internal mental processes as determinants of behavior, rather they espouse that people respond to external events which are strictly stimulus-response reactions. They contend that an adult is a product of his or her childhood conditioning and that neither instincts nor inheritable traits have determined behavior.

"Learning is a process that occurs when experience causes a relatively permanent change in an individual's knowledge or behavior" (Woolfolk, 1990, p. 159). Providing conditions in which learning is generated in children is the ultimate goal in schools. Educational objectives reflect desired changes in children, such as learning to read and add and subtract. Some guidance and counseling objectives reflect children's learned abilities to problem-solve in life situations, make healthy decisions, understand oneself and others, label and express feelings, and develop healthy relationships. Thus, understanding learning theory provides elementary school counselors with knowledge about how to assist change and learning in children. While teachers are teaching academics, counselors are teaching how to grow and develop as a person. The majority of this teaching is done in classroom guidance. Learning theory will be used in your role as consultant and counselor as well.

Counselors consult with teachers and parents and counsel with children on numerous issues related to learning. These include learning disabilities, gifted and talented issues, classroom management, discipline, task completion skills, curriculum advising, motivation, retention, and testing.

This section will briefly describe two behavioral views of learning: classical and operant conditioning, and the cognitive-behavioral view of social learning theory.

Classical Conditioning

Classical conditioning is the learning process that enables an individual (or animal) to respond automatically to a previously neutral stimulus. The response may be emotional, such as a fearful response, or physiological, such as a muscular reaction.

We attribute our understanding of learning through classical conditioning to the Russian physiologist, Ivan Pavlov (1849-1936). Results of his laboratory experiments involving a dog, food, and a bell demonstrated how learning can affect responses in animals and humans.

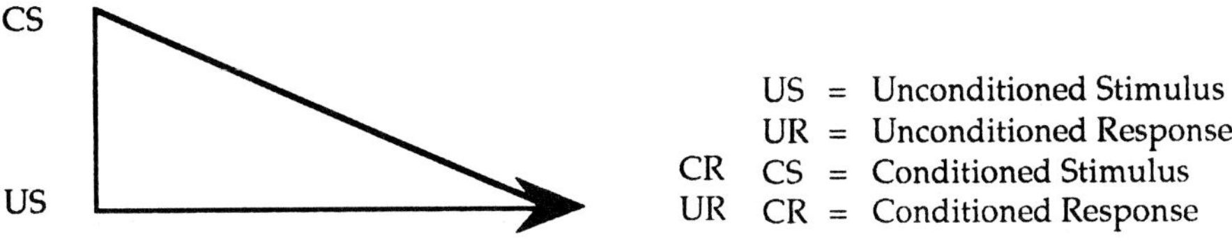

FIGURE 2–2 Illustration Of Classical Conditioning

Concisely, in classical conditioning, a neutral stimulus (the bell), which previously causes no response in the dog, is paired with an unconditional stimulus (food), which does evoke an automatic response (salivation). After repeated pairings, the previously neutral stimulus (the bell) gains the power to elicit the unconditioned response (salivation) in the absence of food.

Learning through classical conditioning occurs in many everyday situations in human beings as well. Of import to elementary school counselors is its applicability in discovering sources of some childhood difficulties. Suppose a teacher expresses concern because suddenly Sandy, a second grader, refuses to go to recess. She complains of stomach-aches at recess time. You, the counselor, help the teacher trace back through previous events that occurred at recess. Together you arrive at the source of difficulty. It was at recess that Sandy, while trying to break up a fight, received a painful hit intended for someone else. Therefore, she associates recess, a previously neutral stimulus (now a conditioned stimulus), with fear and pain, an unconditioned stimulus (now a conditioned stimulus), even in the absence of a fight (the unconditioned stimulus).

Other examples include children learning to fear school or tests when they are repeatedly associated with frightening experiences or failure, respectively. Figure 2-2 illustrates learning through classical conditioning.

Once you know how a child learned, for example, to fear recess, what can you do to dispel the fear and permit the enjoyment of recess again? One answer is to gently reintegrate Sandy into recess in nonthreatening ways. You may suggest that the teacher begin with only a few minutes of recess in which the teacher structures it so that fun activities occur. Longer recess times with constant supervision to ensure that she remains safe will extinguish the fear that was once associated with recess.

Children may learn by classical conditioning to experience positive emotions when school tasks are associated with fun, excitement, and success. Counselors, in a consultant role, provide information to teachers and parents that structure positive events and outcomes for children.

Operant Conditioning

Although some human learning occurs through classical conditioning, it does not explain all learning. Learning through operant conditioning is not automatic and involves only behaviors that people already know. It explains how new behaviors are learned. The individual actively and deliberately "operates" on his or her environment by controlling the consequences of behaviors.

B(urrhus). F(rederick). Skinner (1904-1990) developed the concept of operant conditioning. The earlier work of Edward L. Thorndike (1874-1949), who developed the *law of effect,* provided the basis for Skinner's operant conditioning. The law of effect states that behaviors that produce satisfying effects are more likely to be repeated than those that produce unsatisfying effects. Thus, Thorndike went beyond Pavlov with his interest in stimuli that occur after behaviors, and Skinner went beyond Thorndike's work by focusing on the relationship between behavior and its consequences. For example, behaviors immediately followed by positive consequences are likely to occur more frequently. Therefore, operant conditioning is learning which involves changes in behavior that occur as a result of pleasant and unpleasant consequences.

The apparatus Skinner used to study the effects of consequences on behavior is referred to as the Skinner Box. Many of his experiments involved the study of rats and pigeons in the controlled environment of the Skinner Box. One such box used with rats consisted of a lever or bar that when pressed would release a pellet of food. The rats relinquished their aimless behavior in the box and learned to purposefully press the lever to gain their reward. This is an example of the fact that behavior that is reinforced or rewarded is likely to occur again.

The concept of operant conditioning can be taken from the laboratory into elementary schools by understanding that children learn, from a behavioral view, based on reinforcement and punishment. That is, reinforcement strengthens behavior, and punishment weakens or suppresses behavior. In an elementary classroom, children who receive stickers on good work papers are likely to produce more good work.

Elementary school counselors frequently draw on their knowledge of learning theories when consulting with teachers and parents regarding the behavior of children. Teachers and parents frequently ask for assistance with how to encourage some behaviors and discourage others. Once again, the principles of operant conditioning may be applied in numerous situations.

One helpful guideline is to alert teachers and parents to remember to reinforce positive behavior. If they want certain behaviors to continue, for example, raising hands before talking, they must reinforce those behaviors by saying, "I like the way Joye raises her hand to get my attention."

Before these principles will work, it is also necessary to make sure that reinforcers are meaningful to children. One effective way to discover this is to simply ask children! Another way is to observe what children are doing in their free time. Take note of who is reading, working on the computer, or putting puzzles together.

Many children value free time in class, the opportunity to choose different activities, which may be used as a reinforcer to get less interesting work completed. For example, "Class, when you have finished your math pages, you may choose an activity in one of the centers in our room." Do what I say to do first, then you may do what you want. An example used by a parent to a child is, "After you have cleaned your room, you may go out to play."

As you progress through this chapter, your role as a human development specialist, and the amount of knowledge needed to respond to a wide range of concerns, is most likely becoming real.

Social Learning Theory

Cognitive-behavioral theory indicates by its label the belief that learning is a result of both internal (cognitive) and external (environmental) processes.

Albert Bandura (1925-), a cognitive-behavioral psychologist, believes that explaining behavior in behavioral terms alone is incomplete, not inaccurate. The cognitive-behavioral view of learning is that of a process influenced by the interaction of cognitions, behaviors, and the environment.

Social learning theory was developed by Bandura (1969) as an extension to traditional behavioral learning theory. While most of the principles of behavioral learning theories are accepted, emphasis is placed on what an individual thinks about the consequences of behavior. To provide an overview of this theory we will discuss three principle concepts.

One concept is modeling—learning by imitating actions of others. In this case, models demonstrate behaviors that observers want to learn or behaviors for which they expect reward. Philip models his piano teacher's posture and hand position while playing the piano because he admires her playing and wants to learn.

This concept is useful to elementary school counselors as a tool for consulting with parents and teachers. Many children's behaviors, as well as language and attitudes, can be traced back to their original sources: parents, teachers, other children, and even actors on television.

Teachers and parents may be unaware that they are serving as models for particular behaviors their children are exhibiting. Through consultation, counselors can help them investigate interactions with children that may be providing modeling experiences. Sometimes parents engage in activities unaware that their children are observing. A five-year-old who can describe how to roll a marijuana cigarette has obviously learned through modeling.

Vicarious learning is another principle concept of social learning theory. Individuals observe the rewards and punishments of other's behaviors and decide to imitate, or not to imitate, behaviors of others depending on the consequences. When Elizabeth observes that Joye got good attention from her teacher by raising her hand, it is likely that she will also raise her hand.

Self-regulation is the third important concept of social learning theory. Bandura (1977) posited that people are observers, judgers, and reinforcers or punishers of their own behavior. People base their judgments on their own expectations. We are all aware of feeling good about tasks we know we have completed to the best of our ability and feeling disappointed about the ones we did not finish.

In schools, counselors can use this concept of self-regulation in counseling individuals and small groups. Discussions begin with current feelings about behaviors in question and extend to, "How would you like to feel the next time you take a math test?" Children are helped to recognize that they can take steps to regulate their behaviors to produce outcomes that match the standards they have formulated for themselves.

Observation can be a very effective way of learning and is often referred to as observational learning. According to Bandura (1986) it occurs in four phases: attention, retention, production, and motivation or reinforcement.

Attention

Observational learning requires that the observer pay attention to a model.

Retention

One must remember a behavior in order to imitate it. Rehearsal, mentally and/or in actual practice, is a means by which retention is achieved.

Production

In this phase the learner tries to match his or her behavior to the level of expertise of the model. Often this takes much practice, feedback, and refining.

Motivation or reinforcement

In the final stage of observational learning, the learner repeats a behavior with anticipation of reinforcement. In order to maintain learning, reinforcement must be consistent. If it stops, or is not reinforced at all, it is likely that the behavior will not be imitated again.

Counselors may need to remind teachers and parents of these principles as a means of engaging the steps necessary for achievement in observational learning.

Applications of Learning Theories

To summarize, the importance of knowledge and comprehension of learning theories for elementary school counselors lies in their application of this information to classroom management, discipline, and motivational strategies. These are three major areas of consultation sought by both parents and teachers which warrant your gaining expertise beyond this course.

Social and Personal Development

As we noted at the beginning of this chapter, development of a person occurs simultaneously in four areas. While physical and cognitive skills are developing, so are self-concepts, social skills, values, and belief systems. Schools are environments where education of the whole child is cultivated. While it is important for teachers to understand and attend to children's personal and social development, they teach primarily in the cognitive domain. Part of the counselor's role is to support these efforts through consultation and classroom guidance activities.

As we presuppose throughout this book, the paramount domain in which school counselors function as both teacher and counselor is that of social and personal development. If "it is [truly] better to build children than to repair men and women," then schools must enrich children's development in all domains. To this end, every child deserves a school counselor. To educate the whole child is to build children who are prepared to face successfully all circumstances in their worlds. Consequently, it is imperative that you design guidance curriculums that are adaptable to appropriate levels in all areas of human development.

The Work of Erikson

We will introduce the work of Erik Erikson (1902-) as a framework for understanding personal and social development. Like Piaget, Erikson was not formally trained as a psychologist. He was trained by Sigmund Freud in psychoanalysis.

In *Childhood and Society* (1963), Erikson emphasizes the influence of the social environment on the individual's psychological development which provides a meaningful link between personal and social development. For this reason his theory is called a psychosocial theory. Erikson's theory is comprehensive in that it emphasizes how the self emerges, one's search for identity, and the importance of one's personal relationships in all stages of life. Because children engage in all aspects of development while in schools, psychosocial theory provides counselors with a useful framework for understanding the dynamic impact of the school and home settings on personal and social development.

Like physical and cognitive development, personal and social development proceeds in stages. Erikson posited that people pass through eight psychosocial stages from birth until their death. Each stage consists of a developmental crisis that must be resolved. A conflict is involved with each crisis that will be resolved positively or negatively depending on the reactions of people in her or his world. Successful accomplishments in earlier stages contribute to one's ability to resolve future crises; this creates an interdependence among the stages. Unhealthy resolutions of psychosocial crises may result in difficulties throughout one's life. It is important to note the possibility that unsatisfactory resolutions may be altered to satisfactory outcomes later in life when proper conditions exist.

Often in counseling, issues of trust, autonomy, and guilt, to name just a few, surface in children (and later in adults if not resolved). We will briefly discuss how Erikson's psychosocial theory explains personal and social development. Refer to Table 2-3 for a summary of the eight stages of Erikson's theory.

Infancy: Trust vs. Mistrust (Birth to 18 months)

The development of basic trust in the world is the goal of infancy. According to Erikson (1968), basic trust is "an essential trustfulness of others as well as a fundamental sense of one's own trustworthiness" (p. 96). The duality of this crisis is indicated: the infant's need to have his or her needs met, and their role in meeting their mother's needs. In this stage, babies learn if they can depend on people (parents) in their worlds. Generally the mother is the first important person in the infant's life. Healthy resolution occurs if she satisfies the baby's needs for food and affection. A sense of mistrust develops in the infant if the mother is rejecting or inconsistent in meeting these needs. This mistrust may persist into adulthood.

Autonomy vs. Doubt (18 months to 3 years)

The crisis at this stage involves the toddler's pursuit of independence. Striving toward autonomy involves gaining greater self-control and self-confidence. Feeding and dressing oneself and toilet training are examples of positive outcomes in this stage. Parents must discover how to be protective, yet not overprotective. They must reassure and reinforce the toddler's efforts to master these new skills. If parents are critical of their children's efforts, shame and doubt develop and lead to a lack of self-confidence in their abilities throughout life.

Initiative vs. Guilt (3 to 6 years)

By this stage, children's physical and language development permits them to engage more rigorously in physical and social activities. Parents are encouraged to allow children to run, jump, and play, while helping them realize that some activities are forbidden. Playing and pretending to be grown-ups are important forms of gaining initiative. It is important that adults confirm and value the contributions of children regardless of how small. Giving children responsibilities for chores and confirming their efforts is an example of gaining a healthy resolution to this crisis. Parents who criticize and severely punish attempts at initiative create feelings of guilt in children (and later in adults) who want to explore and do new things.

School counselors can advocate the encouragement of initiative and the avoidance of guilt by participating in and suggesting to parents and teachers the following: encourage children to make their own choices and act on them, set up games and classwork so that all children experience success, stimulate imagination through make-believe activities, be respectful and tolerant of mistakes and accidents as children do things on their own.

Industry vs. Inferiority (6 to 12 years)

Industry indicates that children now want to produce things, to persevere and feel the pleasure of a job well-done. Also, the social world of children increases dramatically with school attendance and actually provides a second world in which to move. The impact of parents decreases while that of teachers and peers increases, thus the child is faced with balancing challenges in both worlds—home and school. Successfully meeting these challenges results in a sense of competence and feeling good about oneself and one's abilities. Feelings of inferiority, inadequacy, and a negative self-image arise when a child fails to succeed in academics or to live up to one's own standards or those of friends and families.

Counselors facilitate the development of industry in children in both counselor and consultant roles. In your role as counselor you will provide support and counseling to children who are discouraged. Consult with teachers and parents about the importance of allowing children to create realistic goals and to work toward them. Encourage that children are given responsibilities and are allowed to be independent.

Identity vs. Role Confusion (12 to 18 years)

During this stage, adolescents search for their identity and ask the question "Who am I?" The answer is sought more from peers than parents. Erikson believes that adolescents are challenged with pursuing a redefinition of their early childhood psychosocial identity. They are emerging physiologically and psychologically from childhood and venturing into adulthood. Therefore, a reorganization of attitudes, beliefs, and actions must occur to produce an image that integrates all the changing aspects into a new whole. This task will be much easier if healthy outcomes have resulted in the previous stages. For example, the sense of trust enables teenagers to find friends they can believe in. Autonomy encourages the freedom of choice in careers and lifestyle. Pretending to be a teacher or engineer as a young child contributes the initiative to pursue those careers as an adult. The accomplishment of industry in stage three furnishes the competence and belief in one's self to prosper in the real world.

Elementary school counselors encourage the establishment of identity by providing activities in individual, small group, and classroom guidance. Counselors allow students to work on personal problems in a safe environment. In addition, suggestions are made to parents and teachers to serve as role models, to invite guest speakers, and to discuss adult roles that will stimulate thinking and reflecting about career choices. Also, suggest that adults tolerate teenage fads and provide realistic feedback to them. Who you are and how you respond will also be an example for them.

Intimacy vs. Isolation (Young Adulthood)

Success in this and the last two stages focuses on the quality of human relations. Once a person knows who they are and who they want to become, sharing that sense with others is an enriching experience. The ability to be intimate refers to communicating with another at a deep level. Developing intimate relationships enhances the identity and further development of both partners. The personal growth of each contributes to the deepening and strengthening of the relationship. An intimate relationship is a beautiful human experience when it is shared by two who are already complete in themselves. Intimacy does not arise from need, rather from trust, respect, and honor for the other.

Sexual relations should not be confused with intimacy since they may exist in the absence of intimacy. Likewise, intimacy may develop in a relationship and not include sexual relations. Experiencing mutual sexual satisfaction within an intimate relationship does intensify the closeness. In both instances, intimacy is a communion between two people that occurs at deep levels of the mind and heart. It involves a communicative ability to deeply recognize another person's being that extends beyond mere thoughts and words. One who has not achieved a

TABLE 2–3 Erikson's Stages of Personal and Social Development

As people grow, they face a series of psychosocial crisis that shape personality, according to Erik Erikson. Each crisis focuses on a particular aspect of personality and each involves the person's relationship with other people.

	Approximate Ages	Psychosocial Crises	Significant Relationships	Psychosocial Emphasis
I	Birth to 18 mo.	Trust vs. mistrust	Maternal person	To get To give in return
II	18 mo. to 3 yr.	Autonomy vs. doubt	Parental persons	To hold on To let go
III	3 to 6 yr.	Initiative vs. guilt	Basic family	To make (= going after) To "make like" (= playing)
IV	6 to 12 yr.	Industry vs. inferiority	Neighborhood, school	To make things To make things together
V	12 to 18 yr.	Identity vs. role confusion	Peer groups and models of leadership	To be oneself (or not to be) To share being oneself
VI	Young adulthood	Intimacy vs. isolation	Partners in friendship, sex, competition, cooperation	To lose and find oneself in another
VII	Middle adulthood	Generativity vs. self-absorbtion	Divided labor and shared household	To take care of
VIII	Late adulthood	Integrity vs. despair	"Mankind" "My kind"	To be, through having been To face not being

strong sense of self tends to retreat from intimate relationships for fear of being consumed by the other. Others who have tried, yet failed, to develop intimate relationships also tend to retreat into isolation.

Generativity vs. Self-absorption (Middle Adulthood)

Generativity refers to the ability to establish and guide the next generation. Typically, this is achieved through having and caring for one's own children. However, the concept of generativity extends to other forms of productivity and creativity, for example, teachers and counselors care for and nurture future generations through their careers. Positive resolution in this stage also occurs in those who contribute to the preservation of this planet and her environment for their enjoyment and that of future generations. In this stage, continued growth is essential to prevent stagnation and self-absorption.

Integrity vs. Despair (Late Adulthood)

The final stage of psychosocial development involves the resolution of the final identity crisis and the coming to terms with death. The now unalterable past, including successes, failures, and limitations, is examined. Acceptance of these, and the ability to take responsibility for one's own life, brings a sense of integrity and fulfillment. Despair comes to those who are regretful of their past and the life they created. They fear death. Table 2–3 summarizes Erikson's eight stages of psychosocial development.

Note that Erikson's theory of psychosocial development, as does Piaget's stages of cognitive development, provides the average time frames for these crises and resolutions to occur. In reality, individual differences in people and circumstances in their worlds determine when the crises actually occur and how they will be resolved. For example, children from dysfunctional families may not develop trust until later in life after more stable conditions are achieved.

It is important to remember that psychosocial development occurs in children and adults throughout their lives and results from continuous interactions with others and their environment. Although conflicts of the first two stages are resolved primarily between children and their families, school counselors gain insight into children's issues of trust and autonomy through understanding the dynamics of these developmental crises. Of particular interest to elementary school counselors is stage III (initiative vs. guilt), since children enter school during this stage. Psychosocial development that transpires in stage IV (industry vs. inferiority) and stage V (identity vs. role confusion) is of fundamental concern to counselors because children are struggling during elementary school years with these conflicts.

For greater clarity and integration, Figure 2–3 illustrates the relationship between Erikson's psychosocial development and Piaget's cognitive stages of development.

Friendships

Friendships are an important area of personal and social development worthy of further discussion. From three to six years of age, in Erikson's initiative versus guilt stage, children become aware of other children. For the first time in their lives they are a participant in three different overlapping worlds: home, neighborhood, and school.

Friendships allow children to learn cooperation, to settle disputes, and to realize that others have thoughts, feelings, and beliefs different from theirs. Playing with friends assists the movement through egocentrism which is characteristic of Piaget's preoperational stage.

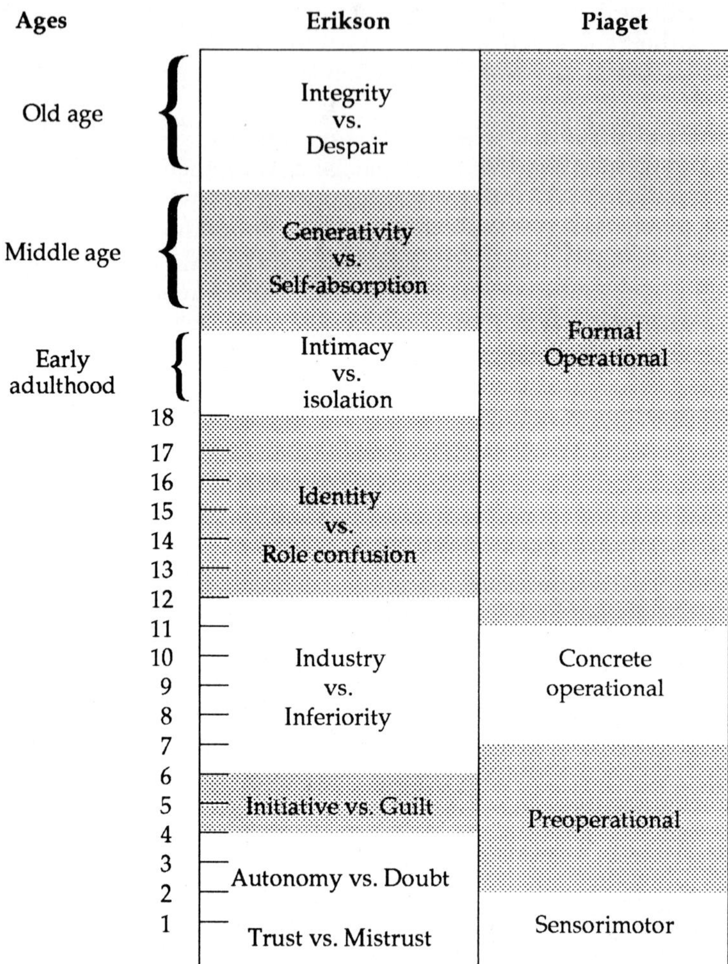

FIGURE 2–3 Stages In Personal And Cognitive Development

From *Educational Psychology*, 3rd Ed. (p. 44) by R. E. Slavin. Copyright © 1991 by Allyn and Bacon. Reprinted by Permission.

Selman and Selman (1979), used Piaget's stages to describe how children's understanding of friendships changes over the years. They report that friendships develop orderly and sequentially relative to the development of thought patterns. A brief description of the five overlapping stages of friendship follows.

Stage 0 (ages 3 to 7)

Friends in this stage are Momentary Playmates depending on who is closeby and who has nice toys. Charlie says to his mom, "Jeffrey is my friend." Why?

"Because he has Nintendo!" Consistent with egocentrism of Piaget's preoperational stage, a child is unable to distinguish between his or her perspective and those of others. A child will play with the child who "acts" kind because she or he is unable to understand possible psychological reasons underlying behaviors that may appear unkind.

Stage 1 (ages 1 to 9)

The stage of *one-way assistance* characterizes a friend as one who does what the other friend wants. The concept of give-and-take has not yet been learned. A child may say, "Paul is not my friend anymore; he would not play Nintendo, and I wanted to."

Stage 2 (ages 6 to 12)

The stage of *two-way fair-weather cooperation* is characterized by reciprocity, each child considers the other's view. Mutual participation must exist for friendship to work, although self-interests are basic rather than mutual interests. "Marty and I are friends. She likes me and I like her."

Stage 3 (ages 9 to 15)

In adolescence, friendship is viewed as systematic and ongoing. There is a shift to collaborating for mutual interests rather than self-interests. In this stage of *intimate, mutually shared relationships*, friends share feelings and help each other. "She is my best friend, I can tell her things I don't tell anyone else. She understands my feelings; we help each other."

As children enter adolescence, they seek friends who share common interests and values. It is no longer necessary to base friendships on concrete behaviors. Moving into Piaget's stage of formal operations allows children to understand more abstract qualities in friends, for example, loyalty. Generally, disputes are no longer powerful enough to destroy friendships because now they have become long-term agreements. Mutual investment in each other warrants the willingness to work through conflicts. Friendships are particularly intense for girls.

Stage 4 (age 12 and older)

In *autonomous interdependent friendships*, both dependency and autonomy are respected and essential. Adolescents and adults in this stage understand that friends give psychological support to each other, yet each allows the other to develop other relationships as well. The nonpossessiveness of this stage is captured by an individual in the Selman & Selman study (1979) who says, "One thing about a good friendship is that it's a real commitment, a risk you have to take. You have to be able to support and trust and give, but you have to be able to let go, too" (p.73).

Of interest to elementary school counselors is the fact that friendships are central to the personal and social development of children. Arguments and rejections among friends may be devastating and necessitate individual and/or group counseling. Friendship groups are effective in elementary schools to facilitate the establishment and maintenance of healthy relationships. Children who learn to establish good communication with others are more likely to progress through the multilevels of relatedness as adults. Friendships provide increasing social and emotional fulfillments that cultivate the development of greater self-awareness.

Self-Concept

Self-concept is the psychological term which refers to our self-perceptions, how we think and feel about ourselves and our strengths and weaknesses. Self-concepts are fluid; sometimes our glass feels half-empty and sometimes it feels half-full. Our behavior is influenced by our current perception of ourselves. Self-concepts are not permanent, they change as we develop and vary in different situations. Children may have a positive self-concept about schoolwork, but a low self-concept as a friend or in sports.

The developing self-concept is shaped by experiences with parents, families, friends, classmates, and teachers. Elementary schools give children opportunities to compare themselves with other children in work and play. Young children perceive themselves concretely in terms of what they can do and how they look.

As they get older and mental processes become more sophisticated, children perceive themselves in more abstract terms of personality, for example, as friendly, kind, and cooperative. Through interactions with others, images are reflected back to children and permit self-evaluation.

To ensure opportunities for the development of a positive self-concept, it is imperative that adults, parents, and teachers set up experiences in work and play that allow children to succeed. Reinforcing children's attempts at tasks and concentrating more on effort than final products helps children feel good about themselves. Encouragement fuels children's interest in continuing to try; criticism crushes the interest and the self. A continued low self-concept can severely impair a child's social development and influence academic achievement as well.

Purkey (1970) suggested that school success more likely occurs in children with positive self-concepts. Also, Metcalfe (1981) states that positive attitudes toward school correlate with positive self-concepts in children. Finding a relationship between self-concept and school achievement, however, does not indicate that positive self-concepts "cause" more school success. It could be the reverse, that doing well in school produces a positive self. Knowing they are related is important information for school counselors.

Characteristics of Elementary School Children

Mini profiles of the development of children from 5 to 12 years old and implications for counseling are listed. These are general nomothetic characteristics that are not intended to identify specific children. As you have learned in this chapter, stage theories provide a sequential and orderly framework within which to understand all types of development. Look for parallels, for example, between Piaget's theory, and this list of age-related behaviors to assist your developmental perspective of children. This list is derived from Muro and Dinkmeyer in *Counseling in the Elementary and Middle Schools* (1977).

The Developmental Ages

Five-Year-Olds

Protect themselves: when allowed the freedom to choose and decide, they will protect themselves by attempting to do only those things that insure success

Good behavior: readily respond to orders and commands; relate well to parents and teachers; seldom display any temper

Prefer to play with those their own age

Enjoy being helpful

Need and want immediate attention from adults

May constantly interrupt adult conversations

Want to relate all experiences as they happen

Can and will sit quietly

Tend to like school

Enjoy and appreciate structure

Attention span is 20–25 minutes

Play is a major part of their world

Thrive on praise

Beyond Five And 1/2

Harsh and combative

Hesitant, dawdling, indecisive, over-demanding, explosive

Behavior characterized by opposite extremes

More restless

May stand up to complete work because cannot remain still for long periods of time

Behave more calmly at school than home

Increase in tantrums

Response to commands not as rapid as before

Increase in reversals of letters and numbers

Implications for Counseling Five-Year-Olds

The classroom is a safe environment for kindergartners. At times your counseling with children from this age group will require that they leave their room. You will develop friendships with them if you make frequent informal visits there, as well as visits for classroom guidance. Keep counseling sessions short and in the here-and-now. Although some children will talk easily, we recommend that discussions are held in tandem with play. Use encouragement and point out his or her strengths as a way to instill a sense of self-worth. Keep a positive attitude.

Six-Year-Olds

Extremely egocentric

Plagued by opposites: perform and rebel, laugh and cry

Express themselves with all parts of the body, particularly with the hands

Possess boundless supply of energy

Tire easily

May encounter difficulty with first-time tasks

Poor habits and classroom problems are more likely to occur in afternoons

Use verbal sounds as tensional outlets

Exhibit explosive behavior

Brash, fresh, argumentative, and silly

May cry easily and fly off into a tantrum

Thrives on praise and encouragement

Can be boastful about abilities

Egocentricity causes interpersonal problems: difficult to share, to take turns, and most especially to lose

Critical of friends

May cheat, but quicker to accuse others of cheating

Relationship with teacher becomes more personal

Perceives teacher as source of all knowledge

Encounters difficulty in making changes

May not always tell the truth

Minimal stealing may occur, but they do not consider it as stealing, rather collecting objects that do not belong to them

Begin to develop sense of time

Implications for Counseling Six-Year-Olds

Continue to work closely with classrooms and to combine play and verbal approaches to counseling. Six-year-olds are dramatic and expressive, therefore, they respond well to role-playing. Because of their impulsive behavior, counselors must set limits to control their behavior. Minimize the minor stealing (borrowing) at this stage. It is sufficiently addressed using bibliotherapy in small groups or in classroom guidance. In essence, bibliotherapy is the therapeutic use of story books and stories as a way to enter and teach in the world of children. Counselors read and discuss stories that contain lessons or generate original relevant stories. Stay in the here-and-now and continue to encourage.

Seven-Year-Olds

More calm, organized, and quiet
Are active thinkers
Able to reason and arrive at conclusions
Can concentrate and reflect—at times leads to moodiness, sullenness, and self-criticism
Express lack of self-confidence
Operate more in world of feeling
Utilize far fewer tensional releases
Internalize and worry
Blame others for things that may be wrong with them
Can and do sit quietly for longer periods of time
More serious, thoughtful, and sensitive
Develop a bit of self-criticism
Relationship with teacher more personal
Encounter problems accepting criticism from others
Like to be group members
Do not enjoy being singled out, even for praise
Balk at corrective action
Do not want to be perceived as problems by anyone
Able to concentrate and complete tasks

Implications for Counseling Seven-Year-Olds

Development of cognitive abilities permits the effective use of a verbal approach to counseling. Since play is still a vivacious form of expression for seven-year-olds, counseling would be remiss without its inclusion at some level. Counselors may focus more on feelings because children in this stage are aware of them and can label them. Unlike younger children, they will also accept counselor interpretations and confrontations. Longer counseling sessions and the use of games are effective.

Eight-Year-Olds

Explosive
Highly dramatic and inquisitive

Undertake more than they can perform

Enthusiastic and curious

Energetic

Few tensional outlets

Anticipate events with great eagerness and often assume "know-it-all" attitudes

Interest is short-lived and impatience is frequently displayed

Demanding of their parents and teachers

Tend to be verbally "fresh"

Exaggerate and become critical

Sometimes capable of extended self-criticism

The group plays an increasingly important role

Peer relationships begin to stabilize

Able to assume more responsibility for their actions

Are active seekers of praise

Implications for Counseling Eight-Year-Olds

Eight-year-olds exhibit a greater degree of self-control which enables them to respond well to group counseling discussions. Games are useful, but not necessary for expression. When counseling for misbehavior, the counselor should focus on the purpose of the behavior and facilitate discovery of alternative behaviors. Eight-year-olds are willing to accept responsibility for their behaviors.

Nine-Year-Olds

Age of general confusion

Age of independence

Distance between child and parents increases

Peer group increasingly important

Lose need for a close adult relationship

Prefer adults on activity level (Little League, Girl Scouts)

Desire to be considered mature and independent

Extremely high activity level

Love to test their strength

Can think independently and critically

Sense of space now includes community

Increasing sense of truthfulness

Prefer groups or clubs to intimate relationships

Test self-concepts against peer standards

Typically not self-confident

May ignore introspection and instead compare themselves with group standards

Can exhibit understanding and feeling for others

Likely to rebel against authority and may choose withdrawal or excessive complaint

Implications for Counseling Nine-Year-Olds

Nine-year-olds enjoy sharing in group counseling with or without games, and talk easily in individual counseling. Increased cognitive development permits analysis of their behaviors and the ability to respond to values clarification activities. The counselor, through modeling, can teach them to be empathic. Nine-year-olds experience feeling "understood" by their counselor and by other children who respond empathically. The ability to understand how others feel as a result of their behavior impacts their desire and willingness to change. Play therapy becomes less effective in this stage.

Ten-Year-Olds

Approach life in casual manner

Television is integral part of their worlds

Obedient, good-natured

Fun to work with

Sense of time includes minutes, years, and even centuries

Capable of getting around alone, running errands

Increased tendency to tell the truth

Self-concept improves

Enjoy life

Positive toward peers, school, and home

Greater acceptance of behavior and attitudes of others

May give compliments freely

Can praise adults and other children

Generally are well-adjusted

Free of most complications

Are quite dependable

Can display sudden and sharp bursts of temper, but, for the most part, can both give and receive affection

Are usually verbal

Enjoy reading and talking more than writing

Form good personal relationships

Have calm, happy personalities

Implications for Counseling Ten-Year-Olds

Ten-year-olds can actively participate in verbal individual and group counseling. Although play is important to them, play therapy is less effective than more cognitively complex activities. This age group can generate their own insights and conclusions from topics. Bibliotherapy is useful in discussing personalities and hypothesizing motives of the characters. Although ten-year-olds can name their weaknesses, it is advantageous for counselors to help them focus more clearly on their strengths. Encouragement from the counselor is an essential element in all developmental stages.

Eleven-Year-Olds

Show more self-assertion, curiosity, and sociability

Restive, love to talk, wiggle a lot

Intensity of emotions

Can label emotional states

Don't like to spend large amounts of time at home

May be frequently frustrated

Competitive

Silly

Use "off-color words"

Emotional mood swings

Can engage in "adultlike" conversation

Observe reactions they produce in adults and peers

Have good peer interests

Are sensitive to the nature of what happens in the group, although still able to make individual judgments despite group pressure

Enjoy group competition

Are curious

Exuberance can lead to tussles and fights with playmates

Will tease

Can be cruel to less fortunate peers

Implications for Counseling Eleven-Year-Olds

Patience is required to work with eleven-year-olds. A roaming memory, unintentional rudeness, and excessive body movements to relieve inner tension may be typical at this stage. On topics of interest, their speech is quick and animated. Counselor effectiveness is increased by interjecting direct leads regarding problematic issues. Once focused, eleven-year-olds can analyze and hypothesize reasonably well regarding their behavior. They respond well to contingency contracts. See Chapter 3 for more information on writing these behavioral contracts. Questions about sexual development may arise. These children respond well to an empathic counselor with a sense of humor. Complaints about the teacher are common and include: too demanding, too strict, too bossy. Listen to these patiently realizing they are likely a reflection of this developmental age perspective. Verbal approaches to counseling are appropriate for both individuals and groups. Mixing boys and girls in groups at this age level may be difficult.

Twelve-Year-Olds

Flow from very childlike behavior to that of mature adulthood

Are spirited, enthusiastic

Have growing sense of intuition and insight

Are capable of remaining seated for longer periods of time, but continue to exhibit twitches and wiggles

Tensional outlets reduced

Girls may show rapid development in both height and weight

Boys may show marked sexual development

More concerned with their bodies and may require more privacy

Emotionally may exhibit less disagreeable or moody patterns of behavior

Generally may be good-natured, warm, and empathic to adults and peers

Moving toward the point of self-control

Become increasingly self-reliant, self-centered, and assured of self-importance

More thoughtful and definite sense of humor

Self-accepted

Can identify and label assets and enjoy focusing on them

Most like school

Peers continue to be very important; strong desire to be one of the group, clothing and fads must not deviate too far from the group

Implications for Counseling Twelve-Year-Olds

Boy-girl barriers are less evident in twelve-year-olds which allows the utilization of mixed sex groups. They respond enthusiastically to groups focused on the identification of their potentials and those of their peers. Sex and sexual activity is an increasingly interesting topic. If the topic is introduced, children benefit from correct information regarding their dramatic body changes from an adult they can trust. Verbal interactions are effective. Contingency contracts are useful with twelve-year-olds when a team agreement is reached between student, counselor, and teacher. Parents should be included in contract writing when applicable. Refer to Chapter 3 on theories for more information on contingency contracts.

Summary

Understanding the developmental characteristics of elementary school children provides a scientific base for planning learning experiences, guiding social and emotional maturation, and monitoring physical motor growth characteristics. This chapter presents a brief review of the development of elementary school children and the implications these developmental characteristics pose for the elementary school counselor.

It is noted that physical growth makes new experiences and new responses possible, determines experiences, affects self-concept, and influences behavioral changes. There is also rapid psychological development of the child. The rapid growth of the child's cognitive processes of understanding, thinking, and language usage from Piaget's four stages of cognitive development is noted. Learning theories are introduced as a means for elementary school counselors to understand classroom management, discipline, and motivational strategies. The academic nature of the school setting necessitates counselors' knowledge of learning theories and enriches their roles as both counselor and consultant with children.

Social and personal development are discussed as primary areas of focus for the elementary counseling and guidance curriculum. The elementary counselor helps children bridge the gap between their two significant worlds: the home and the school. Erik Erikson's theory is cited to give a basic understanding of psychosocial development from birth through old age. A brief description of friendships and self-concepts is included because of their importance in the lives of elementary school children.

Deliberate planning is essential for providing the appropriate positive socialization experiences for *all* children. The importance of each child learning to live socially and harmoniously with others, to create pleasant and rewarding social relationships, and to accept and be accepted by others cannot be underestimated or overlooked. The elementary school counseling program has a major and awesome responsibility to insure conditions conducive to this end.

The importance of a school environment which stimulates learning, socialization, positive self-concept development and feelings of belonging and security cannot be left to chance. The elementary school counselor, the principal, and teachers are team members: architects who are responsible for constructing this environment—one that maximizes the school and social success of every child. Counselors can be cornerstones in developing counseling and guidance programs whose emphasis on valuing and enhancing all areas of child development permeates all areas of the curriculum.

Mini-profiles of the developmental ages of five through twelve are outlined. Implications for counseling children at the various stages of development are included to assist you in matching your counseling approach to their level of understanding. We suggest that you refer back to Piaget's theory of cognitive development which parallels cognitive abilities with the appropriate use of play therapy or verbal counseling.

We have discussed physical, cognitive, personal, and social development in isolated sections in this chapter. In real life, however, these processes unfold concurrently to create the miracle of the whole child.

While you work as a counselor, you will actively communicate that you value and accept children and their difficult, yet dynamic, quests to become the best people they can be. As the counselor, you are the spokesperson, model, and creator for advocating the creation of a safe psychological school environment for all children (and adults).

The counselor is encouraged to be a caring, creative, and expressive advocate for the child. Consequently, school counseling may be considered the "heart" of the school's curriculum. Chapter 3 will discuss ways to further your growth and development as a counselor by providing a theoretical basis for counseling in schools.

Chapter 3

Theories of Counseling

"It is only with the heart
that one can see rightly;
what is essential
is invisible to the eye."
—ANTON DE SAINT-EXUPERY (1971)

An Introduction to Theory

Generating theories is a common practice with most of us. We speculate on what is the best way to teach a class, spend a vacation or sell a new car based on our previous experiences. Parents decide on certain child-rearing practices based on their previous experiences perhaps modified by suggestions from other parents. Children also develop their own theories on a variety of subjects including how to behave in certain situations based on the results such behavior has achieved in the past. In these examples, we can understand that theories are statements that seek to explain connections between events. They are the results of experiences which generate predictions to guide practice.

While the elementary school counselor is primarily interested in "theory" from a psychological viewpoint, we would also note the importance of understanding the whole child from biological and social or sociological viewpoints as well. Therefore, before proceeding to emphasize the psychological, we will take brief note of these other important contributions to understanding children.

From the biological point of view, an organism is viewed as a physical or biochemical system. Disease, physical damage to the body, and/or inadequate development of internal organs may all hamper an individual's ability to get along in the outside world. For example, some forms of mental retardation are due to abnormal development of the brain and nervous system. It is also known that one form of senility is due to a breakdown of the blood vessels of the brain. Physical abnormalities are the main province of medical science. The medical approach to treatment employs medication, surgery, and other physical methods to cure, or at least ameliorate, disorders (Schmolling, Youkeles, Burger, 1989, p. 116).

The social point of view examines the powerful influences of family, schools, neighborhood, and society. To the human services worker, one of the most important social variables is socioeconomic status. This includes specific factors such as income, level of education, and the prestige value of one's occupation. High-level executives, administrators, and professional persons rate higher on this scale than do blue-collar workers and welfare recipients. The majority of those who receive help from human services are concentrated in the lower income levels (Schmolling, Youkeles, Burger, 1989, p. 116).

The psychological point of view is that of a behavioral science examining how and why the individual behaves in varying circumstances and environments. As with any science, the goal of psychology and its related specialties including counseling, are, as a science, to understand, predict, and control natural phenomena; to observe and classify facts for the establishment of hypotheses which when tested can lead to verifiable laws of practice. As a science, we are concerned with accumulating and extending the frontiers of knowledge in a systematic manner through the discovery of general truths. In the professional field of counseling, therefore, we have over the years, generated theoretical structures which in turn have been established on empirical bases providing us with technological knowledge which in turn provides us with guidelines for practice and service to clients.

The process of theory development may be viewed as a four-step one as noted in Table 3–1.

We would conclude this introductory section by noting that there exists controversy and at times confusion among biological, sociological, and psychological theories regarding, for example, such common social concerns as alcoholism, criminality, schizophrenia, and other disorders. Too, within the counseling profession, we must recognize that many differing experiences may exist regarding the same phenomena of human behaviors leading to a conclusion that all human

TABLE 3–1 PROCESS OF THEORY DEVELOPMENT

Step 1.	Experiences leading to speculation
Step 2.	Generation of a theory based on Step 1
Step 3.	Research: Gathering of empirical data that verifies or rejects the theory
Step 4.	Determining of skills and knowledge needed to implement theory and conversion to practice (if verified in step 3)

behavior theories are imperfect. This, in turn, means that a certain amount of overlap in some instances and opposing viewpoints in others may be anticipated as you examine popular counseling theories in the paragraphs which follow. Nonetheless, established counseling theories should be viewed as providing proven guidelines for effective counseling. They provide us with a recognized means for organizing client information and the counseling process itself.

As you examine these theories also keep in mind that you are seeking to identify a theory, or combination of theories, that you would be comfortable with and could implement in practice. You must also keep in mind that some children may respond better to one counseling approach than another and also, that some counseling situations may more effectively utilize one particular theory or combination of theories.

Popular Counseling Theories

The following counseling theories are subsumed under one of the three major forces of psychology: behaviorism, psychoanalysis, or humanistic psychology. Thus, the practice of counseling is guided by the choice of theoretical assumptions adopted by the counselor. As you develop your professional identity, your personal theoretical orientation will evolve based on one of these schools of psychological thought. Coursework in theory of counseling provides an in-depth investigation of each of these. However, in this text only a brief description of their basic principles will be discussed.

Psychoanalysis is based on the notion that people are ruled by unconscious forces (psychic energy). Study in psychoanalytic theory is focused on the conflicts that exist between these forces and the effects these conflicts have on human behavior.

Behaviorists view the human being as a machine which reacts to its environment in a mechanistic manner. Human beings are regarded as passive beings who respond to environmental stimuli. Conscious thought, for example, internal mental processing, is believed to have no influence on behavior.

The third force, humanistic psychology, emphasizes the study of people as human beings rather than as machines. It focuses on conscious experience, free will, spontaneity, and creativity of the whole individual.

Psychoanalysis

The development of psychoanalytic theory is attributed primarily to Sigmund Freud (1856-1939).

> *Freud gave psychology a new look and new horizons. For instance, he called attention to psychodynamic factors that motivate behavior, focused on the role of the unconscious, and developed most of the first therapeutic procedures for understanding and modifying the structure of one's basic character. Freud stim-*

ulated a great deal of controversy, exploration, and further development of personality theory and laid the foundation on which later psychodynamic systems rest. His theory is a benchmark against which many other theories are measured (Corey, 1986, pp. 11–12).

Psychoanalysis became one of the most influential psychological forces of this century and one that has had a profound effect on the development of numerous counseling theories. A brief sketch of the basic principles of psychoanalysis is presented here.

The subject matter of psychoanalysis is abnormal behavior, and its goal is to provide therapy for mentally ill persons. Unlike other psychologies, psychoanalysis deals with the unconscious.

Freud related the laws applicable to energy changes in a physical system to the human being. For the first time in history, Freud regarded man as an energy system who obeyed the same physical laws that regulate physical forces in our universe. Consequently, psychoanalysis is a dynamic psychology in which transformations and exchanges of energy within the personality are studied.

According to Freud, mental energy is released in the individual through instincts, the biological forces which drive the personality. Freud's early work postulated psychic life in three parts: the preconscious, the conscious, and the unconscious. The preconscious consisted of any material that had not been repressed by the individual and thus could be summoned into conscious awareness easily. The conscious part is mental activity that is immediately available to a person's awareness, the visible portion of an iceberg. The unconscious is the enormous portion that lies beneath the surface and is the least accessible part of personality. The instincts that are the powerful propelling forces of all human behavior are contained in the unconscious.

These distinctions were later revised by Freud into the three-part organization of the id, ego, and superego. The id corresponds to the unconscious in that it is the source of all drives and the reservoir of all psychic energy. Its function is to provide release of tension or energy. The id seeks immediate satisfaction regardless of circumstances. It operates on what Freud called the *pleasure principle*. The aim of the pleasure principle is tension reduction. Tension is experienced as pain, and tension release is experienced as pleasure, therefore, the discharge of tension as a function of the pleasure principle is to avoid pain and gain pleasure.

Libido, contained in the id, is our basic psychic energy and is concerned with the manifestation of self-preservation and survival of the species. These instincts include hunger, sex, and thirst. When libidinal energy is increased, tension is increased and the individual attempts tension reduction by interacting with the external world. The id, however, is blind, insistent and passionate, and requires a mediating agent between it and the real world.

The ego serves this function and is the second construct in the mental apparatus. It is characterized by reason and rationality. The ego operates on what Freud called the *reality principle* forcing the id to wait until an appropriate outlet is available for tension release or reduction. Freud compared the relationship between the id and ego to that of a horse and its rider. The horse supplies the power for the rider, but the rider must continuously guide and check the power of the horse or risk being thrown to the ground. Similarly, the ego guides and checks the power of the id so that id satisfactions are met most favorably and with respect to the external world.

The third component in Freud's structure of personality is the superego which represents parental values; it is one's moral code. Freud (1933) stated that the superego represents "every moral restriction, the advocate of a striving towards perfection—it is, in short, as much as we have been able to grasp psychologically of what is described as the higher side of human life" (cited in Schultz and Schultz, 1987, pp. 310-311). The superego strives for perfection rather than for pleasure (id) or reality (ego). Two subsystems constitute the superego: the ego-ideal and the conscience. The ego-ideal represents what a child believes to be morally good by the parents' standards. This is communicated through rewards for "good" behavior. In contrast, the conscience corresponds to what the child perceives as morally bad according to the parents. This is communicated through punishments for "bad" behavior. Conflict exists between the superego and the id. The function of the superego is not to postpone id satisfaction, rather to totally inhibit id impulses. Thus, the ego mediates between the conflicting demands of the id and the superego's attempts to substitute moralistic goals. When the ego cannot maintain balance between these two systems, it is threatened and anxiety develops.

When these three systems work together cooperatively, they allow an individual satisfaction and efficient interactions within the environment. One's basic needs and desires are fulfilled, and the person is considered mentally healthy. However, the person is considered maladjusted when these three systems are not working harmoniously and in a unified fashion.

Counseling (therapy) seeks to construct a normal personality by bringing out that which is repressed so it can be dealt with in conscious awareness. Freud stated that "our scientific work in psychology will consist in translating unconscious processes into conscious ones, and thus filling in the gaps in conscious perceptions" (cited in Hall, 1979, p. 55). Thus, a primary goal of psychoanalysis is to make the unconscious conscious. To this end, several techniques may be used. These

> *techniques are geared to increasing awareness, gaining intellectual insights into the client's behavior, and understanding the meanings of symptoms. The therapeutic progression is from the client's talk to catharsis to insight to working through unconscious material toward the goals of intellectual and emotional understanding and re-education, which, it is hoped, lead to personality change. (Corey, 1986, p. 34)*

Detailed case studies of clients are usually prepared. Free association, dream analysis, and even attention to "Freudian slips" (parapraxes) may all be utilized by the counselor.

As may be noted in Table 3–2, psychoanalytic theory is not particularly popular among practicing elementary school counselors. One disadvantage is the time factor involving such concerns as case study preparation and length of therapy. Too, limits on children's cognitive development and verbal skills must be considered. While children appear to be relatively receptive to dream analysis, Thompson & Rudolph (1983) notes that

> *the problem of free association is more difficult. Children seem to be unable or unwilling to do this. It is now widely believed that non-directive free play, particularly that involving symbolic make-believe (using dolls as particular real people, a stick as a gun, and the like) is closely analogous to free association. The assumption is that children will translate their imagination into symbolic play action rather than words. Some counselors use play therapy as a necessary prelude to verbal psychodynamic counseling and not necessarily as therapy in itself. (Thompson & Rudolph, 1983, p. 168)*

One example, where the use of play therapy by an elementary school counselor served as a prelude to verbal expression, involved an eight-year-old boy whose father had recently died. He was accustomed to spending the first few minutes of his session engaged in sand play. During one session, he used miniature figurines to create what was happening in his family. During the second half of the session he verbally shared with the counselor his pent-up feelings and unanswered questions related to his father's death (Vinturella and James, 1987, p. 229).

Person-Centered

Person-centered theory, like psychoanalytic, represents another historical landmark in both the development of counseling theory and the advancement of the counseling profession. Again, one individual, Carl Ranson Rogers (1902-1987), was largely responsible for both the theoretical formulation and early writings which established its popularity. His books *Counseling and Psychotherapy* (1942), *Client-Centered Therapy* (1951), and *On Becoming a Person* (1961) have become classics in the field. In these and his other writings, Rogers challenged the then traditional viewpoint of the nature of counseling and the directive model which assigned the counselor the role of "expert."

In the six decades that Rogers worked as a psychologist, he developed and crystallized his person-centered (originally labeled non-directive and later client-centered) approach to psychotherapy. He was driven by his personal edict that through the development of a quality interpersonal relationship, the therapist could facilitate within the living human being his or her potential for growth and development.

Unlike other psychologies that investigated animal and human behavior (behaviorism) and mental illness (psychoanalysis), Rogers sought the meaning of personal growth; the conditions necessary for personal growth; how one person can effectively help another; and how to foster creativity. In *Client-Centered Therapy* (1951), Rogers spoke of therapy as "a process, a thing-in-itself, an experience, a relationship, a dynamic . . . therapy is of the essence of life" (pp. ix, x).

Rogers' person-centered counseling places emphasis on the personal relationship that develops between the counselor and the client. His basic premise was that the individual had the capacity to handle all the information that came into awareness during counseling. The role of the counselor was to create an interpersonal relationship which resulted in the client's awareness of previously distorted material.

In person-centered counseling, the counselor stimulates the client's self-actualization. Within the framework of humanistic psychology, self-actualization is defined by Abraham Maslow (1968) as:

> *an episode, or a spurt in which the powers of the person come together in a particularly efficient and intensely enjoyable way, and in which he is more integrated and less split, more open for experience, more idiosyncratic, more perfectly expressive or spontaneous, or fully functioning, more creative, more humorous, more ego-transcending, more independent of his lower needs, etc. He becomes in these episodes more truly himself, more perfectly actualizing his potentialities, closer to the core of his Being, more fully human. (p. viii)*

The person-centered view emphasizes the tremendous potential and belief in the individual client for self-understanding, problem solution and growth. Although the primary responsibility for change rests with the client, the extent to which the therapeutic alliance between the counselor and client promotes growth and development is determined by the quality of the relationship which is the counselor's responsibility. Rogers stated that ". . . it is the quality of the interpersonal encounter with the client which is the most significant element in determining effectiveness" (Rogers and Stevens, 1967, p. 89).

Rogers concluded that effectiveness in relating was due to certain attitudinal ingredients of the therapist which resulted in a growth-promoting climate. He later named these the core conditions necessary for a positive outcome in counseling.

One of these conditions is congruence, which means the counselor is what she or he is. She or he is genuine and open in his or her relationship with the client. The second necessary condition is empathy, the ability to sense the client's inner world and to communicate that understanding to the client. Unconditional positive regard is the third essential attitude. Rogers describes it as "an outgoing, positive feeling without reservation and without evaluation. It means not making judgments" (Rogers and Stevens, p. 94).

In addition to these three conditions, Rogers emphasized the necessity of client perception. He believed that unless the three conditions were communicated unambiguously to the client, therapy would be ineffective. Therefore, it is not enough for the counselor to feel that the conditions exist, rather it is essential that the client perceive their existence in the counselor.

In *Psychotherapist's Casebook* (1986), Rogers noted the "dependence of the person-centered approach on the actualizing tendency of every living organism, that is, the tendency to grow, to develop, to realize its full potential" (cited in Kirschenbaum and Henderson, 1989, p. 137). Client-centered counselors trust this human directional flow toward a more complex and complete development, and it is this flow that humanistic counseling aims to release.

Rogers (1986) wrote about his discovery of a fourth characteristic of a growth-promoting relationship. He discovered that when he was closest to his inner, intuitive self, that simply his presence was helpful and releasing. His inner spirit reached the inner spirit of the other forming a transcendent relationship in which profound growth and healing and energy were present.

He noted that possibly the mystical, spiritual dimension of humanness had been underestimated, and through his own experiences, had encountered its power to promote human growth.

To conclude, Rogers, in 1986, stated the central hypothesis of person-centered therapy in that

> *the individual has within himself or herself vast resources for self-understanding, for altering his or her self-concept, attitudes, and self-directed behavior—and that these resources can be tapped if only a definable climate of facilitative psychological attitudes can be provided. (Kirschenbaum and Henderson, 1989, p. 135)*

Person-centered counseling may be construed, not simply as a technique or a method, but a basic philosophy, a way of being. An approach, that when expressed through the counselor's attitudes and behaviors, creates a growth-promoting climate in which client self-exploration and self-discovery eventuates constructive changes in personality and behavior. Counseling, according to Rogers, is the process in which a therapist accompanies a client in the journey toward the core of the self.

The person-centered approach suggests that elementary school counselors need to consider first of all, the importance of the relationship they establish with the child. We assume that elementary counselors genuinely like children and will be able to convey their caring and understanding to clients at this level, since children are sensitive to congruence and honesty in adults, counselors must be genuine and trustworthy in building a relationship with children. The counselor's attending behavior is also important since verbal capacities may limit elementary children's ability to express themselves, but non-verbal cues may compensate somewhat. Certainly, children, like adults, must be given the opportunity and be encouraged to express themselves in a non-threatening environment.

Williams and Lair (1991) discuss the benefits of elementary school counselors using the person-centered approach with students who have disabilities that may interfere with their education, eventual employment, or both. Examples of these disabilities include: "(a) a loss of vision or hearing; (b) communication disorders; (c) muscular dystrophy; (d) orthopedic impairments; (e) cosmetic disfigurements; (f) mental retardation; (g) psychological disorders; (h) cerebral palsy; and (i) epilepsy" (p. 194).

According to Williams & Lair (1991), the counselor who approaches the student from a person-centered perspective communicates his or her recognition of the student as not merely a person with a disability, but, rather, as someone comprised of a range of attributes that can be applied in the student's pursuing a more rewarding role in his or her life. The following principles, as proposed by Hadley & Brodwin (1988), are suggested as useful in assisting the student in progressing toward this goal:

1. *The elementary school counselor should use precise language so that the whole person of the client is recognized. . . .*
2. *The counselor should avoid the use of subjective expressions that stereotype people who have a disability. . . .*
3. *The counselor should keep the child's disability in perspective. In situations in which the disability has little relevance, one need not make reference to it. . . .*
4. *Children who have disabilities should be portrayed by the counselor as actively going about the business of living as other people do, not as helpless victims, super heroes, or tragedy personified. (p. 200)*

Our inclusion of this example does not imply that the use of person-centered counseling is restricted to children with disabilities. Rather, it is one example of its application in an elementary school setting.

Individual Psychology

The origins of individual psychology are attributed to Alfred Adler, who developed this theory after his split with Sigmund Freud. Frequently referred to as Adlerian counseling, this theory views individuals holistically as unique, purposive, social beings and places more emphasis on conscious rather than unconscious behavior. This theory also presents a positive and growth-oriented view of the individual, one in which humans have the capacity to live positively and cooperatively in society. The label "social interest" is applied to human desires. Humans want to belong and feel accepted. Individuals also are presumed to have the desire to develop their potential; to self-actualize; and, to achieve a position of competence in family and society.

Adlerian psychology, then, focuses on the whole person and the individual's goals and lifestyles in a societal context. Within this framework, counselors help clients change their cognitive perceptions so they can feel good about themselves and can be encouraged to develop socially and acquire healthy attitudes and behaviors. The Adlerian process involves four stages: (1) relationship establishment; (2) diagnosis; (3) interpretation and insight; and, (4) reorientation.

TABLE 3–2 Theoretical Orientations of 68 Elementary School Counselors (Percent Responding)

Eclectic	61%
Individual Psychology (Adlerian)	57%
Person-Centered	46%
Behavioral	44%
Reality	41%
Rational-Emotive	30%
Integrated	14%
Transactional Analysis	4%
Gestalt	4%
Other	2%
Psychoanalytic	0%

During the counseling process, the counselor is caring, committed, uses common sense language and may emphasize social participation and the development of worthwhile goals.

Since the elementary counselor works frequently and closely with families, they should be aware of the fact that Adler was one of the pioneers of family therapy and many of his ideas and constructs are popular in present-day family therapy. In fact, the popularity of Adlerian theory with elementary counselors may be attributed in part to this interest. (See Table 3–2) This point is illustrated by a West Virginia counselor who commented, "Because I spend so much time with the families of my children counselees, I have found the Adlerian approach very helpful."

Kern and Carlson (1981) suggested five levels of intervention that could provide elementary school counselors with a variety of approaches which might help them deal better with families. They are as follows: (1) parent consultation; (2) parent education; (3) family enrichment; (4) family education centers; and (5) ethics and family counseling.

> *The first four interventions are highly educational in their approach and are, in essence, the cornerstone of the Adlerian approach. These interventions can be used successfully with most families and require only minimal advanced training for the elementary school counselor. The last intervention should be employed only if the other four do not seem feasible. The last intervention requires more extensive training and is probably applicable to a small number of families. (Kern and Carlson, 1981, p. 305)*

Also related to family therapy and children's needs are concerns for children of divorce and/or remarriage. The Adlerian approach can be useful to elementary counselors assisting children who are going through these transitions. These changes may lead children to believe that their place in the family is threatened. The resulting misbehaviors may indicate discouragement and cries for help. The elementary school counselor who uses an Adlerian approach works in cooperation with the child and significant others in the child's life to develop coping skills for adjusting to the stresses inherent in changing family constellations.

Counselors who implement Adlerian techniques can recognize the four common goals of misbehavior: attention, power, revenge, and feelings of inadequacy. They know that a misbehaving child is a discouraged child. Along with encouragement to increase self-esteem, Adlerians implement natural and logical consequences instead of punishment. A basic precept is that children are treated with respect and in a democratic fashion rather than an authoritarian one. Alfred Adler believed that the cooperation of children could be won more effectively than it could be demanded.

Counselors may implement Adlerian principles in individual or small group counseling. These become goals of group counseling and "correspond to the four phases that a group goes through: (1) establishing and maintaining the proper therapeutic relationship; (2) exploring the dynamics operating in the individual; (3) communicating to the individual an understanding of self; and (4) seeing new alternatives and making new choices" (Corey, 1990).

While counselors, working with teachers, can help children take responsibility for their behaviors at school, the most effective use of these techniques involves the inclusion of parents as well. A powerful Adlerian concept to remember is that "Children don't do what doesn't work." Therefore, counselors can help all adults in the child's world recognize how their behavior contributes to the child's misbehavior. Children change more quickly and feel more secure when all significant others in their lives maintain consistent expectations and responses to their behavior. Consequently, counselors who become knowledgeable in the practice of Adlerian techniques possess effective tools to share with others in helping children become more productive and self-confident. To help children, Walton & Powers (1978) suggest the following practices:

1. Help the child understand the goal of misbehavior.
2. Stop making the misbehavior worthwhile to the child.
3. Look for ways to encourage the child.
4. Use the class as a group to win children over to friendly and cooperative participation (p. 7).

For more specific information and techniques refer to *Winning Children Over: A manual for Teachers, Counselors, Principals, and Parents* by Francis X. Walton & Robert L. Powers (1978) and *Children: The Challenge* by Rudolf Dreikurs & Vicki Soltz (1987).

A Misbehavior Reaction Checklist for Teachers (Wickers, 1988, pp. 71-73) serves as a useful Adlerian tool for teachers to refer to in assessing how their own reactions might be contributing to a child's misbehavior. The checklist assists the teachers in understanding the student's behavior, as well as learning more effective responses to misconduct. Wickers explains that the checklist can be slightly reworded for use with parents whereby the same goal—understanding how the parent's reactions contribute to continued misbehavior while also educating them regarding more appropriate reactions—is pursued. (For more information regarding the checklist, refer to Wickers, 1988.)

An elementary school counselor in South Carolina formed a group for teachers and aides to inform them and promote the use of Adlerian techniques schoolwide.

Thus, while Adlerian theory was evolving long before elementary counseling was even labeled, elementary counselors today continue to find much of value in the writings of Adler and his later disciples.

Behaviorism

Behavioral therapy is of more recent popularity, having shown significant growth since the 1950s and is currently applied in a wide variety of settings, such as correctional facilities, child welfare agencies, schools, community mental health agencies, and so on. It is also used to treat a wide variety of problems, such as smoking, eating disorders, speech difficulties, substance abuse, and so on. Leaders in the movement have included E. L. Thorndike, John B. Watson, B. F. Skinner, and John D. Krumboltz.

Early behaviorists laid the foundation for behavioral theory by identifying concepts of behavior based on conditioning that influenced behaviors. These were identified as classical conditioning and operant conditioning and discussed in Chapter 2 of this text.

Behaviorists believe that an individual's behavior is the result of stimulus-response effects. They believe that this learned behavior is the product of the environment. Further, they emphasize that since human behavior is learned, it can also be unlearned. If the learned behavior is undesirable, it can be unlearned and new desirable behavior learned as a replacement. The client is viewed as both the producer and product of the environment (Kazdin, 1978), as capable of imagining which behaviors are desirable (Meichenbaum, 1977), and of then working to make those images a behavioral reality (Watson and Tharp, 1981), (cited in Gilliland, James, and Bowman, 1989, p. 157).

Goals are of central importance in behavioral counseling (Corey, 1986). They focus on changing maladaptive behavior, learning how to make appropriate decisions in avoiding problematic behaviors, and, therefore, encourage healthy and adaptive behaviors in the future.

Examples of behavioral techniques which may be useful for elementary school counseling include modeling as it demonstrates to the child appropriate behaviors; identifying peers who are models of the desired behavior; and, use of films, tapes, or dramatic enactments showing desired behaviors.

Tokens or point systems can be provided for rewards and recognition given for appropriate behaviors (and taken away for undesirable behaviors). Behavioral contracts can be used by elementary school counselors as a strategy for involving the student in specifying what behavioral changes are needed. "Contracting has proved highly effective with children in school settings" (Gilliland, James, and Bowman, 1989, p. 167).

"Like other contracts, the behavioral contract is a negotiated agreement between two parties—in this case, between the client and the counselor—in which both parties get something out of the contract and give something to the other individual involved in the contract" (Hansen, Stevic, and Warner, Jr., 1986., p. 174).

"For example, a student who wants to improve classroom behavior might agree that when behavior is appropriate, her or his counselor, teacher, and parents will praise the behavior, and when it is inappropriate, they will either ignore it or criticize it. In either case, the response consequences of both the desired and undesirable behaviors are specified in advance and agreed to by all parties" (Hansen, Stevic, and Warner, Jr., 1986, p. 175).

Behavior modification groups can provide small groups which provide a comfortable and "safe" setting in which children can practice new "replacement" behaviors within the group setting before trying them out in real settings. One such small group, used by Bleck & Bleck (1982) with disruptive third graders, was successful in raising the self-esteem scores and behavior rating scores of these students.

Small groups using peer facilitators can also be successful. Bowman & Myrick (1987) insist that teachers and counselors "need to continue searching for new ways to increase their abilities to reach more students more of the time," and that "peer facilitator programs are a logical strategy for approaching such needs" (p. 377). They discuss the success of a peer facilitator program in Gainesville, Florida which was coordinated and implemented by elementary school counselors in nine elementary schools. Fifth grade students (who were viewed by their teachers as student leaders) served as facilitators in affecting positively the behaviors and attitudes that certain second and third grade students (who were described by their teachers as having classroom behavior problems) had "towards their teachers, peers, and themselves as learners" (p. 374).

Rational-Emotive Therapy (R.E.T.)

Another popular and comparatively recent approach to counseling, *rational emotive theory*, achieved much of its popularity through the writings and presentations of Albert Ellis. Ellis believes that many people develop irrational and emotionally biased ways of thinking and decision-making. We often confuse feeling with thinking. This tendency for irrational thinking is often exacerbated by family and cultural influences. The results are poor decisions, inappropriate behaviors, and so on.

People do, however, have the potential to be rational and replace irrational behaviors and thoughts with those based on rational judgments. R.E.T., therefore, seeks to assist clients in making rational, thought-out, and evaluated decisions and to implement plans. It is a highly cognitive, active-directive, homework-assigning and discipline-oriented process. The counselor's role is one of challenging, suggesting, teaching, and confronting the client. The client thus becomes a learner.

Within this theoretical context, the elementary school counselor would seek to persuade, teach, and/or assign homework to the child in order to facilitate the desired behavior. A popular technique for examining irrational thought and behavior is role reversal (where the counselor plays the role of child).

A strategy through which rational emotive therapy methods can be adapted for use with children in the elementary school is suggested by Watkins (1983). He describes the *Rational Self-Analysis Format* (RSA) which is a tool developed by Maultsby (1976) that is used to assist clients in thinking more rationally. Since Maultsby's (RSA) was not suitable for the cognitive development of most children, Watkins adapted it to the language and understanding of children. The steps involved in using the tool can be understood by referring to Figure 3–1.

There are some limitations of R.E.T. with children which counselors should consider.

> *Studies have shown that children do not generalize well to other situations; that is, the improved behavior is limited to the specific circumstances. Furthermore, Piaget's research would indicate that children in the preformal stages of cognitive development might have difficulty in relating to the rational emotive counseling method. (Thompson & Rudolph, 1983, p. 90)*

Reality Therapy

Reality therapy provides another comparatively modern theory of counseling. William Glasser promoted this concept in the 1970s and his books *Reality Therapy: A New Approach to Psychiatry* (1965), *Schools Without Failure* (1969), and *Stations of the Mind: New Directions for Reality Therapy* (1981) have been extremely popular.

The view of reality therapists is that most psychological problems that people have can be attributed to their denial of the reality in the world around them. There is also some relationship to Maslow's theory of basic needs as reality theory suggests that people choose their behaviors in order to meet their basic needs. Disorders occur when they fail to do this or when others do it for them.

Reality therapy focuses on present behaviors and the need for individuals to have their own identity to feel worthwhile and cared for. Reality therapy also deals with the moral issues of right and wrong.

In reality therapy, the counselors task is to lead the client towards: (a) assuming more responsibility for their own well-being; (b) learning to make better choices; and,(c) establishing their own identity. The counselor functions as a

Step 1. Write down what happened	Step 2. Be a camera. If you were a camera and snapped a picture of what happened, what would you see and hear?	Rational Questions How do you know if you're thinking rationally? Ask, 1. Is my thought really real, say if I were a camera? 2. Does the thought help me stay alive and in good physical shape? 3. Does the thought help me get what I want? 4. Does the thought help me stay out of trouble with others? 5. Does the thought help me feel like I want to?
Step 3. Write down your thoughts about what happened. What did you think? A. B. C.	Step 5. Decide if your thoughts are rational. To do this, look at each thought you had and ask yourself the five questions listed in the upper right corner. Answer yes or no to each question and put your answer below. A. (1) B. (1) C. (1) (2) (2) (2) (3) (3) (3) (4) (4) (4) (5) (5) (5)	Step 7. Write down thoughts you could have that would be more rational than those listed. A. B. C.
Step 4. A. How did you feel? B. What did you do?	Step 6. How do you want to feel?	Step 8. What do you want to do?

FIGURE 3–1 Rational Self Analysis Format for Children

From "Rational Self-Analysis for Children," by C. E. Watkins (p. 305), in 1982. *Elementary School Guidance and Counseling, 17*. Reprinted with permission from the American Counseling Association as was adapted from "The Standard RSA Format" (p. 7), in *Freedom from Alcohol and Tranquilizers: The ABC's of Rational Self-Analysis (Booklet 3)*, by M. C. Maultsby, Jr. (1982). Reprinted with permission.

teacher who praises and/or indicates disapproval when appropriate. Counseling from a reality therapy perspective is simply a special form of teaching or training a person in a fairly short time, what she or he should have learned during normal growth (Glasser, 1965). The more irresponsible the person, the more she or he has to learn in order to perform responsibly. The overriding goal of reality therapy counseling is to teach the client through involvement how he or she can meet needs, using the three R's of right, responsibility, and reality as a guide. (Hansen, Stevic, and Warner, Jr., 1986, p. 186). It is an active, directive, cognitive-behavior oriented approach. The use of contracts is popular in reality therapy.

Guyton and Fielstein (1989) discuss one counselor's reaction to concerns of teachers in one elementary school that focused on their perceptions of students as lacking a sense of ownership for their school progress and learning. The school counselor organized the training of these students to become facilitators of their own student-led parent conferences. As was reported by parents and teachers after the conferences, the students assumed more responsibility for their well-being in regard to school. The students were described as assuming more ownership for their grades and academic progress.

Gestalt Theory

Gestalt therapy is an existentially based theoretical system, originally developed by Fritz Perls. The primary focus of Gestalt therapy is an awareness on "the here and now." This approach suggests that since the past is gone and the future has yet to arrive, only the present is important. This approach assumes individuals are capable of making appropriate choices since they have the potential to be fully aware (of sensations, thoughts, perceptions, and so on), but often they do not because at a younger age they introject ideals and behaviors that may not be suitable. In other words, the individual child has the capacity to cope with life's problems and behave appropriately, but he or she is taught by significant others that he or she is weak, unfair, selfish, and so on. Conflicts may therefore result between individual needs and environmental demands.

The counselor encourages the client to depend less on others; to take responsibility for their own lives; to be all they can be now—in the present; and, to become aware. "The process of 're-owning' parts of oneself that have been disowned and the unification process, proceed step by step until clients become strong enough to carry on their own personal growth" (Corey, 1986, p. 121). The counselor is warm, caring, accepting and supportive. Counseling techniques include "how" and "what" questions, confrontation, "I" statements, and sharing of awareness with clients with emphasis on "this moment" and the present.

Techniques with children can include awareness enhancing activities, fantasy games, incomplete sentence exercises, and self-esteem developing activities. Childers and Basse (1980) noted that

> *The Gestalt goal of awareness is an important affective, developmental skill for elementary school children to learn and practice. Children who experience*

> *awareness training may become more aware of their environment and their internal experiences than children who are not given explicit awareness training. An awareness group can be nourishing and growth producing to all students, not just for those who have a specific concern or difficulty. (p. 120)*

They gave as examples units which encouraged children's (a) awareness of the outside world, (b) internal (self) awareness, and (c) expressive feelings. Schrader & Remer (1980) discussed the effective use of similar Gestalt activities in an elementary classroom guidance program. (Their units were external awareness, internal awareness, and expressing feelings.) They concluded that the three units provided students with a sequential, skill learning experience which was centered on Gestalt awareness goals. The awareness experiences provided an opportunity for students to acquire some important life skills and to learn more about different parts of themselves in an experiential, nonacademic mode. Most important, the units demonstrated that Gestalt activities can appropriately and effectively be used with elementary school children, thus bridging a gap between Gestalt theory and practice.

Other Gestalt techniques include drawing, making things, storytelling, poetry, puppets, play therapy, and sensory experiences, such as music, touch, relaxation, and body movements. The Gestalt approach to counseling is used to increase self-awareness through experiences in "the here-and-now." Counselors provide opportunities that allow expressions through those modalities that are most familiar and fluent for children such as those mentioned above.

It is the specific purpose and type of intervention by the counselor that produces a Gestalt outcome of treatment. *In Windows To Our Children,* Violet Oaklander (1988) describes numerous creative methods which she uses to help children rediscover their own experiences and enable them to "grow strong in spite of the traumas in their lives" (p. 2).

Regardless of what she and the child choose to do at any session, Violet Oaklander (1988) states that her basic purpose is always:

> *. . . to help the child become aware of herself and her existence in her world . . . The process of work with a child is a gently, flowing one—an organic event. What goes on inside you, the therapist, and what goes on inside the child in any one session is a gentle merging. (p. 53)*

Drawing is used as a therapeutic technique in the following Gestalt process. The steps are adapted from an example recommended by Oaklander (1988).

1. *Have the child share the* experience *of drawing—her feelings about approaching and doing the task.*
2. *Have the child share the drawing itself.*
3. *On a deeper level, promote further self-discovery by asking her to elaborate on the parts of the picture; describing the shapes, forms, colors . . .*

4. *Ask the child to describe the picture as if it were the child, using the word "I." "I am this picture; I have red lines all over me and a blue square in my middle."*
5. *Pick specific things in the picture for the child to identify with: "Be the blue square and describe yourself further—what you look like, what your function is, etc."*
6. *Ask the child questions, if necessary, to aid the process: "What do you do?"...*
7. *Further focus the child's attention, and sharpen her awareness by emphasis and exaggeration of a part or parts of a picture ...*
8. *Have the child dialogue between two parts in her picture or two contrast points or opposing points (such as ..., the line around the square ...*
9. *Encourage the child to pay attention to colors ..." What do bright colors mean to you?"...*
10. *Watch for cues in the child's voice tone, body posture, facial and body expression, breathing, silence ...*
11. *Work on identification, help the child to "own" what has been said about the picture or parts of the picture.*
12. *Leave the drawing and work on the child's life situations and unfinished business that comes out of the drawing. Sometimes this is precipitated directly from the question, "Does this fit with your life?"...*
13. *Watch for the missing parts or empty spaces in the pictures and attend to that.*
14. *Stay with the child's foreground flow, or to my own foreground—where I find interest, excitement, and energy ... (pps. 53–56).*

Accompanying a child through a drawing in this manner allows a type of dissection and examination which provides the child with an opportunity to explore the meaningfulness of each part of the whole picture. Drawings of all kinds are representations of meaningful concepts in our lives. Counselors who use the Gestalt approach may use them to intervene therapeutically with children. Other Gestalt techniques are mediums through which symbolic meanings are also discovered and related to the child's life in the present.

Transactional Analysis

Transactional analysis (TA) is frequently associated with the name of Eric Berne who did much to formulate and popularize the theory in the 1960s. TA theory contends that there are three definitive ego states: parent, adult, and child. Each of these states can take charge of the individual to the point that his or her observable behavior indicates "who's in charge" (adult, parent, or child). The client is assisted in gaining social control of his or her life by learning to use all ego states where appropriate. The ultimate goal is to help the client change from inappropriate life positions and behaviors (life scripts) to new more productive behaviors while coming from an "I'm o.k." position.

"Based on messages that we receive in childhood, we make decisions early in life that may later become inappropriate. The redecisional model of TA emphasizes that we react to stresses, receive messages about how we should be in the world, and make early decisions about ourselves and others that become manifest in our current patterns of thinking, feeling, and behaving" (Corey, 1990, p. 94).

TA is a system for treating individuals within the group context. Contracts between counselor and client identify objectives for the client at each step of the counseling process. TA counselors utilize the techniques of giving permissions to the client, using supporting "protective" statements and having the counselor establish the necessary atmosphere. The counseling process itself will utilize interrogation, specification, confrontation, explanation, illustration, confirmation, interpretation, and crystallization.

In upper elementary grades, counselors may use Transactional Analysis concepts with individuals, small groups or in a classroom guidance activity. TA helps children to know themselves better and to recognize which part of their personality (parent, adult, or child) is in charge. In TA groups, the members can examine the context in which they made earlier decisions and thus prepare themselves to make new decisions that are more practical and functional.

The focus is to help children understand that their communications (transactions) with others and their feelings influence their behaviors. The counselor who uses TA teaches children how to communicate more effectively. Helping children achieve "good transactions," those in which their parent, adult, or child does not "cross" with the receiver's parent, adult, or child, produces better communication and less conflict.

Another concept used in Transactional Analysis is that of strokes, which is described as the attention we get and give to others. There are two kinds of strokes—good and bad. Counselors discuss with children that everyone wants and needs strokes. If we cannot get good strokes, then we must settle for bad ones because we would rather have bad strokes than none at all.

T.A. for Tots and Grown-ups Too by Alvyn M. Freed (1990), and *The Warm Fuzzy Tale* by C. Steiner (1977), are stories that illustrate the concept of good strokes, Warm Fuzzies, and bad strokes, Cold Pricklies. Both stories are effective teaching tools with elementary children in classroom guidance and individual and small group counseling.

We have discussed eight theories within three forces of psychology. See Table 3–3 to view the theoretical categorization of each.

TABLE 3–3 Counseling Theories Arranged In Three Forces of Psychology

Psychoanalytic	Behaviorism	Humanistic Psychology
Psychoanalysis	Behavioral	Person-Centered
	Rational-Emotive	Gestalt
	Reality	
	Individual Psychology	
	Transactional Analysis	

Adapted from discussions in George, R.L. and Cristiani, T.S., *Counseling Theory and Practice*, 3rd ed., Prentice Hall: Englewood Cliffs, NJ. (1990), 112–117.

A Case Study from Four Different Theoretical Orientations

This case illustrates how differing theoretical viewpoints will influence different counselor approaches to the same situation. Elementary counselors who adhere to person-centered, behavioral, individual or Adlerian, and reality theories may respond to the case of Jamie in the following ways. Note that there are brief accounts to provide the flavor of the approach, and in actuality the process is a broader extension of these.

"Jamie"

Jamie is a handsome, blond-haired, blue-eyed, third grade student of average height and weight. Often he comes to school dirty and wears tattered clothes; sometimes he wears the same clothes all week. He has been observed as having no friends. His teacher describes him as a loner. Jamie lives with his mother, who does not work. When called to school for a parent conference, she always comes. Their socioeconomic status is low. Jamie's father died three years ago. Jamie is an only child.

The presenting problem at school is that Jamie has no task-completion skills and never brings in homework. The counselor gathers information from teachers, his mother, Jamie, the school psychologist, and from observations in different settings. We suggest assessing the whole child, and not limiting your focus to the presenting problem. During class, Jamie is not disruptive. He sits at his desk, often blankly staring at his work. While the teacher leads a class discussion, he does not participate. When called on to respond, he doesn't know the question. Usually he is left alone since repeated efforts to include him have failed. These behaviors were evident previously in second grade. Non-verbal behavior such as slouching, infrequent eye-contact, and languished physical movements characterize Jamie's low self-esteem. While proceeding from one location to another, he shuffles his feet and dawdles. None of his behavior, academic or social, is indicative of purposefulness. On the playground he is seen standing alone, picking at his fingers, watching sadly while other children are bursting with laughter as they romp and play together. When not exhibiting sadness, Jamie's affect is flat and expressionless.

This is an enigmatic situation since his test scores indicate that Jamie has above-average intelligence, showing that he has the cognitive ability to achieve in school. This type of case is particularly frustrating to teachers and parents since there is no logical explanation for inadequate school performance. Counselors from all theoretical frameworks examine Jamie's functioning in all developmental areas. Thus far, we have noted unsuccessful academic achievement. Psychologically, his self concept is low. Physically, he looks well-developed, but is not observed participating in physical activities on the playground. We conclude his social skills are underdeveloped based on the absence of observed peer interaction. The counselor who encounters Jamie first works from a client-centered theory base.

Person-Centered, Rogerian Approach to Jamie's Case

A counselor using person-centered counseling with Jamie would assess that low self-esteem is resulting in a lack of motivation. The focus of counseling is on the relationship between the counselor and the child. Building rapport with Jamie and creating a safe and warm environment is of primary interest. The counselor will communicate to Jamie feelings of acceptance, unconditional positive regard, and caring. You will discover that person-centered counseling is the only approach of the four examples that places emphasis on Jamie's feelings, rather than on his behaviors.

Carl Rogers advocated an "If, then" approach to counseling. He suggested that *if* the proper conditions for growth are established—empathic understanding, congruence, and unconditional positive regard, *then* growthful changes can occur in the client.

In this case, the counselor responds empathically to Jamie and to his present life circumstance, reflecting how lonely it must feel not to have any friends; and how frustrating it must feel to never complete classwork. The client-centered counselor actively listens to Jamie and reflects his feelings regarding issues of home, school, and self. This counselor does not direct Jamie to a particular topic of discussion. He or she takes the lead of the client. However, the session, itself, is directed by the counselor to a feelings level by focusing, reflecting, paraphrasing, and summarizing the important themes as they emerge from Jamie's content. Exploring these feelings can enable Jamie to understand his feelings and how they influence his behavior.

As he becomes more self-actualizing and aware of himself and his experience, he can learn to accept himself, like some parts of himself, and discover ways to change the things he does not like about himself. Thus, he can begin to move toward more productive behaviors. Self-esteem will be enhanced, as will motivation to work and play.

Behavioral Approach to Jamie's Case

A behavioral counselor recognizes Jamie's lack of motivation and believes that his behavior can be modified through environmental stimuli. Little, if any, attention would be given to the other aspects such as home environment and lack of friends.

It is likely that the counselor would consult with the classroom teacher to set up a variety of behavior modification techniques to increase classwork. These techniques would include positive reinforcement, shaping, the Premack principle, and contingency contracts. An application of each technique is described here.

An example of using positive reinforcement is that the teacher will present Jamie with a desired consequence, such as a lollipop, after his work is completed. The counselor may consult with the teacher alone and suggest these techniques which the teacher would then implement. Another scenario is that the counselor, Jamie, and his teacher meet together to discuss a plan of action which involves presenting these reinforcers after the desired behavior: classwork. The critical issue for the behaviorist counselor is to choose reinforcers that are meaningful enough to motivate Jamie to work to receive them.

Shaping would be effective since Jamie has not been completing any classwork. It would be unrealistic to expect that suddenly he would begin to complete it all. An example would be to suggest to the teacher that she divide Jamie's work into small increments. She would discuss with him that after the completion of each small unit, he would be rewarded with something they both agreed upon. Possibly he would earn minutes on the computer later in the day or some tangible reward such as a sticker. As his task-completion skills become more developed, larger units of work will be assigned until eventually the rewards are phased out.

The counselor would inform the teacher of the Premack principle. Using this technique, the teacher would say, "Jamie, after you finish your math problems, you may go to the computer or work on the puzzle." This concept requires Jamie to do what his teacher wants him to do first, then he is allowed to do what he wants.

Another behavioral technique which modifies behavior is the use of the contingency contract. An agreement is decided upon between the teacher and Jamie regarding how much work will be done in a specific time period. His mother may also be included. For example, after he has completed the agreed upon amount of work in a specified time period, his mother will agree to take him for a treat of his choice, for example, invite a friend for a pizza. All parties sign the contract. Consequences must be decided upon should the stipulations not be met. A kitchen timer is often effective in helping children structure their time.

Behavioral counselors facilitate teachers in using environmental stimuli to reinforce desired behaviors. Caution must be taken to eventually phase out reinforcers so that children do not place more emphasis on the reward than on the learning task that is accomplished.

Adlerian Approach to Jamie's Case

The Adlerian counselor would assess immediately that Jamie is a discouraged child. His goal of misbehavior, in this case, not completing work, would be identified as related to feelings of inadequacy. After initially meeting with Jamie, you would ask if it would be acceptable for his teacher and you to work together to help him. Jamie, as well as other children, will be eager for you to do that. Consultation with his teacher provides a time to suggest techniques that produce effective and efficient change. The counselor would suggest that his teacher eliminate situations that substantiate his deficiencies. First of all, her expectations for him must be lowered. She must shorten assignments or find examples of things she knows he can accomplish. Since Jamie feels discouraged and inadequate, he must be convinced that he is capable of succeeding. Telling him he has an above-average IQ and "should" be able to do his work will be meaningless and fruitless. Discouraged children must be encouraged and given opportunities to succeed. Teachers are encouraged to recognize Jamie's behaviors that contribute to the class in any positive way.

Jamie's lack of completing homework and his coming to school unbathed may also be indicators of the discouragement he is experiencing as the result of his family life; this behavior may be his cry for help. Since his mother is unemployed and widowed, the counselor would assess how her situation is contributing to Jamie's behavior. A parent conference would be held to enlist her efforts in the encouragement process. At this time, the counselor would ascertain the mother's understanding of Jamie's needs and the problems he is experiencing. Parent and family education might be necessary in order to assist the mother in comprehending the importance of and tasks required in encouraging Jamie to bathe regularly, dress in clean clothing, and complete homework assignments. By explaining the positive impact that she can have in improving his appearance, his mother can be encouraged to cooperate.

A parent conference would be held to enlist efforts of Jamie's mother in the encouragement process. She would be informed of the plans discussed which involve his teacher. There are specific ways in which the mother can help. Suggestions of ways she can encourage her son would be given. For example, it would be encouraging that he be required to take a bath in the evenings after playing. It would be acceptable to mention that you have noticed his clothes are often dirty. An encouraging act would be to send him to school in clean clothes. His mother can assist in improving his appearance, and usually after these types of conferences, parents do cooperate. If, after a time, they become negligent, call another conference.

The Adlerian counselor would further formulate a plan for Jamie's mother to look over his school work every afternoon. You may suggest setting a specific time in the afternoon for homework everyday. Jamie is given a choice to have homework time either after milk and cookies or after an hour of play time. This provides an opportunity for him to take ownership and some responsibility for a portion of his life. Thus, he is more likely to respond positively. Of course, this requires that Jamie's mother be responsible and provide the appropriate environment and limitations to make this work.

As Jamie becomes more encouraged and experiences successes, he will begin to feel less inadequate. He will experience self-confidence and feelings of belongingness and acceptance in his class. These feelings will lead to his taking more responsibility for his classwork. It is encouraging that his mother takes an active role in his life, as well. They work now as a team.

A Reality Therapy Approach to Jamie's Case

Using a reality-based theoretical orientation, the counselor will help Jamie evaluate his behavior of not completing his classwork. She or he will ask "How is this behavior helpful to you?" Certainly he will answer cognitively that it is not helpful at all. She will then ask, "How is this behavior hurtful to you?" The child is given the opportunity to "think" of ways that it is hurtful. Reality therapy is a cognitive-behavioral approach in which Jamie discovers how his behaviors influence his feelings.

The counselor works with Jamie so that he may decide if his behaviors are responsible or not. The goal with Jamie in reality counseling is to facilitate his taking responsibility for his work. It will be a cognitive process in which he must convince himself that completing his work is what he "needs" to do. This also addresses the problem of identity. Jamie thinks of himself as a failure, therefore, when his behavior becomes responsible and realistic, how he identifies himself will change. The use of contracts is also an effective reality-based technique which counselors may implement.

Note that behavior change in Jamie is possible based on any and all of the four counseling approaches discussed. As you proceed through your counselor training you will adopt one or a few of these theories as your own, and work from those principles. Regardless of the theory you use, it is critical to persevere even though behavior change is slow. In some cases, change will be almost immediate, and other cases change will be only slight or not at all. In all cases and all theories, we encourage you to be a caring and resourceful counselor, communicating your commitment and interest in the school and personal success of the children you serve.

Eclecticism

As previously noted, an understanding of theories assists the neophyte counselor in identifying a model that he or she can follow with some assurances of its validity or "workability." Too, the many theories give the beginning counselor an opportunity to identify a theory with which they feel comfortable; a theory that is a "good fit" for them.

For some, perhaps the majority, however, an eclectic approach may be a more desirable option. This avoids the necessity of totally accepting one theory in favor of an approach which allows the counselor to pick and choose from the smorgasbord of proven theories according to the dictates of the situation, the client, and the counselor him or herself. As one North Carolina counselor stated, "I am rather eclectic in my theoretical approach because each situation determines a need for a certain approach. For example, I am currently using behavioral methods in dealing with a school phobia case, but I use rational-emotive techniques with a student who exhibits disruptive behaviors. I may also use a combination of R.E.T. and Reality."

Eclecticism, while a long standing traditional theoretical option, has also been the subject of criticism over the years as an approach lacking consistency and integration. However, eclectic theory when properly developed can play an acceptable role for guiding counseling practice. This is not easy, however, as Wallace (1986) notes:

Student-counselors cannot shelve their responsibility for constructing a personal theory of counseling by turning it into an intellectual game or academic exercise. Their obligation to their clients is far too real for that. Developing an eclectic approach to therapy requires an enterprising juxtaposition and a genuine confrontation of their work with the values, thoughts, and research of others. And, while independence of observation and thought is essential to an eclectic stance, so are understanding, respect, and tolerance for other theorists. Before students in search of a personal theory of counseling and psychotherapy can choose the best, they must become fully aware of all that are available—no small achievement in a discipline overburdened with diverse and contradictory theories. The eclectic approach, then, is no shortcut to theory formulation. Indeed, when properly traveled, it is a most difficult path to follow. (Wallace, 1986, p. 310)

Integrated Theories

Integration of various theories has become increasingly popular in recent years as a means of not only reinforcing and expanding on traditional theories, but also to develop new multi-dimensional and integrated models. For example, Ivey, Ivey, and Simek-Downing (1987) noted that an integrated knowledge of skills, theory and practice is essential for their culturally intentional counseling and therapy model. They described this integration as follows:

Skills form the foundation of effective theory and practice: The culturally intentional therapist knows how to construct a creative decision-making interview and can use microskills to attend to and influence clients in a predicted direction. Important in this process are individual and cultural empathy, client observation skills, assessment of person and environment, and the application of positive techniques of growth and change.

Theory provides organizing principles for counseling and therapy: The culturally intentional counselor has knowledge of alternative theoretical approaches and treatment modalities. Practice is the integration of skills and theory: the culturally intentional counselor or therapist is competent in skills and theory, and is able to apply them to research and practice for client benefit.

Undergirding integrated competence in skills, theory, and practice is an intentional awareness of one's own personal worldview and how that worldview may be similar to and/or different from the worldview and personal constructions of the client and other professionals. (p. 413)

Summary

Established theories of counseling offer proven guidelines for the beginning elementary school counselor. They provide a recognized and effective means for organizing client information and the counseling process itself. Popular theories include psychoanalytic, client-centered (person-centered), individual (Adlerian) psychology, behavioral, reality, rational-emotive, integrated, transactional analysis, and Gestalt. Eclectic and integrated approaches using several theoretical viewpoints may also be appropriate. The discussion of these theories also notes major contributors to their development and to the field of counseling, such as Sigmund Freud (psychoanalytic), Carl Rogers (person-centered), Alfred Adler (individual psychology), B. F. Skinner, John Krumboltz, and others (Behavioral), Albert Ellis (Rational-emotive), William Glasser (Reality) and Fritz Perls (Gestalt).

The authors conducted a survey in which sixty-eight practicing elementary school counselors indicated the eclectic and individual psychology theories as most popular, although strong support was also shown for person-centered, behavioral and reality therapy as well (See Table 3–2). In practice, over half of these counselors used two or more of these orientations, suggesting that no one single approach is applicable to all situations.

Table 3–4 summarizes major counseling theories and their implications for practice in the elementary school. Respondents could indicate one or more theoretical preferences. Forty-four (44) percent of those responding indicated three preferences; 20 percent indicated two choices; 17 percent selected one theory. The remaining 19 percent selected four or more possiblities. Eclectic was the popular choice among those indicating a single theory or two theoretical options.

TABLE 3–4 Counseling Theories And Their Implications For Counseling Children

Theory	Major Premises	Implications for Counseling Elementary Children
Psychoanalytical (Freudian)	• Primary goal to make the unconscious conscious • Counseling techniques used are catharsis, free association and interpretation of dreams • Once repressed information is brought to the conscious level, it can be examined in a traditional manner by the child and counselor	• Play therapy allows child to express symbolic messages • Dream-analysis for conflict resolution • Use of verbal games to elicit free association • Children's limited verbal skills and cognitive development are limiting factors
Individual (Adlerian)	• Lives are holistic • Emphasis on the conscious positive growth • Individuals desire to self-actualize—develop their potential • Focus on goals, life-styles, and self-concept • Stages (a) relationship, (b) diagnosis, (c) insight, and(d) reorientation	• Counselors focus on ways to develop in children attitudes of responsibility and cooperation • Keep goals of misbehavior in mind and find ways to stop making misbehavior worthwhile • Help children discover their potential for positively contributing to their classes and families

TABLE 3–4 ***Continued***

Individual (Adlerian)		• Encourage parents to do nothing for their children that they can do for themselves • Use lifestyle interviews of children based on their present and past recollections of themselves, their families, and school experiences, and so on
Person-Centered (Rogerian)	• Emphasis on the potential of the individual to solve own problems • Counselor is a skilled listener whose role is that of a reflector and facilitator	• Counselors use empathic understanding to communicate to children an unconditional regard in order to build rapport and create a safe environment in which children feel safe • Limited by limited insight and reasoning of child
Behavioral (Skinner)	• Behavior is learned (a product of heredity and environment)... thus, • Behavior can also be unlearned • Conditioning is also important in the process • Useful in treating eating disorders, smoking, substance abuse, and so on	• Often elementary school counselors collude with teachers to modify the behaviors of children • Techniques that counselors use with teachers include: • *Systematic desensitization*, as to treat school phobia • *Positive reinforcement*—the application of a desired consequence to increase behavior • *Shaping*—the approach that reinforces successive approximation to desired behaviors (subgoals) • *Premack Principle*—using a high-frequency behavior to reinforce a low-frequency behavior, such as "After you finish your math problem, you may go to the computer lab." • Help teachers set up a *token economy*—an environment in which behaviors are reinforced by presenting tokens or coupons which may be "cashed in" later • *Contingency contracts*—agreements between student and counselor or teacher that involve the condition for behavior change
Reality (Glasser)	• Children need to feel loved to feel worthwhile	• Counselor helps children examine their behavior and place value judgments on it

Continued

TABLE 3–4 *Continued*

Reality (Glasser)	• Children can learn to meet their needs and become responsible individuals • When clients deny reality, they need help. Focus on right and wrong. Focus on present and future • Counselor functions as a teacher as well as a therapist	• Children are asked how their behavior is helpful or hurtful to themselves and others • Children are encouraged to assume responsibility for their own behavior, to establish their own identity, and to make better decisions based on what they value
RET (Ellis)	• People confuse feeling with thinking and make poor emotional-based decisions • Irrational thought is often furthered by family and culture • Counselor promotes rationality (teaches, assigns, and pressures)	• Counselors are concerned with discovering the illogical thinking of children and then teaching them to rethink situations to avoid self-defeating behaviors
Gestalt (Perls)	• Clients make poor decisions because they have acquired behaviors, ideals, etc., that inhibit them • Clients are helped to become "aware" (of all the variables) in the "here and now" (as currently existing) • Clients take responsibility (don't depend on others) to become all that they can be • Counselor is supportive, confronting, using "How" and "What" questions	• Counselors use drawing, puppets, clay, and other forms of play to increase a child's self-awareness • Children are asked to express themselves as if they were certain objects or parts of a drawing • Attention is given to changes in body movements and breathing • Counselors may ask "What's happening now?" in order to focus feelings in the present that are achieved through the therapeutic process
TA (Berne)	• Three states of parent, adult, and child each of which can dominate one's behavior • Used primarily in group settings • Clients learn to gain control by using the adult primarily and they use the others where appropriate	• Counselor helps children understand that each person may communicate with others from these ego states: parent, adult, or child • The focus of activities is to help children communicate more effectively by recognizing whether their parent, adult or child is in control

Chapter 4

Counseling the Elementary School Child: Process and Skills

A Counselor's Task
You have been chosen to be touchers
Touch through me
You have been chosen to be healers
Heal through me
You have been chosen to be providers
Provide through me
You have been chosen to be enablers
Enable through me
You have chosen to be validators
Validate through me
You have chosen to be lovers
Love through me.
For as we touch each other, we
experience healing
As we provide for each other, we
find fulfillment
As we enable each other, we
stimulate growth
As we hear each other, we
discover release
As we validate each other, we
expand horizons
As we love each other, we
generate strength.
-MARY JOE HANNEFORD (1985)

Introduction

As often stated, individual counseling is the heart of any school program of counseling and/or guidance services. It is the core or critical counselor activity. It is that professional activity, more than any other, that distinguishes the counselor and his or her special expertise from other educators and human services providers in the school setting. It is the basis for deserving the title and role of *counselor*.

And what is this near magical process called counseling? Individual counseling is, first of all, a social interaction process, involving the counselor and her or his client, in this context—the elementary student. The client is the focus of the process. The counselor is the facilitator of the process. This process may be guided by a theoretical context such as those discussed earlier in Chapter 3. The intent, of course, is assistance to the client. Blackham (1977) suggests that "counseling is a unique helping relationship in which the client is provided the opportunity to learn, feel, think, experience, and change in ways that he or she thinks is desirable" (p. 7). Shertzer and Stone (1980) define counseling as "an interaction process which facilitates meaningful understanding of self and environment and results in the establishment and/or clarification of goals and values for future behavior" (pp. 19-20). Kottler and Brown (1985) suggest that "counseling is a profession and a process that involves a relationship between persons and demands a special set of skills and knowledge that can be communicated to influence a client to change" (p. 6). Another popular (and earlier) definition identified

> *individual counseling as a personal, face-to-face relationship between two people, in which the counselor, by means of the relationship and his special competencies, provides a learning situation in which the counselee, a normal sort of person, is helped to know himself and his present and possible future situations so that he can make use of characteristics and potentialities in a way that is both satisfying to himself and beneficial to society, and further, can learn how to solve future problems and meet future needs. (Tolbert, 1982, p. 9)*

While there are many definitions of counseling, George and Cristiani (1990) point out the common elements in these definitions:

> *One is the notion that counseling is aimed at helping people make choices and act on them. A second is the notion of learning, although there are some sharp differences as to what facilitates learning and how learning occurs. Still another element is that of personality development, with relatively little agreement as to how personality development is best facilitated (p. 2).*

The Goals of Counseling

While the elementary school counselor's role and function integrates the two major thrusts of prevention and intervention, the activities and skills required for each service are distinct. In this chapter, counseling process and skills, the emphasis is on skills essential for intervention. When children experience a crisis situation, for example, death of a loved one, divorce, disruptive behavior, or any threat to their school success, counselors intervene. Counselors are human service providers who initiate changes in children that make their lives more pleasant. Although counselors cannot prevent death and divorce, they can increase children's coping skills.

Major concerns of children may be clustered into three broad categories: (1) conception of self; (2) interpersonal relations; and (3) how to gain and maintain power and control in their lives. Maladaptive behaviors at home and in school may result when children experience difficulties in these areas. It is not the intent of counseling to rob children of their natural concerns, rather to facilitate a change in behavior that represents improvement in handling them. When school success is threatened, Baharoglu (1989), states that "counselors help children learn alternative ways to foster adaptive behavior in the classroom" (p. 25).

The assistance provided by the counselor in the elementary school must focus upon some desired change in behavior which is the goal of counseling. Since teachers and parents refer children for counseling, counselors collaborate with them to arrive at counseling goals. The counselor's first step is to ask teachers and parents to describe the following: a) the child's behaviors, b) their feelings about the child, c) what changes need to occur, and 4) what they have tried so far.

Broadly speaking, counseling goals may be separated into the following categories.

Developmental Goals

Developmental goals are those wherein the child/client is assisted in meeting or advancing her or his anticipated human growth and development (that is, socially, personally, emotionally, cognitively, physical wellness, and so on.)

As stated in Chapter 2, children naturally encounter numerous developmental crises concurrent with their growth process. While the evolution of growth and development is a challenge to all children, some are more prepared and have greater resources to successfully resolve these crises. The presence of the school counselor ensures that all students have available to them a caring adult who shares accurate information regarding the complex process of growing up. Counselors help all children to understand the normalcy of physical and psychological changes while increasing their skills to adapt to these changes.

Preventive Goals

Prevention is a goal in which the counselor helps the client avoid some undesired outcome. Elementary school counselors counsel children individually who are faced with issues that endanger their lives and threaten their personal and school success. These issues include, but are not limited to, substance abuse, academic failure, and inappropriate behavior. Counselors allow children to discuss openly and without judgment their behavioral options and the resulting consequences of those behaviors. The opportunity for a child to develop a trusting therapeutic relationship with a professionally skilled adult increases the chances that children will be equipped to make informed personal decisions and acquire personal habits that foster wellness throughout the lifespan.

Enhancement Goals

If the client possesses special skills and abilities, enhancement means they can be identified and/or further developed through the assistance of a counselor. Expertise in both child growth and development and in counseling creates the combination of skills conducive to the development of human potential in children. Elementary school counselors heighten awareness of strengths in children and spark motivation to develop them fully. Note that enhancement goals of counseling are not reserved for gifted and talented children, but are the prerogative of all children.

Remedial Goals

Remeditation involves assisting a client to overcome and/or treat an undesirable development. These may be academic, but they may also be social/personal, emotional, psychological or environmental in nature.

In individual counseling, counselors facilitate remediation by focusing on the undesirable behavior of children. For example, counselors help children unravel goals of misbehavior and discover more appropriate and healthy ways to meet their needs. It is not that children deliberately act out or want to misbehave. Often they are using the only means they know to achieve, for example, their goals of attention or power. Counselors help children discover and understand these goals while instilling the notion that they have the option of replacing misbehavior with appropriate alternative behaviors that increase self-esteem and productivity.

Exploratory Goals

Exploration represents goals appropriate to the examining of options, the testing of skills, and trying new and different activities, environments, relationships, and so on.

Within the safety of the counselor's office, children have the opportunity to practice, role play, and discuss new and more effective ways of interacting. This type of counseling builds self-confidence and self-esteem and prepares children, for example, who are shy, for successful interactions in real-life situations.

Reinforcement Goals

Reinforcement is used those instances where clients need help in recognizing that what they are doing, thinking, and/or feeling is okay. Counselors give children the freedom to experience being who they are while facilitating the understanding, in their terms, of what it means to be real. Counselors validate the experiences of children; they teach them that they are not powerless to become who they want to be.

Another approach to specifying goals may be to examine them in terms of expectancies which are common to the elementary school. That is, counselors work in tandem with other school personnel to provide a rich and full total education program for all children. Thus, counseling goals also include enrichment of educational goals.

Cognitive goals

Cognition involves acquiring the basic foundations of learning and cognitive skills. Counselors encourage children to enjoy learning, to experience the intrinsic rewards of learning.

Physiological goals

Physiology involves acquiring the basic understandings and habits for good health. Counselors encourage children to respect and nurture their bodies.

Psychological goals

Psychology aids in developing good social interaction skills, learning emotional control, developing a positive self concept, and so on.

Protective Goals

A final goal which is not so easy to categorize or describe may be labeled "the protection of childhood." It represents the efforts of the elementary school and counseling program and their staff to prevent the occurrence, to every extent possible, of those experiences which destroy the hopes and happiness of the childhood years. They include such common concerns as child abuse, parental conflict and divorce, substance abuse, peer group punishment, death and dying of loved ones, and so on . . . and still more subtle destroyers, such as retention, failure to participate in significant events, lack of parental interest, and moving away from old friends into a new and strange environment.

Childhood should include years of happiness, excitement, eager anticipation, security, and the enjoyment of self, family, and others. The elementary school can and should be one of the positive experiences of everyone's childhood.

Counselors and the elementary school programs they serve can be a major force in seeing that their children experience the joys of childhood.

The Process of Counseling Applied to Children

As suggested earlier in this chapter, individual counseling is a social interaction process. This means that there are two individuals involved—the professional counselor and her or his client, with the focus on the needs of the client. Moreover, since it is a social interaction process, there must be ongoing communication between counselor and client. This social interaction process moves through a series of stages.

The *first stage* in the counseling process is the establishment of an environment conducive to open, shared, and rewarding communication. It is the counselor's responsibility to take the lead in creating such an environment.

Initially, we must recognize that children do not bring to the counseling office the same degree of understanding, levels of maturity, and expectancies that can be anticipated in older and more sophisticated clients. Thompson and Rudolph (1983) note that

> *children often have the idea that going for counseling means you are "sick in the head," "mentally ill," or "weird" in some way. They may have heard the counselor referred to as a shrink or head doctor. Many have erroneous ideas about counseling and the role of a counselor (p. 213).*

They go on to suggest that:

> *some counselors prefer to ease the anxiety of the initial meeting by just talking in general conversation with the child for a few minutes. They may introduce themselves and then start to talk with the child about home, school, friends, hobbies, or other interests. For nonverbal clients or extremely anxious children, the first session or two may include only techniques of play therapy (p. 213).*

To prevent erroneous beliefs, it is imperative that counselors routinely orient children, parents, and school staff to their role and function. (Refer to Chapter 6 for more information on orientation to counseling and guidance.) Particularly when children are exposed to counselors in classroom guidance (Chapter 6), they develop an understanding that counselors are in schools for all children and are available to everyone upon request. Children both enjoy and benefit from the opportunity to talk freely with a knowledgeable, caring, and attentive adult who is significant in their academic community.

Whether the child is self-referred or referred by a teacher or parent, begin the initial visit with a welcoming gesture such as a handshake, suggesting your level of respect for the child's presence in your office. Often during first visits, it is advisable to use familiar objects such as puppets, drawing with crayons and markers, or games, to convey that you acknowledge and operate in the child's world. When you sense that rapport is established, begin talking with the child about the presenting problem.

Always during counseling, and other communications with children, literally get on their level. Bend down, get on your knees, or sit in a small chair to equalize this personal interaction. This nonverbal explicit behavior communicates dramatically to children that you value and respect them and their concerns.

Regardless of the techniques utilized, the skillful counselor is seeking to put his or her client at ease, to gain her or his trust and confidence and to open up lines of communication between the two of them. Too, in this initial stage, the counselor has the responsibility to educate the child client in the process of counseling itself, and to the roles and responsibilities that each must assume.

The *second stage* of the counseling process is frequently called the assessment or, as we prefer, the understanding stage. It is the process of gathering and examining data that help us and the client to better understand him or herself, the circumstances or problems that have led to the need for counseling and the environmental or "systems" setting involved. Obviously in some crisis situations very little data can be accumulated at the moment. However, in most situations, the skillful counselor will be seeking all the pertinent information that can be reasonably obtained and will contribute to a clear understanding of the client, his or her concerns or needs, plus the relevant settings.

Although immature and often unsophisticated in communication styles, children typically know when they are in trouble and what problematic behaviors led to their referral to the counselor. It is acceptable to say after establishing rapport, "Tell me the reason your teacher (or parent) suggested that you come for a talk with me." When appropriate, you may reply supportively, "I believe that you and I working together can arrive at a good solution to help you feel better, improve school work, get along with classmates, and so on."

More often than not, children do not know how to generate solutions and alternative behaviors by themselves. Counseling helps children explore present behaviors and consequences in a nonjudgmental environment. A counselor may probe, "Tell me what occurs in your classroom before you get in trouble (for example, before you are sent out of the room)." After listening carefully to the child, using the counseling skills of attending, the counselor proceeds with reflecting and facilitating skills discussed in the next section of this chapter. Generally, counselors use the skills of attending, reflecting, and facilitating to achieve effective communication in all stages as the process of counseling unfolds.

The *third stage* of the counseling process is the examination of the client's/child's needs in light of the various action options or solutions available to him or her. It is important to again emphasize that clients may have developmental, enhancement or enrichment, and preventive needs as well as intervention or remediation needs. Keep in mind at this stage that even though the client is a child, the final decision as to what to do must be hers or his and may involve the parents as well. Counseling initiates the brainstorming of alternative behaviors and encourages thinking of anticipated outcomes. Each option is examined in terms of its feasibility, its likelihood to be helpful, and the consequences it might generate.

A counselor, after attending to a child's discourse on what happens prior to getting in trouble, may reflect by saying, "You said that after you _____, your teacher _____, and then you felt _____." You could then facilitate by an encouraging lead, "I wonder what you could do instead of _____." The child is urged to consider, and describe, an alternative behavior. To facilitate use a query: "What do you suppose would happen if you actually did that in your classroom?" This process is continued until the child considers several optional behaviors before choosing the most acceptable. You could summarize and facilitate this decision-making by saying, "You have reported feeling unhappy about how things have been going in your classroom. You have thought of many ways to do things differently (reiterate them for the child). Which one of your ideas would you prefer trying?"

The *fourth stage* in this process, having decided on what would work best to serve the client's/child's needs, is planning a suitable course of action for implementing the decision. The primary responsibility for this implementation must be the client's, despite the lack of maturity of the elementary school pupil. Of course, parents and teachers too, can contribute to the child's implementation, but she or he must learn to take responsibility for her or his own actions at this point.

In this stage, the counselor helps the child by formulating a framework within which to implement her or his new plan of action. One example may be to suggest writing an outline of things to do first, second, third, and so on, to reach the desired goal. The counselor accommodates by giving the child paper and a pencil, or writing it for the child if these skills are not yet developed. It is useful to concretely state the new plan in writing even though the child may not be able to read. When the child consents, the plan is shared with the teacher and parents. One way to progress through this stage is to say, "You have chosen to _____. Let's consider how you will put your new plan into action. At the very beginning of the school day what will you do to get off to a good start?" After the child learns this system, you continue with what would happen second, third, and so on, and then summarize. At the end of this session, we suggest that you say, "Let's make an appointment in a few days so you can tell me how your new plan is working."

A *fifth* and final *stage* could be designated as the follow-up, evaluation, and termination stage. At this point, the counselor is ascertaining the effectiveness of the client's applied plan of action, following along to see if additional counseling assistance, such as reinforcement, is needed and moving to conclude the counseling process while, at the same time, keeping the door open for further contact if desired.

An opening comment to the child may be, "Last time you were here, we discussed .... So, tell me how your new plan is working." Remember to attend and remain nonjudgmental regardless of the child's progress. If the plan has not been working, listen to the child to discover what went wrong and proceed with your skills of reflecting and facilitating. Use your judgment in deciding whether it is likely that the child will succeed with a revision of this plan or to allow the child to consider another option.

In either case, follow-up and evaluation will proceed followed by eventual termination. Counselors must keep in mind that termination should never be abrupt and unanticipated by the client. When you near the end of counseling, say to the child, for example, "After today, I will meet with you two more times."

Skills for the Effective Counseling of Children

As already discussed in this chapter, to be effective, counseling must be aimed at achieving desired and specified outcomes or goals. We have also noted the counseling process through which the goals of counseling may be realized. Next, we will examine basic skills which counselors must acquire in order for the counseling process to achieve its goals. We have chosen to categorize these as attending, reflecting, and facilitating skills.

Attending Skills

Attending behavior on the part of the counselor indicates to the child that she or he is the center of your attention. It conveys the sense of your attentiveness, your focus on the client and his or her concerns. It is being with the counselee both psychologically and physiologically. This attentiveness is expressed nonverbally through normal eye contact, a natural body posture that indicates your interest and appropriate gestures, (such as head nodding, hand movements, and so on.) Verbally, attentiveness may be reflected through noninterruptive responses to client statements. This attentiveness and obvious interest in her or him further encourages the client to trust the counselor and communicate more freely. It is important for counselors to recognize that different cultural groups, and individuals also, frequently require differing patterns of attending (for example, in many middle Eastern cultures eye-to-eye contact is acceptable between males but not between a male and female). Good attending can be characterized as "focused intensity." Poor attending is marked by a kind of "detached passivity."

In examining this skill further, we can anticipate that attending behavior by others is something most of us enjoy. It makes us feel that the person attending is genuinely interested in us—wants to get better acquainted, know more about us—and we usually respond in a positive way. Children, no less than adults, also want and need attention. And so it is with attending behavior as a counseling skill in the counseling setting. The client senses one's genuine interest, becomes more at ease, more willing to talk. Attentiveness also increases the counselor's awareness of client's feelings and behaviors and sensitivity to subtle cues that may elude the less attentive counselor. It is the prerequisite for counselors "learning to hear."

Attending to a client's verbal and nonverbal communication is a physically and psychologically draining task. Intense concentration and focus on what your client, the child, says and does not say, are critical and rudimentary skills to the process of counseling. Counselors listen to words, observe body language, and sense the child's feelings. With practice, counselors develop a sense to "hear" what the client does not say and to gain entry into the child's frame of reference.

Reflecting

Reflecting is a way of letting the child, your client, know that we understand or are seeking to understand her or his feelings, observations, and expressions. It subtly signals to the client the efforts of the counselor to enter, understand, and perceive the client's frame of reference—in this instance, the child's world as he or she sees, feels, and acts in it. Reflection of feelings is a way of letting the client know how we recognize and understand their feelings and also, to assist the client in recognizing, understanding and owning their feelings. Brammer (1988) notes that

> *this is why we usually begin the reflecting method with "you feel" as an attempt to help him re-own the feeling. You will know when your reflection is accurate because the helpee will tend to respond with something like, "Yeah, that's it." Skillful use of reflecting depends on the helper's ability to identify feelings and cues for feelings, from body cues as well as words (p. 76).*

Reflecting of counselor observations is descriptive feedback to the client behavior as observed by the counselor, including attitudes, feelings, and so on, that may be implied from the client's actions, reactions, and nonverbal communiqués during the counseling process. Reflecting a client's verbal expression is paraphrasing and repeating the client's statements or ideas back to him or her.

Brammer (1988) suggests the following guidelines for reflecting:

1. *Read the total message—stated feelings, nonverbal body feelings, and content.*
2. *Select the best mix of content and feelings to fulfill the goals for understanding at this stage of the helping process.*
3. *Reflect the experience just perceived.*
4. *Wait for helpee's confirming or denying response to your reflection as a cue about what to do next (p. 79).*

We are stating that it is not enough simply to attend to and understand where the child hurts. It is essential that you become skillful at communicating that understanding to the child. When this is achieved, the dynamic process of growth and change in your client will begin.

Table 4–1 consists of a list of general categories of both positive and negative emotions which can be used by the counselor in reflecting feelings to the client. Peterson and Nisenholz (1987) emphasize the importance of the counselor

TABLE 4–1

Relative Intensity of Words	Feeling Category				
	Anger	**Conflict**	**Fear**	**Happiness**	**Sadness**
Mild Feeling	Annoyed Bothered Bugged Irked Irritated Peeved Ticked	Blocked Bound Caught Caught in a bind Pulled	Apprehensive Concerned Tense Tight Uneasy	Amused Anticipating Comfortable Confident Contented Glad Pleased Relieved	Apathetic Bored Confused Disappointed Discontented Mixed up Resigned Unsure
Moderate Feeling	Disgusted Hacked Harassed Mad Provoked Put upon Resentful Set up Spiteful Used	Locked Pressured Torn	Afraid Alarmed Anxious Fearful Frightened Shook Threatened Worried	Delighted Eager Happy Hopeful Joyful Surprised Up	Abandoned Burdened Discouraged Distressed Down Drained Empty Hurt Lonely Lost Sad Unhappy Weighted
Intense Feeling	Angry Boiled Burned Contemptful Enraged Fuming Furious Hateful Hot Infuriated Pissed Smoldering Steamed	Ripped Wrenched	Desperate Overwhelmed Panicky Petrified Scared Terrified Terror-stricken Tortured	Bursting Ecstatic Elated Enthusiastic Enthralled Excited Free Fulfilled Moved Proud Terrific Thrilled Turned on	Anguished Crushed Deadened Depressed Despairing Helpless Hopeless Humiliated Miserable Overwhelmed Smothered Tortured

From *Helping Relationships and Strategies* by D.E. Hutchins and C.G. Cole, 1986 (Monterey, CA: Wadsworth).

communicating his or her understanding of the client's feelings at the same general level of intensity as the client is experiencing them. In examining the table, it is obvious that using the word *annoyed* to describe a feeling would be perceived as less intense than using the word *enraged*.

Facilitating

The skill of facilitating embodies those techniques which the counselor employs to encourage the flow of meaningful client communications. They are designed to keep the conversation moving in a purposeful way. A wide range of options are available to the counselor for this purpose. They include leading the client to focus more specifically on the topic through anticipation and encouraging the client to verbalize or continue to verbalize their feelings and thoughts. Leading may be both direct and non-direct with the latter being especially useful in the early stages of the interview (for example, "Maybe we could begin by your telling me in your own words why you decided to come here").

Another facilitative technique is the use of encouraging or motivating statements (for example, "That's very interesting. Tell me more about that," or "I'd like you to tell me more about how you felt about that"). Encouraging statements can also be used to focus the conversation more specifically, to keep it from straying away from the major focus of the interview, and to cut off meaningless rambling.

Another common facilitative technique is the use of questions. Questions can be either non-directive or directive. Non-directive questions are designed to elicit additional information and encourage the client to elaborate or provide more detail (for example, "What were your feelings when you weren't chosen?"). They may also be used to avoid associating the client directly with an undesirable event or sensitive issue (for example, "How do you feel about students who cheat on tests?"—rather than "Have you ever cheated on a test and why?"). Direct questions, on the other hand, may be used to secure a specific response, to focus the conversation, to focus responsibility or to cut down on extraneous conversation. Of course, too many questions arouse client suspicions and harm the rapport. Questions are valuable only when used in a timely and considerate manner.

Other useful facilitative techniques are those of confrontation, summarization and feedback, interpretation, paraphrasing, repeating, and clarification. Even counselor silence may be facilitative on occasion when the young client needs to pause, contemplate, perhaps rethink, find the words to express, and so on before proceeding.

In applying the skills of effective counseling, the elementary school counselor recognizes the uniqueness of the elementary school pupil-client. Here again we must stress the significance of the child's developmental stage—their maturity, ability to verbalize and express their feelings as well as their willingness to do so; the degree to which they understand the "why" of their concerns plus differences that may be reflective of their family and/or cultural backgrounds. Garbarino, Stott, and Faculty of the Erikson Institute (1989) state that

> *as adults learn more about the child's perspective, they will begin to see children as intelligent, respected actors in the adult-child communication process. As they learn that children have a comprehensible point of view, even though it is immature compared to the adult perspective, adults can improve the validity and*

ethical soundness of their efforts to communicate with children. What they do and how they do it will become more effective and in greater harmony with the needs and rights of children. (p. 1)

Children can be good candidates for effective individual counseling. However, the degree to which they are, and in turn, can benefit from this counseling, will be in no small measure dependent upon the counselor who recognizes that they are first and foremost children living in and experiencing their childhood years.

While counseling children, remain cognizant that children are at various stages of development and parallel your interventions to the child's level of understanding. Paramount to effective counseling with children is believing that children are unique and possess their own blueprints of who they will become. A counselor who attempts to instill one's own values or to influence the child to become who the counselor believes the child should be, will be not only unsuccessful, but grossly unethical. This misdeed would be in violation of the ethical code of the counseling profession and in desecration of the belief that all human beings possess the potential to be all that they are capable of being.

The Use of Imagery in Counseling

In this chapter we suggest that the goals of counseling pervade all areas of human development. Counseling utilizes specific skills and progresses through stages. Counselors may also choose to become trained in the technique of *visualization and guided-imagery* (VGI) for use in counseling children. Imagery is a means by which counselors can help clients find their dreams: to visualize concepts they have been unable to express. When children (and adults) gain a vision of how they can grow and become, they can actually move toward that goal. As a friend once said, "If you do not have a dream, how are you going to get a dream to come true?"

Emphasis on affective/holistic education has increased the use of visualization and guided-imagery techniques in school settings at all levels (Galyean, 1985). Research data regarding the outcomes of imagery work warrant its inclusion here as a viable technique which can be used individually or in groups in elementary school counseling. Some of the outcomes are compiled by Sheikh and Sheikh in *Imagery in Education: Imagery in the Educational Process* by A. Sheikh and K. Sheikh, 1985. (Reprinted with permission from Baywood Publishing Company, Inc. Copyright 1985 by Baywood Publishing Company.)

Gowan (1978) found that enriched art and music programs designed to encourage creativity led to improvement in students' performance in general (p. 9). Toomin (1982) found that visualization and guided-imagery activities combined with various stress-reducing techniques help elementary school children perform better academically, reduce physical and emotional tension, improve test-taking skills, handwriting skills, I.Q.; and learning-disabled students improved in reading recognition, comprehension, and spelling. (pp. 168-169)

Sheikh and Sheikh (1985) conclude that "visualization and guided-imagery activities are a potentially powerful aspect of the curriculum and can serve to effect highly desirable gains in: (1) cognitive areas of academic skills acquisition and proficiency; (2) affective areas of attention, creativity, initiative, listening, and self-esteem; and (3) the interpersonal area of cohesiveness" (p. 173).

According to Galyean (1985), educators ordinarily use visualization and guided-imagery activities in one or more of four ways:

1. *They employ it as a means of relaxing, centering, and sharpening perception (focusing), thereby preparing individuals for the learning task at hand.*
2. *They use it for teaching basic subject matter. This is referred to as 'guided cognitive imagery.'*
3. *They see imagery as a vehicle for affective development, such as the increased awareness of inner senses and feelings and the expression of these wherever appropriate, expanded inner cognizance of personal images and symbols, introspective means to conflict resolution, culling feelings of self-love and appreciation, strengthening one's personal values schema and belief systems, and bonding with others. This is called 'guided affective imagery.'*
4. *They utilize imagery as a means of recognizing and working with altered states of consciousness, experiencing energies beyond the normal field of awakened consciousness, probing the spiritual, mystical, and transcendental aspects of life, experiencing concepts such as unity of being, oneness, wisdom, beauty, joy, love, and self. This is labeled 'guided transpersonal imagery.'*

   These four types of imagery techniques often encompass health-producing or health-maintaining activities . . . . These activities are being recommended by a growing number of health professionals in hopes that individuals will become increasingly more responsible for managing their own health care. (p. 161)

Counselors interested in implementing imagery work may find these six suggested steps helpful:

1. Relaxing/centering—*teaching children to assume a comfortable position while breathing deeply and relaxing body-muscular tension.*
2. Focusing—*they are presented with a series of short focusing exercises, such as, "Close your eyes and picture a red circle in front of you . . . Now change the color to orange . . . now to green . . ." Focusing exercises help students to sharpen inner perception, to pay greater attention to detail, and to control their images.*
3. Multisensing—*next they are prompted to experience simple sensory images and to 'see, feel, touch, hear, taste, and smell' their images. This exercise enables them to experience their images in much greater depth than if they were only to 'look at' them. This mode targets all learners: visual, auditory, and kinesthetic imagers are given an equal opportunity.*

4. Imaging—*imagery journeys take children to various places, involve them in new situations, and bring them in contact with different people and objects.*
5. Communicating—*when the journeys are completed, students communicate their experiences orally, through writing and/or the arts.*
6. Reflecting/interpreting—*finally, they are invited to reflect upon the deeper meaning of their images and to determine what new insights might be gleaned from the imagery work. (cited in Sheikh and Sheikh, p. 166)*

The goals of counseling include attending to both intervention and prevention. Facilitating and educating the whole child may occur through a number of counseling techniques and skills. Eventually the educational focus may be redirected to include educating both hemispheres of the brain to maximize the learning experience. Visualization and guided-imagery provide a means for counselors to integrate development in both the cognitive and affective domains and to nurture all the senses and inner resources.

With increasing understanding of the positive effects of the imaging mind on physical and emotional material, visualization and guided imagery has the potential of becoming a basic life skill. According to Sheikh and Sheikh (1985),

> *this basic skill promises to enhance intellectual functioning, expand previously conceived Cartesian-Newtonian mental limitations [that mind and body are two separate entities], enlist intellectual energies beyond those of ordinary awakened consciousness, transcend ordinary values and biased perceptions of human possibility, and heal physical matter. (p. 174)*

Thus, the technique of visualization and guided-imagery is worthy of further investigation. Other information regarding how visualization and imagery can be helpful may be obtained through professional workshops and books such as Bernie Siegel's *Love, Medicine, and Miracles.* (1987)

Play Therapy

This text reflects, among others, the theory that personality development in all individuals is characterized by an inner force which drives them to self-actualization, maturity, and independence. Further, it is the birthright of every human being to have opportunities to develop every potential. Just as any living thing requires nourishment, children too, benefit from enrichment during the formative years of childhood.

Elementary school counselors regard childhood with genuine appreciation and are committed, not only to protect it, but to enrich it, and in so doing, to maximize the process of growth for all children. Experiences of childhood, the forces of life that impact on children and determine their patterns of development, are characterized by complexities that require clarification and acceptance. In *Play Therapy* (1969), Virginia Axline states that:

> *through the process of therapy, children acquired the necessary feeling of personal worth, a feeling that they were capable of self-direction, a growing awareness that they had within themselves the ability to stand on their own two feet, to accept themselves, to assume the responsibility for their conscious personalities, and by so doing synchronize the two projections of their personalities—what the individual is within [her or] himself and how [she or] he outwardly manifests this inner self.* (pp. 14-15)

While this quote summarizes outcomes of counseling children in crises, we suggest the usefulness of play therapy as intervention and prevention in elementary school counseling.

According to Axline (1969), the eight basic principles which guide the therapist in all non-directive therapeutic contacts are as follows:

> 1. *The therapist must develop a warm, friendly relationship with the child, in which good rapport is established as soon as possible.*
> 2. *The therapist accepts the child exactly as he is.*
> 3. *The therapist establishes a feeling of permissiveness in the relationship so that the child feels free to express his feelings completely.*
> 4. *The therapist is alert to recognize the feelings the child is expressing and reflects those feelings back to him in such a manner that he gains insight into his behavior.*
> 5. *The therapist maintains a deep respect for the child's ability to solve his own problems if given an opportunity to do so. The responsibility to make choices and to institute change is the child's.*
> 6. *The therapist does not attempt to direct the child's actions or conversation in any manner. The child leads the way; the therapist follows.*
> 7. *The therapist does not attempt to hurry the therapy along. It is a gradual process and is recognized as such by the therapist.*
> 8. *The therapist establishes only those limitations that are necessary to anchor the therapy to the world of reality and to make the child aware of his responsibility in the relationship.* (pp. 73-74)

In play therapy, children are given the opportunity to "play out" their feelings. Play is regarded as practice of basic developmental skills and behaviors within a safe environment that allows freedom to experiment and explore. The purpose of play is to rehearse adult life. Children substitute experiences for cognitions. Communication in play therapy is indirect, suggesting that the counselor observe children's association through metaphors. One source which counselors may refer to for understanding these metaphors is *Therapeutic Metaphors for Children and the Child Within* (1986) by J. Mills and R. Crowley. The observation of play may culminate in a therapeutic process just as counseling is a therapeutic process. Particularly with nonverbal children, the counselor observes the child's choices of toys and how the child interacts with them.

In the context of play therapy, consider imaginative play. Singer and Singer (1976) view it as

> *a cognitive skill that enables the child to explore both his/her internal and external environment and that allows for the processing and reprocessing of material until it is fully assimilated. In this mode, the brain is seen as endlessly processing and reprocessing material, with a set towards attending to it, rather than as functioning as a static computer. (cited in Sheikh and Sheikh, 1985, p. 42)*

Imaginative play may be used as an adjunct procedure to other preventive, remedial, and interventive counseling modalities. When a counselor encourages a child to play, she or he is inviting the child to participate in a natural form of expression, not an aimless act, rather, one which requires skill in combining scattered elements into some meaningful form. A child uses her or his imagination to make sense of her or his reality. Dewey (1934) stressed

> *the importance of children's active investigation as a means of learning from the environment. Play was regarded as the starting point which led to the child's reasoning, discovery, and thought . . . . The popular American interpretation of Dewey's theories led to an emphasis on the provision of an enriched and spacious [educational] environment. (Smilansky, 1968, cited in Sheikh and Sheikh, 1985, p. 55)*

Imaginative play is an activity that produces outward expression of one's inner experience, fostering the development of a personal reservoir of resourcefulness, creativity, and self-esteem; the child's tendency toward exploration and curiosity is gratified; and organization skills are practiced.

In a school setting, one benefit of imaginative play to the developing child is its likelihood to increase levels of joy, happiness, and the experience of positive interactions.

> *Empirical studies (Singer, 1973, 1977; Pulaski, 1973; Udwin and Shmukler, 1981; and Marshall and Hahn, 1967) consistently show positive relationships between high levels of imaginative play and positive affect . . . . Observations by Marshall and Hahn (1967) and Smilansky (1968) included benefits to disadvantaged children as changing apathy and lack of motivation to positive goal-directed behavior. (cited in Sheikh and Sheikh, 1985, p. 43)*

While play therapy has its limitations, as is illustrated in Figure 4–1, it is regarded as a valid and useful means of expression by children.

Special Counseling Concerns

The elementary school counselor faces the challenging task of dealing with the wide range and variety of counseling needs of children. While many of these

FIGURE 4–1 Life in Hell

may be unique to the childhood years, there are those special counseling concerns that are reflective of societal problems and educational issues affecting large segments of our population, including elementary school children. A sampling of some of the more visible of these concerns and issues will be briefly addressed in this section. They include substance abuse, child abuse, family problems, minority youth, "mainstreaming," gifted children, and retention. This section discusses these topics as special concerns for elementary school counselors. Some of these will be addressed further in Chapter 8 on prevention.

Substance Abuse

Certainly a major threat to the wellness of our society has resulted from the rapid growth of substance abuse in recent generations. The habitual and harmful use of addictive substances has reached alarming and epidemic proportions in our society. Further compounding the problem is the realization that substance abuse is not a problem of just the adult world or even the adult and adolescent world, but that it has already dramatically invaded the elementary school years as well. Roth and Friedman (1987) emphasize that:

> *it is no longer unusual for ten and twelve-year-olds to have serious alcohol or other drug problems. Alcohol is considered to be a "gateway" drug. That is, it is the first mood altering substance children use and the one most likely to be associated with other risk-taking behaviors such as smoking, use of illicit drugs, early sexual activity leading to adolescent pregnancy and dropping out of school. (p. 186)*

The disturbing statistics that are highlighted in the media almost daily remind us that the numbers of children who are active users of drugs and alcohol numbers in the disturbing millions. In addition, there are countless other millions who are affected by living in homes with addicted parents or environments where addiction thrives. Ostrower (1987) explains that the counselor who works with children in the school often sees the consequences of alcohol abuse translated into various school problems for children. These include "poor academic performance, low self-esteem, truancy, school phobia, aggressive or disruptive classroom behavior, withdrawal, depression, or difficulty relating to peers" (p. 209). These consequences result among children exposed to all types of substance abuse.

Finally, completing this dismal picture is the realization that the treatment and cure of the drug addict and/or alcoholic has met with only limited success to date. The inevitable conclusion has to be that the only programs of hope for combating this terrible menace to our national wellness are programs that prevent the occurrence of the problem in the first place. Two other conclusions *must* be equally obvious: (1) to be successful, such programs must be located in our elementary schools—*every* elementary school; (2) such programs must be a part of the total social/personal, developmental effort of the school, while under the direction and leadership of the elementary school counselor. These programs will not succeed when directed by amateurs. They must be the responsibility of the trained professional counselor since they must be aimed at populations, not solitary individuals or even selected families. Everyone in the elementary school must be addressed by this counseling effort.

A variety of factors appear to contribute to children becoming substance abusers. A prime contributor, which appears consistently across the literature is peer pressure or pressure from older children, adolescents, and young adults to "join the fun." One survey involving 500,000 school children nationwide found thirty percent of fourth-graders reporting that children their age were pressuring others to drink beer, wine, or liquor (Roth and Friedman, 1987, p. 121). Certainly families in which alcohol or drugs are prominent and/or in which there are weak sanctions against their use, encourage their use. Other factors contributing to substance abuse in children include poor school performances, family problems, no active religious affiliation, low self-esteem, and lack of respect by others.

Medical treatment alone has not proven adequate in the treatment of substance abuse. In fact, counseling appears to be a major factor in successful treatment. This includes individual, group, and family therapy. Since specialized courses and programs are recommended for counselors working with substance abuse counseling, elementary school counselors will usually refer children who are substance abusers or will work as a team member with specialists.

Those children who live in homes where alcohol or drug abuse is prevalent will experience varying degrees of adjustments, and feelings. They often feel:

1. Responsible either directly or indirectly for their parents' drinking
2. Their parents drinking equates with their not being loved
3. Angry with the parent who does not drink for not changing the situation and providing safety for them
4. Afraid of harm coming to the alcoholic as a result of drinking
5. Confused by the difference of behavior when the parent is drinking from when the parent is not drinking
6. Afraid to bring friends home since it is hard to know what to expect at home
7. Ashamed and embarrassed about the parents' behavior

Counseling with children who live in an alcoholic environment should focus on: (a) providing empathy and support, and (b) helping clients to develop coping skills which will facilitate their ability to handle the situation.

Edwards and Zander (1985) advise the use of the following strategies for counselors who are working with children from an alcoholic environment.

1. *Establish a trusting relationship by demonstrating consistent care and interest in the child (e.g., setting limits, keeping promises, and being on time) and by avoiding the replication of destructive attitudes and behavior patterns of the parents.*
2. *Help the child overcome denial of parental alcoholism. Denial should be presented as a phenomenon experienced by family members as well as by the alcoholic (Black, 1981). Counseling should focus on common examples of denial by the alcoholic (e.g., "I don't have a problem."), the spouse (e.g., "He's just overworked; the situation will remedy itself."), and the children (e.g., "That's okay that he forgot my birthday.").*
3. *Explain and discuss alcoholism with the child. Concepts that need to be addressed are alcoholism as a disease, blackouts, personality changes, broken promises, enabling, reinforcement of drinking behavior, and relapses.* My Dad

Loves Me, My Dad Has a Disease *(Black, 1979) is a useful workbook and picturebook for conveying this information to children between the ages of 6 and 14.*

4. *Help the child to identify his or her diverse feelings and healthy ways to express these feelings. Black's (1979) workbook is excellent for helping children to understand and share their thoughts and feelings.*
5. *Help the child develop positive relationships with others. Friendship skills can be taught and extracurricular and community activities and relationships should be encouraged and supported. Coaching isolated children in specific social skills (i.e., starting a conversation, asking for and giving information, and exhibiting inviting behaviors) in the context of a small group seems to be effective in teaching friendship-making skills.* Teaching Social Skills to Children *by Cartledge and Milburn (1980) is a valuable resource book for modifying children's social behavior.*
6. *Incorporate a success component in the exercises and activities used with the child. This should include breaking tasks into manageable steps and the acknowledgment of success by both the counselor and the child. In addition, the child should receive assistance in developing coping strategies to deal with failure. For example, the child can be taught to use self-talk that encourages continued problem-solving efforts and instills a self-concept of "learned resourcefulness" (as contrasted with "learned helplessness"). Specifically, the child can be trained through a combination of procedures (modeling, overt and covert rehearsal, prompts, and feedback) to use such statements as "What else can I try?" "What can I learn from this mistake" or "I'll try harder next time."* Cognitive Behavior Modification *by Meichenbaum (1977) is a useful resource book for teaching children how to use self-instructions.*
7. *Encourage opportunities that provide the child with recognition as a worthwhile person. This involves more than global statements (e.g., "You are such a nice little girl") or indiscriminate praise. Praise should be offered for specific behaviors and attitudes that are within the control of the child (e.g., in-class recognition, strength bombardment exercises).*
8. *Provide the child with a sense of control and preparedness in facing family situations. This can be accomplished through honest, straightforward discussions about what the child might expect, exploration of coping alternatives, and role playing.*
9. *Discuss the prevention of alcoholism and family breakdown through education on the disease of alcoholism. This will afford the child freedom from guilt and responsibility for the family situation and provide a realistic sense of hope. (Edwards and Zander, 1985, pp. 124-125)*

Many children of substance abusing families may go undetected because they have developed superb coping/survival skills. These children may appear responsible, make good grades, and act socially adjusted. That is, they could appear, and actually be, model students, and therefore, not be referred for counseling intervention. Very often these children are taught in dysfunctional homes

ATTENTION! ATTENTION! BOYS AND GIRLS, SOMETIMES PARENTS OR OTHER GROWN-UPS THAT YOU LOVE TAKE DRUGS AND DRINK TOO MUCH ALCOHOL. SOMETIMES THEY ACT IN WAYS THAT SCARE YOU. THEY MAY EVEN HURT YOU SOMETIMES. IF THIS IS HAPPENING IN YOUR HOME, YOU ARE INVITED TO UNDERSTAND HOW THIS HAPPENS AND FIND OUT WHAT YOU CAN DO TO FEEL BETTER. JUST ASK YOUR TEACHER, IN PRIVATE, TO EXCUSE YOU TO THE COUNSELOR'S OFFICE.

YOUR SCHOOL COUNSELOR,

CAREY E. NOUGH

FIGURE 4–2 Sample Announcement to Children

to ignore the "elephant in the living room", the alcoholic parent, and to go on living as if nothing were out of the ordinary. To some extent, many children are able to do this and "appear" very healthy. The difficulty eventually ensues when they can no longer live the lie. This situation, among others that occur in substance abusing families, is confusing and often harmful to children.

These children can benefit from counseling intervention. However, first, the counselor must discover who these children are and invite them to counseling. To prevent these children from "falling through the cracks," letting their emotional needs and insecurities go undetected, it is suggested that counselors send out flyers to classrooms inviting children to sign up for groups pertaining to this population. An example announcement may read as shown in figure 4–2.

The counselor will see each child who responds to this announcement individually to discuss the concerns. Children may be counseled individually for a few sessions. It is suggested that eventually children be placed in homogeneous groups for maximum benefits. One benefit is realizing the universality of this problem which dispels feelings of isolation, embarrassment, and loneliness. Refer to Chapter 5, group counseling, for details about setting up and running groups.

Abused Children

Child abuse is one of the most prevalent destroyers of childhood. The joys of early life which every child has the right to anticipate are destroyed for not only the tens of thousands affected by reported incidents, but possibly equal numbers of the unreported as well. According to a review of research findings on developmental effects of abuse (Augoustinos, 1987), there is sufficient empirical evidence to support the widely held assumption that child abuse and neglect have deleterious effects on the physical, neurological, intellectual, and emotional development of the child (p. 15).

While media attention has created a heightened public awareness of the problem in recent generations, there is no evidence that this awareness has resulted in a decline in this, our national childhood tragedy.

While the exact legal definitions of what constitutes child abuse differs from state to state, they all include categories of physical, sexual, and emotional (or psychological) abuse. In a broad general sense, child abuse may be viewed as the mistreatment of a child (minor) by a parent or other adult. The actions of the adult go beyond the label "unwarranted." They are damaging or harmful in a physical and/or psychological sense not only in the present but usually over the long-term as well. Their consequences can be deep and disturbing throughout the life of the victim. One study demonstrated that abused children tend to blame themselves for the abuse; however, the extent of the blame is mediated by the type and extent of abuse. For example, physically abused children accepted the blame for abuse that was mild but not for severe abuse, while children who were sexually or verbally abused appeared to be affected more severely by the abuse (Gerler, 1988). In fact, one of the worst aspects of family violence is its natural reproduction of itself. Studies by Kempe and Kempe (1978) and Polansky, Chalmers, Buttenweiser, and Williams (1981), among others, show that one of the best predictors of abuse is whether the parent was also abused as a child.

In the United States, elementary school counselors are at the forefront of efforts to improve understanding of child abuse and to develop educational programs aimed at preventing and treating child abuse (Downing, 1982; Holtgraves, 1986). Counselors in elementary schools of course need to be aware of their legal responsibilities as mandated reporters of suspected abuse. The key words that counselors must keep in mind in guiding their actions are that they are reporters—not investigators of suspected—not necessarily proven incidents of abuse. On this point, in a published interview by Susan and Michael Crabbs, Mr. David Sandberg, a researcher and practitioner of law relating to children's issues, noted that:

> *counselors basically report and that child protective services workers investigate . . . . Counselors, in my opinion, have a duty to remain alert and make discreet inquiries in cases where there is little hard evidence but a strong feeling persists that abuse is occurring. Even more than this, anyone working with chronic problem children should have child abuse in mind as a possible contributory factor. This duty becomes distorted and trouble begins when a counselor progresses to a zealous crusade in the search for evidence.*

In other cases where there is "reason to suspect" abuse or there is a "suspicion" of abuse, which inferentially implies some specific evidence such as black-and-blue marks or behavioral indicators, there is no duty to investigate further. At this point, a report is compelled (Sandberg, Crabbs, & Crabbs, 1988, p. 270).

In any event, it would appear highly desirable that elementary school counselors receive annual legal advice from the legal counsel for their school system in order that misunderstandings and possible violations of the law can be avoided.

Beyond their legal responsibilities, however, counselors have an even broader responsibility as reflected in the American School Counselor Association (ASCA) position statement of 1985. This statement points out:

> *it is not simply a legal issue of reporting child abuse, but also a moral and ethical responsibility of school counselors to help children and adults cope with abusive behavior, facilitate behavioral changes, and prepare for parenting styles and positive interpersonal relationships. Counselors must commit themselves to providing strategies to help break the cycle of child abuse. (American School Counselor Association, 1988, p. 261)*

Definitions and examples from this statement are as follows:

Definitions

Abuse: *The infliction by other than accidental means of physical harm upon the body of a child, continual psychological damage or denial of emotional needs.*
Corporal Punishment: *Any act of physical force upon a pupil for the purpose of punishing that pupil.*

This definition specifically excludes any reasonable force exercised by a school employee which is used in self-defense, in defense of other persons or property or to restrain or remove a pupil who is disrupting school functions and who refuses to comply with a request to stop.

Some examples of child abuse are:

1. *Extensive bruises or patterns of bruises*
2. *Burns or burn patterns*
3. *Lacerations, welts or abrasions*
4. *Injuries inconsistent with information offered*
5. *Sexual abuse is any act or acts involving sexual molestation or exploitation, including but not limited to rape, carnal knowledge, sodomy, or unnatural sexual practices*
6. *Emotional disturbances caused by continuous friction in the home, marital discord, or mentally ill parents*
7. *Cruel treatment*

Neglect: *The failure to provide necessary food, care, clothing, shelter, supervision, or medical attention for a child.*

Examples of child neglect are:

1. *Malnourished, ill clad, dirty, without proper shelter or sleeping arrangements, lacking appropriate health care*
2. *Unattended, lacking adequate supervision*
3. *Ill and lacking essential medical attention*
4. *Irregular/illegal absences from school*
5. *Exploited, overworked*
6. *Lacking essential psychological/emotional nurturance*
7. *Abandonment (American School Counselor Association, 1988, p. 262)*

School counselors are the central helpers in any school system's child abuse prevention efforts. They must recognize the symptoms of possible abuse and their legal reporting responsibilities. They must also recognize their responsibility to take a leadership role in developing and implementing an effective program of child abuse prevention. Allsopp & Prosen (1988) emphasize the increasing need for counselors to provide appropriate training and information for school personnel who might be involved in cases of suspected child abuse. They discuss a model program which has been successfully implemented in the training of over 2,000 teachers and administrators to deal with sexual abuse cases. The program consisted of: (a) information related to offenders, victims, and non-offending family members; (b) present laws and proposed legislation; (c) requirements and procedures for school systems in reporting suspected child sexual abuse; and (d) available community resources for victim's use. Ninety-eight percent of teachers reported that the program increased their awareness of victims and offenders; 92 percent stated that the program provided them with a clearer understanding of the school system's procedures for reporting child sexual abuse; 93 percent expressed they had increased their knowledge of county services currently available to victims; and 98 percent reported that as a result of participation in the program they felt more adequately prepared to deal with a situation in which a child was sexually abused. The American School Counselor Association's (1985) position statement:

encourages its members to participate in the implementation of the following guidance and counseling activities:

- *Coordinate team efforts involving the principal, teacher, counselor, school nurse, protective services workers, and the child.*
- *Serve as a support to teachers, and other school personnel especially if the child was abused as a result of a report sent home about the child from school.*

- *Emphasize the non-punitive role of protective services and allay fears that the child will be removed immediately from the home.*
- *Facilitate the contact between the child and the social worker. The issue of confidentiality and re-establishing the trust of the child after the report is made is critical to the child-counselor relationship.*
- *Provide ongoing counseling services to the child and/or family after the crisis is over, or refer to an appropriate community agency.*
- *Provide programs designed to help prevent child abuse. Counselors can help children with coping skills and ways to prevent their own abuse by improving their self-concepts, being able to recognize stress in their parents, and being sensitive to cues that abuse may occur if their own behavior is not changed.*
- *Help teachers and administrators in understanding the dynamics of abuse and abusive parents, and in developing a nonjudgmental attitude so they can react more appropriately in crisis situations.*
- *Provide developmental workshops and/or support groups for parents focusing upon alternative methods of discipline, handling anger and frustration, and enhancing parenting skills (American School Counselor Association, 1988, p. 263).*

It is the counselor's responsibility to advocate and work toward effective treatment programs for abused children while also implementing programs focusing on prevention of abuse.

Although Gerler (1988) emphasizes the difficulty in developing preventive programs, and Garbarino (1986) notes the major problems that exist in measuring the success of preventive programs

> *one successful preventive approach seems to be the health visitor program studied by Olds, Chamberlin, Henderson, and Tatelbaum (in press). Their rigorous study showed that a registered nurse assigned to a family judged to be at high risk for abuse resulted in significant preventive effects. . . . A parent education program developed and studied by Golub, Espinosa, Damon, and Card (1987) for groups of abusive parents offers the hope that preventive group programs are within reach.*
>
> *This program, entitled "Hugs 'n Kids," incorporates videotapes of 13 episodes depicting typical problem situations between parents and their preschool children . . . . Results indicated that abusive parents and high-risk parents who completed the program had improved their knowledge of alternatives to physical punishment and had changed their attitudes toward children's misbehavior. (p. 326)*

Straus and Gelles (1986) suggest:

> *that the effort to change public attitudes and standards concerning family violence have achieved a certain measure of success . . . . Moreover, a change in attitudes and cultural norms is an important part of the process leading to*

change in overt behavior. If all that has been accomplished in the last 10 years is to instill new standards for parents and husbands about the inappropriateness of violence, that is a key element in the process of reducing the actual rate of child abuse. (p. 475)

In elementary schools, teachers often alert counselors to a suspected case of child abuse. Upon notification, see this child in private immediately. You may say while looking at the bruised eye or cigarette burns, "Your teacher is concerned about this bruise (or these burns). It looks like it hurts very badly. Tell me how you got that." Then listen to the child and be alert to nonverbal clues and underlying feelings, for example, fear of telling. Keep in mind that this may not be a case of child abuse. However, if you suspect that the child is not telling the truth, you may add, "Sometimes grown-ups get angry with little kids and hurt them when they really may not intend to do that. I am wondering if anyone got angry with you, and if you are afraid to tell on that person." Sometimes children are very afraid and protective of people they care about and will not tell on them. Our experience has been that generally children do tell the truth about who abused them, in which case you are mandated by law to report it to the authorities. The authorities are usually the Department of Social Services where is housed the child protective agency in your community. Again, consult with your principal or your school system's legal advisor.

In some school districts, when a counselor reports a sexual abuse case, the social worker will come immediately to the school to interview the child. The counselor's role is to prepare the child for this process. The counselor may say that she or he will be visited by someone who will help them. They will ask the child to repeat what was told to you. It is obviously advisable to develop a positive professional relationship with the social workers and other helping professionals in your community. In many situations, you will ask the social worker if you may be present during the interview with the child. As counselor, you are the child's advocate and someone the child knows and trusts. The interview process with a stranger and the stressful nature of the topic warrant your presence. When a child divulges that she or he is being sexually abused, enormous amounts of support, understanding, reassurance, and patience will be required to help this child over a long period of time.

Gifted and Talented

An obvious and fundamental goal for elementary counseling and guidance programs is facilitating the optimal development of all children during their elementary school years. This presumes the development of their potential and the enhancement of whatever special aptitudes they may possess. This implies program activities which: (a) assess and identify areas of special ability; (b) aiding children and their parents in recognizing their strengths; and (c) curricular and other program planning facilitating the development and enhancement of special abilities. These special abilities or talents may be academic, artistic, athletic or social in nature. Those with extraordinary talents in one or more of these areas may be said to be *gifted*, or perhaps more accurately in the elementary school, as *potentially* gifted.

The identification of giftedness in the elementary school, especially in the early years will be largely dependent on teacher assessments (including those with specialties in arts or sports) and to a lesser degree diagnostic psychological measures.

It is important to avoid an overemphasis on gifted assessments with endless testing, checklists, and so on, to the detriment of the major goal of the program, which is the enhancement of the giftedness. Too, excessive assessment often leads to labeling and while *recognition* of potential giftedness is important, the *labeling* of elementary school children is not. In addressing this point, Colangelo and Fleuridas (1986) indicate that:

> *in reviewing a number of publications in the last few years and listening to presentations at conferences, we have noticed how often gifted children have been referred to as the nation's most "precious natural resource." The danger is that gifted children will be seen first as natural resources and second as children . . . . Labeling of young children is practically never useful. Labels help educators, parents, and society at large to forget that gifted children are normal children with exceptional ability, not abnormal children . . . . Counselors, perhaps more than other educators, are in a position to advocate the recognition of children as, first and foremost, children. Counselors should also help school officials recognize that children may have rather extraordinary variations in abilities, even at a very young age. These abilities should be developed for the good of the child. (p. 562)*

This is not to suggest that giftedness be overlooked. Rather, it is suggested that special talents should be identified as early as possible and their development attended to and accommodated, for the most part, through the elementary school's total educational program, where their total development can be attended to as well as their special abilities. This suggests a stimulating environment with opportunities for exploration and enrichment and the building of a solid foundation for the later development of their talents without the abdication of their childhood. Various authors (Culross, 1982; Dettman and Colangelo, 1980; North Carolina Association for the Gifted and Talented (NCAG) Task Force, 1986) have discussed the significant role school counselors have in assuring that educational needs of gifted students are met. Their conclusions, along with the results of a four-year study by Cox (1986), demonstrate that counselors' services are essential in successful programs of education for gifted students (Conroy, 1987). The elementary school counselor can play a major role in the identification of children with this potential, in conferring with pupils and their parents for awareness and motivational purposes and in developing appropriate enhancement opportunities and experiences.

Counseling concerns of gifted and talented children may include: how to deal with pressure from parents; how to develop positive peer relationships; and how to cope with feelings of being different, of being singled out, and of failure. We are not suggesting that all gifted and talented children will be referred for counseling or that they will encounter possible adjustment problems. As a school counselor, awareness of potential concerns will prepare you if, and when, cases occur.

Minority Children

We have noted previously the importance of the elementary school as the societal institution responsible for the foundational years of our youth and eventual adult population. These are the years that provide the experiences that will significantly influence one's later educational, career, and personal accomplishments. Elementary school counselors have the responsibility to see that all children have these opportunities, including those from racial minorities.

Understanding the impact that cultural influences have on the elementary school student's basic values, beliefs and behavior is of critical importance. "When individuals from different cultures attempt to relate to one another, they may begin with very different perceptions about the nature of people, what people need, how people succeed, and the relationship of people to nature" (Brown and Srebalus, 1988, p. 139). The school counselor must recognize the likelihood for these differences in perceptions in attempting to be of assistance to students from all cultural backgrounds.

The information in Table 4–2 can be useful in beginning to identify cultural differences that might influence these differences in perceptions as mentioned above. Caution must be taken in using this table as a guideline in understanding possible differences and not as a set of generalizations to be applied to any person who is a member of the ethnic categories.

African-Americans

It is important to recognize that despite significant legislative enactments at the federal and state level that seek to address inequalities in educational opportunities, and which are coupled with many local programs addressing minority issues and concerns in schools, many problems still exist. They are in great need of attention by elementary school educators including counselors. Parker and McDavis (1989) identified six such problems facing African-American elementary school students as follows:

- *One problem Black children face is that they often do not achieve or perform at their full potential as a result of a lack of self-confidence and self-esteem. (Harper, 1977; Stephan and Rosenfield, 1979; Bewley, 1977; Lee and Lindsey, 1985)*
- *A second problem is that many questions concerning the career development needs of Black students have not been clarified. (Johnson, 1980; Griffith, 1980; Gunnings and Gunnings, 1983)*

TABLE 4–2 Cultural Differences That May Influence Cross-Cultural Counseling

Clients	Language	Views of Human Nature	Goals of Human Relationships	Time Orientation	Relationship with Nature	Action Orientation
White Americans	Standard English	Individual has primary responsibility	Competition, dominance	Adhere to rigid time schedule	Must Dominate	Action-oriented
Black Americans	Nonstandard English, nonverbal communication important	Affiliation with others valued	Support	Schedules less important	Accept nature	Action-oriented, meet immediate short-term goals
Hispanics	Bilingual or Spanish speaking	Group-centered	Cooperation *not* competition	Time Unimportant	Unite with nature	Action-oriented to meet present needs
Asian Americans	Nonstandard English for some, standard English for others, Asian language for others	Emphasis on group, particularly family	Cooperation stressed but can be competitive, respect for authority stressed	Schedules less important	Appreciation for nature	Action-oriented to meet short- and long-term goals

From *An Introduction to the Counseling Profession* (p. 140) by D. Brown and D. J. Srebalus, 1988 (Needham Heights, MA: Allyn and Bacon). Copyright 1988 by Prentice-Hall. Adapted and reprinted from D. W. Sue, *Counseling the Culturally Different* (pp. 30–31) by permission of John Wiley & Sons, Inc. Copyright © 1981 John Wiley and Sons, Inc., Adapted and Reprinted from J. H. Katz, "The Sociopolitical Nature of Counseling," in *The Counseling Psychologist, 13* (p. 618) by permission of Sage Publications, Inc. Copyright © 1985 Sage Publications, Inc.

- *Another problem is that many Black students still have not learned how to establish social relations effectively among themselves or with students from other racial or ethnic groups (Asher and Singleton, 1978).*
- *A fourth problem is that some Black students have not learned how to solve problems effectively; thus, their educational process is continuously interrupted by suspensions throughout their school years (Goldsmith, 1979; Kaeser, 1979; Larkin, 1979).*
- *A fifth problem is that many Black students perform poorly in their classes because they never learn how to study. Effective study skills are crucial to the acquisition of the vast and varied amount of information students are required to comprehend.*
- *A sixth and final problem is the poor performance by Black students on standardized tests, which indicates a need for them to learn specific strategies for taking standardized tests. (McPhail, 1979; Simmons, Brown, Bush, and Blyth, 1978; Berk, Bridges, and Shih, 1981, p. 244)*

Various strategies to confront these issues faced by African-American children, are suggested by Parker and McDavis (1989). They present a personal development model that counselors can use to facilitate the development of African-American elementary school students' self-confidence, career goals, social- and work-relationship skills, and standardized test-taking skills. They refer to this model as one more tool that elementary counselors can use to assist African-American children in acquiring necessary skills to build a strong academic foundation for their future. Counselors from fifteen African-American elementary schools, who used the model, reported that it made a major contribution toward meeting some of the personal, career development, and educational needs of African-American elementary school children.

Elementary school counselors must become fully aware of difficulties faced by African-American students and implement strategies to deal with these often overwhelming and challenging issues.

Asian-Americans

Asian-American students also bring their cultural differences to the elementary school and counseling setting. These usually include a much greater sense of obligation to family, a great pressure to succeed academically and emotional restraint (Sue, 1981). Sue and Sue (1977) identified three types of goals or expectations in counseling which may be a source of conflict with these minority group members:

> *First, most counselors expect their clients to exhibit openness and psychological mindedness. To do so, however, the client must be facile with the standard form of English. Because many Asian-Americans come from a bilingual background, they may be disadvantaged in this form of verbal expression. Asian clients also have learned to restrain emotional expression and feel that this repression represents a sign of maturity.*
>
> *Second, the process of counseling involves the revelation of intimate details on the part of the client. The cultural upbringing of Chinese and Japanese clients may be in opposition to this goal. Discussion of personal problems is difficult because such disclosure is felt to reflect not only on the individual but also on the whole family.*
>
> *Third, the counseling environment is often an ambiguous one for the client. The therapist listens while the client talks about the problem. In many cases, little direction is given. The unstructured nature of the counseling environment adds additional stress to Asian-American clients who prefer concrete, tangible, and structured approaches to problems. (Vacc and Wittmer, 1980, p. 190)*

Hispanic-Americans

Hyland (1989) stresses:

> *that in the last twenty years, the Hispanic American population subgroup has experienced the most dramatic growth . . . . Currently, Hispanics have the*

> *highest dropout rate of all major population subgroups at around 36 percent . . . . Further, Hispanic children tend to be over-represented in remedial tracks and under-represented in gifted programs and to exhibit low academic achievement levels overall. This group also has the distinction of being the most highly segregated of all school children, both within and among public schools . . . . The Hispanic population in America has entered a tremendous period of growth which, according to projections, will result in an American demographic picture in the year 2020 composed of 47 million Hispanics out of 265 million people. (p. 132)*

Hyland (1989) states further that "counselors must keep in mind that there are several different subgroups of Hispanics in America with similar, yet sometimes distinctive, characteristics" (p. 134).

Hispanic-Americans exhibit similar attitudes toward the family and its importance as previously noted for Asian-Americans. Designation of the family as of primary significance, along with respect and loyalty to parents as authority figures is stressed. Sue and Sue (1977) discuss the mistaken notion of regarding all Hispanics as just alike. They also refute one stereotypical belief that sex roles for Hispanics are unique and rigid and that the male is macho in the sense that he is physically aggressive and dominant over women. They insist instead that for Hispanics real masculinity "involves dignity in personal conduct, respect for others, love for the family and affection for children" (p. 192).

An elementary school counselor, in working with children of Hispanic heritage, could learn much about the Hispanic culture by referring to the book *Crossing Cultures in Therapy—Pluralistic Counseling for the Hispanic* (1980), by Levine and Padilla. Counseling techniques that focus on the cultural, linguistic, and socioeconomic conditions of Hispanics, and other minorities, are illustrated.

Native-Americans

The pre-European Native-American population reached 2.5 million in the Continental United States; however, by the end of the 19th century, the number had decreased to 25,000 (Herring, 1989). Presently, it has grown to over 1.5 million and continues to increase (Ashabranner, 1984). Special needs exist for Native-American children; however, because of their limited number in schools, they have received less attention from school counselors than any other minority group (Mitchum, 1989) Mitchum explains that although they represent a unique culture which is plagued with severe problems, programs offered to them through the schools are the same as those offered to their non-Indian peers. These approaches are reported as ineffective in dealing with the problems faced by the Native-American children. For example, Mitchum discusses how the use of the "strength bombardment" exercise (through which children are singled out and given positive feedback) has been quite successful in increasing the self-esteem for non-Indian children, but, on the other hand, has met with no success among the Native-American children. One might comprehend why the exercise would not succeed with these students by understanding the following values as reported by Mitchum (1989):

> *Cooperation and harmony are highly valued in Indian culture (Lazarus, 1982). Honoring these Indian values would make it difficult for a child to be singled out and praised for his or her uniqueness. Competition is not valued in Native-American culture. Being first, best, fastest, smartest, or any similar superlative implies standing out, being different. Native Americans consider it ill-mannered to speak of one's own accomplishments (Youngman and Sadongei, 1974, p. 267).*

Because more value is placed on contributing to the group than on individual success and accomplishments amongst the Native American culture, Mitchum (1989) suggests the use of group counseling with Native American students in which the actual dynamics of the group are adapted in order that they can mirror aspects of their own culture. Groups of this type have shown promising results with Native-American children in boarding schools. Mitchum emphasizes the need to now integrate them into the public school setting.

Diversity is also an aspect that characterizes the Native-American population, as Thomason (1991) emphasizes "there are 505 federally recognized tribal entities and an additional 365 state-recognized tribes and bands" (p. 321). Heinrich, Corbine and Thomas (1990) insist that while keeping the enormous diversity among native-Americans in mind, there are similarities in values that exist across tribes and regions (Blanchard and Mackey, 1971; Lazarus, 1982; National Indian Child Abuse and Neglect Resource Center, 1980; Richardson, 1981; Trimble, 1981). They illustrate major value differences between White mainstream culture and traditional Native-American culture through the use of Table 4–3. The contents of the table were derived from a list of value differences as provided by Richardson (1981) in the book *Counseling the Culturally Different* which was written by Sue (1981).

TABLE 4–3 Comparison of Value Orientations

Contemporary Native American Values	Traditional Native American Values
Subjugation of nature	Harmony with nature
Future, progress, change	Present, following the old ways
Competition (each person maximizing own welfare will maximize the general welfare)	Cooperation, conscious submission of self to the welfare of the tribe
Private property, acquisition of wealth	Sharing freely, working only for present needs
Fame, recognition	Anonymity, humility
Reliance on experts	Reliance on extended family
Verbal expression	Keeping to oneself
Analytic	Holistic

From "Counseling Native Americans," by R. K. Heinrich, J. L. Corbine, and K. R. Thomas in the 1988 *Journal for Counseling and Development, 69*, p. 129. Reprinted with permission from the American Counseling Association. Reprinted from D. W. Sue, *Counseling the Culturally Different* (pp. 225–227) by permission of John Wiley and Sons, Inc., Copyright © 1981 John Wiley and Sons, Inc.

Richardson (1981) suggests that counselors use such techniques as silence, restatement, and general leads in beginning counseling with Native-Americans, while Lazarus (1982) recommends nonverbal interaction including play and art, becoming comfortable with long pauses in conversations, the use of the Native-American family as a resource, and the facilitation of group work rather than individual counseling (Heinrich, Corbine, Thomas, 1990).

In recognizing that there are enormous differences among tribes, Vacc & Wittmer (1980) suggest that several basic points should be kept in mind:

1. *The Indian-American has a culture, a cultural heritage, and a right to that culture as inalienable as any other basic human right.*
2. *Most Indians do not prefer assimilation; they do not want all of the "advantages" of the non-Indian life.*
3. *There may be differences between Indians and others in the kinds of pressure with which they have to contend given their particular culture and the dominant society in which they live. (pp. 112-113)*

The illustrating of cultural differences for African-American, Asian-Americans, Latin-Americans, and Native-Americans is not meant to suggest that these are the only cultural minorities with which counselors will work, but rather, to simply illustrate with these groups, examples of cultural differences and attending problems which counselors must anticipate in working with cultural populations different from their own. Nearly all minority groups have shared certain undesirable experiences in common such as:

1. Experiencing bias, prejudices, and stereotyping
2. Experiencing hostility, aggression and violence related to their ethnicity
3. Facing socio-economic and career disadvantages
4. Experiencing stress and trauma, especially in the early elementary years when they initially encounter overt acts of prejudice and hostility
5. Learning to maintain their own ethnic identity while learning to live in a "different world."

Bennett (1988) refers to three factors that prevent the development of an effective relationship as suggested by Padilla, Ruiz & Alvarez (1975). They include language barriers, class-bound values, and culture-bound values. Communication, according to Bennett, is seriously hindered and distorted as the result of these factors.

In order to effectively engage in the counseling of minority children and at the same time to develop programs that meet their needs, counselors must develop an awareness of cultural differences and similarities. Pedersen (1988) suggests such an awareness would require an individual to have:

- *ability to recognize direct and indirect communication styles;*
- *sensitivity to nonverbal cues;*

- *awareness of cultural and linguistic differences;*
- *interest in the culture;*
- *sensitivity to the myths and stereotypes of the culture;*
- *concern for the welfare of persons from another culture;*
- *appreciation of the importance of multicultural teaching;*
- *awareness of the relationships between cultural groups; and*
- *accurate criteria for objectively judging "goodness" and "badness" in the other culture. (p. 9)*

The American School Counselor Association's position statement (1983) on cross/multicultural counseling is presented here in its entirety as follows:

> *The American School Counselor Association recognizes cultural diversities as important factors deserving increased awareness and understanding on the part of all school personnel, especially the school counselor. A definition of cross/multi-cultural counseling is the facilitation of human development through the understanding and appreciation of cultural diversities with respect to language, values, ethics, morals, and racial variables.*
>
> *The American School Counselor Association encourages school counselors to take action to assure students of culturally diverse backgrounds access to appropriate services and opportunities which promote maximum development. Counselors may utilize the following strategies to increase the sensitivity of students and parents to culturally diverse persons and enhance the total school and community environment.*

1. *Conduct self-examinations of personal values, attitudes, and beliefs toward cultural diversity.*
2. *Maintain awareness of concepts and techniques with a current library of cultural information.*
3. *Foster the interest of culturally diverse students in careers which have been traditionally closed.*
4. *Continue to upgrade materials utilized in the awareness and sensitivity groups.*
5. *Provide educational awareness workshops for teachers and culturally diverse parents at the local PTO/PTA meetings.*
6. *Develop a resource list of educational and community support services to meet the socioeconomic and cultural needs of culturally diverse students and their families.*
7. *Conduct student small groups to enhance self-esteem and cultural awareness.*
8. *Conduct classroom activities which develop acceptance and appreciation of cultural diversities.*
9. *Work within the larger community to identify cultural diversities and assist in the development of community-based programs which will propagate community acceptance of all culturally diverse populations in the larger population. (Adopted 1983)*

School counselors can encourage school districts to implement the following strategies to increase awareness of culturally diverse populations:

1. To include culturally diverse parents on curriculum development planning boards, committees, and other school projects.
2. Provide awareness workshops for faculty and staff on culturally diverse people.
3. Incorporate culturally diverse family resources into the educational process.
4. Develop workshops for culturally diverse parents to educate them on the school system's philosophy of education.
5. Promote schoolwide activities that focus on individual differences and contributions made by culturally diverse persons.
6. Provide liaison services to facilitate communication between diverse populations in the school and community.
7. Adopt classroom materials that are free of culturally biased information and urge classroom teachers not to utilize any material of that caliber.

> *School counselors have the responsibility of insuring that the special needs of all students are met. Counselors have the skills necessary to consult with school personnel to identify alienating factors in attitudes and policies that impede the learning process. School counselors need to continue to be aware of and strive to insure that the rights of all students exists (sic) so as to maximize their potential in an environment that supports and encourages growth and development of the person. (American School Counselor Association, 1989, pp. 322-323)*

Bennett (1988) argues that cooperative learning strategies serve as useful approaches in the student's learning about multicultural issues. These strategies are based on Allport (1954) and the *Social Science Statement for Positive Effects of Desegregation on Race Relations*. Cooperation across all race lines, status roles of equality for students of various races, contact among students of different races which allows them to learn about one another as individuals; and the communication of clear support from school personnel for interracial interacting are all aspects of cooperative learning (Slavin, 1981).

These specific cooperative learning activities, as suggested by Slavin have had a major impact for creating a multicultural environment within schools. Other specific learning activities suggested by Bennett (1988) are Student Teams—Achievement Divisions, STAD (Slavin, 1978), and Teams—Games-Tournament (Devries and Slavin, 1978; and Aronson, 1978).

The number of immigrant school-age children (5-18 years of age) falls between 2.1 and 2.7 million (Haney, 1987). Esquivel and Keitel (1990) stress the need for elementary school counselors to address the social and emotional needs of these children. They encourage school counselors to use folk stories as an effective means of fostering ego development in children. Counselors can be helpful by reflecting on the human values which are illustrated in the stories as well as on the application of the stories to U.S. society.

Lewis and Hayes (1991) refer to the following books as providing instructional support for counselors as they examine specific counseling skills which are necessary in working effectively with persons from differing cultural backgrounds. They include:

- *Counseling Across Cultures* by Pedersen, Draguns, Lonner, and Trimble (1989).
- *Counseling American Minorities: A Cross Cultural Perspective* by Atkinson, Morten and Sue (1989).
- *Counseling the Culturally Different* by Sue and Sue (1990).
- *Handbook of Cross-Cultural Counseling and Therapy* by Pedersen (1985).
- *Multicultural Counseling: Toward Ethnic and Cultural Relevance in Human Encounters* by Dillard (1983).
- *Understanding and Counseling Ethnic Minorities* by Henderson, 1979.

In further heightening awareness of multicultural issues and practices in counseling we would also call the attention of our readers to the Association for Multicultural Counseling and Development (AMCD), a division of the American Counseling Association (ACA), which publishes a journal of the same name as well as a newsletter.

We would also note the importance of increasing the number and ratio of counselors from culturally different/minority backgrounds in our elementary schools. Not only should minority children have access to counselors of similar ethnicity, but all children should have exposure to role models representing the great cultural diversity of our country.

Our country is no longer considered a "melting pot" of many cultures, one in which emphasis is placed on all cultures becoming the same as the majority culture. Rather, the concept of cultural pluralism has been adopted which focuses on the retention and value of the diverse aspects of every culture that constitutes our nation. In this regard, counselors can advocate the preservation of cultural diversity and model the respect and acceptance that all minorities deserve.

In schools, counselors can ensure that minorities are included in group activities and that classroom guidance activities are utilized to educate the school population about cultural diversity (See examples in Chapter 5). Too, counselors must always be mindful that diversity exists within every cultural/racial population. There are no exact profiles for any minority group. The only "stereotype" is that individual differences exist in all populations.

Retention

Another group of children who have special concerns are those who have been retained. Few events in the elementary school threaten a child's self-esteem more than feeling that one has "failed" a grade. Humiliated in their peer group, assailed in the home and the general self-assessment that they don't measure up are all common after-effects. Yet, in U.S. schools each year numerous students are retained . As a result, many elementary school counselors will work in school districts that implement a retention policy for low-achieving children.

In graded school systems, curricula are generally designed to teach children information at developmentally appropriate age levels. When test scores and teacher judgment indicate that a student's performance does not meet the required standards of a grade level, one alternative is to have the child repeat the same grade. Short attention span, immaturity, poor social skills, emotional problems, and differences in abilities could all be factors that contribute to below-average performance in school.

Retention is intended to give children a chance to catch up. Proponents of retention argue that students who do not understand material at one grade level will find it difficult or impossible to benefit from material at the next level. However, as noted, this solution is often accompanied by adverse effects on the individual children who are retained. The stigma of "flunking" is damaging to the social and personal development of low-achieving students. Daily failures in schoolwork have probably already triggered a low self-esteem. As a result, it is likely that these children, feeling like failures, become increasingly unmotivated to attempt tasks at school. Children who do not, will not, or cannot perform academically, baffle and frustrate teachers and parents alike.

As Nancy Golden, an internationally known specialist in teaching self-esteem to at-risk students, puts it, "Failure is not the falling but the staying down" (cited in Rubinstein, 1991, p. 4).

Rubinstein (1991) confirms this point by emphasizing that

> *Many at-risk students stay down not because they lack the intelligence to achieve, but because they lack the skills, the guidance and self-confidence to acquire knowledge and to succeed (p. 4).*

One approach used to redirect this downward spiral is to consult with the school counselor. Facilitating a team effort which includes the child, parents, and teachers is an effective skill that counselors use to ameliorate effects of retention. First of all, it is critical that a counselor become aware of the policies in the school. From the beginning, a counselor can communicate to faculty and parents that she or he is available as a specialist in promoting school success for children. When teachers are alert to early signs of at-risk children (for example, a lack of task-completion skills, low self-esteem, and inability to communicate difficulties in class), an early intervention can begin. It is crucial that counselors guide teachers in understanding how both of their roles interconnect with that of parents to insure the least damaging effects of retention on children. Differences in abilities and concurrent difficulties that are monitored and addressed early can possibly lessen or prevent more adverse effects later. Therefore, it is critical that teachers communicate concerns for low-achievers early so that intervention may begin. In addition, it is advisable for teachers to inform parents as soon as possible about academic expectations of children. In essence, the message to be conveyed to parents is that their primary interest is the long-term welfare and their education of their children.

Once the general theme of a caring team approach is woven into the school environment, a counselor can become more effective, in as short a period of time as possible, at insuring that the foundation and all integral pieces are in place. Again, the counselor is at all times a resource to children, parents, and teachers both individually and collectively. The facilitation of interactions between all these groups illustrates the counselor's ultimate goal of coordinating energies for everyone's optimum benefit. Children cannot be the counselor's sole contact because they touch and are touched by others in their process of becoming. Therefore, the counselor must integrate all the forces influencing children to enhance more fully their education.

Obviously, retention results from low achievement. By working with parents whose children are experiencing low achievement, counselors help the parents to discover strategies for encouraging improvement in the areas of concern. Navin and Bates (1987) report the benefits of group work that included parents of children who were in a remedial reading program. As a result of the group participation, the parents gained a clearer understanding of their children's reading problems while they were also able to learn effective and positive techniques for helping their children with reading. Topics covered in the group included:

1. The personal feelings of the parents regarding their children's reading difficulty
2. The significance of the self-concept of the children as it relates to learning
3. Helping the children with reading
4. Helping the children deal with homework assignments
5. Assisting the parents in dealing with school personnel

Esters and Levant (1983) pointed to the significant increase in grade point average GPA that resulted for students in third and fourth grade (who were considered low-achievers) after their parents participated in parent counseling groups led by the school counselor (Wilson, 1986).

These are just two of many examples where counselors have been successful in helping parents to assist their children in handling problems with low achievement. In order for children, as well as their parents, to be further assisted in this area, school counselors must continue to play a vital role in working with issues of low achievement and retention.

How can counselors be helpful to children who must confront retention? First, as previously noted, counselors help by counseling children and consulting with parents and teachers. Initially, it is useful to help children understand that they learn at different rates. Ask children to describe the children who excel in different subject areas. This is one way to illustrate differences among children and to communicate respect for these differences. Provide opportunities for descriptions of their progress in school. This will permit ownership for their achievement. They will be less likely to perceive the differences in their achievement as criticisms by adults. Counselors provide an atmosphere of objectivity and caring where children become aware of difficulties. Counselors respond by asking for options that will close the gaps in achievement. (A counselor may ask, "Exactly what is it that they can do for themselves, and what do they need from others as well?") Early interventions empower children to become a part of the solution and thus instill the self-confidence and hope necessary for future success.

Secondly, counselors help children by maintaining contact with their parents. Perhaps the most crucial factor influencing how children handle retention is parental attitude. Therefore, it is critical for parents to become aware that the attitudes of their children are largely reflections of their own. Parents can communicate that retention is a chance to catch up rather than punishment for not learning enough. This attitude alone could determine whether children respond positively or negatively to their experience.

Teachers are the third group through which counselors help children who are being retained. Counselors can better prepare teachers to meet the special needs of children who are failing by first recognizing that self-esteem requires nurturance. Teachers who design class assignments that allow children to succeed will produce the desired effect. Low-achievers will continue to experience failure whether promoted or retained unless classroom activities are adjusted to the ability level of the individual child. Activities can be sequenced to insure completion and success which will build self-confidence and raise self-esteem. It is erroneous to believe that simply sending a child through the same grade again, sometimes with the same teacher, the identical format, and the same material will guarantee the child's success in that grade. Encourage teachers to discover alternative ways of tapping the child's resources, and arrange assignments that can, and will be, successfully completed.

Rubinstein (1991) recommends stories and storytelling as unique and powerful ways to reach these at-risk students. Among the rationales for this are:

1. At-risk students frequently come from families that are affected by sexual or physical abuse, divorce, drug and/or alcohol addiction, or neglect whereby examples of loving relationships and moral values may be lacking in the family.
2. Tales "provide structure, give direction, reinforce morals and societal guidelines and promote family and positive relationships" (p. 4-5).
3. Folktales usually focus on such values as love, respect, and responsibility among people. They convey these essential values with enchantment rather than through learning.
4. It is often the case that the characters in the tales, who are experiencing the same or worse conditions than the students, through persistence, manage to succeed. These stories serve as alleys toward insight amongst the listeners since they can relate their own problems to those of the characters and can learn possible ways to deal with them .

Teachers may also reframe prior experiences of repeaters into opportunities for the development of leadership skills and peer tutoring. Giving children responsibilities increases self-confidence which cements a firm foundation on which to build future, more complex learning. To summarize, counselors can help children who are retained by reducing negative associations with "flunking."

Children of Divorce

Between 1970-1985 the divorce rate tripled in the United States and continues into the 1990s to suggest that many marriages are "at risk." As a result, the homes of many elementary age school children are disrupted. Divorce follows only the death of a parent in stressfulness for the child. The severity of the reaction by the child depends on his or her age, the sex of the child, the psychological health of the parents after the divorce, and the child's self-concept (Burke and Van de Streek, 1989). Children do not escape the adverse effects of divorce. Emotions such as anger, hostility, sadness, guilt, confusion, and loneliness often precipitate difficulties in academic performance and peer relations. Sonnenshein-Schneider, & Baird (1980) discuss the difficulties experienced by these children:

> *School counselors, teachers, and other school personnel have observed various behavioral manifestations exhibited by children who are affected by divorce, including poor concentration, verbal outbursts, physical aggression, withdrawal, and inferior schoolwork. (Cited in Cantrell, 1986, p. 186)*

Given the psychological struggles erupting from divorce, parents and children can benefit from support outside the home. Burke and Van de Streek (1989) state that school systems in the past decade have made a number of attempts to assuage the negative effects of divorce on a child's academic abilities. Emotional distress of divorce sometimes causes changes in academic performance, as well as behavior. School counselors provide a support system to assist children through these stressful times.

Counseling individually and in small groups provides a safe and nurturing environment where children can be guided to carefully unravel the tangles acquired through the transitions of divorce. Here, counselors can concentrate on clarifying two major issues for children of divorce. One is that divorce is not their fault; children do not cause divorce. The second is fear of abandonment by the custodial parent. A word of caution to counselors before reassuring children is to be certain that this is not a possibility. Sadly, in some cases, both parents do abandon their children. It is noteworthy to add that typically noncustodial parents do not consider themselves abandoning their children at all. However, children may interpret their absence as such. A counselor's awareness of these two concerns helps direct the focus of counseling to insure that facilitation occurs wherever children need it most.

In individual counseling, a child begins to develop an understanding of divorce. Through exploration children expose, experience, accept, and understand their feelings.

Generally, after individual counseling, children are invited to participate in small group counseling. Groups are dynamic and powerful experiences that expedite adjustment. As Robson (1982) points out:

> *Children's groups on divorce, led by elementary school counselors with specific strategies to meet the needs of these children, have been extremely successful.*

> *The basic benefit of these groups is the development of individual problem-solving skills that can be applied at home and in the school. In addition, group counseling can help diffuse feelings and offer a supportive environment as the children learn that others are experiencing similar concerns. (Kurdek, 1981; Kurdek & Siesky, 1980; Sonnenshein-Schneider & Baird, 1980, cited in Cantrell, 1986, p. 165)*

Learning of the universality of divorce typically dispels the loneliness and isolation felt by children of divorce. Exposure to others who have survived divorce gives children hope for their futures. They are usually eager to discuss this nightmare openly.

In counseling, feelings associated with divorce are listed, drawn, role-played, guessed, described, pointed to on the body, and studied until clarity, acceptance, and resolutions are reached. Topics range from how monster feelings inhabit their stomachs to what makes a happy marriage. Rather than allowing their feelings to consume them, children share ideas about how to cope. They begin to see past the turmoil in their lives. Counseling frees children to understand divorce on their level and thus empowers them to find in themselves the strength to cope and continue. Initially, there is exploration of the difficult, painful feelings of divorce. However, counselors eventually allow children to weave love and forgiveness back into their lives. To help children understand that they can love and be loved by parents who may not live in the same house with them can be very healing.

Death and Dying

Although not a high percentage, some elementary school children will be affected by the death of someone close to them. However, many adults are uncomfortable discussing death and dying, especially with children. Consequently, greater need is created for elementary school counselors to assume some responsibility for easing the passage for these children through the grieving process.

How Children View Death: Developmental Stages of Awareness

In Chapter 2, you read about the stages of cognitive development posited by Jean Piaget. The level at which children function cognitively influences their understanding of concepts in their worlds. One of Piaget's followers, M. H. Negy (1948), developed a three-stage approach to conceptualizing death. According to Negy, the developmental (age-related) stages of death awareness are:

1. Stage One, Before age 5: *Children in this stage deny the irreversibility of death. They regard death as a departure or a sleep. Children under the age of 5 acknowledge that the dead person is gone and experience the loss in terms of sep-*

aration. They may ask when the dead person will return, where that person is now, and how that person feels.

2. Stage Two, Ages 5–9: *Children in Stage Two tend to personify death. For example, they perceive death as a skeleton, a "bogeyman," or a killer. Though death may also be an invisible entity to children in this group, it nevertheless has a personality and literally carries people away.*
3. Stage Three, After age 9: *Children after age 9 realize that death marks the end of life, and that it is related to the body's inability to function. To children in this stage, death is irreversible, inevitable, and results in the end of bodily life.*

Children's attitudes and feelings about death are the reflections of various factors. In particular, their stage of cognitive development and previous personal experiences with death and separation affect their responses. Although children may not have developed the cognitive abilities to understand death in adult terms, they are aware of its existence. This awareness warrants that adults provide children the opportunity to share their feelings, thoughts, and concerns (cited in Kalish, 1981).

Death is understood by children differently depending on their developmental levels. According to Bertoia and Allan (1988), elementary school children before age six believe death is gradual, happening only to the very old, and that it is reversible. By middle childhood, ages six to ten, most children understand the finality and universality of death. Cases for counselors include: sudden death of relatives or friends, prolonged illness of a family member, terminal illness of a child, suicide, and death of a pet.

Children who experience loss will react in various ways. Bertoia and Allan (1988) state that there is no right way to grieve: crying, joking, mood swings, acting out, and regression are all normal reactions. Therefore, counselors get information from teachers, significant others, and children themselves to find the relevant starting point for counseling.

While death and dying of loved ones results in a different set of emotional responses and potential problems, it is important to keep in mind that regardless of the counseling issue, intervention and prevention are the two major thrusts in helping children. Counselors intervene to provide support and guidance through the grieving process. Hence, the second goal is addressed which is to prevent psychological problems later in life should the loss go unresolved.

Furman (1984) explains that the bereaved child is faced with coming to terms with death, grieving and then resuming progression, as is appropriate, toward the development of personality. Therefore, initially children need simply to get through the puzzling parts for them. Consequently, counselors need first to meet children where they are emotionally with death. The simplicity of discovering this point follows: allow them to talk first. Use sentence stems that allow their completions to be most informative to you. An example of a sentence stem is, "I am very sad that your brother died last week. Maybe you are confused because . . . or Maybe you are angry because . . ." If it is necessary to use questions, begin them with "how" and "what." An example of a question you may ask them is, "What is it about the funeral that you do not understand?" Allow them to ask you questions about what puzzles them most. A question a child may ask you is, "My sister was wearing her seatbelt; how come that did not save her?" Others are: "What will happen to my daddy's body when it is buried?"; "How come dead people cannot talk?"; "What do they eat?"; "When will my mother stop crying?"; "Will I die?"; and "Why do people die?"

Your goal as counselor is to help children understand that life is at times difficult to understand and that it sometimes hurts. You want to provide safety for their explorations. You will listen and reflect the reality of their experience back to them in understandable terms. Once you help them to examine the pieces, they begin to place them into a meaningful order that makes sense to them. Acceptance, adjustment, and healing become the results.

Counselors can prepare themselves by learning specifically about grief counseling, as well as by discovering their level of comfort with discussing death and dying. According to Cunningham & Hare (1989), because of their expertise in dealing with personal, socio-emotional concerns of students, counselors are in an excellent position to provide training to teachers in the area of bereavement. They suggest that after counselors examine their own attitudes toward death, they can conduct in-service programs for teachers. These programs would include:

> *(a) awareness of children's bereavement behaviors; (b) awareness of children's perceptions of death; (c) awareness of personal attitudes toward death; (d) exercises in dealing with bereaved children's concerns; and (3) awareness of curricular and community resources. (Cunningham & Hare, 1989, p. 181)*

Death of a loved one does occur with elementary school students. It is essential that school counselors be prepared to assist them and their teachers with death as it touches their lives. For more information on this topic, refer to *On Death and Dying* by Elisabeth Kübler-Ross (1969). *The Fall of Freddie the Leaf* by Leo Buscaglia (1983) and *The Tenth Good Thing About Barney* by Judith Viorst (1983) are children's stories to help in counseling children on death.

A Case of Counseling a Child About Death

Early one morning a sobbing little girl in first grade was brought to the counselor's office by her teacher. The child's explanation was that her brother had been killed by a car during the night. Puzzled that the girl had been sent to school, the counselor began comforting the child and drying the tears.

Many questions remained unanswered after the counseling session. The child's mother was phoned. When she answered, sadness and distress were not detected in her voice. The counselor asked if anything had happened that may have upset her daughter. The mother responded with an apology for sending her crying daughter to school. She added that she felt it was best to get her daughter's mind off the death of her cat. He had been hit by a car and was found in the street that morning.

It was her beloved cat that had been killed, not her brother; in fact, she did not even have a brother! As the mother listened, the counselor emphasized that her daughter experienced a deep sense of loss accompanied by feelings of sadness and confusion.

One explanation for this incidence may be that since the child received no help through the grieving process from her mother, she felt it necessary to have the death pertain to someone "significant" to allow her to grieve. Her assumption was correct. The child learned that it was not okay to grieve over the loss of a pet and felt helpless, confused, and misunderstood. One may marvel at how much this little girl knew about our society's system of handling death and dying. Generally, this complex topic arouses discomfort and feelings of inadequacy in adults. Therefore, processing is limited, if at all engaged, particularly with children.

This little girl accurately assumed that in order to legitimize her feelings of pain and sadness, she had to make up a story of death "worthy" of the grieving experience. She could not stop crying until someone listened. She needed someone to allow her to express and own feelings of loss and sadness, even for her cat.

Gaining a Counseling Perspective from a Parent

While the counselor's role is to counsel grieving children, most often counselors do not personally know the relative, friend, or pet that died. However, a child may die who is a student at your school, the son of one of your teachers and friends, and the friend of hundreds of children that you see everyday. Therefore, part of your preparation for becoming a school counselor can be to come to terms with the devastating, yet inevitable, truth that at times children suffer and die.

The following excerpts are included to illustrate the reality and depth of trauma that occurs in families who experience the illness and death of a child. As elementary school counselors, an awareness of the depth of pain and the number of lives touched by one child, as well as the hope derived from these excruciating experiences, will possibly deepen the level of your helpfulness and presence to families in similar situations. Your gift to grieving families is to communicate compassion and a willingness to be open to the extremely fearful issue of death.

To express the often untold and misunderstood stories of pain and triumph we have selected the following excerpts from an unpublished manuscript written by a father whose child died of leukemia at age seven.

> *. . . The one thing I did't want one of my children to ever get was leukemia. Nevertheless. . . with Laura [daughter] less than a week old and Philip three weeks shy of his third birthday, the flow of our lives had been suddenly and drastically interrupted and altered. Nothing would ever be the same again, or even resemble the vision we had of our lives. A Meteoric Life Event had exploded upon us, just that sudden; just that dramatic; just that unforgiving. Philip died nearly four and one-half years later. . .*

The life of a child with cancer is a life of needles, a life of blood tests, chemotherapy, bone marrow tests, lumbar punctures. One thorn after another producing pain, anxiety, fear, dread, resentment, tears, and blood. Philip knew the unfairness of life. He knew the unfairness of being hospitalized for days at a time; he knew the unfairness of being isolated from friends and from people because of fear of infection; he knew the unfairness of feeling bad and feeling sick more days than not for four and one-half years. He knew the unfairness of having to guard his play because of low platelet counts and the fear of hemorrhaging. He knew the unfairness of struggling with school life and with school work. He knew the unfairness of being bald many times and being chubby because of the effects of chemotherapy. He knew the unfairness of the regimen of pills and pain and the relentless necessity of needles. . .

It takes a strong parent not to let a child's tears be his emotional guide in the exercise of his parental responsibility as guardian, teacher, and nurturer. It takes a wise parent to know when tears are to be dried and when tears are to be ignored. It takes a compassionate parent to know when to act and when to cry with his child when the child needs a companion in his pain. . .

Philip cried often. They were complicated tears. They were mixed with all kinds of feelings and motives. They affected me in a way that is hard to describe. He cried out of pain; he cried out of fear; he cried out of frustration and anger; he cried out of anxiety. He cried because he was spoiled and didn't always get his way. He cried because he was disciplined. He cried sometimes and didn't know why. We longed for a Johnson's Baby Shampoo remedy for his tears. I'm still moved by his tears. I still see them after four years. How I wanted to make every unfair reason for his tears to disappear. . .

Philip's protocol called for three years of treatment as long as he remained in remission. At first, three years seemed like forever. If we dreamed at all, it was for his 6th birthday. His three-year protocol would end somewhere around that time. After about the end of two years, with all of its ups and downs, we could begin to see the light at the end of the tunnel. We were beginning to feel more confident that perhaps Philip was going to be one of those among a growing number of children who survived the disease. One more year to go; four more scheduled hospitalizations; four more bone marrows. This was the countdown. During that year each bone marrow exam took on more and more significance for us, and with each reported clear exam we dreamed a little more. We began to dream what Philips's life would be like after leukemia, and what our family life would be like not having such a negative focus.

The next to the last scheduled hospitalization, Philip's doctor happily reported a clear bone marrow and began to explain the specifics of the last phase of treatment. Philip was to continue the chemotherapy for the next three months, then, on that last hospitalization would have a bone marrow and a testicular biopsy. If these were clear, he would discontinue chemotherapy and come in only periodically to monitor his health.

The spring of 1984 was an exciting time. We celebrated Philip's sixth birthday on March 17th and for once couldn't wait to get to the hospital in a couple of weeks to put the nightmare behind us and resume with normal living. The day we entered the hospital was like Jesus entering Jerusalem for the last time. The doctors and nurses, all whom had become like clan members in another city, greeted us triumphantly. We were never happier to be at the hospital. This was the moment for which we had been praying and waiting for three years.

Philip looked absolutely wonderful to us. He was getting taller and thinner. His hair was full and his complexion was rosy. He had recuperated normally from a typical viral infection, and his energy level was excellent. We had every reason to be upbeat and celebrative. In fact, we had planned to take Philip out to the restaurant of his choice as soon as his last hospital trip was over. The plans were set. The spirit of celebration was mounting. All that was needed was a clear bone marrow and a negative biopsy and an appetite for pizza!

What transpired after the triumphal entry into the hospital on that day in April of 1984 I cannot adequately describe. Philip was taken to the Treatment Room as always, only this time we wanted the results as quickly as possible. Usually it took no longer than an hour or two for the slides to be read, and our doctors always brought us the reports as soon as they could get them.

On this pivotal afternoon hours passed without a word from the doctors. We had no clear understanding, but we had assumed that they would tell us something before they went home for the day. As the evening hours approached we concluded that no news was good news. . .

The next morning I was cheerfully walking down the hall and met up with the two oncologists who had been so wonderful and supportive throughout Philip's illness. They asked me to step inside a private room with them, and with tears rolling down their cheeks one of them said, "We can't believe it, but Philip's bone marrow is in relapse." As they wept, I remember sitting there in stonelike silence, too stunned to cry, crack, or collapse. I sat in disbelief. If you've been there, and I know that multitudes have, I don't have to explain to you the way I felt. If you haven't been there the best I can do is call it a devastating disappointment.

For Philip, Elliott [mother], Laura [sister], and myself and our families, this was the unkindest, most unfair part of the whole drama of Philip's story. It would have been disappointing enough for relapse to have come at any time during his treatment, but for it to come on the very last hospitalization was the most unjust turn of events imaginable. There is no disappointment to compare to the disappointment one feels when a celebration is quelled by tragic news, when all the plans and preparations are in place, the band is on the stage, and the participants are ready to dance, but the music never plays. . .

A parent invests more energy in a sick and dying child than he thinks is within him to give. Physically, emotionally, and spiritually a parent pours himself out day and night to care for such a child. He gives and gives and gives so much that there are times he doesn't think there is anymore to give, but he keeps on giving. I am not describing drudgery. I am describing love. . .

Looking back on it now, our investment in Philip was staggering. . . as much as Elliott and I gave of ourselves to and for Philip, Philip gave back as much and more to us, and not just to us, he gave to everyone who knew him more than they could ever give to him. . .

It does not follow that a child who gets ill and dies does not contribute to life and to those who love him. It does not follow that one's life value has worth in proportion as the number of his years. I believe it was Corrie ten Boom who said, "One's life is not measured by its duration but by its donation."

We in this great country of ours don't expect our children to die young. We expect them to survive and thrive. The American dream, we suppose, includes health as well as wealth. But the fact is, our children do die young. Some don't survive, and many don't thrive. In spite of the remarkable advances in science, medicine, and technology, children are dying in this country at a rate that would shock most Americans. . .

The tendency we all have with regard to the death of children is to say, "But his story is incomplete; it's not finished; it's too short!" But as a father who has seen a child die along with his dreams of a long, happy life, I must find comfort in the fact that Philip's life is indeed a story. It's a great story, a wonderful story of bravery, triumph, and donation. If I cannot say that there is a story to tell, then either I did not perceive the story that was there, and that's to my shame, or his life was meaningless. But Philip's life, and I believe every child's life, has a story and a powerful and meaningful one at that. . .

To number your days means that you recognize that any day may be your last day, or the last day for someone you love, and so you want to live it wisely, productively, redemptively. Someone has said that life is what happens to you while you're making other plans. That, of course, is not living wisely. . .

When a child dies it is so easy to lament the untold story and fail to celebrate the story that is actually there. We need to learn to celebrate and rejoice in the story of our children's lives. They have written much of their stories in our very own hearts. To deny it or to fail to recognize it is to deny who we are. When our children die, we so often close up our hearts, but in doing so we not only lock away the pain, but we also lock away the joys and pleasures of our relationship and experience with the child. It does not have to happen overnight, but as time allows we must begin to read within our hearts the lovely things our children have written there. The pain will come out too, but the pleasure of shared love and tenderness and innocence will unfold in abundance. I believe that real healing and reconciliation occurs when we courageously open up our hearts again and begin to read the beautiful story that is written there. . . It is there, as it is for anyone who knew and loved the child. . . . West, H. N., Jr. (1989).

This personal and emotion-filled passage has been included to alert you, as counselors in training, to a crisis in which your understanding will be needed. Your ability to search for and feel the feelings of sensitive issues before they occur increases your ability to be spontaneously helpful when others are truly in need.

Other Special Concerns

The special counseling concerns highlighted in the previous sections were not selected as ones which are present in every elementary school or which may be even societally the most pressing; rather, they were discussed as representative of issues of national concern that will also need to be attended to in many elementary schools.

While certainly an extensive list of additional concerns could be generated, we have chosen to conclude this section with, again, a few of the many, additional concerns for which elementary school counselors may need to plan.

Family Problems

Chief among these are those family settings in which there is discord between parents, even abuse, unemployment, and homelessness. Any of these events can be traumatic for the elementary school child, frequently resulting in feelings of guilt, low self-esteem, withdrawal, and poor school performance. Counseling programs can provide support groups, individual counseling opportunities to channel their emotions and express their feelings, assistance with coping styles, and referral (of families) to appropriate agencies. It is important to keep in mind that for many of these children, the school is their only "haven," the only stable institution in their experience, the only environment in which they have a chance to feel secure.

Latch Key Children

Long and Long (1984) describe latch key children as those who are home alone or are cared for by an underage sibling during a significant period of the day. It was estimated that by 1990, the number of children in this category would reach 18 million (Scofield and Page, 1983). The increase in the number of single-parent families (Bundy and Gumaer, 1984); the increase in the number of mothers who are working (Levitan and Belous, 1981); the necessity for dual wage earners in the family (Waldman, 1983); and the unlikelihood that grandparents or other relatives can be available to care for children all contribute to the increase in unsupervised children (Bundy and Boser, 1987). Research findings point to various negative effects that result for children who are left without adult supervision. Included by Bundy and Boser are high levels of worry and fear (Long and Long, 1984; Strother, 1984, Zill, 1983), feelings of loneliness and boredom (Long and Long, 1984), stress and anxiety (Long and Long, 1983), and diminished performance in school work (Robinson, 1983; Strother, 1984).

The dual career family is no longer the exception but is now the norm. As the movement towards both parents working became more recognizable as well as widespread in recent decades, many dire predictions were made regarding negative effects on children. Recent research however, has not supported these contentions. Nevertheless,

> *counselors who have accurate information about dual-earner families and who can teach effective family living skills to their clients are in an excellent position*

> *to help parents, children, schools, and communities address the challenges and biases experienced by working families and their members. (Boyer and Horne, 1988, p. 11)*

Transfer Pupils

Hometowns today are more often temporary than not for millions of the U.S. mobile society. This mobility is reflected yearly in the increasing number of transfers in and out of our nation's elementary schools.

According to the 1986 United States Bureau of Census report, about one-fifth of all families in the United States relocate every year (Matter and Matter, 1988) and as Matter and Matter indicate, more than 12 million children are involved in these moves.

> *At all ages youngsters lose their credentials every time they move (Packard, 1983, p. 56). In some instances, just one move, particularly in elementary school, can be quite traumatic (Allan and Bardsley, 1983).*
>
> *Probably some of the most important understandings of the effects of moving comes to us indirectly from the work of Bowlby (1980) on attachment and loss. Moving for young children, he argues, parallels the experience of death and grief. With moving, children often lose the feelings of place security, continuity with their psychological roots, pets, and friends. The response to the loss may take many forms, but is often characterized by hurt, sadness, anger and possibly aloof detachment. (Allan and Bardsley, 1983, p. 163)*

Matter and Matter (1988) point to signs of withdrawal, negativism to an unusual degree, psychosomatic type ailments, and regression developmentally as indicators of the stress that the relocating child may be experiencing. They insist that elementary school counselors

> *have a unique opportunity to help lessen the anxieties children experience upon relocation. In doing so, they also may be able to help children re-establish their credentials and take advantage of the positive aspects of relocation—new friendships, new experiences, and new opportunities. (Matter and Matter, 1988, p. 28)*

Matter and Matter (1988) refer to one source of help that counselors can alert parents to as the Moving Monster Extermination Kit. The Kit is offered to relocating families by a major moving company and is described as a "learning package that explains moving from a kids-eye view" (p. 159).

The authors also suggest a variety of books written for children regarding relocation. They recommend these books to provide information and role models for relocating children, as well as to provide assistance to children who are preparing to welcome a newcomer to their classroom or neighborhood. The list of books includes the following:

Bourke, L. (1981). *It's your move. Picking up, packing up, and settling in* (Reading, MA: Addison-Wesley).

Conrad, P. (1984). *I don't live here* (New York: Dutton).

Hickman, M. (1974). *I'm moving* (Nashville: Abingdon).

Jones, P. (1980). *I'm not moving* (Scarsdale, NY: Bradbury).

Tobias, T. (1976) *Moving day* (Westminister, MD: Knopf).

Watson, W. (1978). *Moving* (New York: Crowell).

These transfers are not without their traumas for many of the children involved, some, who for the first time, will be experiencing a completely new and strange environment without friends or familiar faces. To help ease this transition, many elementary schools have ongoing orientation programs, buddy systems, big brother/sister programs, planned support groups, and newcomers clubs. Special programs for parents are also common. For these programs to work effectively, elementary counselors and administrators work cooperatively to insure the instant identification of newcomers to the school environment.

Summary

Individual counseling is the core professional activity for the professional counselor. It is a one-to-one process in which a trained professional counselor assists one's client with developmental, preventive, enhancement, remedial, exploratory, and/or reinforcement needs. This process usually proceeds through the stage of environment/relationship establishment, client and problem assessment, possible options or solutions, planning and implementing a course of action, and termination with probable subsequent follow-up and evaluation. The effectiveness of the process will be dependent on the counselor's professional skills in utilizing attending behavior, reflection of feeling, and facilitative techniques for keeping the conversation moving and on track. Of course, the entire process is modified to adapt to the developmental level of the elementary school client.

Elementary school counselors must be prepared to apply their skills to such special concerns as substance abuse, child abuse, needs of the gifted and talented, minority youth, discrimination and prejudice, pupil retention, parental divorce, and death and dying. To address these concerns, group counseling is a popular, and often more effective alternative, or supplementary activity to individual counseling. In Chapter 5, which follows, we will note the similarities between individual and group counseling in the stages and skills involved.

Chapter 5

Group Counseling for Elementary School Children

Whenever you are with a brother,
you are learning what you are
because you are teaching what you are.
He will respond either with pain or with joy,
depending on what teacher you are following.
He will be imprisoned or released
according to your decision,
and so will you.
Never forget your responsibility to him,
because it is your responsibility to yourself.
—FRANCES VAUGHAN AND ROGER WALSH, Eds.
(Portions from "A Course in Miracles," © copyright 1975, reprinted by permission of the Foundation for Inner Peace, Inc., PO Box 1104, Glen Ellen, CA 95442)

Introduction

In the first chapter, the importance of the elementary school in the development of the individual child's social-personal foundations for lifelong living was noted. In this sense, the school becomes what sociologists refer to as "an agent of socialization." Socialization itself is a process of learning to interact with others according to the norms of a society. It is a learning of society's values and roles and the important social behaviors that accompany these norms, roles, and values. This socialization is basically a group process for which the school, as a societal institution for educating its citizenry, should provide ample opportunities. These opportunities for social development through the natural process of groups can be provided by various experiences in a variety of settings in the elementary school. These include instructional groups, activity groups, guidance groups, and counseling groups, all of which are discussed in later chapters.

This rationale for these group experiences can be stated as follows:

1. Human beings are attracted to their own species—by human nature they are group-oriented.

2. The human species meet most of their basic needs through groups.

3. Thus, groups are influential in how individuals develop and grow, acquire values, adopt coping style, behave, and learn.

4. Consequently, groups provide a powerful medium for influencing the individual and his or her behaviors.

5. Therefore, counselors use groups for the purpose of assisting clients in their personal/social/educational growth and/or adjustment.

In addition, group counseling is a very effective and efficient use of the counselor's time. Effective in that counselors use their skills as group leaders in two ways: one way is that the counselor creates an environment properly suited to the understanding of self and others; a second way is that the counselor becomes a role model for children so that they learn and develop communication and social skills. Thus, children learn to give to and receive help from their leader and from other children. This phenomenon contributes to the effectiveness of groups.

The dynamics that are produced through group interaction provide diverse opportunities for growth unlike those in individual counseling. One example is that children may respond more readily to feedback received from another child than from an adult. Another factor related to the effectiveness of groups is the sense of universality gained through group interaction. According to Yalom (1985), universality is the therapeutic factor present in groups that enables group members to feel a sense of relief from hearing that others share similar problems (p. 8). Children no longer feel that they have to face their difficulties alone. Also, hope is instilled through the presence of children in the group who have successfully overcome similar crises in their lives (Yalom, 1985, p. 6). For example, eight-year-old Billy, whose father severely abuses alcohol, might enter a group feeling ashamed and embarrassed about his father's problems. He may believe that he is the only child whose father is not perfect. Through group interactions, Billy realizes that other children's parents have problems too. Billy learns that he is not alone, and most importantly, that other children "understand where he is coming from." He feels more understood and accepted because others have shared similar feelings. Further hope results as he listens to Kim, whose mother abuses drugs. Kim has learned to successfully cope with the anger and fear related to her mother's abusive behavior.

Group counseling is also an efficient use of the elementary counselor's time in that six to eight children can be helped in the same amount of time that it takes to counsel one individually. One will discover that all issues requiring help from counselors are not conducive to group work. However, some issues are best addressed in groups, and thus result in effective and efficient use of the counselor's time and energy. The elementary school counselor must take precautions to make sure group work is appropriate for the individual student at that specific time.

According to the Council for the Accreditation of Counseling and Related Education Programs (CACREP), school counselors facilitate self-understanding and self-development through individual and small group activities. Emphasis on group work as a major component of school counseling was noted by Morse and Russell (1989) who surveyed counselors and found that the five highest ideal roles are:

> 1. *Helping teachers better understand individual student needs by discussing student's behaviors, attitudes, and progress*
> 2. *Working with students in groups to help them learn appropriate social skills*
> 3. *Working with students in groups to enhance self-concepts*
> 4. *Working with students in groups to help them understand their feelings*
> 5. *Working with students in groups to help them develop problem-solving skills (cited in Rotter, 1990, p. 182)*

Group Definitions

Most of us belong to and participate in a number of different groups over a given time period such as a day or a month. We recognize these "groups" as collections of individuals sharing some experience in common. We would probably also agree that in a technical sense, a group is one that is deliberately organized to serve a purpose as opposed to a happenstance gathering of individuals. As counselors, however, we are interested in groups in a more recognized and formalized sense as we would use them professionally for the advantage of our clients—to help children in the elementary school grow, develop, and adjust.

From a broad sociological viewpoint, we are interested in definitions of groups that are useful for classification and analysis purposes. These are primary and secondary groups.

> *A primary group is used to refer to small, informal groups of people who interact in a personal, direct, and intimate way. This category includes such groups as the family and play groups, which are important in shaping the human personality. Primary groups involve intimate face-to-face association and interaction, and their members have a sense of "we-ness" involving mutual identification and shared feelings. Their members tend to be emotionally attached to one another and involved with other group members as whole people, not just with those aspects of a person that pertain to work, school, or some other isolated part of one's life. Your family, close friends, and certain neighbors and work associates are likely to be members of your primary group.*
>
> *A secondary group is a group whose members interact in an impersonal manner, have few emotional ties, and come together for a specific practical*

purpose. Like primary groups, they are usually small and involve face-to-face contacts. Although the interactions may be cordial or friendly, they are more formal than primary group interactions. Sociologically, however, they are just as important. Most of our time is spent in secondary groups, sales-related groups, classroom groups, or neighborhood groups. The key difference between primary and secondary groups is in the quality of the relationships and the extent of personal intimacy and involvement. Primary groups are person-oriented, whereas secondary groups tend to be goal-oriented. (Eshleman, Cashion, and Basirico, 1988, p. 142)

Counselors are, of course, interested in the impact of both primary and secondary groups on children. Primary groups are important in personality and self-concept formation; in becoming accepted; and as sources of intimacy and trust. Children who are not accepted members of such important primary groups as the family or peer groups are clearly "at risk" from a mental health standpoint. Secondary groups are important to counselors in school settings as presenting opportunities for group guidance and guidance instruction; for the observation of children in controlled or organized settings; and for assessment of certain personal traits or behaviors of children.

Elementary school counselors are directly involved in guidance groups and counseling groups. Guidance groups are group activities that focus on providing information or experiences through a planned and organized group activity (Gibson and Mitchell, 1990, p. 182).

Group counseling is the routine adjustment or developmental experiences provided in a group setting. Group counseling focuses on assisting counselees to cope with their day-to-day adjustment and development concerns (Gibson and Mitchell, 1990, p. 142).

Types of Groups

While the focus of this chapter is on group counseling, elementary school counselors should be familiar with the different types of groups in which they may serve as leaders or co-leaders, organizers, referrers, or observers. As with individual counseling, these may initially be classified according to the following counseling skills levels :

1. Guidance level: Provides information, instruction, orientation, experiences, and so on, appropriate to the developmental/preventive/educational needs of populations (such as, all new pupils, all sixth graders, a drug education program). Requires the group leader to have special knowledge and on occasion, experience related to the topic. Usually large groups.

2. Counseling level: Focuses on the routine adjustment/developmental/remedial needs of individuals where more personalized assistance is needed.

Group leader is expected to be a counselor or other appropriately trained helping professional. Group membership is limited.

3. Therapy level: Provides remedial/adjustment assistance to individuals suffering severe personality and/or emotional disorders. This treatment is usually a part of in-patient therapy for institutionalized patients who have serious mental health disorders. Group leaders are usually trained to the Ph.D. or M.D. level. Groups are limited in size.

Obviously, elementary school counselors would only be directly involved in guidance and counseling groups.

Another system for classifying groups would be according to their major purpose. While this brief listing includes most of the popular types of groups in this era of group popularity, we are not suggesting that our listing is all inclusive. We have chosen those appropriate to the elementary school as growth, learning, social skills training, and values clarification.

1. Growth Groups: Groups are designed to provide members with the opportunity for personal growth or enhancement through motivation, the acquiring or advancing of specific skills and "learning how to learn." "Succeeding in School" (Gerler & Anderson, 1986, p. 79), a guidance program which took place in 18 different elementary schools in North Carolina, involved group work of this type. The groups, which were facilitated by elementary school counselors, focused on enhancing the students' attitude toward school, along with encouraging improvement in the area of classroom behavior. Students who participated in the groups were reported to have positively improved their attitude toward school and improved their classroom behavior. It appears that through their involvement in the guidance groups, the students developed motivation and skills which contributed to much growth in their learning how to be successful in school.

2. Learning Groups: Those groups formed for the purpose of acquiring specific knowledge. George and Dustin (1988) point out that:

> *such groups are typically more structured, with carefully defined goals and more explicit, generally accepted expectations of the group members. Although the focus is on learning specific information, the process involves a great deal of group interaction, with members of the group sharing feelings, attitudes, and values. (p. 12)*

Colao and Hosansky (1983), Fontana (1982), and Hitchcock and Young (1986) all advocate a preventive approach to sexual abuse in that they stress the importance of children learning to deal more effectively with issues of sexual abuse which they someday may be forced to confront (Vernon and Hay, 1986). Vernon and Hay discuss how one elementary school counselor facilitated learning groups which focused on the students acquiring specific knowledge in the area of sexual abuse prevention. The children who participated learned how to "identify and discuss different types of touch, ways to ask for help, and assertive ways to say no to inappropriate touch" (p. 311).

3. Social Skills Training Groups: Since a function of the elementary school is to further the socialization of the individual, groups which provide for social skills training can be helpful. Like T-groups, they represent a type of training and like sensitivity groups, they focus on personal issues (or social skills) and personal growth (in social skills). Research cited in Omizo and Omizo (1988) has pointed to the fact that:

> *children with learning disabilities tend to have poor interpersonal skills, which contribute to their behaving inappropriately (Bryan, 1974). They also seem to be less empathic (Bachara, 1976; Borke, 1971; Feshbach and Roe, 1968), less sociable (Rosenberg and Gaier, 1977; and Pihl and McLarnon, 1984), and less popular (Bruininks, 1978; Bryan, 1974, 1978; Rosenberg and Gaier, 1977). Their inappropriate behaviors make it likely that they will be rejected by others. (Bryan, 1974), (p. 109)*

4. Values Clarification Groups: These groups utilize values clarification techniques to assist group members in identifying those values that can give positive meaning to their individual goals and behavior. They involve a process of identifying, examining, and comparing what is important to the individual, determining or verifying those values that are truly worthwhile and then learning to implement these true values in their daily living.

The group activity entitled "Ideas about Divorce" is a divorce clarification activity suggested by Morganett (1990). The goals of the group are

1. *To illustrate a wide range of beliefs about divorce and to help students clarify what they believe about it.*
2. *To help students learn that it is all right for people to have different views.*
3. *To show that, even though many kids believe they are the cause of their parents' divorce, in fact, they are not. (p. 20)*

Through involvement in this group, the members have the opportunity to identify their own values and beliefs related to divorce, examine how these values affect their feelings, thoughts and behaviors regarding the issue of divorce, and to clarify which values are worthwhile to hold onto in trying to deal effectively with the divorce of their parents. The children also have the chance to explore which values they can let go of in their attempts to adjust.

Organizing Counseling Groups

In the structuring of groups for counseling purposes, the elementary school counselor must determine: (a) when children should be referred to groups; (b) the size of the group; and subsequently, (c) the goals of the group.

There are a number of occasions when children may benefit from a group counseling experience. One or more of the following occasions may suggest that such an experience would be appropriate.

1. When learning, growth, development, adjustment and/or enhancement will be facilitated by the group experience

2. For interpersonal/social problems, including the need to "belong"; where the group can provide a mini-social context for working through such problems

3. For better self-understanding, and also understanding how their behavior impacts others. Groups can help children understand who they are. For example, a group referred to as the "Disruptive Child's Play Group" (Bleck and Bleck, 1982, p. 138) was facilitated in 13 Florida elementary schools. The group was comprised of students who exhibited disruptive behavior in the classroom. Participation in the group resulted in an improvement in self-concepts for the students while at the same time, a decrease in disruptive behavior occurred

4. To gain reinforcement for desired behaviors and/or for the prevention of the undesirable

5. To explore personal concerns and issues including exposing them to the feelings and experiences of others

6. To establish goals and work towards their achievement; to receive the rewards and recognition that comes from worthy accomplishments

7. To explore, identify and clarify one's values

8. To experience growth through helping others

Not all children who have these needs are good candidates for a counseling group. Some children may be too emotional or in a state of crisis where individual counseling would be more appropriate. Others may be too aggressive or have a need to dominate. Some may be too immature, have grossly inadequate social or communications skills or be too shy or withdrawn to benefit.

It therefore becomes important before setting up groups in elementary school, that preliminary steps are taken by the counselor to ensure that the members will benefit from the experience. From a practical standpoint, this suggests a time frame within which counselors prepare to run groups that could appropriately begin about one month after school starts. Preparation for forming groups involves initial individual counseling or a pregroup screening session.

Corey and Corey (1987) describe a pregroup screening session as a private session between the candidate and their leader in which the leader looks for evidence that the group will be beneficial to the candidate. Here we should note that initial individual counseling in the elementary school consists of providing and gathering the same types of information necessary to place children in groups. It is of utmost importance that counselors form a workable blend of personalities, ages, and sexes to insure the best possible outcome of the group experience for all members. Distinct individual characteristics must be considered when forming groups because an optimum fit among members increases group dynamics. Therefore, during initial individual counseling sessions (usually from one to three or more sessions depending on the readiness of the child and circumstances), counselors gain needed information and prepare children to work in groups.

The following practical considerations are suggested for forming groups with children:

1. *Age*—children of approximately the same age, such as seven and eight year olds or eight and nine year olds, may be grouped together. However, more important than age is that group members share the same level of social maturity.
2. *Sex*—a heterogeneous mix of boys and girls is possible with kindergartners through third graders. Opinions differ regarding fifth graders; therefore some counselors prefer to separate boys and girls and others group them together.
3. *Size of group*—six to eight children is ideal, although groups may operate with as few as three. Corey and Corey (1987) caution that larger numbers lead to these counselor concerns:

   a. inability to relate intensely to individuals
   b. slipping into role of disciplinarian; distractions
   c. frustrated by the number of children competing for your attention
   d. not enough time to pay attention to group dynamics, and children become impatient if they must wait too long to speak (p. 259)

5. *Length and frequency*—depends on the age of children; because of limited attention spans, younger children require shorter and more frequent sessions. They may meet twice a week for thirty minutes, while older children could meet once a week for forty-five minutes.
6. *Duration*—six to eight weeks
7. *Open versus closed*—open groups allow the addition of group members after the group has begun. Closed groups do not allow entry to new members after original members have been selected.
8. *Personality*—include peers who have successfully coped with concerns; those who can serve as role models; and personalities that will mix well together.
9. Some children will be unable to function in a group. Feel free to take them out and provide individual counseling, a smaller group, or a group with a different composition.

Participation in counseling groups should be preceded by individual sessions in which a thorough explanation to prospective group members regarding group goals, activities that may be anticipated, roles and responsibilities, and expectancies for those who do participate. These expectancies include participation in the group by talking about feelings and giving positive feedback.

Counselors discuss with children in the group the anticipated number of sessions, times, and dates of group meetings. It is important that children be given an understanding of the time frame within which they will participate as a member. (For example, at the first meeting, the counselor explains that the group meets on Tuesdays and Thursdays at 10:15 until 11:00, and the group will meet eight times altogether.) After these explanations, ask the children to repeat the information to be clear that they understand. At subsequent sessions, ask how many sessions they have met and how many they have left.

From the beginning, children are taught that groups are places where people come together to work on the exploration of feelings, coping strategies, and changing behaviors. To increase the probability that this will indeed occur, it is good for counselors to determine which children are motivated and really care about changing behaviors that are not serving them well. These more motivated members can serve as models to the other members. By providing positive encouragement to the motivated students for specific behaviors which demonstrate their willingness to work hard and make changes, the counselor can indirectly suggest to other members that this is expected and approved-of behavior. Expectations for children include: appropriate behavior; arriving on time; adherence to rules set by the group; and group participation. Ask them to specify personal goals they hope to attain while working in the group. We suggest that counselors keep a written log on each group member for future reference.

While discussing with children expected outcomes of the group experience, indicate that simultaneously groups may be work and fun. Emphasize, nevertheless, that groups are not merely opportunities to bypass work in class. Arrangements to participate in groups must include that all class assignments are completed satisfactorily.

Organized ways of keeping information on individual children may be also helpful in the overall process of setting up groups. Although counselors will feel freer to develop personal styles of planning and organization as time goes by, one possible model is indicated below.

In a separate notebook labeled *groups*, the counselor writes at the top of a page the title of a specific group, for example, Children of Divorce. The page is then divided into fourths by drawing a line down the middle vertically and one across the middle horizontally. This allows the counselor to organize up to four different sections for children who are in need of group counseling on this topic.

After initial individual counseling, the first name is placed in a section. Additional children are added to sections according to personality (who would get along with whom), sex (do you prefer to mix boys and girls depending on age), grade level (you may find it acceptable in some instances to overlap), level of maturity, suitability as a role model, and amounts of attention required. Other pages in the notebook are designed similarly for all topics for which group counseling is offered.

As sections approach five names, the counselor will begin to set up the group. Times and dates for group sessions should be discussed with, and approved by, homeroom teachers.

Planning for Group Counseling

The potential for effectiveness of a counseling group is based on certain basic assumptions. As previously noted, the human species are meant to complement, assist, and enjoy each other. Therefore, humans find that groups are a natural way to carry out many interactions, including learning. Since counseling is a learning process, group counseling then can be an effective process for group members to learn, for example, how to cope, adjust, relate to others, plan ahead, be responsible, and so on. However, in order for counseling groups to be effective sources for client learning, to be productive and achieve their potential to positively influence the children of the group, certain conditions must be met. These are:

1. The counselor's management of the group is effective, sensitive, efficient and non-threatening.

2. The purposes of the group are clearly understood, accepted by and participated in by the membership.

3. The processes of the group and the individual group members' responsibilities in the process are also recognized and accepted by each group member.

4. As the group progresses, meaningful participation should increase as members become more trusting, open and sharing with each other. The counselor's role and skill as a facilitator, as one to help individuals and the group over "rough spots," is critical throughout the process. The counselor also ensures the equitable involvement of all group members.

5. Further, this progress should result in increasingly rewarding experiences leading to enjoyment of participation, loyalty and attraction to the group, all of which increases the impact and influence of the group experience on the individual. This in turn, enhances the possibilities for desired outcomes.

6. In his or her initial planning and throughout the process, the counselor is alert to those situations where techniques need to be modified to accommodate the uniqueness of cultural/ethnic minority group members.

In planning for group counseling, the counselor must also keep in mind that some children, perhaps most, are accustomed to and have become acculturated to doing what the adult authority figures in their lives tell them to. Thus, they will wait for directions, assignments, and so on, from the counselor/group leader. Too, children have often had their feelings identified for them at home (as, "I'm hungry"—no you're not, you're just tired!) Also, even in these early years, children learn to mask or hold back the expression of their feelings. Even the sharing of the groups efforts may be difficult in those schools where individual effort and evaluation is stressed.

As children learn and try out new behaviors in the group, the counselor emphasizes to them that these changes might not be as readily accepted by people who know them outside the group. The group serves as a safe environment where the children can take risks in changing behaviors. By developing confidence and receiving support from within the group, they can be encouraged to gradually make similar changes outside of group.

In recognizing the uniqueness of children, VanderKolk (1985) suggests eight aspects of a therapeutic approach for group therapy with children:

1. Total acceptance of the child
2. A simple invitation to play without explanations, goals, reasons, questions, or expectations
3. Helping the child learn to express himself and to enjoy respect
4. Permitting, but not encouraging, regressive behavior early in therapy
5. Permissiveness of all "symbolic behavior" with limits on destructive behavior
6. Prohibiting children from physically attacking each other
7. Enforcing limits calmly, noncritically, and briefly, mentioning limits only as necessary
8. Empathy (p. 304)

The counselor must realize the significance of his or her role to group members. The more gently, but firmly, she or he interacts with the students, the more likely it is that members will react similarly to the counselor and to their peers.

Generally, counselors follow a structured format when running groups for children. Various activities such as filmstrips, books, games, and puppetry are available on a number of topics. These activities function as catalysts for discussion with children. To acquaint you with actual groups, their structure and implementation, we have included the following illustrations.

Group Topic

Multicultural Awareness

One example is suggested by Locke (1989) to use in groups that are meant to "foster multiculturalism in general, and positive images for African-American children in particular" (p. 255). The activity called "African-American People" is encouraged for third grade level (although it can be played at other age levels). The purpose of this activity is to introduce young children to noted personalities within both the African and African-American culture. The counselor as well as students collect photographs of famous African-American people and discuss what made them famous. A "Win, Lose, or Draw" game, using all gathered information is then developed. Locke emphasizes that participation in the group can greatly enhance the self-esteem of children as it focuses on diversity.

Another approach which focuses on concerns of elementary immigrant children, as suggested by Esquivel and Keitel (1990), is for elementary students in the higher grades to represent symbolic parents or older siblings who care for and nurture the younger students through therapeutically oriented group interactions. The interactions might take place in playground circle groups, recreational activities in arts, crafts, or in sports.

Ponterotto (1991) suggests specific roles that counselors may play in becoming more involved in multicultural awareness training. These roles include parent training, faculty and administrative consultation, group counseling and support, and individual and family counseling. Further, *young children, particularly, need the approval of their parents, and if "white superiority" is the family norm, then young children will nourish this norm. Counselors can consider speaking to parent groups as most schools already have formed informal mechanisms for school-parent dialogue. Again, parents must be instilled with the attitude that cultural diversity in and of itself is rewarding, and that the students are academically and socially enriched by diversity. Counselors can collaborate with teachers and administrators in the development of culturally diverse and multilingual pamphlets focusing on cultural pluralism. The innovative work of Casas and Furlong (in press) with bilingual story books for children and their parents provides an effective model. (Ponterotto, 1991, p. 222)*

Counselors may use group experiences to play games that enhance multicultural awareness in children. Nickell and Kennedy (1987) explain that play is universal, culturally specific and is a form of cultural expression through which the values of the society from where it originated are revealed. They suggest that students can learn from games much about the aspects of cultures that make them unique (Hatcher, Pape, and Nicosia, 1988). Wulff (1987) also recommends the use of games in encouraging students to develop a global perspective. Various games from other cultures promote the value of cooperation and the accomplishment of a common goal.

Two such games, suggested by Hatcher, Pape and Nicosia (1988), are presented. The games can be led by counselors, as well as teachers, to promote multicultural understanding among students.

Antelope in the Net *This is an example of a game from the Congo based on the importance of skill and cunning in trapping food. Sudanese children play a similar game entitled "Hyena and Sheep."*

Space Required: Outdoor play area

Appropriate for Ages 7-10.

Equipment needed: none.

Directions: (1) from 10 to 30 children can play. (2) After one child is chosen as the antelope, the others form a net (circle) around the child. They hold hands and chant "Kasha Mu Bukondi! Kasha Mu Bukondi!" (3) The antelope tries to break out of the net by crawling under, climbing over or running against the tightly joined hands. (4) When escaping, the antelope is pursued by the others. (5) The player who catches the antelope becomes the new antelope and the game begins again. (McWhirter, 1970, p.)

Helping Harvest the Lane *This game is symbolic of the cooperative efforts in farming and communal living found in the People's Republic of China.*

Space Required: Playground outdoors.

Appropriate for Ages 7 and 8.

Equipment needed: For each team, garden hoe, cardboard or plastic flowers, watering can, basket and tricycle.

Directions:

1. *Group players into teams of four members.*
2. *Equipment for each team is placed at the far end of the playground and the teams line up at the opposite end.*
3 *The first team member runs to the team's equipment, picks up the hoe and hoes the ground five times, then runs back.*
4. *The second team member plants the flowers and runs back.*
5. *The third team member waters the flowers and returns.*
6. *The fourth team member waters the flowers and returns.*
7. *The fourth team member picks the flowers, places them in a basket and rides the tricycle back, taking the flowers to market. (Orlick, 1978)*

Just as small group counseling utilizes discussion, processing purposeful group play is also central to ensuring that learning has occurred.

Children of Divorce

The goals of one successful divorce counseling group for elementary school students were to:

> *(a) clarify the children's feelings toward the divorce, (b) help the children become aware that other children were in similar situations and were experiencing similar feelings, (c) help the children gain a realistic picture of their situations, (d) teach the children ways to cope with their feelings associated with the divorce, and (e) enhance the children's self-concept. (Omizo and Omizo, 1987, p. 48)*

Counselors who structure groups using these goals can make a difference in helping children adjust to the crisis of divorce.

Latchkey Children

This program was implemented by an elementary school counselor with students who were latchkey children (Bundy and Boser, 1987). Latchkey children are described as those whose parents are not at home when they return from school. At times, children are at home alone before and after school and must be responsible for their own safety, meals, and activities. This program consisted of a guidance unit called "Being in Charge" (p. 60). An outline follows:

> Objective and Content for Each Session *"Being in Charge" was written to be presented in six 45-minute sessions. The objectives and content for each session of the program are:*

> Session 1: Introduction *Students are told the purpose and given an overview of the program. They also develop a combined list of their existing home rules and current responsibilities when home alone.*
>
> Session 2: Setting up a self-care arrangement *A model is presented, showing how children should work with their parents to set up their self-care arrangement (for example, finding a contact person, establishing routine communication, and determining special home rules and responsibilities).*
>
> Session 3: Personal safety when home alone *During this session, students rehearse ways of safely answering the door and telephone when home alone. Group discussion focuses on the reasons for each of the safety tips that are listed on specially developed handouts.*
>
> Session 4: Emergency and non-emergency situations *Group discussion focuses on helping children distinguish between emergency and non-emergency situations. Role-playing activities help students practice emergency action procedures.*
>
> Session 5: Special problems of being in charge *Group members brainstorm ways to overcome boredom and loneliness when home alone. A group discussion generates tips for coping with worries and fears.*
>
> Session 6: Other topics for being in charge *Role-playing activities help students practice ways to talk with their parents about concerns and problems that arise while home alone. Tips are provided to help students learn how to take care of younger children. (Bundy and Boser, 1987, pp. 60-61)*

Bundy and Boser (1987) indicated that children who participated became more knowledgeable about approaches they should use in self-care. Their parents reported more confidence in their children's skills in caring for themselves after participation in "Being in Charge."

Great demands are placed on children in caring for themselves in today's society. This program is one example of how a school counselor can intervene to help children and their parents deal more successfully with these demands.

Gifted and Talented Students

One study (Conroy, 1987), that touched on parental concerns regarding their gifted elementary school children, involved the implementation, by a school counselor, of a three-session parent workshop that was aimed at helping parents to develop a better understanding of their children as well as increasing their comfort in raising the gifted child.

After participating in the workshop, parents reported a greater understanding of the need for gifted children to: (a) develop higher-level thinking skills; (b) pursue their own interests; and (c) learn self-discipline. The personal comfort level associated with parenting a child with special abilities also increased as the result of parents having the opportunity to discuss the needs and problems faced by their children.

This is only a few of many examples in which a school counselor has intervened successfully in helping children through participation in a group.

Unstructured Groups

At times, and after more experience running groups, counselors may prefer to run unstructured groups in which topics of interest are discussed verbally and spontaneously with no use of additional or pre-planned activities. This procedure requires clear understanding of group process and outstanding group leadership skills to be utilized effectively.

Group Summary Sheet

To counselors who run groups, we suggest that you prepare a *Group Summary Sheet* which lists: group topic, names of group members and homeroom teachers, times and dates of sessions, duration of group, and activities for each group session. Reproduce this and give a copy to each homeroom teacher for their information (and as a gesture of their inclusion in the group process by the counselor). Refer to Figure 5–1 for an example of a group summary sheet.

Prior to the first group meeting, send a letter to the parents or guardians describing the nature of the group and its purpose. Incidentally, all correspondence to parents should be written on school letterhead, appear professional as well as personal, and show kind regard for and interest in their child. See Figure 5–2 for a sample letter to parents.

In the interest of parental cooperation and to a degree, for the counselor's protection, it is best to receive written permission from the parent or guardian for counseling their child in a group. In fact, "in many school corporations, parents or legal guardians must provide a written informed consent in order for minor children to participate in group counseling. Informed consent involves the provision of specific information about the group so that the client (and, in the case of the minor child, the parent/guardian) can make an intelligent decision about whether or not to participate" (Morganett, 1990, p. 3). Parents are also invited to ask questions or seek clarification.

A counselor's periodic exposure to children during classroom guidance enables counselors to become familiar with the personalities and needs of children in their schools. This awareness expedites the task of planning for groups and ensures a "proper fit" among members.

Once the counselor has completed the initial preparations, group work can begin. Counselors will gain more cooperation from teachers when they begin and end groups on time. There are a number of ways of reminding children of the group meeting. Some include: notes placed in the teachers' mail boxes; prearranged instructions that children stop by the rooms of other group members on their way; children are met by the counselor at their rooms; or they are called on the intercom in their room, depending on the school's procedures for its use.

Group Summary Sheet

Topic____
Goals____

____

Dates of Sessions: Begin ________________ End ________________
Time of Group ________________ Number of Sessions ________________

Participant	**Homeroom Teacher**
1. ________________	________________
2. ________________	________________
3. ________________	________________
4. ________________	________________
5. ________________	________________
6. ________________	________________
7. ________________	________________
8. ________________	________________

Activities and Materials Needed

Session1 ________________________________
Session2 ________________________________
Session3 ________________________________
Session4 ________________________________
Session5 ________________________________
Session6 ________________________________
Session7 ________________________________
Session8 ________________________________

FIGURE 5–1 Sample Group Summary Sheet

The Group Counseling Process

As with individual counseling, group counseling is planned to follow a logical process, usually defined by stages, phases, or steps in a sequential order. In the paragraphs that follow, these are discussed as the orientation, identification, application, and termination stages.

Orientation

A good beginning is a significant first step towards a worthwhile group experience. In this beginning, the orientation stage, the counselor will be introducing the children of the group, to not only each other, if they are unacquainted, but, in addition, to new and unfamiliar processes. As in individual counseling, positive interpersonal relationships are a counselor's goal during this stage. The counselor may initially review the purposes, the beginning process and some "ground

Archway Elementary School

Date ____________________

Dear Parents:

The elementary school of today is no longer protected and isolated from society's problems and concerns. Our children are increasingly vulnerable to outside pressures as they attempt to acquire personal and social skills in addition to academic competencies.

Some early symptoms of these pressures are underachivement in school and low self-concept. Without early intervention, these symptoms could increase to far worse problems in the future.

The elementary school counselor is the professional uniquely qualified to implement programs of appropriate intervention for all our children. I am interested in helping our children learn all they can and grow into a happy successful adult. This can begin by increasing their skills to become successful in school.

I want to work with your child ______________________, in a small group on ______________________. There may be times when I need your help.

Please feel free to call me at school, ___phone number___ if you have any questions.

Warmly and with much interest,

Carey E. Nough
Counselor
Archway Elementary School

FIGURE 5–2 Sample Letter to Parents

rules," which include the rule of confidentiality and one person talking at a time. Various introductory-personal interaction activities may follow in an attempt to begin the relationship process.

For example, according to Morganett (1990):

> *One of the leader's most important roles is to help establish positive norms for expression and conduct in the group. One set of norms, ground rules, consists of explicit (generally written) statements concerning behaviors and issues that affect the group. These statements are developed by the leader and are added to by the members, usually at the first session. It is important that the members be allowed to have some input into the creation of these rules so that they develop "ownership" of them and will be more willing to abide by them. The confidentiality rule is an especially important norm; others include such matters as being on time, allowing everyone to have a chance to talk, and freedom to decline participation, if desired. Other norms are unwritten, but no less important. The leader has a special role in developing the norms of a group because of his or her position as a behavioral model. (p. 8)*

One such exercise involves the use of a *Record of Me Form* (Morganett, 1990). Morganett suggests that:

1. *Students can be instructed to choose six categories from the following list:*

   My Favorite Song
   My Favorite Place to Go with Friends
   My Best Friend
   Month of Birth
   My Pet(s)
   Best Vacation Ever
   Class I Like Best
   Sport I Like/Do Best
   Favorite Movie
   Favorite Movie Star
   Favorite Performing Artist
   Favorite Food
   Where I Was Born
   Best Friend in Elementary School
   Favorite Restaurant
   What I Hope to Accomplish in Group. (p. 33)

One category must be "What I hope to accomplish in group." Children create their own record similar to the example in Figure 5–3.

Of course, counselors may add their own favorites to the list as they pertain to specific group topics. Students may be encouraged to add ideas for categories also.

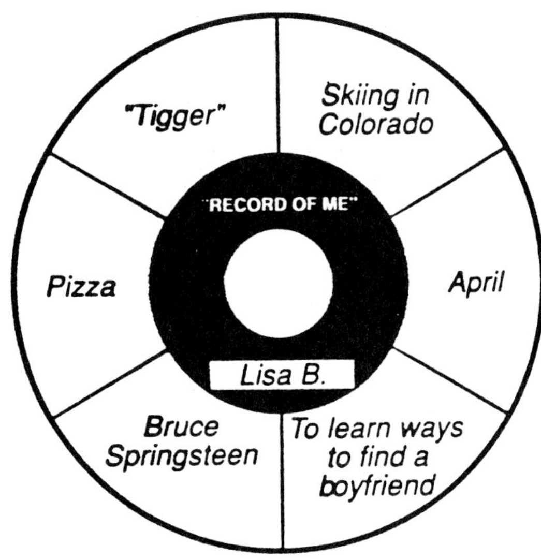

FIGURE 5–3 Record of Me Form

From *Skills for Living: Group Counseling Activities for Young Adolescents* (p. 35) by R.S. Morganett, 1990, Champaign, IL: Research Press. Copyright 1990 by the author. Reprinted by permission.

2. *Students should have approximately five minutes to work, and then should pair up with the person next to them and share the information they have written about themselves.*
3. *Students can be asked to take turns introducing their partners and telling what they have learned about each other.*

The outcome of the orientation stage should include open communications among all children in the group, acceptance of each other which includes receptiveness of viewpoints and feelings, a sense of working together and feeling comfortable together, and the beginning of experiencing openness and trust. "Without such trust, group interaction will be superficial, with little self-exploration . . . . As a result, the group will operate under the handicap of hidden feelings, and it faces the risk of never moving beyond the first stage" (George and Dustin, 1988, p. 103).

Identification

There is often a gradual transition from the orientation, or getting started, stage into the identification stage. During this stage, the group identity should emerge, individual roles should develop and group and individual goals should be identified. Corey and Corey (1987) suggest examples of group goals which include:

(a) the creation of a climate of trust and acceptance among the group members; (b) encouragement of sharing of themselves; and (c) promotion of risk-taking (p. 116). The counselor must play a significant role in helping the members to establish the group goals as well as helping individual members to clarify concrete and attainable individual goals. For example, if Helen states that her goal is to learn how to make new friends, the counselor can help her to identify steps or subgoals which she can work toward in attempting to accomplish the bigger goal. One such subgoal can be Helen's learning how to remain quiet while another person is speaking so that the other person feels that she is being listened to.

Group members should continue to learn about and share their feelings and perceptions, to examine their behavior and to assume more responsibility for their actions. Against this background, each group member is encouraged to begin not only identification, but also exploration of their own concerns that have brought them into the group or of the common concern of the group as it applies to them.

The counselor is the facilitator of this process and recognizes that during this phase conflicts, confrontations, or more passive resistance such as silence will probably occur. He or she may therefore be called upon to resolve feelings of resistance or ambivalence by group members as she or he seeks to further the group's working relationship by helping members learn the advantages of sharing, trusting and working together.

George and Dustin (1988) point out that:

> *a major force in this transition phase is resistance. Resistance may be directed at the subject matter, the group, or the leader, and may take the form of withdrawal, absence from the group, attacking others, or questioning the purpose of the group. While this emergence of hostility may be a struggle for control of the group, the resistance is more likely to have its source in the unrealistic, sometimes magical, expectations which group members have for the group leader. Such expectations are so extreme that the group members are bound to be disappointed by the group leader, no matter how he or she conducts the group. Although this is rarely a conscious process, the group members react to it by showing behaviors of resentment and resistance toward the group's activities and process. (p. 104)*

An outcome of this stage should be a statement of group goals which in turn are converted into behavioral objectives for the group members. The counselor must keep in mind that these goals are jointly arrived at by the counselor and the group members. What do the group members expect will be the outcomes of their group experience? Does this relate to what they actually want and need? It is important at this stage that the counselor ensures that the goals of the group are not only stated so that they are clearly understood by all the members, but that they also represent what the membership wants to achieve.

Application

This stage is the working stage for the group. It is a time of movement towards the goals of the group and its membership. There are specific commitments from group members to act; to change their lives; and to develop alternatives for coping with their concerns or situations. Actions or behavior changes which signal goal-related progress may be observable. Discussions should be more frank and open during this stage and group members should now be assuming more responsibility for their behaviors and their consequences as they begin the application of their "group learnings" to real-life situations.

During this stage the counselor is constantly reinforcing positive initiatives of the group collectively and its members individually. This includes support for members' willingness to take risks as they venture into new ways of dealing with others and their daily experiences. In this regard, the counselor assists members of the group in examining their options for dealing with troublesome situations. Throughout this stage, the counselor may need to (a) remind members to verify and seek what they want from the group and (b) stress the need to translate insight into action.

Elementary school counselors must always be flexible in their group work as sometimes unexpected and seemingly insignificant events can lead to very valuable discussions for children. For example, one spring day an elementary school counselor held a group outdoors under an oak tree, surrounded by azalea bushes. While there, a child quietly unearthed an earthworm. His eyes beamed with immediate attachment to this unexpected treasure. The counselor acknowledged, "John, how would you and the others feel about that worm joining our group today?" This particular earthworm was allowed by the group to remain for the session.

During group that day, issues of inclusion and exclusion, and feelings around these issues, were introduced and processed by the children and translated to other people and situations in their lives. This example illustrates the counselor's flexibility of content and props in that she originally did not intend to see, touch, nor discuss an earthworm! Nevertheless, when relevant issues are presented extraneously, it is advisable to respond by allowing the process to unfold naturally. Otherwise, you may experience the frustration which often accompanies a need to stick rigidly to a preplanned activity, as well as risk losing the efficacy of the moment.

Various activities can act as catalysts to get children started on the real issues. The counselor as group leader has the task of facilitating the group process to enable children to discover, explore, and accept their feelings. The counselor helps children see the relationship between how they feel and how they act. Previous choices and alternative choices for behavior may be processed by the group. Children are aided by the counselor in responding to others at appropriate feeling levels rather than merely to content, for this is the realm in which growth and change occurs. Counselors are role models in this process and insure that all members have an opportunity to interact.

It is critical that members are attuned to each other. This requires that children learn skills in listening. To develop this in children, the counselor may ask that a group member repeat what was said by the other child before responding. Children can be compassionate and empathic and therefore help create an environment in which change can occur for themselves and others. Elementary school children learn the value of talking about their feelings and accepting them. From this level, they can learn acceptable behaviors for expressing their negative feelings which, in the past, have gotten them into trouble.

The group setting also provides opportunities for learning life skills that involve self-expression and relating and communicating effectively with others. These are skills which illustrate for children their potential to solve problems as they arise throughout life. Practicing these skills within the safety of a group and under the leadership of the counselor helps children develop the self-confidence needed to use the skills outside the group.

During the group meetings, the elementary school counselor is aware that change occurs in some children faster than in others, and for some it may be temporary or not occur at all. Counseling children in groups is a method of intervention that has potential but no guarantees for positive outcomes. The end of one group in which little or no change occurred is not an indication that a child cannot be helped. Yalom (1985) writes that the end of a group signifies the beginning to further group work or to go forth into the world and implement new process. There is potential for growth and additional change in both. Human beings are always in the process of becoming. School counselors contribute their skills, and a safe environment in which to maximize this process, to those who are in need.

Termination

The familiar quote that "all good things must come to an end" is an appropriate reminder to members of a successful group. Another popular phrase "no one ever said it was going to be easy" may also be a useful reminder to the counselor (leader) of a successful group in the termination stage. During this stage, the group is functioning to help members understand what they have learned from the group experience and how they can now apply these learnings to their daily living but without the support of the group to fall back on. It is essential that the members be encouraged to express their reactions and feelings regarding the ending of the group.

> *They may have fears or concerns about separating, and leaving the group may be as anxiety-producing for some as entering it . . . . The members are likely to need encouragement in facing the fact that their group is terminating, and some mourning over this separation can be expected if the group has become a cohesive one. (Corey and Corey, 1987, p. 208)*

The counselor also ensures that no member has any "unfinished business" but, at the same time, members are informed of resources for future assistance.

Indicate your future availability, if that is an option. The importance of continuing confidentiality may need to be addressed also. Counselor follow-up procedures may also be planned during this final stage of the group process. Of course, this phase is never an abrupt one, but rather, one for which the membership has been alerted, and one in which the final meeting itself is anticipated in advance of the final session. Counselors can implement various activities which can assist members in consolidating what they have learned from the group experience.

One exercise involves the members as well as the counselor writing down and stating openly two things that they have learned, as the result of participating in the group. Another activity that allows the member to both give and receive positive feedback is referred to as the strength-bombardment activity. Each person (including the leader) writes their name on a large sheet of newsprint and writes their strengths on the back. They then hang the sheet on the wall in order for other people to write a positive strength describing them. Each person then reads the strengths that they have written, as well as those that others have written about them, aloud. The list of positive strengths can serve as reminders to the members of what they contributed to the group and what positive attributes they possess that can help them in interacting with people outside the group.

An excellent summary of group counseling skills related to stages of the process, developed by Gill and Barry (1982), is presented in Table 5–1.

In the first stage, *Group Formation*, it is clear that skills related to the facilitation of acceptance, trust and openness are necessary. As the group moves to the second stage, *Group Awareness*, the counselor utilizes skills that help the members to identify group norms, take risks in communicating their thoughts and feelings and develop understanding of how their presence impacts the group. The awareness of what impact the group has on members as individuals is also facilitated.

Group Action, the final stage, requires the counselor to use techniques that encourage the members to act on "getting out of the group" what they need. The co-leaders focus on individual, and group goals, and facilitate the members taking action to solve problems, as well as, to evaluate the results of such action.

A Group Model Format

We suggest the following model as a format applicable to any group topic:

Session 1 - Orientation: Introductions of group members, group expectations, responsibilities of group members and the leader, purpose of the group, goals, rules, and norms (such as, confidentiality and only one member talks at a time). You may facilitate a "getting to know you activity", such as a name game. Discuss meeting dates, times, and the number of sessions they will meet. If writing,

TABLE 5–1 Classification System for Group-Focused Counseling Skills

Stage I Group Formation:	Stage II Group Awareness:	Stage III Group Action:
Facilitating cooperation toward common goals through development of group identity	Facilitating a shared understanding of the group's behavior	Facilitating cooperative decision-making and problem-solving
1. *Norming*: Stating Explicitly the expected group behavior.	1. *Labeling Group Behavior*: Identifying and describing group feelings and performance.	1. *Identifying Group Needs*: Asking questions and making statements that clarify the wants and needs of members.
2. *Elicit Group Responses*: Inquiries or invitations to members that encourage comments, questions or observations.	2. *Implicit Norming*: Describing behavior that has become typical of the group through common practice.	2. *Identifying Group Goals*: Asking questions and making statements that clarify group objectives.
3. *Eliciting Empathic Reactions*: Inquiries or invitations to members that encourage disclosure of experiences or feelings similar to those being expressed.	3. *Eliciting Group Observations*: Inquiries or invitations to members that encourage observations about group process.	3. *Attributing Meaning*: Providing concepts for understanding group thought, feelings, and behavior.
4. *Identifying Commonalities and Differences*: Describing comparative characteristics of participants.	4. *Eliciting Mutual Feedback*: Inquiries or invitations to members that encourage sharing of perceptions about each other's behavior.	4. *Eliciting Alternatives*: Providing descriptions of possible courses of action and inviting members to contribute alternatives
5. *Eliciting Empathic Reactions*: Inquiries or invitations to members that encourage reflection of one member's expressed content or feeling.	5. *Identifying Conflict*: Labeling discordant elements of communication between members.	5. *Exploring Consequences*: Inquiries or invitations to the group that evaluate actions and potential outcomes
6. *Task Focusing*: Redirecting conversation to immediate objectives; restating themes being expressed by more than one member.	6. *Identifying Nonverbal Behavior*: Labeling unspoken communications between members' facial expression, posture, hand gestures, voice tone, and intensity, etc.)	6. *Consensus Testing*: Requesting group agreement on a decision or course of action
	7. *Validating*: Requesting group confirmation of the accuracy of leader or members' perceptions.	
	8. *Transitioning*: Changing the group's focus on content or feelings being expressed.	
	9. *Connecting*: Relating material from group events at a particular time or session to what is happening currently.	
	10. *Extinguishing*: Ignoring, cutting off, or diverting inappropriate talk or actions of members.	

From S. J. Gill, and R. A. Barry, "Group-Focussed Counseling: Classifying the Essential Skills" (p. 304) in *The Personnel and Guidance Journal, 60*, 1982. Reprinted with permission from the American Counseling Association.

drawing, or other creative activities will be used, it is advisable to allow them to make a folder to keep their materials in until the last group meeting.

Sessions 2–7 - Identification and Application: In structured groups, the following activities may be used to stimulate the processing of feelings: games, painting, drawing, roleplaying, handout sheets, books, play dough, or filmstrips. Whether structured or an unstructured group, the counselor facilitates sharing and interactions among group members relative to the group topic. In session five or six, begin preparation for termination.

Session 8 - Termination: Process feelings of saying good-bye to group members. Consolidate learning. You may have them complete (orally or written) the sentence: "In group, I learned . . ." Discuss what they liked and did not like about the group. Summarize how in-group behavior has created more effective out-of-group behavior.

Summary

Groups provide a natural setting for many developmental and adjustment experiences in the elementary schools. Counselors utilize many of these opportunities not only because groups may promote greater efficiency in terms of time utilization, but also because groups are frequently more effective than individual counseling or other techniques. An important initial step is that of screening and selection of group members.

The group counseling process is very similar to individual counseling in that it passes through stages beginning with the identification of goals and roles and relationship establishment, to the application or working stage of the group, and finally termination or closure. At each of these stages, the elementary school counselor is sensitive to the developmental characteristic of his or her elementary age clients.

Chapter 6 will continue this discussion of group activities with a focus on classroom guidance.

Chapter 6

Classroom Guidance Instruction

Your greatest contribution to mankind is to be sure there is a teacher in every classroom who cares that every student every day learns and grows and feels like a real human being.
—DONALD CLIFTON

Identifying Goals

The two major thrusts of an elementary school counseling and guidance program are intervention and prevention. In Chapter 4, we discussed the counseling process and skills required for intervention. Intervention is commonly used by the counselor in a number of situations to assist the elementary school client, including crisis situations related to home and school.

Classroom guidance instruction, on the other hand, is designed for prevention and utilizes the counselor as a teacher for all children in the school. Counselors periodically schedule times to go into classrooms to teach a classroom guidance lesson. Prevention involves the continual investment of time by both teachers and counselors who prepare each child to become fully productive and to thrive in the world. This chapter will discuss the design and implementation of a developmental guidance curriculum. The goal of this curriculum is prevention, that is, to educate the whole child in life skills while instilling hope and purpose to assist each one in becoming a healthy self-actualizing adult.

Because our nation is one at risk, it is imperative that we capitalize on all available resources to ameliorate and extinguish the ensuing pressures and dangers that accompany growing up in a rapidly changing and unstable world. One resource is our school systems which can provide a comprehensive education to all children. Schools can prepare students to meet the challenges of life and provide opportunities to grow and develop to their maximum capacity academically and personally with the help of school counselors.

Within school systems, school counseling programs, if comprehensively and developmentally designed, can play a critical role in the education and development of the whole child. This chapter will discuss the development and implementation of a developmental guidance curriculum aimed toward the most effective use of a school counselor's time. Excerpts from *A Model for Developmental School Counseling Programs* in Indiana are presented and four classroom guidance activities are described in detail. The purpose of this chapter is to provide a model for the form and function of a developmental school counseling program which will "Let each become all that he or she is capable of being." (State University of New York motto)

Trotzer (1980) stated that "classroom guidance is the process of providing personally relevant information and skills and encouraging interpersonal interaction, discussion, and sharing in order to help participants understand themselves, their development, and their world, thereby facilitating effective decision-making, appropriate adjustment, and satisfactory personal growth" (p. 342). In classroom guidance, the counselor chooses topics and teaches children about personally relevant issues that are not found in the academic curriculum. A topic may range from "Being a Friend in School" to "Study Skills."

Counselors teach children life skills to effectively deal with situations in their lives. They learn how to problem-solve and make good decisions. Through an exploration of their feelings, they learn about resulting behaviors and consequences and options for alternative behaviors.

Although problems will always be an aspect of the human condition, their impacts can be lessened if children are taught healthy coping skills. Some problems, however, can be avoided, for example drug abuse and AIDS. Classroom guidance instruction educates children about dangers and how to make healthy decisions. It is likely that children will be faced with life choices which could endanger their health in adulthood. Therefore, our schools are faced with the monumental task of insuring the preservation of our country's greatest natural resource: our children, our future. To this end, classroom guidance instruction is a crucial supplement to academic instruction in our schools.

Gail Sheehy's statement in 1987 at the American Association for Counseling and Development (AACD) National Convention suggests that, "Counselors help the victorious personality find itself." Personality development is an aspect of human development, as you remember from Chapter 2. Children and adults learn through their experiences and learning results in personal growth. In elementary school, counselors help children understand their experiences. Learning and growth occur throughout life as children and adults encounter their own strengths, weaknesses, potentials, feelings, behaviors, and thoughts, and the complexities resulting from interactions with others. In classroom guidance instruction, counselors initiate discussions on these topics to increase children's awareness and potential to act responsibly. They learn to accept responsibility for who they will become as adults. Childhoods provide practice for developing adults. Counselors use their knowledge and skill to guide children to discover their human potential, their "victorious personality." "Guidance promotes maximum personal development in all spheres of life" (Dagley, 1987, p. 102). To this end, it is critical that school counselors invest major energy in prevention strategies through the development and implementation of a developmental guidance curriculum.

Designing a Guidance Curriculum

The American School Counselor Association (ASCA) adopted the following definition of developmental guidance in 1978 and reaffirmed it in 1984:

> *Developmental guidance is that component of all guidance efforts which fosters planned intervention within the educational and other human development services programs at all points in the human life cycle to vigorously stimulate and actively facilitate the total development of individuals in all areas—personal, social, emotional, career, moral-ethical, cognitive, aesthetic—and to promote the integration of the several components into an individual lifestyle. (Cited in Rotter, 1990, p. 1)*

As noted above and in Chapter 2 as well, elementary school counselors are human development specialists. Therefore, knowledge of the developmental stages of children is essential. This content provides the foundation upon which a guidance curriculum is designed. Counselors provide activities for children that correspond to their developmental stage. Thus, a sequential format of guidance activities throughout elementary school provides parallel progression through the natural maturational stages as children grow. As certain competencies are gained, counselors can introduce concepts and information at more complex levels as cognitive and emotional development progresses.

A useful format to design a developmental guidance curriculum might include the four steps described here.

Development of a Rationale

The first step is the development of a rationale. The purpose of a developmental guidance curriculum is to enhance the development of human potential through age-related activities. Counselors provide instruction in life skills, interpersonal relationships, awareness of self and others, and careers.

In developing a rationale for a developmental guidance curriculum, the counselor must assess the special needs of the population in the school. In addition to brainstorming all the developmental needs of the students, often a counselor will ask for suggestions from children, parents, teachers, and administrators by distributing a questionnaire. These needs and interests provide the foundation for proceeding to the next step. Refer to Table 6–1 for a sample questionnaire.

TABLE 6–1 Sample Guidance Questionnaire

Counseling and Guidance Questionnaire

To: Teachers, students, parents, administrators

From: Your Counselor, Carey E. Nough

I am developing (or revising) the guidance curriculum at Archway Elementary School. To more fully meet the needs of our growing and diverse population of students, please share with me any areas of interest or need that I can address. One example may be to suggest topics for classroom guidance instruction.

Your ideas are appreciated. Many thanks!

Statement of Goals

Next, needs of your population are then translated into workable goals. One example of a goal is to increase children's awareness of feelings in themselves and others. Other goals include:

Orientation to counseling and guidance
Individual appraisal of students
Teaching student behavior management programs
Creating and maintaining a counseling and guidance information center
Self-concept improvement
Career awareness and education
Provide knowledge of a pluralistic society
Counseling and guidance program evaluation

Some of these goals are met through classroom guidance instruction. Table 6–2 lists some topics of classroom guidance lessons.

Implementation

Once the counselor becomes sensitive to the needs of the population, a guidance program gains effectiveness through the counselor's response to those needs. The third step, implementation, involves: orienting children, parents, teachers, and administrators to your program; choosing topics; preparing presentations; gathering resource materials, such as, audiovisual aids, posters, filmstrips, activities, and so on; preparing handouts for distribution; scheduling; presenting; and evaluating. These will be discussed in detail in the activities section of this chapter which follows the fourth step, evaluation.

TABLE 6–2 Topics for classroom guidance in elementary school

self-concept
awareness and acceptance of feelings
social skills: e.g., politeness and helping
communication skills, including listening
friendship
values clarification
problem-solving skills
task-completion skills
career awareness
study skills
organizational skills
test-taking skills
decision-making skills
conflict resolution
peer pressure
appreciating similarities and differences
multicultural issues

Evaluation

Receiving feedback from children, teachers, parents, and administrators provides counselors with information regarding what is actually effective and what, if anything, needs improvement. Counselors can design questionnaires to be completed by the above audiences so that feedback is received in a constructive manner. It is not necessary to gather written evaluative comments after every presentation. However, periodically, they provide useful information and increase communication among your team members. Often feedback is verbal and serves, as well, to indicate the progress and effectiveness of your program. As a counselor, your caring attitude and commitment to the education of the child is reflected in your work. Through your work, everyone in your school environment will begin to see you as a support person, a person dedicated to improving the school success and personal development of every child. See Table 6–3 for a sample evaluation.

Activities for Implementation of a Guidance Curriculum:

Orientation

Orientation is a means by which counselors describe their role and function to everyone they serve and to the community. Teachers and administrators may be

TABLE 6–3 Sample Classroom Guidance Evaluation

Classroom Guidance Evaluation

Archway Elementary School

Dear Teachers,

Please complete this form and leave it in my mailbox. Periodic assessment of our guidance program is useful to keep it effective. Please circle your responses.

	Highest				Lowest
1. Content appropriate to grade level	1	2	3	4	5
2. Ability to maintain student interest	1	2	3	4	5
3. Topics relevant to learning and growing	1	2	3	4	5
4. Attitude of counselor is positive	1	2	3	4	5
5. Length of presentations appropriate	1	2	3	4	5

6. Strengths ______________________________

____

7. Weaknesses ______________________________

____

8. Comments ______________________________

____

9. Suggestions ______________________________

____

Warm Fuzzily,

Carey E. Nough
Your Counselor

addressed in faculty meetings. It is fun and informative to present a brief demonstration of a guidance lesson periodically to your teachers. Counselors may choose to orient school board members at one of their meetings. Parents, teachers, and members of the community are oriented through presentations at Parent Teacher Organizations. The first classroom guidance lesson of the school year is typically used for students' orientation to the school's program of counseling and guidance. Children in every classroom need to be reminded each year of the role and function of the counselor and that she or he is in the school for everyone.

Many activities are available for purchase by the elementary school, or school district, for implementation in a guidance curriculum. The counselor's own resourcefulness plus the characteristics of the school and community will influence the planning and scheduling of these activities.

Choose Topics

A questionnaire similar to Table 6–1, will provide topics that need attention in your particular school setting. Guidelines for a school or systemwide needs assessment may be found in Gibson, Mitchell, Higgins (1983). Prepare classroom guidance lessons to address these needs. In addition, teachers may make personal requests of the counselor when other issues arise in their classrooms. Of course, when there is a special schoolwide or districtwide observance (such as, *Warm Fuzzy Week* or *I am Lovable and Capable (IALAC) Day*), counselors create applicable lessons to coincide with the event. Needs of children and faculty, as well as, areas of personal interest are broad and provide counselors with an array of topics from which to choose.

Prepare Presentations

Since classroom guidance is the primary mode through which prevention occurs, it is an essential and fundamental function. The counselor's effectiveness in the classroom will be increased through thorough preparation. Lesson plans are prepared for classroom guidance just as they are for academic classes. They will include an introduction, explanation, discussion, questions and answers, activity, and summary. Counselors are required to have a clear understanding of concepts and, like all effective teachers and counselors, the ability to relate to children. Plus, practice makes perfect!

Gather Resource Materials

Resource materials are valuable teaching aids. They may include posters, filmstrips, puppets, games, or anything concrete through which concepts are presented more clearly. In many schools, counselors are given a budget each year to purchase guidance materials. Necessities would include: puppets, books, clay, cassette player, filmstrip projector, and markers (usually preferred by children over crayons, but both are good). Many commercial catalogues are available from which to choose materials. They are frequently displayed at conventions and workshops and may be purchased there. Districts that employ guidance coordinators may have a library where counselors check out materials for use in their schools.

Prepare Handouts

Handouts related to classroom guidance presentations serve two purposes: one is to enhance the learning process for children; and the other is to maintain public relations. Handouts provide a concrete activity related to the content which children must think about and complete. The use of handouts increases the likelihood of retention and makes learning more meaningful. Handout exercises should be fun, simple, consistent with grade level, and generally brief. Children may be instructed to take them home and discuss them with their parents. This serves as a reinforcement technique, and parents will become aware of the guidance activities of the school (public relations). All handouts should include your name as counselor and your school's name (for example, Classroom Guidance Activity from your counselor, Carey E. Nough, Archway Elementary School.)

Schedule

Setting aside the same blocks of time each week is recommended because the consistency and structure is appealing to teachers. Classroom guidance may be scheduled by principals, as are other special area classes, for example, art or music, but assisted by consultation with the elementary school counselor. In any event, it is beneficial to schedule it so that it is least disruptive to the regular classroom schedule. For example, first period before regular activities begin, and the period before lunch is a time when many schedules shift temporarily out of academic instruction, as to go to the bathroom or to lunch. However, since children are more receptive to learning earlier in the day, classroom teachers may regard this as "prime time" and be reluctant to give up that time to classroom guidance. While the counselor understands that improved self-concepts, peer relations, social skills, and understanding of self and others all contribute to mentally healthier individuals, the teacher is impressed by their contributions to school success. Counselors can ensure that students are more completely prepared for success in school. The classroom teacher may need to be tactfully convinced—usually through one-on-one contacts—to share this valuable time slot. Nevertheless, teachers give some choice in the decision of the day of the week and time. An example of a classroom guidance schedule planning sheet is in Figure 6–1.

The topic of your presentation and the available dates and time slots are written in. This is passed among the teachers. They indicate their selection by signing their name in the appropriate box. Involving teachers as often as possible is a reminder that guidance and counseling is a team effort. It is helpful for

FIGURE 6–1 Classroom Guidance Schedule Planning Sheet

TABLE 6–4 Sample Classroom Guidance Reminder

CLASSROOM GUIDANCE REMINDER

Archway Elementary School

Teacher ______________________
I will be in your room for classroom guidance on __________ (day) at __________ (time). The topic is __________ See you then!

Carey E. Nough
Your Counselor

counselors to design a brief reminder to be placed in the teacher's mailbox the day before your scheduled visit. Table 6–4 is an example.

Presentation

It is critical to be aware that classroom guidance in elementary schools involves the transfer of information, from you to the child, in an activity-oriented style. Since the audience is children, every instructor must consider developmental issues such as attention span and learning styles. Visual, auditory, and kinesthetic factors are included in the design of classroom guidance presentations. Children and adults respond to a delivery technique that captures their attention and maintains it. It helps to be enthusiastic and use colorful props. Effective teachers and counselors stimulate discussion and encourage verbalization of the concepts during the presentation to insure that children understand and retain the information. Visual aids and occasional magic tricks are very impressive with children. Use them to transform mediocre lectures into dynamite and fun learning experiences. Children will remember the concepts when they are introduced with enthusiasm, and their retention is your goal! Always at the conclusion of your presentation, thank the children and teacher for allowing you time to share with them.

Evaluation

Criteria used to evaluate the guidance program are based on the original goals which result from your needs assessment. Measuring the extent to which these goals were achieved will provide an evaluation. In this process, questionnaires (similar to Table 6–3) may be developed by you and completed by children, parents, teachers, and administrators. Verbal feedback is a less formal means of evaluation. Counselor perception of the extent to which goals were achieved is a personal evaluation.

Following any type of evaluation, written, verbal, or perceived, process the information with significant others in your school. Evaluations provide constructive feedback, praise you for effective activities, and give direction to areas needing improvement. It is seldom that guidance curricula remain unchanged over time since the needs of your population change as new children enter school and as society places new demands on their lives. Evaluations are not to be feared, rather appreciated, so that the design of the elementary school counseling and guidance program becomes more effective, preventive, and relevant to the needs of your student population.

Excerpts from a Model Developmental School Counseling Program

The beginning of this chapter has outlined the design and implementation of a developmental guidance curriculum. To strengthen the understanding of this concept, we have included in the next section excerpts from *The Model for Developmental School Counseling Programs* in Indiana (1991). This program is developmental and comprehensive in nature and encompasses prekindergarten through grade twelve. You will find in Table 6–5 the *Rationale,* in Table 6–6 the *Definition,* and in Table 6–7 the *Competencies* as they appear in the model's complete form. Read the following and focus on the developmental aspect of the model and the theme that school counselors empower students and adults in a broad range of competencies useful in school, home, and beyond. Be mindful that these learned competencies are intended to become a part of students and to remain useful throughout their lives.

TABLE 6–5 Rationale

The school counseling program is an integral part of the total educational experience. Given that student growth and development evolve over time, school counseling is developmental by design, comprehensive in scope, and systematic in its implementation. It follows that the need for a counseling program begins with prekindergarten and continues through graduation from senior high school. All students can benefit from participation in school counseling activities which are designed to maximize each individual's personal-social, educational, and career development potential. This kind of orientation contrasts with the traditional approach to school counseling which is more crisis-focused and reactive, dedicated to information dissemination, unplanned and unstructured, and burdened by scheduling and other noncounseling functions. Comprehensive developmental school counseling is preventive and proactive in orientation. It is comprised of four major program components: school counseling curriculum, individual planning, responsive services, and system support; consequently, it is well planned, goal-oriented, and accountable.
Benefits of developmental school counseling are cited below

For Students:

1. Promotes knowledge and assistance in career exploration and development
2. Develops decision-making skills
3. Increases knowledge of self and how to relate effectively to others
4. Broadens knowledge of our changing world
5. Increases opportunities for counselor-student interaction

TABLE 6–5 *Continued*

For Parents:

1. Provides support for parents regarding their child's educational development
2. Develops a system for a child's long-range planning
3. Increases opportunities for parent/counselor interaction
4. Enables parents to obtain resources when needed

For Teachers:

1. Encourages positive, supportive working relationships
2. Entails a team effort to address competencies
3. Enhances the role of the counselor as a resource person

For Administrators:

1. Provides a program structure with specific content
2. Provides a means of evaluating schools, counseling program efforts (accountability)
3. Enhances the image of the school counseling program in the community

For Boards of Education:

1. Provides rationale for implementing a comprehensive counseling program in the school system
2. Provides program information to district patrons
3. Provides ongoing information about student competencies attained through school counseling program efforts
4. Provides a basis for allocating funds for school counseling programs

For School Counselors:

1. Provides a clearly defined role and function
2. Eliminates non counseling functions
3. Offers the opportunity to reach all students
4. Provides a tool for program management.
5. Outlines clearly defined responsibilities for specific student competencies

For Student Services Staff:

1. Provides school psychologists, social workers, and other student services staff with a clearly defined role and function of the counselor
2. Clarifies areas of overlapping responsibilities
3. Encourages a positive team approach which enhances cooperative working relationships

For Business, Industry, and Labor:

1. Provides increased opportunity for collaboration among counselors and business, industry, and labor communities
2. Enhances the role of the counselor as a resource program
3. Increases opportunities for business, industry, and labor to participate actively in the total school program
4. Provides a potential work force with decision-making skills, preemployment skills, and increased worker maturity

From "A Model for Developmental School Counseling Programs in Indiana" A Joint Department of Education-Indiana School Counselors Association Project. Indiana Department of Education, State House, Indianapolis, Indiana, 46204-2798. Reprinted with permission of the Indiana Department of Education.

TABLE 6–6 Definition

The Developmental Approach

Comprehensive school counseling forms a partnership with the instructional program. Developmental by design, it includes sequentially presented activities and responsive services which address student growth and development as priority goals. Collaborative in practice, the developmental approach to school counseling focuses on the attainment of student competencies which accommodate the personal-social, educational, and career development needs of all students at each grade level.

The Personal-Social Domain LEARNING TO LIVE

The *Learning to Live* dimension consists of the competencies which concentrate on successfully relating to others as individuals and in groups. The focus of intervention in this area has to do with educational, career, and general life success—the development of a strong positive self-concept. Awareness of self—"Who am I?"—persists as a major theme in education today.

The Educational Domain LEARNING TO LEARN

Activities clustered in the *Learning to Learn* area are designed to help students achieve educational success in each learning situation. Competencies include the "new basics" necessary for survival in this age of information and high technology: decision-making and problem-solving skills, goal-setting, dealing with change, organizing and managing information and one's time.

The Career Development Domain LEARNING TO WORK

The *Learning to Work* category includes the competencies which target a positive attitude toward work and the development of skills which enable students to make a successful transition from school to the world of work and from job to job across the life-career span.

From "A Model for Developmental School Counseling Programs in Indiana." A Joint Department of Education-Indiana School Counselors Association Project. Indiana Department of Education, Sate House, Indianapolis, Indiana, 46204-2798. Reprinted with permission of the Indiana Department of Education.

Note that the rationale emphasizes the developmental, comprehensive, and systematic nature of the model. It is to be used with all students to facilitate the maximum development of human potential. Benefits of the school counseling program are listed.

In the definition, note the developmental and collaborative approach suggesting that guidance and counseling does not stand alone, but operates in conjunction with all school systems. There is comprehensive emphasis on three major areas of learning: learning to live, learning to learn, and learning to work.

The competencies section lists the learning in three areas of competence gained from school counseling services. The focus here is on self-discovery, understanding others, interpersonal relationships, and understanding and exploring the world of work. This section lists specific life skills that school counselors teach during classroom guidance instruction and summarize the thrust of preventive activities.

TABLE 6–7 Competencies

In addition to nurturing student growth and development in the areas of learning to live, learn, and work, the competencies which comprise the Indiana Developmental School Counseling Program naturally cluster in Categories. These competency categories are as follows:

LEARNING TO LIVE

Understanding and appreciating self.
Understanding and appreciating others.
Understanding and appreciating home and family.
Developing a sense of community.
Making decisions and setting goals.
Understanding safety and survival.

LEARNING TO LEARN

Understanding the relationships between personal qualities and school.
Understanding factors which affect school environment.
Making decisions, settings goals, and taking action.
Understanding interaction between home/family and school.
Understanding interaction between school and community.

LEARNING TO WORK

Understanding the relationships between personal qualities and work.
Making decisions, setting goals, and taking action.
Exploring careers.
Learning how to use leisure time.
Learning to work together.
Understanding how community awareness relates to work.

From "A Model for Developmental School Counseling Programs in Indiana." A Joint Department of Education-Indiana School Counselors Association Project. Indiana Department of Education, State House, Indianapolis, Indiana, 46204-2798. Reprinted with permission of the Indiana Department of Education.

Challenges to Developmental Guidance and Materials

There have been cases in which parents have challenged developmental guidance materials or activities. They contended that schools taught children what parents should teach at home. The question may be more specifically whether or not the sole responsibility for teaching life skills does indeed reside in the home. Challenges such as these need not be reasons to discontinue developmental guidance programs. Rather, counselors need only be equipped with information of the value of these programs and how they parallel district and state educational goals. We have included in Table 6–8 strategies for dealing with these challenges.

TABLE 6–8 Strategies for Dealing with Challenges to Developmental Guidance Materials and Activities

I. Relate your program to district and state goals.
II. Establish an advisory committee to select/reconsider developmental guidance materials. Include teachers and community members on the committee.
III. Require that all complaints be made in writing to the "Central Office."
IV. Have written goals and objectives for guidance and especially for the classroom developmental guidance activities.
V. Have copies of the materials you use available for review.
VI. Use activities and terms that are less likely to upset fundamentalists. For example, avoid the term values clarification. Replace it with thinking exercises. Use the term guidance rather than psychological education. A developmental guidance activity is not group counseling.
VII. Use debriefing time if a student reacts emotionally to something that is done in developmental guidance classes.
VIII. If necessary allow parents to exempt students from some curricular activities.
IX. Keep the focus of the complaint on the materials rather than on the guidance program or counselor.
X. Communicate with the challengers as representatives of their organizations. Let them know that you know about Eagle Forum, etc. To get a mailing list of the opposition contact 1-800-A-FAMILY.
XI. Avoid engaging in continuing "letters to the editor" debates. Send letters to people who complained signed by faculty, school board, etc.
XII. Check the guidelines from PEOPLE for the American Way. 2000 M. Street, N.W., Suite 400, Washington, D.C. 20036.

From *Strategies for Dealing with Challenges to Developmental Guidance Materials and Activities*, by W. Poppen, 1991, Department of Educational and Counseling Psychology, University of Tennessee, Knoxville, TN. Reprinted with permission of the author.

Numerous activities for classroom guidance instruction are available to the elementary school counselor. Some of these are commercially prepared "packages" that may be purchased through professional publications. Other ideas are gained through attendance at counseling workshops, conferences, and conventions.

When selecting activities, give consideration to developmental characteristics of the student group, for example, level of maturity and length of attention span. Amount of time available for classroom guidance, special materials needed, and expense must be appraised as well. Some examples of classroom guidance activities are described in the remainder of this chapter.

Classroom Guidance Activities

Activity 1 The Giving Tree

The book, *The Giving Tree*, by S. Silverstein (1964), is a parable about the gift of giving of oneself and another's capacity to love in return. It can be used any time in the school year. Because the "giving" theme of the book correlates with the Christmas season, where religiously acceptable, it could be used then. Our culture has emphasized the giving of tangible gifts at Christmas. This book is a touching illustration for children (and adults) of the value of giving of oneself, for example, through acts of kindness. When beginning any story or activity, children profit from a thorough introduction. Using the title of the book, have them discuss what it means to be a "giving tree." Ask, "What are some things that trees give us? Does the tree pay money for these things? In what ways do people give to each other? Are there things you can give that do not cost money? What are some of those things?" These ideas are listed on the chalkboard. Ask, "Who would you give these things to?" Help the children realize the value of giving to friends and neighbors and not just to people who are related to them.

After the introduction, give them ideas of what they should listen for in the story. Test for listening skills by asking after reading the first couple of pages, "Is this a boy or girl tree?" and "How do you know?" There are many ways to incorporate the reinforcement of basic skills in guidance lessons. Be mindful, discover and implement these reinforcers. Learn to read stories with feeling and expression, and *always* show children the pictures. Learn to read a story holding the book open, facing the children. Your interaction with them while reading and their ability to see the pages provides an inviting, participatory atmosphere. Reading while holding the book to one side of you may be easier than reading upside down, although it can be done. Eventually you will memorize the story verbatim and not need to look at the words at all, freeing you to interact more dramatically with the children. Pause and walk among the children giving them a closer look at the pictures. At the end of the story, processing is absolutely essential. If some children cry when the boy cuts down the trunk of the tree, process these sad feelings. Understanding feelings regarding giving and receiving is the essence of this story. Help children understand the concept of giving

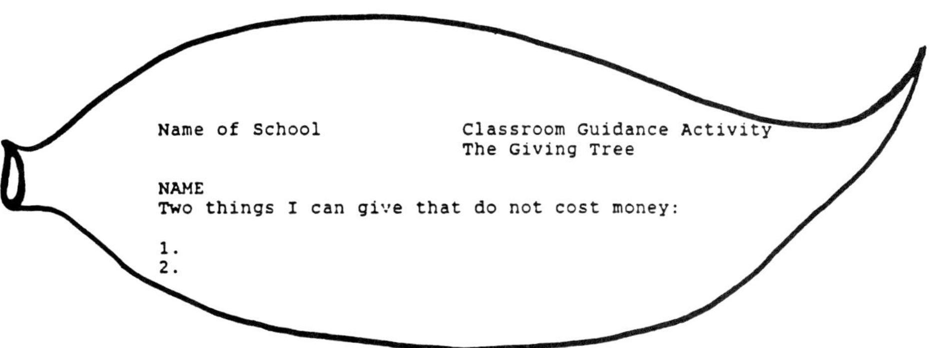
Name of School
Classroom Guidance Activity
The Giving Tree

NAME
Two things I can give that do not cost money:

1.
2.

FIGURE 6–2 Sample Activity

FIGURE 6–3 The Giving Tree

and of giving unselfishly. If you believe, instill the concept that often it is much more difficult, and of much more value, to give of oneself than to give things that cost money. This is an example of exploration and teaching in the affective domain. An activity is used at the end of the presentation to strengthen learning.

After the story is processed, a leaf, Figure 6–2 is given to each child and to the teacher. After it is completed, colored, and cut out, it is pasted or taped on a large paper tree (see Figure 6–3), which the counselor provides for display in the classroom.

In addition, the counselor draws a tree and duplicates it on construction paper for distribution to the children, Figure 6–4. Each child cuts it out and tapes it on another sheet of construction paper. The limbs and trunk are complete with perforations so that children may retell the story themselves and remove parts of the tree as it becomes more giving in the story.

Activity 2 Free to be You and Me

Free to be You and Me by Marlo Thomas (1971), is a collection of humor, songs, stories, poems, and pictures. Growing up, autonomy, and interdependence are emphasized. The major theme is that we are free to choose who we want to become. It is incorporated in the delightful celebration that people are similar and different; that people are in this world together; and that people need each other. The songs and stories included in this series touch on various aspects of growing up. They state clearly that it is not always easy, but it is always worth it to be the best you can be. Individual sections may be used for one lesson, or a few may be combined to form a unit. Introduce the concepts you are teaching so children will be alert to listen for details while you teach. If songs are used,

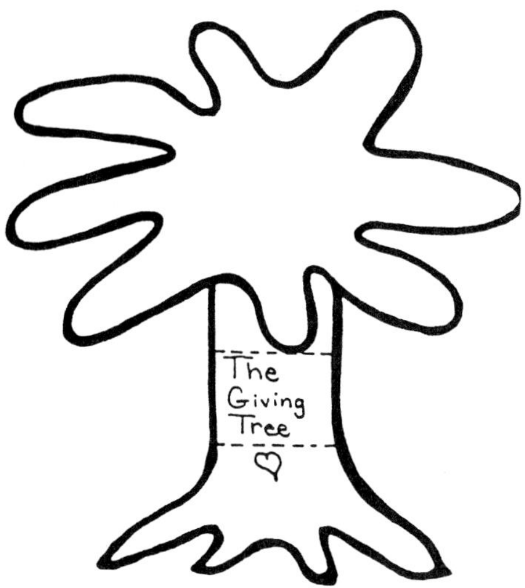

FIGURE 6–4 Sample Activity

discuss the words and what they mean before you play the music. At times, give each child a copy of the words and have them sing along. These activities are about life, people, feelings, and growth. Include handouts at the end of your presentation, for example, a coloring sheet, or have the children draw a picture, write a poem, or write a story which describes who they want to be or become. Figure 6–4 is a sample coloring sheet.

FIGURE 6–5 Sample Handout

Activity 3 Homework Hoopla

In elementary schools, teachers often refer children because they lack task-completion skills, which means they have not learned to take responsibility for their school work. If children do not complete their work in class, it is unlikely that they bring in their homework. Classroom guidance can facilitate children in taking more responsibility for homework and classwork. This presentation focuses on explaining three reasons why homework is beneficial. They are: (1) to promote honesty, since doing homework prevents children from feeling a need to make up an excuse to convince the teacher that they really did it, but that somehow it did not make it in their bookbag; (2) to give children the responsibility of completing an assignment and returning it—they learn that homework is children's work and that parents can be helpful by checking over it after its completion; and (3) to provide practice for material taught in class—they learn that practice increases learning. During the introduction, children are asked why they are given homework. These ideas are written on the chalkboard and discussed. The three points above are practically woven into the discussion. Activities below are included in this presentation.

Activities to accompany Homework Hoopla

1. *Banners*—Since this presentation can be done in all grade levels, place banners around the school a week in advance to arouse interest. These could be printed by computer or by hand.
Examples For Banners:

COMING SOON!! HOMEWORK HOOPLA
HOMEWORK HELPS US LEARN!
HOMEWORK IS FOR KIDS!
HUG A HOMEWORK HONEY!
HOORAY FOR HOMEWORK!

2. *Homework Honey Bee Form*
This handout, Figure 6–6, is a summary of the points discussed during the lesson. It is developmentally appropriate for grades two and up (also for advanced first graders).

3. *"I'm a Homework Honey" Badges*
Make badges by drawing a circle around the Homework Honey Bee pictured in Figure 6–6. You can draw several on colorful construction paper or cardstock which can be duplicated. Cut them out and show them to the children with the explanation that they are for those who bring in their homework. Leave one for each child with the teacher at the end of classroom guidance.

4. *My Checklist for Learning Responsibilities*
After your presentation, children are instructed to take this form home so parents can post it on the refrigerator as a way to organize responsibilities. Teachers are encouraged to keep copies to send home periodically. See Figure 6–7.

HOMEWORK HONEY BEE FORM

Classroom Guidance Sheet

Fact #1 Part of a teacher's job is to give children HOMEWORK. They're supposed to and it's not for punishment.

Fact #2 To kids, HOMEWORK may feel horrible. However, there are at least three good things that HOMEWORK can do for you.

Three good things that HOMEWORK can do for you:

1. HOMEWORK teaches you about the importance of honesty.
2. HOMEWORK helps you grow up because you learn about responsibility.
3. HOMEWORK helps you learn schoolwork because you get to practice what your teacher knows you need to learn.

Complete these sentences:

1. Homework is important because ______________________________

____

2. Learning responsibility is important to me because ______________________________

____

3. Honesty is a good quality to have because ______________________________

____

FIGURE 6–6 Homework Honey Bee Form

5. *My Checklist for Learning to be Responsible for School and Careers*

Discuss that the development of the listed habits increases school success and prepares them for the world of work. These checklists are kept in the classroom until the end of the week. Some teachers choose to fasten them on the children's desks. Others have children keep them in folders. Filling in the checklist is the responsibility of the children. The teacher keeps a master copy with the option to reproduce them weekly. See Figure 6–8.

My Checklist
For Learning Responsibilities

	Mon.	Tues.	Wed.	Thurs.	Fri.
1. Homework					
2. Chores without being reminded					
3. Going to bed on time—no fuss					
4. Cooperate with family					
5. Getting up when called					
6. Clean body and clothes					
7. Brush teeth					
8. Pick out clothes and dress self					

FIGURE 6–7 Sample Handout

My Checklist
For Learning to be Responsible
for School and Careers

	Mon.	Tues.	Wed.	Thurs.	Fri.
1. Complete Work					
2. Neat Work					
3. Appearance					
4. Friendly					
5. Homework					
6. Punctuality					
7. Neat Desk and Cubby					
8. Manners					
BONUS **1.** Brainstorming **2.** Problem-Solving					

Figure 6–8 Sample Handout

6. *The Homework Song (R. P. Bowman, 1985)*
Singing "The Homework Song" is a fun way to end this presentation. At the end, discuss the words; they reinforce the issue of honesty and homework. If you play the guitar, add chords to this song, typically in the key of G and create your own melody. Teach the children the chorus so they can sing along. You sing the individual verses. There are two verses at the end which you invite the teacher to sing with you. This is a treat for children and teachers. If you do not play guitar, the music teacher or someone you know may be helpful in producing a musical arrangement on cassette tape for you to carry into the classroom. See Table 6–9.

Activity 4 Study Skills

1. Begin the introduction with a discussion of these questions: What are study skills? How can they help? Why do you come to school? Eventually, lead your discussion to the fact that improved study skills increase learning.

2. Give a fun test which assesses the children's ability to follow directions. See sample in Figure 6–9.

3. Next, ask a child to give you a book from his or her desk. Ask if anyone can tell you the exact title of that book, the picture on the front, and describe the colors. Discuss how much they can or cannot recall and why.

TABLE 6–9 The Homework Song

Chorus:
We really did our homework,
And now we could just cry.
Cause we don't have it with us,
And here's the reason why.

My little brother sure likes art,
He's only three and not too smart.
He draws on anything he can find,
He scribbled up the homework that was mine.

I ride my bike to school each day,
But a big black dog chased me today.
He jumped at my leg and tried to bite,
But he missed and bit the homework I did last night.

My mom just bought a parakeet,
And so the cage would stay very neat,
Underneath that little birdie,
My homework became very dirty.

Last night when it rained so hard,
It made a lake in my front yard.
I had to swim to get to school,
My homework would get wet, I'm no fool.

You won't believe this but it's true,
A gator escaped from the local zoo.
I'm so lucky I didn't get hurt,
When it had my homework for dessert.

Teacher, you've got to understand,
An eagle snatched it from my hand.
And as I saw it fly away,
I yelled something I shouldn't say.

Last night I saw the strangest sight.
Down from the sky there came a light.
An alien spaceship did appear,
And took my homework as a souvenir.

Teacher's Verses:
I really hoped for recess,
And now I could just cry.
Cause you must do your homework,
And here's the reason why.

Lots of dangerous things outside,
Birds and gators and a lake that's wide.
In here you will be protected,
'Till your homework's all collected.

From *The Homework Song*, by R. P. Bowman, 1985, Columbia, SC. Presented at the 1985 South Carolina Association for Counseling and Development Conference in Hilton Head, SC. Reprinted with permission of the author.

FIGURE 6–9 SAMPLE ACTIVITY

FOLLOW THESE DIRECTIONS:

1. Read all the statements before you do anything.
2. Write your name in the upper right hand corner of the paper.
3. Put a circle ◯ around the word go.

   To Put Go One
4. Write the first letter of your first name on the line.
5. Add the number, put the answer *under* the line.
6. Draw a square, put a number 2 inside the square.
7. Only answer Number 2 of this test.

---

4. Explain the concept of self-disciplined student, and ask how many believe they are one. Read to the class the items in Figure 6–10. Instruct the children to respond by signaling with thumbs up for agree and thumbs down for disagree. There is no need to become concerned if they look around the room to see how their classmates are responding. You will have made your point with them.

5. Ask for reasons children do not pay attention in class. List their answers on the board and discuss.

6. Perform the Four Rules for Reading magic trick. Introduce this activity by discussing the importance of learning to read and remembering what is read. If you use this activity, you must practice first. You will hold an open medium-sized paper bag at the top. You will pretend that you are finding invisible magic balls in the classroom. For example, you may find one behind the ear of a child or in a desk. Shape your hand as if you were holding that invisible ball, and tell the children that one of the rules for reading is written on it. Read the words to them: "Expect to remember what you read." Discuss what that means. Next, pretend to throw the ball into the air and catch the ball in the paper bag you are holding. While holding the top rim of the bag with your thumb on the inside and fingers on the outside, you will snap your fingers. This creates a pop and the illusion that the ball has been caught in the bag! Really! Practice this trick. Children and adults are fascinated which adds a twist of remembrance to the concept of reading. You will find three more magic balls. Repeat the procedures above. The three remaining rules are: (1) Reading is thinking with the author; (2) Concentrate on the meaning of the words; and (3) Look for main ideas while you read. Children will catch on to this magic and play along. For reinforcement, ask a child to take a magic ball out of the bag and read from it to you. (They really can use their imaginations to do this!) Then let him or her throw it to you and, of course, you catch it in the bag with your secret snap. Do this for all four magic balls. Summarize and move on to the next part of the lesson.

7. With older children, introduce and discuss the PQ4R (Thomas & Robinson, 1972) study method. Revised from SQ3R (Robinson, 1961).

Preview
Question
Read
Reflect
Recite
Review

List these on the board and discuss each one with the children. Use one of their textbooks as an example to illustrate this study method process.

FIGURE 6–10 Self-Discipline Handout

Am I a Self-Disciplined Student?

Answer the following questions about yourself.
Check the answer that describes you best. A=Always B=Most of the time C=Some of the time D=Usually E=Hardly ever.

_____ **1.** I get myself up in the morning.
_____ **2.** I get to breakfast when it is ready.
_____ **3.** I get myself dressed for school in plenty of time.
_____ **4.** I brush my teeth and hair before I leave.
_____ **5.** I remember my books, lunch, and materials needed for that day.
_____ **6.** I get to the bus stop before the bus arrives.
_____ **7.** I get to my classroom on time.
_____ **8.** I keep my desk and the area around it clean and picked up.
_____ **9.** I remember my homework assignments and turn them in on time.
____ **10.** I complete my homework assignments during the day.
____ **11.** I am careful not to disturb my friends when they are studying.
____ **12.** I remember other students are working when I walk down the hall and I talk softly.
____ **13.** I bring my lunch money or remember my lunch every day.
____ **14.** I copy my homework assignments down and prepare my books to take home with me.
____ **15.** I get in the bus line in time to walk to the bus.
____ **16.** I hang up my coat and put my books away when I arrive home.
____ **17.** I remember to do my homework.
____ **18.** I remember to do my jobs or chores at home.
____ **19.** I get myself to bed at my bedtime without being reminded.

Name ______________________________

8. *Mnemonics:* The art of memory, or techniques for remembering. A mnemonic method that helps children remember is the use of acronyms, words formed from the first letters of a series of words, such as:

IALAC - I am Loveable and Capable
ROY G. BIV - Colors of spectrum: Red, Orange, Yellow, Green, Blue, Indigo, Violet
HOMES - The Great Lakes: Huron, Ontario, Michigan, Erie, Superior

Another mnemonic is an acrostic, an arrangement of words in which certain letters taken in order spell out a word, such as:

ARITHMETIC: A Rat In Tom's House Might Eat Tom's Ice Cream.
EGBDF: Notes on the lines of a staff are remembered by Every Good Bird Does Fly.

Another mnemonic is write i before e except after c.

Have a piece of pie.
You can't believe a lie.
February makes one say "br."
Potatoes have toes.
Together = to get her.

9. Compare the brain and thinking to riding a bike on grass. Ask how it feels to ride a bike on grass. What happens as you travel that same route on the grass day after day? Answer: the grass is worn down and a path is created which makes riding easier. The brain creates a similar process because the more you think the same things over and over, the easier it is to remember them. You create pathways in your brain that makes remembering easier.

10. *Flash cards:* instruct children to use flash cards in a more productive manner. Say: Put the ones you know in one stack and the ones you don't in another, rather than repeating the whole stack.

11. *Why test?* discuss how testing is a learning activity. Tests tell teachers how much you have learned. Discuss some test-taking skills: write your name first; use a pencil; read all questions first; answer the ones you know first; then go back to the others.

12. Distribute schedule and pointers for parents' sheets. See Figure 6–11.

13. If time allows, lead children in making up a rhyme, song, or poem about some facts they are learning.

14. Distribute gold (or any color) coding dots, purchased from any office supply store, or stickers, to children as symbols and reminders of what they have learned. Others will see them during the day and also ask what the dot or sticker means. This reinforces learning since the children will be prepared to respond about study skills!

FIGURE 6–11 Sample Parent Handout

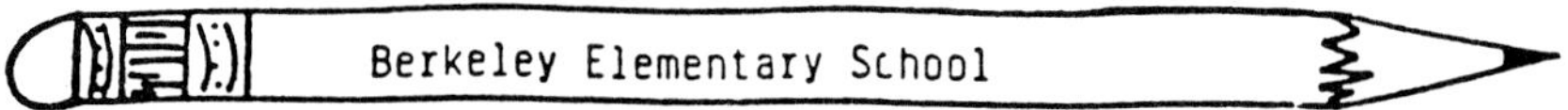

HELP SHARPEN YOUR CHILD'S STUDY HABITS

1. Provide a proper environment for homework.

   A quiet place (no TV)
   A place to be alone
   Enough light
   Flat table or desk and chair
   Sharp pencils and an eraser
   Paper
   Books the child needs
   Dictionary

2. Work with your child to organize his/her time.
   Make a schedule. Fill in chores, dinner, football practice, homework.
   The child should be allowed flexibility to choose homework time as long as it isn't put off until late at night.

3:00–4:00
4:00–5:00
5:00–6:00
6:00–7:00
7:00–8:00

   Once a schedule has been agreed upon, post it somewhere and try to stick with it.

3. Encourage good habits.

   Read to your child.
   Listen to your child read.
   Drill math facts and/or spelling words.
   Talk about what is being learned at school.

4. Maintain regular contact with teachers.

5. Be aware of changes in family and home conditions which may interfere with your child's learning, and seek appropriate guidance.

6. Give lots of "warm fuzzies" for effort and improvement.

PARENT HANDOUT ON STUDY SKILLS

Summary

In this chapter classroom guidance instruction is identified as a major function and anticipated responsibility of the elementary school counselor. A developmental guidance program is suggested to match the changing needs of children at different age levels. A format to design this type of guidance curriculum is outlined, along with excerpts from a model program. The thrust is prevention of problems later in life and the development of a "victorious personality" so that all children have the opportunity to become all they are capable of being.

Since the elementary school counselor provides information during classroom guidance, the role of teacher is assumed, rather than that of a counselor. Unlike the content of academic subject areas, counselor instruction consists of life skills development such as problem-solving, awareness and exploration of feelings, and decision-making. As human development specialists, counselors help children by teaching them skills that will enable them to be the best persons they can be, now and as adults. Four classroom guidance presentations are described in detail to illustrate the planning and delivery techniques of this type of teaching.

Chapter 7

Career Development in Elementary School

You work that you may keep pace with the earth
and the soul of the earth.
For to be idle is to become a stranger unto the seasons,
and to step out of life's procession,
that marches in majesty and proud submission
towards the infinite. . . .
. . . When you work you fulfill a part
of earth's furthest dream,
assigned to you when that dream was born,
and in keeping yourself with labour
you are in truth loving life,
and to love life through labour
is to be intimate with life's inmost secret. . . .
And what is it to work with love?
It is to weave the cloth with threads
drawn from your heart. . . .
It is to build a house with affection. . . .
It is to sow seeds with tenderness
and reap the harvest with joy. . . .
It is to charge all things you fashion
with a breath of your own spirit. . . .
—KAHILL GIBRAN (1923)

Introduction

As noted earlier in Chapter 1, during the early years organized guidance in U.S. education consisted primarily of career guidance. Despite the traditional attention given career guidance at the secondary level, little organized emphasis has been given at the elementary level until recent decades. Certainly many elementary teachers discussed occupations and the world of work in their classes while field trips to industries, farms, and other fields of employment were not uncommon. Too, as Herr and Cramer (1988) noted

> *the provision of career guidance in the elementary school is not a new add-on to or a dramatic reversal of typical elementary school emphases. Self-knowledge, knowledge of future educational and occupational alternatives, and development of the rudiments of decision-making by students generally have been considered important in both elementary school philosophy and practice (p. 226).*

However, few planned, systematically-based, developmental programs which provided all elementary pupils with experiences and information for later career decision-making and related adjustments had been instituted until the 1970s. Miller (1986) contends that since the 1970s, career-focused work with elementary school children has become a major focus of developmental guidance programs.

Few would argue that the elementary school years are important in preparing youth to make appropriate occupational educational decisions and related personal-social adjustments. Staley and Mangiesi (1984) have observed that it is widely acknowledged that children begin to formulate career decisions at a relatively young age. At these early ages, they acquire impressions of the work people do, the kinds of people employed, the compensations offered, and the abilities required for acceptable performance. These are the years of curiosity and inquiry, trial and exploration, and relative freedom from prejudice. As such the elementary grades encompass the natural years for developing appropriate career foundations. It is within the role of the elementary school's program of counseling and guidance to see that these opportunities are not lost.

Further, career development and related programs of career guidance are important in the total development of the individual at all educational levels. This total development of the individual must include attention to his or her career-educational and social-personal needs.

While the various aspects of the individual's total development should receive individualized and specialized attention, the functioning whole of the individual indicates the desirability of learning programs which themselves integrate these educational, vocational, social, and personal factors. In the elementary school, the guidance counselor can serve as a consultant and resource to the classroom teacher in developing this integrative approach which would include attention to the role of career development.

The Basis for Career Development in the Elementary School

Although the introductory paragraphs of this chapter have presented a general rationale for career development assistance in the elementary years, more specific reasons can be suggested. While these reasons may be essentially those cited in behalf of career guidance at higher educational levels, they are no less appropriate to the elementary years. Such factors as the complexity of the world of work, the complexity of career preparation, the need to develop broader career concepts, the importance of career development in total development, and the importance of career development in human resource development, to mention but a few, are indices of a need for career development at all educational levels. Their discussion at this point also presents a basis for a program of career development activities in the elementary school.

Complexity of the World of Work

Career guidance has, since its earliest inception, ascribed its need, at least in part, to the complexity of the world of work. While this world, as known by Parsons and the early fathers of career guidance, would appear strikingly simple when contrasted to today's scientific-technological society, there can be little doubt that counseling and guidance programs have, down through the generations, been helpful in assisting thousands of youth in making appropriate career decisions, placements, and adjustments in a complex working world.

We should note that this complexity of the world of work has steadily increased as a result of the changing character of many traditional careers and their training requirements, the emergence of new and the disappearance of old careers, the changing nature of our economic-industrial structure, and countless other unforeseen and unpredicted factors. If today's youth is to cope with these complexities, their preparedness in this regard cannot be initiated too soon.

Complexity of Career Preparation

Many earlier writers in the field of career guidance stressed the decline of the apprentice and other on-the-job training opportunities and the increased complexity of preparation to enter the world of work. Today, over half a century later, the complexity of occupational preparation itself continues to be a reality influencing our educational and related pupil guidance programs.

While few would underestimate the desirability of earlier career decision-making and entry into appropriate training programs, our understandings of human growth and development, coupled with our recognition of the rapidly changing requirements and nature of the world of work, indicate the impracticality of such a possibility. We can, however, ready youth to cope with the complexities of both career choice and preparation, and this training can and should begin in the early years of his or her elementary schooling.

Need to Develop Broader Career Concepts

There is much evidence indicating that young people approach career decision-making with a narrow, and often unrealistic "choice field." Later a few youth will enter the world of work with a realistic concept of what full-time employment means. The elementary school guidance program can contribute to broadening the career understandings of youth from these several standpoints. One objective is to broaden the range of occupational familiarity to enable the individual student to ultimately make his or her choice from a wide variety of possibilities commensurate with his or her potential. In addition, the program also seeks to broaden the concept of an occupation from that of the "job description" to a "work as a way of life" viewpoint. Too, children frequently acquire sexual stereotyping of work roles if not exposed to career information that discourages these concepts.

Gottfredson (1981) hypothesized that the development of occupational aspirations is a process of "successive circumscription of occupational alternatives that are considered acceptable" (p. 549). As children grow older, they reduce the occupational options acceptable to them. Gottfredson concluded that this circumscription process begins early within the individual and continues through four stages: orientation to size and power (3 to 5 years); orientation to sex roles (6 to 8 years); orientation to social valuation (9 to 13 years); and orientation to the internal, unique self (beginning around age 14). Gottfredson hypothesized that the circumscription process is active in the elementary school years. "Primary" children (6 to 8 years) eliminate potential occupations on the basis of gender. Girls rule out aspirations of careers perceived as "male only jobs" and boys remove aspirations they consider "female only jobs" (Gottfredson, 1981, p. 549 as seen in Bailey and Nihlen, 1989, pp. 135-136).

It is clear from Gottfredson's perspective that this sexual stereotyping of career roles begins at an early age for children. If dissuasion of this stereotyping is not attempted through the offering of career information at the elementary level, many children will, unfortunately, count out career opportunities that would have fit their needs, goals, and aspirations in later life. It is the responsibility of adults to do whatever is possible to prevent this from happening.

Miller (1986) insists that teachers and counselors can help by inviting guest speakers who work in atypical occupations into the classroom and also by taking field trips to places where atypical models are working. She further states that

> *Because books are central to a child's education, teachers and counselors should obtain career education materials, classroom textbooks, and readers that portray girls and women and boys and men engaging in a wide variety of nonstereotypical activities and careers (p. 253).*

The list of books at the end of this chapter is recommended by Miller. They can be suggested for reading to children by counselors and teachers as well as parents. Children can even read them on their own, although it will prove even more beneficial for them to have the opportunity to discuss what they have learned through their reading with an adult. The counselor is in an optimal position to be this adult (Bailey and Nihlen, 1989).

The development of these concepts cannot wait until the time when youth must make decisions but rather must be a part of a longitudinal process of career development which has its beginnings in the elementary school.

Career Development—Importance in Total Development

While much academic ado has been made over educating "the whole child," the fact is that little attention has been given in the elementary years to the career aspects of this education. Nor have most of the early elementary school guidance programs focused upon career guidance. Career development will take place whether planned or not. Obviously, this uncharted possibility is not conducive to developing the individual's potential and the development of our society's human resources.

Career Development—Important in Human Development

As frequently mentioned, a major role of the school counseling program is facilitating the development of the individual child's potential. The formative years in the elementary school can make a major contribution to implementing this concept. A planned program of career guidance is one vehicle for this implementation. The national implications should not be ignored. Any program that assists the individual in realizing his or her potential is, in a very direct manner, contributing to the human resource development of the individual and of society. The elementary school provides a time and setting for initial assessment and identification of the unique strengths of each child and their potential for future enhancement. This potential may also provide a basis for later career examinations. Too, the motivational effects of discovering what one is good at cannot be discounted. Enhancing self-awareness is a desired outcome of the growth stage in elementary schools and learning to build an understanding of strengths and limitations provides a foundation for self-understanding. In the upper elementary and later middle school grades, the classroom teacher, assisted by the school counselor, has the opportunity to motivate students in the study of both subject matter and career development through the integrating of related and meaningful career materials and experiences into class presentations. It provides opportunities to understand why people work; why all worthwhile work should be respected; and awareness of the differences among people and careers.

Importance for the Disadvantaged

One of the themes of educational reform in recent decades has focused on efforts to equalize educational opportunity. Perhaps synonymous with this theme is the need to develop programs which also equalize career opportunity. In this regard, the importance of programs facilitating the early and continuous career development of our youth from disadvantaged environments can hardly be overemphasized. In view of the high proportion of these youth who leave school at the earliest opportunity, and the high unemployment rate of youth from disadvantaged socio-economic environments, it is obvious that career guidance programs which concentrate on secondary school youth are "too little and too late."

Evidence from a variety of studies indicate that both the school dropout problem and the problems of underachievement and resultant talent wastage have their basis in the students' experiences of early childhood and early schooling. If it is to achieve success with this group, the school counseling program must have meaningful and early (elementary school) involvement with the problems and world that are real to the disadvantaged.

Parker and McDavis (1989) discuss the problems of the high unemployment rate among young African-American adults and the fact that many African-American students graduate from or leave high school without making any type of career decision. They suggest the following career awareness and exploration activities as beneficial in encouraging the development of career goals among African-American students. These activities can be used at the elementary level. The first activity is entitled "What is Your Job?" (p. 247). The purpose of the activity is to assist the students in developing career objectives by their learning about and increasing their familiarity with thirty traditional and nontraditional careers. Five steps are involved in this activity:

1. The counselor gives a description of the traditional and nontraditional careers.

2. The counselor places a cardboard label with the name of one of these thirty careers on it around the neck of each student.

3. The students pretend that they are at a meeting and describe their careers to other professionals (students).

4. The students discuss their thoughts and feelings about these careers.

Another exercise recommended by the authors is entitled "A Day in Your Future" (p. 24). Helping African-American students to learn the values of work through a guided vocational fantasy about a work day in the future is the goal of the activity. Three steps are involved:

1. The students are asked by the counselor to pretend they are adults working in their favorite jobs.

2. The students are then asked by the counselor to describe their families, homes, clothes, cars, work environments, job duties and responsibilities, and evening activities as they play these roles.

3. The students are then encouraged to discuss their fantasized work days.

These activities can be useful in initiating these students' awareness of career goals and possibilities. They also provide avenues for the counselor to use in learning of the knowledge, aspirations, and possible obstacles that the elementary student is dealing with in terms of career awareness. In terms of using these activities with disadvantaged students, the exercise provides the students with the opportunity to apply their real-life perceptions and situations in fantasizing about future careers. They are also given the chance to learn about careers that they may never have learned about elsewhere had they not experienced the career activities (Parker and McDavis, 1989).

The elementary school guidance program, in seeking to provide the types of career development experiences to benefit all their pupils, must consider that different kinds of experiences must be provided which recognize the differing backgrounds and needs of the students from a disadvantaged background. Such programs must be a planned part of the disadvantaged child's experiences beginning in the primary grades if he or she is to truly have "equality of opportunity."

Theories of Occupational Choice

Those teachers and counselors who seek to assist elementary school youth in their career development must have some understanding of the process through which an individual ultimately identifies with a career. In addition, they must be cognizant of the implications of these processes for the career guidance program in the elementary school. Theories of occupational choice provide some guidelines for these understandings. However, readers should be aware that these theories were developed primarily from studies of white males, thereby limiting severely their current application. Further, to the elementary school oriented counselor, these theories will appear to focus, for the most part, on adolescence and beyond career planning. Given that, however, there are meaningful implications for the elementary school counseling and guidance program. From a multitude of theories which might be presented at this point, only a few of the more popular approaches will be discussed. These have been rather arbitrarily grouped for discussion purposes into developmental, personality, and "other" categories.

Developmental and Process Theories

Developmental theories of career decision-making and entry suggest, as noted earlier in this chapter, that career development is a part of one's total development. This development is an ongoing process across the lifespan of the individual. A leading researcher in the field, Super (1975) identifies the stages of career growth as exploration, establishment, maintenance and decline. The current propositions of Super's theory (Super, 1984; Bell, Super and Dunn, 1988) are as follows:

1. People differ in their abilities, interests, and personalities (Super, 1984, p. 194).

2. The occupational level attained, and the sequence, frequency, and duration of trial and stable jobs, is determined by the individual's parental socioeconomic level, mental ability, and personality characteristics, and by the opportunities to which he or she is exposed (Super, 1984, p. 195).

3. Development through the life stages can be guided, partly by facilitating the maturing of abilities and interests and partly by aiding in reality testing and developing self-concepts (Super, 1984, p. 195).

4. The process of career development is essentially that of developing and implementing self-concepts; it is a synthesizing and compromising process in which the self-concept is a product of the interaction of inherited aptitudes, physical makeup, and opportunity to play various roles (Super, 1984, p. 195).

5. Work and occupation provide a focus for personality organization for most men and many women, although for some persons this focus is peripheral, incidental, or even nonexistent, and other foci, such as leisure activities, are central (Super, 1984, p. 196).

6. A series of developmental stages comprises the life "maxicycle" (Super, 1984, p. 200).

7. Coping behaviors relevant to vocational development tasks are described as drifting, floundering, trial, instrumentation, establishment, stagnation, and disengaging (Super, Kowalski, and Gotkin, 1967).

8. A variety of determinants affect the career decision process (Super et al., 1957).

9. Self-concepts are critical to vocational development, with occupational choice being the expression of the self (Super, 1963, 1984).

10. Career maturity involves readiness to meet vocational development tasks (Super, 1955, 1984; Super et al., 1957; Super and Kidd, 1979; Super and Thompson, 1979).

11. Salience of the various life roles determines the impact of one role upon another (Super, 1984) (cited in Bell, Super, and Dunn, 1988, pp. 14-18).

Themes characteristic of other areas of human development parallel the stages of career growth as well. Six of Super's propositions can be integrated into the career guidance section of an elementary comprehensive developmental counseling and guidance program.

1. Individual differences as an influence on careers—counselors integrate explorations and acceptance of individual differences with regard to career interests. For example, counselors may begin a career awareness discussion by asking children to name their various strengths and interests. Next, they are asked which jobs would provide expression of their interests and talents.

2. Influence of parents and home environments on career decision-making—Counselors invite children to become aware of ways in which parents and their home environments influence their career knowledge and aspirations. Children learn that although they are influenced by their families, they are not necessarily limited to those careers or levels of education.

3. Developmental emphasis—Knowledge of the developmental stages of children allows counselors to provide career emphasis relative to levels of maturation. For example, in early elementary grades, counselors focus on career awareness. As children mature cognitively and personally, the focus extends to the more complex task of career exploration.

4. Self-concept development—Super (1963, 1984) suggests that human beings have the tendency to express themselves through their careers. School counselors who acknowledge this concept increase children's awareness of how they might manifest their personal inclinations in their life's work. Pursuing a career in which the self-concept is allowed expression increases the likelihood of high job satisfaction. "Work is love made visible" (Kahlil Gibran, 1923, p. 28).

5. Coping strategies—while counselors teach coping skills to children to be used in their childhoods, it is useful to instill that these skills are transferable to other life situations as they grow older. Children can be taught early to anticipate varying levels of stress in their workplaces and to consider alternatives for stress management.

6. Various life roles—the current status of our economy necessitates, in many households, dual career families. Children observe firsthand that mothers and fathers juggle family, career, friends, and community services. Elementary school counselors develop an appreciation in children for the demands of each role. A preventive measure of enormous value in adulthood centers around elementary school counselors and teachers teaching these skills related to numerous life roles: (a) effective time management; (b) ability to establish quality personal connections; and (c) ability to maintain a balanced and harmonious integration of all the life roles required in being a fully functioning human being.

While it is useful to direct the career attention of children into their futures, counselors must not neglect to emphasize that the current "job" of children is to become educated, and the current workplace is their school. Therefore, counselors facilitate success on the job, school success, by clarifying and integrating these propositions into the educational experiences of children.

Another popular developmental theorist, Havighurst (1964) described career development as a lifelong process also, consisting of six stages from childhood to old age. Each age/stage period has developmental tasks which must be achieved if one is to be prepared to accomplish those which follow in the next stages. The basic stages associated with elementary-age pupils are (1) identification with a worker and (2) acquiring the basic habits of industry. Career process theories may also be classified as developmental inasmuch as they view career choice as a process that consists of stages that an individual passes through enroute to a career entry. Ginzberg, Ginsburg, Axelrad, and Herma (1951) were early proponents of this theoretical approach. They identified the process as encompassing the three periods of fantasy, tentative and realistic choices. In a 1984 update of this original theory, Ginzberg continued to stress the importance of early choices in the career decision-making process and occupational choice as a lifelong process for those who view their work as a major source of satisfaction in their life.

Personality and Trait-Factor Theories

As the label implies, personality theories emphasize the relationship between personality variables and career choice. One of the most popular of these theories currently is John Holland's theory matching personal styles with occupational environments. The personal styles are linked with the occupational environments through six rather broad themes: (1) realistic, (2) investigative, (3) artistic, (4) social, (5) enterprising, and (6) conventional. (Holland, 1966, 1973, 1985a and b) assumes:

1. *In our culture, most persons can be categorized as one of six types: realistic, intellectual, social, conventional, enterprising, and artistic.*
2. *There are six kinds of environments: realistic, intellectual, social, conventional, enterprising, and artistic.*
3. *People search for environments and vocations that will permit them to exercise their skills and abilities, to express their attitudes and values, to take on agreeable problems and roles, and to avoid disagreeable ones.*
4. *A person's behavior can be explained by the interaction of his personality and his environment. (1966, pp. 8-12)*

The relationship among these personality types and environments, as demonstrated by the hexagonal model shown in Figure 7–1, is one of the most significant features of Holland's theory.

According to Holland, the shorter the distance between any two types, the greater will be their similarity or psychological resemblance to each other (Holland, 1985a and b). For example, *realistic* and *investigative* are next to each other on the model so they resemble each other more closely. *Realistic* and *social* are much more different from each other and this is demonstrated by their being in opposition to each other on the hexagonal model. Lock (1988) explains that the model also illustrates the degree of consistency in personality patterns. Adjacent types such as *social* and *enterprising* make up the most consistent patterns and have more traits in common. Personality patterns composed of opposite types, such as *realistic* and *social* are described by Lock as the least consistent since they include many traits that are opposites of each other.

Holland's model can be quite useful in assessing the degree of agreement between an individual as a person and a particular work environment (Lock, 1988). "A social person would feel most comfortable in a social environment but would be most incongruent in a realistic environment, since social and realistic are quite opposite types (p. 136).

The implication for school counselors is to provide activities that focus on these six personal styles. Children gain an awareness of where their strengths lie and, at early ages, may choose to build on these strengths and/or to develop their weaknesses if they are also of interest. At young ages, children are not required to state a preferable style, but rather to gain exposure to all. Continued development will naturally result in the most salient style of preference.

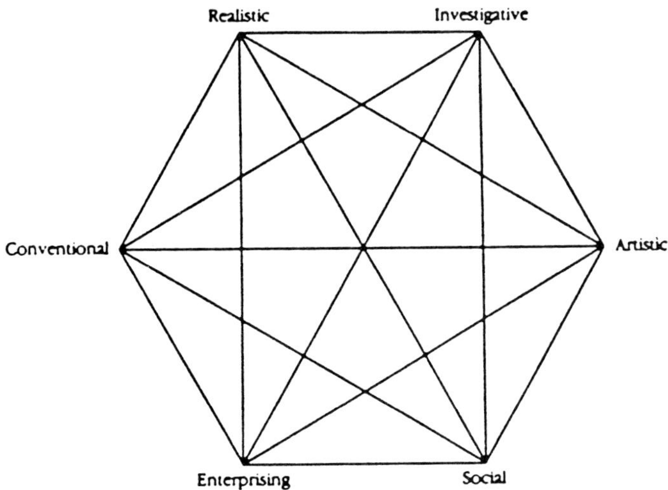

FIGURE 7–1 Hexagonal Model for Types and Environments

Reproduced by permission of Psychological Assessment Resources, Inc., from *Making Vocational Choices: A Theory of Vocational Personalities and Work Environments*, by J. L. Holland, 1985, copyright 1973, 1985 by Psychological Assessment Resources, Inc., Odessa, FL. All rights reserved.

Perhaps the oldest theory of career choice and one that may be classified as a counseling approach, personality theory or as a theory under its own label, is the trait-factor theory. This approach consists of procedures for (1) self-understanding, (2) an understanding of requirements and expectancies for different vocations, and (3) relating (1) to (2).

The nature of the trait-and-factor was summarized by Kutz as follows:

1. *Each person is "keyed" to one or several "correct" occupations.*
2. *If left alone, people will gravitate toward the right occupational choices.*
3. *However, counseling can make the process of occupational choice more effective and efficient.*
4. *The "key" can and should be learned during early adolescence.*
5. *The right occupational choice has a great influence on educational decisions.*
6. *Both the occupational choice and secondary decisions should remain constant over a period of time.*
7. *The final occupational goal should be known early and should determine decisions related to and leading toward that goal. (Seligman, 1980, p. 18)*

The trait-factor approach has made extensive use of standardized psychological measures over the years for the assessment of individual traits useful in career planning and decision-making.

Although elementary school children are not administered career placement batteries, school counselors help children build the foundations for their eventual career decision-making tasks. Specifically, counselors facilitate self-understanding in children and elicit responses pertaining to how their current strengths would match a potential career choice. The theme of career guidance in elementary schools is awareness and exploration of career choices, and the development of personal habits characteristic of a good employee.

Other Theories

A number of other career theories might also be mentioned at this point. They should include the social learning theory of career selection of Krumboltz, Mitchell, and Gellat (1975) and subsequently revised Mitchell, Jones, and Krumboltz (1979) and Mitchell and Krumboltz (1984). This theory identifies four influential factors as: (1) genetic endowments and special abilities; (2) environmental conditions and events; (3) learning experiences; and (4) task approach skills.

Another theory of career choice which has always had popular or romantic appeal is the suggestion that many individuals end up in a particular career more by "chance" or "accident" than through deliberate planning. The careers of popular entertainers, politicians, scientists, and sports figures who were discovered by chance or who accidentally tested their talents lend public credence to these theories. Counselors may choose a classroom guidance or small group activity to expose children to this theory. The counselor may know of, or investigate to find, a popular childhood figure whose career development has been a result of "chance" or "accident." Stories of human interest are particularly effective with children because they make the learning meaningful to them. Not only do you gain their attention, but you increase the chances of retention of concepts.

Finally, we would note, that as in counseling theory itself, there are those who have drawn from prominent theories of career choice to provide an "eclectic summary." One such summary, presented by Isaacson (1985) presents eight major points as follows:

1. *The career development process is an ongoing, lifelong aspect of human existence.*
2. *Since the process is essentially developmental in nature, it is generally predictable but also can be modified by changing circumstances, even to the point of being reversible as the individual attempts to optimize the benefits and satisfactions derived from the worker-job relationship.*
3. *Individuals have differing patterns of abilities, interests, and personality as a result of the interaction of genetic inheritance and environmental factors.*
4. *Occupations also have differing patterns of characteristics required or expected of successful workers.*
5. *The extent to which a person develops and applies his or her unique pattern of individual characteristics depends on attitudes, motivations, and values. These patterns can be approached from either the basis of psychological need or the development of self-concept.*

6. *The individual learns about jobs and their relationship to the individual specifically and to society generally from many sources, including the family, peer groups, community, school, media, and the planned and unplanned experiences of everyday life. The attitudes toward and knowledge of work developed in the growth, exploration, and crystallization periods of childhood and adolescence will have lasting influence on the worker job relationship of the adult years.*
7. *The optimization that the individual seeks in the worker job relationship is the product of the interaction between the individual and the realities of his or her situation. The ability and desire of the individual to capitalize on these interactions influence the level of optimization.*
8. *The degree of satisfaction experienced by the worker is largely determined by the extent to which the potential for optimization is apparent to the individual and is viewed as agreeable and acceptable. (pp. 76-77)*

Of interest to the elementary school counselor is the theme of these eight major points. The theme is that individuals pursue the development of their human potential in all areas of humanness. Since work consumes a vast portion of one's time and energy, the most effective use of that time is achieved while loving one's work. School counselors help children make potentially good career choices by: (a) increasing their awareness of themselves; and (b) instilling the belief that they gain happiness through their life's work when it is congruent with who they are as a person.

Implications for the Elementary School Guidance Program

A review of the various theories of occupational choice would appear, first of all, to suggest that the basic emphasis of the elementary school guidance program should be on providing appropriate developmental career experiences. While pupils may, at any age, be able to identify their occupational preference, these early choices should serve as a basis for exploration only and not long-range planning or semi-permanent decision-making.

In addition, during his or her elementary schooling, the pupil should develop an awareness of the meaning and significance of work and of the inevitability of occupational decision-making. She or he must also acquire an understanding of the relationships between one's educational opportunities and one's ultimate career possibilities. Positive attitudes towards education should be encouraged as pupils should also be guided into the development of basic habits of value for their education and also their eventual world of work. These would include learning to organize and use one's time effectively, being punctual with assignments, and giving appropriate priorities to work over play.

The elementary pupil must acquire foundations for occupational assessment and self-assessment. They must recognize that one's life work should be an occupation one can do well and enjoy doing and that therefore both self-understanding and occupational understanding are important.

TABLE 7–1 Career Development Competencies by Area and Level

	Elementary Level
Self-Knowledge	Knowledge of the importance of self-concept Skills to interact with others Awareness of the importance of growth and change
Educational & Occupational Exploration	Awareness of the benefits of educational achievement Awareness of the relationship between work and learning Skills to understand and use career information Awareness of the importance of personal responsibility and good work habits Awareness of how work relates to the needs and functions of society
Career Planning	Understanding how to make decisions Awareness of the interrelationship of life roles Awareness of different occupations and changing male/female roles Awareness of the career planning process

From *The National Career Development Guidelines* (p. 1) by the National Occupational Information Coordinating Committee, 1989 (Washington, DC: NOICC). Copyright 1989 by NOICC. Adapted by permission.

Career Development Competencies

The developmental approach to the career development of the elementary school pupil is based on the identification of those competencies that they should acquire during this period of their schooling. These competencies represent the desired outcomes for the school's comprehensive career guidance program. These competencies provide a basis for activity planning (a cooperative effort between counselors and faculty).

The National Occupation Information Coordinating Committee (1989) suggests the following career development competencies for elementary school pupils. See Table 7–1.

For another view, we note the Wisconsin Department of Public Instruction (1986) in their *School Counseling Programs: Resources and Planning Guide* suggested the following career/vocational competencies for elementary school pupils. They suggest that they should be learning about, understanding, and applying five competencies. These competencies are used as a basis for an example of a comprehensive career developmental plan for grades one through six as noted in Table 7–2.

Providing Appropriate Career Development Experiences

All aspects of a child's planned learning and development in the elementary school are dependent upon and enriched by the utilization of appropriate experiences. A wealth of these have been identified, organized, and provided

TABLE 7–2 Comprehensive Career Development Plan by Grades

Competencies	Grade 1	Grade 2	Grade 3	Grade 4	Grade 5	Grade 6
acquire knowledge about different occupations	parent interviews field trips →	interview neighbors →	interview community workers →	→	shadow community workers →	→
learn about changing male/female roles			male/female careers in different periods of history, review job ads in newspapers			community surveys of where men and women work
become aware of personal interests and preferences	various "what I like to do," "what I'm good at," exercises "what I want to be as an adult" exercise		add: sharing hobbies, leisure time activities →	→	→	→
learn how to cooperate and co-exist with others in work and play	games puzzles →	→ add: group projects, plays, etc. →	→	→	→	→
understand what it means to work and how school work relates to future plans	relate skills learned in class to careers →	→	→ examine careers in terms of training needed →	→	→	→
become aware of world beyond immediate experience	speakers come in to discuss careers →	→	study of geography-examines careers unique to locales →	examine & work in other countries creative writing assignments →	visit to area technical schools, colleges and universities →	→

with resources over the years for the various academic and artistic areas of the curriculum. These experiences have been planned to reflect appropriate principles of learning, characteristics of child growth and development, the objectives of the educational program they represent, and the development of desired competencies reflective of these objectives.

TABLE 7–3 Elementary School Student Competencies

Career/Vocational
1. Acquire knowledge about different occupations and changing male/female roles.
2. Become aware of personal interests and preferences.
3. Learn how to cooperate and co-exist with others in work and play.
4. Understand what it means to work and how school work relates to future plans.
5. Become aware of worlds beyond the immediate experience.

Reprinted/excerpted from *School Counseling Programs: A Resource and Planning Guide* (1986) with permission from the Wisconsin Department of Public Instruction, 125 S. Webster Street, Madison, WI 53702.

The career development program for the elementary school pupil must similarly provide for appropriate experiences and the utilization of relevant resources for facilitating career development competencies. These experiences should be planned within a framework of principles that recognizes child growth and development characteristics as well as school objectives and competency acquisition.

The American School Counselor Association (ASCA), in 1984, issued a career development policy statement that called for school counselors to take leadership in the implementation of developmental career guidance programs for all students in their schools and to begin this no later than kindergarten (Hoffman and McDaniels, 1991).

The following outline of a developmental elementary school curriculum provides the foundation for elementary school counselors in Virginia's public schools as they incorporate career activities that are developmentally appropriate for their students. Further details regarding the use of this curriculum by the Roanoke County Public Schools in Virginia can be found in "The Best for our Kids" by Gerstein and Lichtman, 1990 (Hoffman and McDaniels, 1991, p. 168).

Resources for Career Development

One concept for viewing and organizing these career developmental experiences is a chronological one which presumes that the child's early significant experiences will occur primarily in the home, the school, and the community in which he lives. As the child grows and develops, she or he will become increasingly subject to secondary influences from beyond this immediate environment. Such a concept might be visually depicted as an expanding pool or resources. (See Figure 7–2)

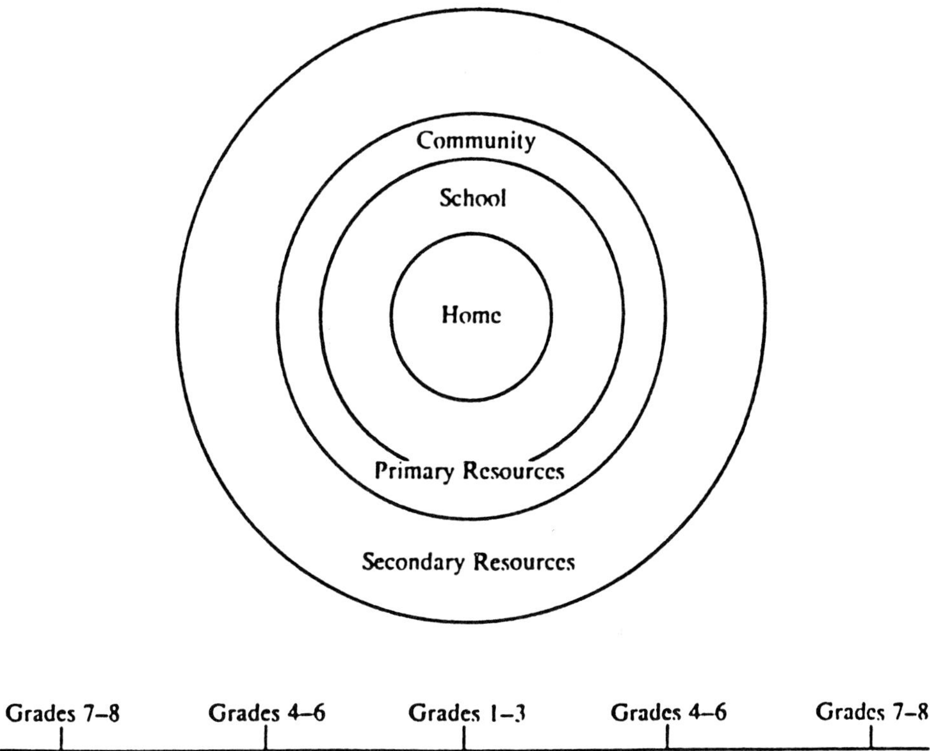

FIGURE 7–2 Pool of Resources

From *Career Development in the Elementary School* (p. 34) by R. L. Gibson, 1972. Copyright 1972 by Robert L. Gibson. Reprinted by permission from the author.

Primary Resources

The primary or initial resources for career guidance might be described as: (a) those careers with which the child lives and learns, such as those represented by his parents and teachers; (b) those careers with which children readily identify and are familiar, such as the mail carrier, police, minister, and bus driver; and (c) those careers which they can readily observe and relate to through such experiences as field trips, worker visits to the classroom, and simulated work experiences. The relating of career information to family, school, and community occupations can thus be both meaningful and interesting. The utilization of these local resources also provides increased opportunities to incorporate many "direct" learning experiences into the program and is an effective method for introducing children to the world of work.

An activity called "How Does McDonald's Affect My Life?" (Miller, 1989, p. 174) can help children understand just what workers do impact their important early experiences. The exercise involves having children in a class list all the workers whose work contributes to their life from the time they wake up in the morning until the time they go to bed at night. (This might include such people as the house cleaner, paper carrier, bus driver, or dairy farmer.) The class is then split into groups whereby children are asked to compare lists and attempt to determine whether one field of work is more important than another. They are then asked to give reasons for their choices. Discussions that follow assist the children in understanding the significance of various professions as they impact their lives.

Secondary Resources

In addition to those primary resources immediately available within the home-school-community complex, the child's career horizons can be further expanded through the utilization of various other media which can in a real sense acquaint them with the "world of work." Published materials, tapes, films, television programs, and other resources are readily available and should be increasingly utilized as the child moves up the career development ladder. While these materials can never replace first hand contacts or actual experiences, they are useful for supplementing and expanding the career understandings of the student.

Career Development Experiences

Career Development in the Home The home provides the elementary pupil with their first, most persistent, and most important contact with a worker. In the home the child has not only the opportunity to study the occupation of parents "in depth," but also to comprehend the significance and results of work in terms of the family's daily living. It is obvious, too, that one's parents will play an early and significant role in the child's development of attitude and habits conducive to their career development and later career success. Therefore, the study of occupations in the elementary school is usually best initiated through the child's exploration of her or his parents' world of work.

This exploration may be initiated by asking each pupil to "interview" their parents about their jobs and report to the class what they found out. They may act our or role play their parents' careers, draw pictures depicting their parents working, or engage in games such as "charades" or "occupations please."

Of course, parents should be alerted to their involvement and role and may even be profitably involved in planning their own child's experiences. This involvement can be even more rewarding for all concerned when parents are educated to the developmental characteristics and needs of their children, what the school is doing about it and how they, the parents, can help. The following is an example of correspondence for the purpose of alerting and explaining to parents their involvement in a career development unit.

Dear Parent:

Next week the third grade classes of the Edward Moore Elementary School will study a unit entitled, "Introduction to the World of Work." A lesson plan for this unit is enclosed for your information and also because we hope that you may be willing to assist us in making this a meaningful learning experience for our pupils. You will note that, as an assignment for this unit, your son, Paul, will be asked to interview you about your job. His interview will be based on the kinds of information he and his fellow pupils decide they would like to have about "workers and the world of work." In addition, I will ask him to ask you "what makes a good worker?"

The following week we will be discussing in our classes good home habits that lead to good work habits, and your cooperation will again be elicited. Each pupil will have "homework" as a "home worker." At the end of the week you will be asked to complete a "homework check sheet" that he will bring home with him.

May I thank you in advance for your anticipated cooperation. If you have any questions or suggestions, please don't hesitate to call me.

Sincerely yours,

Ms. Nancy Lee
Counselor

Parents may also become involved by going to their children's classrooms and telling students about their careers.

Whitson (1989) explains that parents often wish to help their children in making career decisions but lack the knowledge and skills to encourage effective decision-making in this area of career development. It has been found by Otto and Call (1985) that involvement of parents is a visible way of responding to public expectations that schools assist young students in their establishment of career plans. The past success of a group which focuses on maximal involvement

Dear Parent: Please place a check mark beside each item your son/daughter accomplishes for each day of the week beginning Monday.

	M	T	W	T	F
1. Gets up on time					
2. Makes bed					
3. Straightens up his room					
4. Is on time for meals					
5. Washes hands and face before meals					
6. Brushes teeth after meals					
7. Helps with house work					
8. Is considerate of others					
9. Is dependable					
10. Goes to bed on time					

Comments:

Please ask Paul to bring this form to school with him on Friday, October 16. Thank you for your help.

(Miss) Nancy Lee
3rd Grade Teacher
Munger Elementary School

FIGURE 7–3 Homeworker's Checklist

From *Career Development in the Elementary School* (p. 36) by R. L. Gibson, 1972. Copyright 1972 by Robert L. Gibson. Reprinted by permission from author.

of parents in the career development of their children is discussed by Whitson (1989).

> *Parents who have participated in this group have reported that they gain insight into the complexity of effective career decision–making and communication patterns within their families (p. 344).*

Career Development in the Classroom

The elementary school classroom offers the most natural, consistent, and effective approach to providing pupil career guidance. The classroom teacher has the daily opportunity to demonstrate attitudes, provide learning experiences, and dispense information which contributes to the child's career development and guidance. These opportunities may be further enhanced by planned provisions for the integration of career and related educational information into the on-going subject matter discussions, the presenting of special career units, and the utilization of special activities.

To supplement the teacher's career activities, counselors may use classroom guidance sessions to teach about careers. An example of a career unit is included here.

Unit Title: Introduction to the World of Work

Unit Objectives:

1. To become more aware of the significance of the "world of work"
2. To become more knowledgeable about one specific career
3. To become aware of the many different jobs in the world of work
4. To learn about some of the characteristics that make a good worker
5. To practice good home habits that can become good work habits.

Methods for Achieving Unit Objectives:

1. "The World of Work," film, will be presented followed by class discussion.
2. *Assignment:* Each pupil will be asked to "interview" at least one of their parents about his or her career. Class members will discuss kinds of information and questions to ask. Following the completion of the assignment, each class member will identify the career she or he explored, present findings, and answer any questions classmates may ask.
3. *Bulletin board display:* Each child will be asked to cut out an illustration from a magazine or newspaper which illustrates his or her parents' careers. These will be grouped by the teacher so as to illustrate clusters of similar careers as well as the many different jobs represented in even this relatively small group of people. The display will be studied and reacted to in class discussions.
4. The pupil will be requested to ask their parent "what makes a good worker?" Each pupil will report these responses to the class and a discussion will follow. Their teacher will conclude the discussion by presenting composite characteristics of the good worker.
5. From the previous exercise, a list of good work habits will be prepared. Those that can be practiced in the home will then comprise a check list which parents will be asked to keep on their child as a "home worker" for a week.
6. Unit will be concluded with a review and discussion.

Period of Time for Unit: Two Weeks Related Activities

Art Class: Pupils will be asked to draw pictures depicting their parents at work.

Music Class: Class will learn songs about work and workers ("I've Been Working on the Railroad, There's No Business Like Show Business").

Integrating Career and Education Information

From the very beginning of a child's formal learning experiences and throughout elementary schooling, understandings of the world of work and the various academic areas can be made more alive, enriched, and meaningful when career information becomes a natural and integrated part of subject matter content. Even the youngest first grader must see some meaning or purpose in educational opportunities, while the upper elementary pupil begins demanding to see the application potential of what he or she is asked to learn. The relationship between "learning in school" to "living out of school" thus becomes increasingly significant to pupil achievement, motivation, and retention. In the primary grades, the identifying of jobs and hobbies related to a subject or topic, the relating of classroom material to common everyday living needs, and the accomplishments of well known personalities in the news are examples of techniques for integrating career and educational development. In the upper elementary grades more detailed descriptions of related careers and their training requirements, the reading of job stories, the study of biographies, and field trips to employment sites are but a few of many useful approaches.

The Teaching of Career Units

As a supplement to the daily integrating of career information with the academic, the teaching of career units at appropriate times has considerable merit. Some of the potential values of career units are listed below.

1. Assures that concentrated attention will be given at some time each year to career information
2. Indicates to pupils the importance of occupations and the world of work
3. May make more of an impact than items fed into the classroom on a bit-by-bit basis
4. Offers an opportunity to "tie together" the various career discussions and activities that pupils have participated in over a period of time
5. Can also serve as a "preview" to the career relevance of upcoming subject matter content and experiences
6. Provides a specific opportunity to take advantage of the "expertise" of the elementary school counselor through utilizing him or her in such capacities as a resource person, a team-teacher of the unit, or a consultant to individual pupils
7. May facilitate the undertaking of special activities and the utilization of special resources.

Classroom Activities for Career Development

There are numerous special activities which can be appropriately incorporated into the on–going instructional program or utilized as a planned experience of a career unit. In either situation, such activities have at least the two-fold purpose of: (1) presenting meaningful career information and development opportunities to pupils; and (2) stimulating pupils to utilize the opportunity.

In the primary grades, activities should be planned which help pupils learn about jobs from such primary and familiar sources as the home, school, neighborhood, and community. Activities of this nature which capitalize on the child's imagination, natural curiosity, and enjoyment of role playing can be profitably planned.

Miller (1989) indicates also that the activities at the introductory stage of the child's career development should address the students' "(a) awareness of self; (b) feelings of autonomy and control; (c) need for planful behavior, and (d) desire for exploration" (p. 173). A career education activity that Miller has used with elementary school children is called "Student as Worker" (Miller, 1988, p. 246). Students pretend that being a student at school is their job and answer the following questions. "What are some things that are expected of you on the job?" and "What are some things you need to do to be a good worker (that is, student?" (p. 246). This activity helps students to explore rules, regulations and expectations related to work and school, while it also encourages them to realize that "the requirements for being a student and for being an adult worker are similar" (p. 248).

In the upper elementary grades, career development activities can become increasingly sophisticated and realistic without losing their appeal. "Relevant" experiences must be provided and actual work opportunities, even if limited, should be available.

"Mission Venus" (Harvath, 1980) is an excellent activity for students in this age group. According to Miller (1989) it involves:

1. *Informing students that a space shuttle will be sent to Venus on which only machines can be sent to do the work, along with some astronauts who have been equipped with special atmosphere-resistant suits.*
2. *Each student taking the role of a specific occupation which might include a dentist, mother, father, nurse, teacher, doctor, veterinarian, draftsperson, engineer, or manager.*
3. *Students having the responsibility of designing a machine to do the work of their occupation. They are required to (a) draw the machine and place labels on all parts and (b) include with their machines a set of directions which describe the function of the machine to the astronaut.*
4. *Asking students to discuss the significance of people and human interaction while including a "caution" for each machine which lists its drawbacks.*
5. *Discussing the activity following the presentations.*

This activity is useful in reinforcing the responsibilities of planfulness and decision-making in students.

> *Children at the elementary school level enjoy "let's pretend." They roam the world, assume a multitude of roles, and run a gamut of unbelievable experiences in their make-believe worlds. It is an ideal age to capitalize on their imagination in stimulating their acquaintance with the world of work. Role-playing and simulation projects are popular techniques suited to this purpose.*

Among the many interesting activities noted in elementary schools have been those simulating preparation of astronaut crews for a trip into outer space or to a specific planet, the establishment and operation of in-school post-offices, making a movie, running a school store, publishing a school newspaper, and setting up a "factory" that produces a saleable product for a reasonable profit—complete with advertising and sales personnel.

Career Development Activities in the Community

During elementary school years, pupils should expand contacts and deepen understandings of the community. Such contacts are particularly appropriate to such subject matter areas as history, government, economics, and geography. In fact, there is hardly a subject matter which cannot find enriching examples in community life.

Every community has a wide variety of careers and workers. A review of local census and employment data will usually indicate the diversity of careers in even the smallest community. A simple listing of every career which they can identify in their community will illustrate this point to students.

Careers are dependent on each other. Pupils can select a career and show dependent relationships with other careers. For example, the doctor needs (1) the nurse to assist him or her; (2) the postal carrier to deliver needed goods; (2) the pharmacist to prepare prescriptions; (4) the bank to handle the physician's money; and (5) stores to provide the physician with food and clothing. . .

One's career opportunities in any community are related to need versus supply plus the individual's own educational and experiential background. Youth should also become aware of the uncertainties of employment and the problems of the underemployed and jobless.

All honest careers in the community are important and make a contribution to society. It is important to stress respect for one's fellow worker regardless of what he or she does, where it is done, or how much one earns for it. Discriminatory practices and prejudices directed at low-income workers and disadvantaged minority groups can also be appropriately discussed at this junction.

One activity that can lead into a discussion of discriminating and prejudicial practices is one which Tomlinson (1991) used in dealing with children who were putting down others because of differences. The counselor enters the classroom with stick-on dots, covering his or her face, arms, hands, and neck. The students are encouraged to ask questions of the counselor that show curiosity and interest.

They also practice making statements which demonstrate caring and acceptance to the counselor even though he or she appears different. Various objectives associated with this activity include:

1. *helping children understand differences in one another;*
2. *assisting the children in acknowledging differences;*
3. *assisting the children in accepting and valuing differences;*
4. *providing children with practice and positive reinforcement for displaying interest in one's differences (p. 233).*

Counselors can use this activity as a way to facilitate students' discussion of what it is like to feel different, inferior, and/or excluded. They can encourage students to explore careers in which a person is contributing significantly to society, although the occupation might not be regarded as a high status field. The counselor can have the children imagine that they are someone working in a job of low monetary compensation and status and that they are criticized and discriminated against. Then the counselor can have each child write a short story telling what it was like to be in such a position. Finally a discussion of the stories should take place. Children are highly influenced by these types of activities as they allow the children to express concerns which they might not understand or have the opportunity to discuss in other situations.

Community Career Surveys These surveys can involve students in a variety of career information gathering activities. Surveys can be conducted through class group projects of all careers represented by pupils' parents or of all the different kinds of workers pupils notice over a specific period of time. Career checklists, graphs, charts, and posters may be used to stimulate the collection and presentation of findings.

Reviewing help wanted and situation wanted ads in the local newspaper covering a selected time span may provide insights into job needs and requirements as well as how one may use this source in seeking a job. Comparing similar ads from the local newspaper's back issue file for the same day last year and five, ten, and perhaps even twenty years ago will enable pupils to better understand changes in the career structure of their community and in working conditions and salaries over a period of time. Other comparisons may also be made utilizing newspapers representing several communities. Pupils might also write papers or present oral reports contrasting "worker's world" of today with the "worker's world" of twenty years ago. In such an assignment they might even speculate on the world of work twenty years in the future.

Model Community Projects A project of this nature requires an entire class to work together. It promises both enjoyment and information for the student. In such a project the pupils set out to design their model community. They draw up their plans, determine zoning and other restrictions, and identify the industries and careers of adults living in their community. They may even go further and adopt the role of workers in the community and describe this role to their "fellow workers."

A reversal of this procedure can also be interesting. Pupils may identify their career interests first and then seek to build a community around these jobs noting the kinds of industries needed, critical careers where workers might have to be recruited, and other resultant problems. . . .

Career Days Such traditional secondary school activities as career conferences, career novels, and career days can also be useful in providing elementary students with the opportunity to meet individually or in small groups with one or more representatives of specific career areas. At the elementary level, these activities should not be planned on the grandiose scale witnessed in some secondary school "days" but will be more effective if limited in number and kept informal.

Another approach, particularly appropriate to the elementary pupil, is one in which each pupil chooses a career and prepares to represent this career to the rest of the class. He or she might, for example, describe the history of the job, past and present working conditions, general public importance, training required, and future prospects for workers in the field. To increase realism in his or her presentation, one might dress in clothing appropriate to the job and even present tools or equipment used.

"Career Days" may also focus on certain occupational areas such as education, women in the world of work, traveling jobs, or sports. . . .

The Field Trip This is a traditional, yet still worthwhile activity, for acquainting the elementary school pupil with careers and industries within one's community and the immediate geographic area. The potential is limited only by the career-industrial resources of the area and the "effectiveness" of the activity itself.

Whether or not a field trip is a worthwhile educational experience or simply a get-out-of-school excursion will depend on how well it has been planned. This planning includes the preparatory details, the field trip results, and the follow-through.

The primary responsibility for adequate preparatory planning rests with the classroom teacher. This planning may be shared with, and should involve, the pupils who will participate and the representatives of the site to be visited. Parents may also be involved. This planning would include administrative and transportation arrangements, the identification of field trip objectives, specifics to observe for, possible questions to ask, and anticipated follow-through.

Guide sheets, time tables, and checklists can give direction to the field trip itself. Plans should be made for rest stops and, where warranted, meals. Field trip "discipline" is important in preventing stragglers, undue confusion, and diversion from the purpose of the experience. Provisions should also be made for those pupils of the group who may not be participating.

Summary

Career development is an important component of the individual's total development at all educational levels. In the elementary school, the opportunity exists to provide elementary school pupils with an appropriate foundation of career information and competencies for later career planning and decision-making.

Acquisition of information and competencies is near mandatory as a result of the complexity of the world of work; the complexity of career preparation; the need for individuals to develop broader concepts of the world of work; the importance of career development in human development; and the individual's total development and the important assistance it can give to the potentially disadvantaged.

Theories of career decision-making, though limited in some respects, are noted as providing indicators for how individuals may ultimately arrive at a career choice. Career competencies desired in elementary pupils are indicated and examples of resources and experiences are discussed.

Of course, the elementary school counselor has a responsibility and leadership role in the development of a planned schoolwide program for acquiring information and developing these competencies. Included here is a list of children's books with occupational models that are atypical by sex.

Children's Books with Occupational Models that are Atypical by Sex (Miller, R. M., 1986, p.254)

Bauer, C.F. (1981). *My mom travels a lot* (New York: Frederick Warne). A child reports on the good and bad points of her mother's work.

Burton, V.L. (1967). *Katy and the big snow* (Boston: Houghton Mifflin). Katy is a tractor who is strong enough to plow out an entire snowed-in city.

Eichler, M. (1971). *Martin's father* (Chapel Hill, NC: Lollipop Power). A simple story of a nurturing father who performs all of the housekeeping tasks.

Foote. P. (1980). *Girls can be anything they want* (New York: Julian Messner). The true stories of women in nontraditional careers such as law, psychiatry, firefighting, politics (for grades five and up).

Goble, P. (1978). *The girl who loved wild horses* (Scarsdale, NY: Bradbury Press). A Native-American girl gets separated from her family while riding horses in a storm. When her parents find her, the girl decides she prefers the independence of living with horses.

Hughes, S. (1977). *George the babysitter* (Englewood Cliffs, NJ: Prentice-Hall). George babysits for three children while their mother is working. George washes dishes and clothes and cleans house.

Mendoza, G. (1981). *Need a house? Call Ms. Mouse!* (New York: Grossett & Dunlap). Henrietta is a world famous decorator, artist, designer, builder, and creator. She designs homes for a cat, a squirrel, a trout, a mole, and a worm.

Pogrebin, L. C. (1981). *Stories for free children* (New York: Ms. Foundation). A collection of short stories that have been published in Ms. Magazine.

Reavin, S. (1971) *Hurrah for Captain Jane* (New York: Parents Magazine Press). While in the bathtub, Jane fantasizes about being the first woman captain of an ocean liner.

Williams, J. (1973). *Petronella* (New York: Parents Magazine Press). A smart princess rescues a prince.

Wolde, G. (1972) *Tommy goes to the doctor* (Boston, MA: Houghton Mifflin). Tommy treats his teddy bear just like the doctor (a woman) treated him.

Chapter 8

Prevention

It is better to build children
than to repair men and women
-ANONYMOUS

Introduction: The Role of Prevention in the Elementary School

Adults in the United States are prevention conscious today. We are constantly reminded of the danger signs of cancer; foods to avoid and foods we can eat for a healthy tomorrow; to meditate an hour each day (when the boss isn't looking) to prevent stress; to stuff ourselves with oat bran to lower our cholesterol and prevent heart attack; to brush with fluoride toothpaste to prevent tooth decay, etc., etc. . .nor are we neglected by the commercial entrepreneurs whose major nutrition and vitamin formulas promise to prevent nearly every physical disorder known to humankind including miracle cremes that prevent aging (wrinkling).

While the "prevention and wellness revolution" appears to be rapidly—and with good cause—raising the health consciousness of adults, a quieter but equally important prevention and wellness movement involving our children has been taking place in our nation's elementary schools. This movement has as its goals the psychological, physiological, and sociological well-being of our children of today—our adults of tomorrow. It recognizes that prevention is always more desirable than cure. It further recognizes that such social disorders as substance abuse, AIDS, teen pregnancies, school dropouts, crime, and delinquency, and so on, can never be eliminated by remediation and treatment—quite the opposite in fact! It also is congruent with the fact that to be successful, prevention efforts must occur well in advance of the possible onset of the undesired disorder. Too, this movement recognizes that to be successful, prevention programs must impact populations—not just individuals—and that these populations are most effectively dealt with when they are within organizational structures. Such populations are frequently labeled for program identification purposes as at-risk. At-risk children can be viewed as those who, according to present indicators, are considered highly likely to experience some undesirable outcome and/or behavior in the future, such as substance abuse, child abuse, school dropout, juvenile delinquency, and so on. Common indicators of at-risk children most frequently include at least several of the following: failing grades, disruptive behavior, poverty background, frequent absences, stress, and social immaturity.

These programs recognize that personal habits conducive to prevention and wellness must be established early and constantly reinforced for a healthy adulthood.

Hence, from every standpoint, the elementary school, is the ideal setting for initiating programs of prevention and wellness. Further, recent studies indicate that elementary schools are cognizant of this responsibility. For example, a study by Gibson (1989) reported that 85 percent of 96 elementary schools surveyed reported prevention as a major emphasis of their programs and all other schools reported some preventive and related wellness activities. Table 8–1 presents the prevention objectives of these elementary school counseling and guidance programs.

Other studies have reported positive outcomes from preventive activities. A number of these (Cobb and Richards, 1983; Myrick and Dixon, 1985), Myrick, Merbell and Swanson, 1986) reported programs for the prevention of maladaptive social behavior, which resulted in improved attitudes and behaviors as the result of classroom guidance activities, including small-group sessions. Chandler, Weissberg, Cowen, and Guarez (1984) reported positive results for fourth-grade

TABLE 8–1 Prevention Objectives of Elementary School Counseling and Guidance Programs

Prevention Objectives	Percentage
1. To prevent child and/or sexual abuse	69.7
2. To prevent substance abuse	64.9
3. To promote self-concept development	35.8
4. To promote personal safety	17.6
5. To promote social-skills development	15.0
6. To prevent teenage pregnancy	6.3
7. To prevent premature school leaving	4.4
8. To prevent school vandalism	2.1

From "Prevention and the elementary school counselor" by R. L. Gibson, 1989, *Journal of Elementary School Guidance and Counseling*, 24, p. 34. Copyright 1989 by the American Counseling Association. Reprinted by permission.

children who had been seen two to five years earlier in a prevention intervention program for children who were experiencing school adjustment problems. Bleck and Bleck (1982) reported that third-grade pupils who participated in a series of group counseling sessions for five weeks showed significant improvement in both self-concept scores and the disrespect defiance factor, when compared to the control group. Anderson and Lemoncelli (1982) used assessment data as a basis for identifying pupils when behavior would place them at risk and then designed strategies for behavior improvement. Results indicated success of these programs (Gibson, 1989, pp. 30-31).

Early intervention with low-achieving elementary school students was effective in preventing their continued underachievement in studies reported by Jackson, Cleveland, and Merander (1975) and Esters and Levant (1983). The former study provided the experimental group with two and one-half years of counseling and consultation directed primarily at parents and teachers. This study found differences in favor of the counseled students over those in the control group. The Esters and Levant study used parent training for parents and self-esteem groups for students (Gibson, 1989, p. 31).

Blotner and Lilly (1986) and Forman and Neal (1987) reported comprehensive school-based substance abuse prevention programs. These programs provided drug education, peer intervention, and behavioral self-management programs. Positive changes in student attitudes toward drugs resulted (Gibson, 1989, p. 32).

Thus, it can be concluded that: (1) prevention is preferable to remediation; (2) the elementary school is the prime setting for organized programs of prevention; and (3) programs of prevention have been successful with elementary school populations. The sections of this chapter which follow will examine such major goals of prevention programs as building self-esteem, the development of coping and stress management skills, and nutrition and wellness. Special prevention concerns such as substance abuse, child abuse, school dropouts and so on, will also be discussed.

Prevention Through Building Self-Esteem in Children

The core or center piece of an effective prevention program in the elementary school has to be the building of self-esteem in children. This development of self-esteem or a positive self-concept is significant inasmuch as one's view of self is a major determinant in the development of one's behavior: in the security one feels and in the development of self-respect. The development of this behavior, which enables an individual to interact positively and productively with others, is a part of the socialization process that takes place for all children in the elementary school. This development cannot be left to chance but requires careful planning, since it is evident that to relate effectively to others, the child must first of all feel good about him or herself. In this regard, Conyne (1987), Dodge (1983) and others have cited a body of evidence that has accumulated to demonstrate that children who cannot adjust during their elementary school years are at high risk for a variety of later problems including excessive absenteeism, dropping out from school, delinquency, and psychiatric impairment. To this we might add that they are also more prone to substance abuse, irresponsible sexual behavior, and criminal activity. Thus, the development of the child's self-esteem is a major prevention strategy in efforts to deal with many of the major problems confronting our society.

In planning for this development we, of course, recognize that the formation of the child's self-esteem is acquired from and is a result of interactions with others. Charles Horton Cooley (1864-1929) coined the phrase "looking-glass self" to refer to the origins and nature of self-concepts. McGee (1980) described the three elements of this self-concept as

> *(l) our imagination or image of how we appear or present ourselves to others; (2) an imagination or image of the other's judgment of that appearance or presentation; and (3) some self-feeling about that judgment, such as pride or shame that another sees us in that way. Thus, we accumulate a set of beliefs and evaluations about ourselves, and about whom and what we are and what that means in our society. This is our self-concept. (McGee, 1980, p. 88)*

Lickona (1988) points out that

> *Building self-esteem in the elementary school years fosters the sense of competence and mastery that is at the core of the child's self-concept. Building self-esteem also teaches children to value themselves as persons, to have the kind of respect for themselves that enables them to stand up for their rights and command the respect of others. (Annual Editions/Educational Psychology, 89/90, p. 48)*

Some of the goals of public education are: to prepare our children to enter the world of work; to be well-equipped with problem-solving skills and task completion skills; to instill the desire to be the best person they can be; to provide maintenance of a positive self-concept; to experience successful careers at individual aptitude levels; to prepare them to live satisfying personal lives; and to be assets to society. The list is not exhaustive. Yet, to prepare children to fulfill those aspects of their lives is to prepare children to meet most any challenge in the future.

How does a positive self-concept help a child achieve? It is enabling. It is the inner feeling and cognitive belief that one is worthwhile. It is enabling because if children believe in themselves—if they believe they can do something, then they can. Often determination accompanies a positive self-concept. Similarly, self-efficacy, "the belief that you can execute behavior to achieve an outcome" can also be derived from a positive self-concept. According to Albert Bandura's social cognitive theory (1977), children can be all they believe they can be. Bandura stated in the *American Psychologist* (1989), "There is a growing body of evidence that human attainments and positive well-being require an optimistic sense of personal efficacy (Bandura, 1989). This is because ordinary social realities are strewn with difficulties. They are full of impediments, failures, adversities, setbacks, frustrations, and inequities. People must have a robust sense of personal efficacy to sustain the perserverant effort needed to succeed" (p. 1176). To equip young children as early as possible with "perseverance and strong beliefs in themselves" is an exercise in prevention.

The importance of self-esteem or the affective dimension of self-concept in children cannot be overemphasized. For example, Clemes and Dean (1981) found that children with high self-esteem acted positively, assumed responsibility, tolerated frustration well, felt able to influence their environments, and were proud of their accomplishments. On the other hand, children with low self-esteem were easily manipulated by others, were easily frustrated, blamed others for their failures, and avoided difficult situations. Similarly, Wiggins (1987) found a positive correlation between self-esteem scores and earned grades for boys and girls in grades 4, 6, 8, 10 and 12 (Childers, Jr., 1989, p. 204). The importance of successful, confidence-building experiences for children in building their self-esteem is stressed repeatedly in educational and psychological literature.

Jarolimek and Foster (1989) point out that it is imperative:

> *that the teacher establish a social climate and a classroom environment where children learn to feel good about themselves. It should be a place in which people are more valued than things. It must be a place where everyone counts for something. Whether or not they have learning problems, as almost everyone does at some time, is beside the point. This should have nothing to do with making children feel that they are worthy human beings. Human beings of any age, but most especially the young, should not have to prove their worth. The teacher must convey genuine affection for the children.*
>
> *Healthy self-images develop in caring environments that help children build backlogs of success experiences. Self-images are destroyed in environments in which children get the impression that no one really cares about them, and where they experience constant failure. Also, it is doubtful whether children can perceive themselves positively if they do not have a personal liking for the teacher, or if they feel the teacher does not like them. It is the teacher, therefore, who sets the good emotional climate of the classroom, the climate that facilitates social interaction based on trust, respect, and integrity. (p. 248) (Reprinted with permission of Macmillan Publishing Company from* Teaching and Learning in the Elementary School *by John Jarolimek and Clifford D. Foster, Sr. Copyright 1989 by Macmillan Publishing Company.)*

In any organized effort for developing pupil self-esteem, the classroom teacher and school counselor must work closely together. Burnett (1983) noted that during the 1970s and 1980s,

> *there has been a push to have children exposed to self-concept programs in the classroom with the teacher as a leader. Schulman, Ford, and Bush (1973)*

> *reported that a self-concept unit presented to 502 children in 33 classrooms produced significant changes in the pupil's self-concept as measured by instruments devised by the authors. In 1970 the* Developing Understanding of Self and Others (DUSO) Kit *was devised (Dinkmeyer, 1970) for use in the classroom by teachers. The DUSO Kit is structured for implementation during 1 or 2 school years. Canfield and Wells (1976) contributed to the area of self-concept enhancement with their book,* One Hundred Ways to Enhance Self-Concept in the Classroom. *Again, their ideas and activities are for use in the classroom with the teacher as leader. (1983, p. 101)*

Various commercial companies have also developed activities for teacher (or counselor) use in improving self-esteem in the elementary classroom. Other examples of specific activities are classroom bulletin board displays highlighting "pupils of the week" or "ego ads" in which individual student strengths are advertised. Collages can be prepared in which students cut out ads and other pictures from magazines and newspapers which are descriptive of their own traits and characteristics and paste them on art paper or cardboard for display. Compliment cards and "strength bombardment" exercises are helpful as well as fun.

Childers (1989) describes the activity called "Looking at Yourself Through Loving Eyes" as an activity that can be helpful in increasing self-esteem in school-age children in various settings. These include one-to-one work, group counseling, and classroom guidance. There are seven steps for implementing this exercise. They include:

Step 1: Establish the experience of being an artist.
Step 2: Identify someone you know who loves you.
Step 3: Describe to yourself the characteristics that make that person special.
Step 4: Draw a picture of the person who loves you.
Step 5: Imagine being this special person and able to see yourself through his or her loving eyes.
Step 6: Describe and draw what they love about the person they saw through loving eyes.
Step 7: Re-associate into own body, bring back lovable feelings. (p. 205-206)

Childers (1989) emphasizes the importance of reassuring children early in the activity that the artistic quality of their work is not going to be evaluated. Art is used because for many children drawing appears to be a comfortable method of expressing themselves. In some situations, children cannot identify anyone who loves them or who has ever loved them. Childers (1989) suggests that the counselor do the following in helping the child create a person who he or she knows loves him or her by saying:

> *Pretend for a moment, as if this special person existed—this person who loves you. How would you describe this person's special qualities? How would you*

describe his or her interactions with you? What qualities does he or she possess that makes him or her so valued, so special to you? If you were to name this special person, what name would you give him or her? As you continue to listen to your own description of ____ (name of this loving person), begin to be aware of the emerging feelings within you. Perhaps you are beginning to experience feelings of loving, caring, and prizing. Please continue, for a few minutes, to think about how you would describe this special person who loves you. (p. 206-207)

At the completion of the activity, it is suggested that each student consider giving this picture to the person who loves him or her. The completed drawings can be used in one-to-one counseling, small group work, and classroom guidance activities as stimuli to encourage self-esteem discussion. Teachers can also be asked by the counselor to hang the pictures up in the classroom. For a more detailed description of the activity, refer to "Looking at Yourself Through Loving Eyes," by John H. Childers, Jr., in Volume 23 of the *Journal of Elementary School Guidance and Counseling*, 1989.

In addition to classroom programs for enhancing self-esteem, the elementary school counselor may run small group sessions for this purpose. These small groups may be designed to serve special populations. In fact, Burnett (1983) states that much of the literature

regarding small group self-enhancement or affective education refers to programs directed toward specific populations. The groups of children include first-grade repeaters (Fournier, 1977), seventh grade behavior problems (McCurdy, Ciucevich and Walker, 1977), gifted children (Gumaer and Voorneveld, 1975), and children of divorce (Green, 1978). The results of these studies seem to indicate that children have more positive attitudes and feelings about themselves after being exposed to a self-enhancement program. (Burnett, p. 101)

Developing Coping Skills

Counselors will come in contact with many children whose circumstances at home create for them a state of constant emotional turmoil. Some examples are: alcoholic or substance-abusing parents, families in transition, and transient families. Children often live in dysfunctional families and as a result need help coping with situations out of their control. It is likely that these children will not have positive self-concepts. Of course, helping these children to build a positive self-concept is critical. In this regard, children can benefit from individual or small group counseling in which they are taught basic coping skills. These groups could include children from a wide variety of different situations including those previously indicated. For example, sometimes children face temporary challenges with which they need help to cope, such as moving to a new school and community. Counselors provide children with hope and the skills to cope with temporary or semi-permanent situations.

Often children become hopeless when conditions appear to be out of their control. Hopelessness is derived from helplessness because generally they feel they are helpless to change anything in their environment.

> *Learned helplessness is a phenomenon that occurs when people are repeatedly exposed to situations over which they do not have control . . . . Once children develop learned helplessness behaviors, they are reluctant to attempt the initial task in which failure was experienced and tend to avoid related activities . . . . other behaviors displayed are listlessness, passivity, depression, lack of motivation, and negative beliefs about oneself and abilities. Another characteristic of children who develop learned helplessness is a difficulty in seeing relationships between responses and outcomes. As a result, many children do not recognize the successes that they have achieved, whereas, on the other hand, they take personal responsibility for all perceived failures.* (Greer and Wethered, 1987, p. 157)

Not knowing how to cope in situations of discomfort may eventually lead to juvenile delinquency, school dropouts, poor grades, and problems with peers and teachers. Some children may give up easily when faced with tasks at school, cry, throw temper tantrums, or withdraw. These are symptoms that can alert teachers and counselors to their need.

How can counselors help these children cope with their less than perfect worlds? Individual counseling is usually desirable initially and then small groups which can become good, safe places to work and explore options. It is in these settings that counselors teach children coping skills. Again the instillation of hope is critical from the beginning. Let them know there are ways of getting through tough times in their lives. Also, it is helpful when appropriate to discuss that life doesn't have to be that way when they grow up. Ask them what things they would change and how. What things, if any, are they able to change now? What would help them feel better under these circumstances? Invite these young children/clients to tell you and others how it feels to be them. When they become specifically in touch with the unpleasant factors, counselors can help them choose coping strategies suitable for each individual situation. What strategies help children cope? One technique is to have children think of, write, and discuss things they enjoy doing. This enables them to build a repertoire of activities to which they may turn when they feel sad and hopeless. (Children may list things such as: call a friend and talk, go to a friend's house, ride bikes, take a walk, play a game, and listen to music.) Another approach is to teach children to use imagery by using imagery with them in the group setting. Encourage them to create their own imagination vacations in times of need.

Counselors can also assist children in breaking the helplessness cycle by teaching them to identify realistic reasons for failure and success. They can point out the reasons for failure by emphasizing those causes that are specific to the incident. Greer and Wethered (1987) emphasize that children can learn how to recognize personal success experiences related to their own ability (an internal, consistent quality) as well as learn skills which can be utilized in various situations (global). Table 8–2 lists strategies that counselors can use in dealing with children's beliefs about reasons for their failure or success. These reasons are referred to as attributions and they are categorized as either internal-external (who or what do the children see as the reason for the lack of control), consistent-inconsistent (how consistent does the child perceive the lack of control to be?), and global-specific (How widespread is the helplessness? Does it occur for a single task or across a number of activities?). Table 8–2 suggests various strategies that counselors can use in assisting children with these specified attributions.

It is important to make children aware that they have choices. Even in the confines of their homes they can choose activities that are calming. Making them aware of alternative activities is helpful in guiding them to more useful and less stressful experiences. Even though circumstances may be out of their control, they may stay in control of themselves by choosing activities that help them feel better. They learn to cope by distracting themselves and understanding that someday life can be different. They learn to talk through difficult situations with friends or the counselor. They must endure unpleasant circumstances sometimes now, but they may use these times to be creative. They can learn what they do not want to be when they grow up!

Health and Wellness

The individual elementary school pupil's developing physical and mental health is of concern to all the school's professional personnel. Along with the child's parents, the classroom teacher is the daily observer of the child's wellness. The elementary school counselor obviously must consult continuously with both parents and teachers regarding the development and maintenance of programs for monitoring and facilitating pupil wellness.

Among the many dimensions of wellness is that most basic one of the healthy diet. While the public in general has become more health food conscious, the junk food industries are spending millions annually to attract children to sugared cereals, fatty french fries and burgers, carbonated beverages, and a holocaust of candies, cakes, and other sweets. Not surprisingly, many children are malnourished in terms of the absence of basic nutritional needs and sometimes even in the number of calories consumed. A "check" on the child's diet may be aided by asking children to keep a careful record over a week or two of everything they've eaten, by specific meals and between meal periods. The results of these exercises are usually dismaying. At this point, the counselor may want to enlist the help of nutritional specialists, such as school dieticians, home economics teachers from the high school, nutritional specialists from local hospitals, and so on, to fight television food propaganda with "food facts" disseminated to both children and their parents through a variety of means, such as classroom and parent teacher association presentations, newsletters, healthy menus, bulletin board displays, "healthy eating week," and so on.

TABLE 8–2 Counselor Strategies for Specific Attributions

Attributions	Student verbalizations	Counselor strategies
Internal	I must be dumb. I try and try, but I can't do this stuff. I don't understand math. I just can't spell.	Focus on less personal responsibility. Cite external influences.
External	I couldn't hear what to do because it was so noisy outside. I just didn't study hard enough. My dog ate it. My test was blurry.	When appropriate, validate external attribution. Encourage accurate attributions.
Consistent	I never do that right. I always have trouble with that. I can never please my teacher.	Focus on past control and successes achieved. Reinforce that the student has, in fact, done "it" correctly. Stress that this failure was not part of a consistent predictable pattern.
Inconsistent	Sometimes I can do it right and sometimes I can't. I only got a few wrong this time.	Reinforce the accuracy of the student's observations and partial successes. Discuss success and failures.
Global	I have this same problem in all of my classes. Nobody likes me. I can't do any thing right.	Focus on control and successful experiences. Minimize the global attribution.
Specific	I can't do subtraction problems. That's only hard for me when I do it on the blackboard. My teacher doesn't like my writing.	When appropriate validate specific attribution. Reinforce successes that are accepted by the student.

From "Learned helplessness and the elementary student: Implications for counselors," by J. G. Greer and C. E. Wethered, 1987. *Journal of Elementary School Guidance and Counseling*, 22, p. 162. Copyright 1987 by the American Counseling Association. Reprinted by permission.

Tuckman and Hinkle (1986) emphasize that children are made to spend school time becoming proficient in such subjects as math and reading and that if we as educators want fitness to happen, we must educate children in this direction.

> *Educating children for fitness means more than telling them about it; it means having them engage in fitness producing exercise. Exercise . . . may not inherently be any more "fun" for children than any other kind of activity aimed at self-improvement. But it is equally important.(Tuckman and Hinkle, 1986, p. 34).*

They insist further that we must include girls as well as boys and ensure that exercise is maintained among the girls. Girls can and should experience the needed benefits of exercise. Considering their potential for increased body fat in adolescence, elementary school is a prime time for them to begin fitness habits that can prevent excessive gains in weight in the future (Tuckman and Hinkle, 1986).

As a helping professional, the elementary school counselor also has the responsibility of maintaining linkages with the health care helping professionals employed by the school system including the school nurse, school dental technician, school eye care clinician, and those who serve the children of the community, doctors, dentists, and other medical specialists. Governmental health agencies can also make valuable contributions to school health care programs. Persons from the various healthcare professions can be invited in to the school to speak to the children. This might take place as part of a career guidance activity where both future health and future careers are discussed.

In addition to attention to the physical well-being of the elementary school child, his or her mental health must also be given planned attention. As often noted, physical and mental health are frequently interrelated and both affect the child's performance in school. Certainly the previously discussed needs to build self-esteem and develop adequate coping styles are major contributors to the mental health of the elementary school pupil. Another broad general category of concern in this area is stress and its management. While considerable public attention has been focused on the impact of stress on the mental health of adults, we must also recognize that the complex demands of everyday living can be equally stressful to children who are even less prepared to cope or adapt and who have even less control of their world. Typical stressors for youngsters include: prolonged absence of a parent, separation, or divorce; change in parent's health or employment; change in family responsibility or income; addition or loss of a sibling; family vacations (or lack of them); loss of a friend; death of a pet; illness and injury; physical growth and puberty; change of teacher or school; changes within the school system, such as in the lunch programs or busing arrangements; academic difficulties and successes; racial or cultural tensions; and peer pressure and developmental issues. Special needs groups may face additional, unique stressors. (Herbert, 1983, p. 1)

A variety of approaches have been successfully utilized to assist the prevention and management of stress by young children. These include humorous exercises that generate laughter and play activities (for example, clay modeling, flower planting, puppets, blocks, games, musical activities, exercising, relaxation techniques, and guided imagery). Counselors may use small groups to develop coping skills and individual counseling may be utilized as well.

Arming children with tools for combating stress can assist them in reducing stress-related disorders in later life (Zaichkowsky, Zaichkowsky, and Yeager, 1986). One stress management program, which was designed to help children learn how to deal with stress, was implemented with children in grades one through four in two school districts. The following concepts were focused on throughout the program:

1. *Theoretical lessons focusing on what stress is, how the body responds, and student perceptions of stress*
2. *Abdominal breathing exercise*
3. *Progressive muscular relaxation exercise*
4. *Mental imagery exercises*
5. *Practice of techniques with the use of biofeedback apparatus (Zaichkowsky, Zaichkowsky, and Yeager, 1986, p. 262)*

Special Prevention Concerns

Substance Abuse Prevention

It is doubtful that any issue in the history of American education has received the prevention attention that has been focused on substance abuse in recent years. From former First Lady Nancy Reagan's "Just Say No" effort to more formally organized programs, a wide range of prevention efforts have reflected the nation's concern that our elementary children are indeed an "endangered species," since they are threatened by the growing epidemic of drugs and alcohol usage among our youth of elementary school age. While an enormous body of literature has been written in recent years describing existing programs or suggesting new approaches, very little of it is useful to practicing counselors seeking to identify empirically, verifiable successful prevention programs (Horan, Kerns, and Olson, 1988).

Lacking "absolute" guidelines at this point, counselors must turn to the "next best" lineup of possibilities, guidelines that seem to offer promise. For example, Resnick (1988) does suggest that after two decades of trial and error some basic premises are beginning to emerge as follows:

1. *It is time to put behind us the notion of a "quick fix" to the drug problem. School assemblies, informational pamphlets, and even widely publicized drug awareness and health events are not enough. Although they can be helpful in a more comprehensive prevention effort, there is little evidence that, by themselves and isolated from other prevention activities, they can change young people's behavior.*

2. *Parent and family involvement is central to effective prevention programming. At one time, it was considered helpful and desirable; increasingly, it is being recognized as a key element.*
3. *Effective prevention programming takes time. A commitment of as much as three to five years is not overly ambitious. This does not mean that after three to five years a prevention program is "over." Rather, by that time, it should have been thoroughly internalized and institutionalized.*
4. *Good drug education and prevention programs are positive, constructive elements in the life of a school and its community. They lead to a community-wide emphasis on healthy living, positive activities for youth, improved education, and family involvement. A good program does not focus exclusively on the drug and alcohol problem; rather, it promotes a long-lasting, community-wide commitment to the development of human potential, especially the well-being of children and youth.*
5. *For school-based programs, effective prevention programming is closely associated with better teaching, happier and more successful kids, more involved parents—in a nutshell, better schools. (Resnik, 1988, p. 93)*

In addition, other factors frequently mentioned in surveys of programs showing promise are: (a) the developing of profiles for identifying pupils who are highly vulnerable—viewed as "at risk"; (b) recognizing the prime factor of "peer pressure," how to use it positively, such as peer tutoring programs and how to combat its negative pressures, since research shows a high correlation between an individual's drug use and that of his or her friends; (c) training in social skills and assertiveness on the assumption that many turn to substances when they are socially rejected or limited and that learning to be assertive may help youth offset peer pressures; (d) values clarification techniques; and (e) working to provide positive school experiences for all elementary pupils.

As studies indicate, pupils in the early elementary years who fail, who exhibit discipline problems, and who are socially isolated are more apt to encounter substance abuse problems ten years later (Bernard, Fafoglia, and Perone, 1987). These programs which show promise can help these troubled children avoid turning to drugs as a solution to their problems. However, they must be implemented in early elementary school so the children become aware of the dangers of drug use and the healthy outlets for confronting problems.

Finally, for this section, two conclusions are obvious: (1) any and every elementary school counseling program must develop a rigorous program of substance abuse prevention; and (2) substance abuse is a complex and difficult problem to attack that will require great skill, knowledge, use of a wide range of tactics, local follow-up studies to verify "what works," and unswerving persistence.

Bradley (1988) indicates that several programs have been developed for sequential use with elementary school-age children. They address the topics of self-esteem and decision-making and provide accurate information on substances that are abused. They are suitable for children from kindergarten to sixth grade. The programs include the following:

- "Here's Looking at You"
  This program was developed by the National Institute on Alcohol Abuse and Alcoholism
- *CASPAR* - Cambridge and Somerville Program for Alcoholism Rehabilitation
- *Project Charlie* (Chemical Abuse Resolution Lies in Education (Guild, 1984).

Specific organizations, such as *Children are People, Inc.* (Lerner and Naiditch, 1985), provide training and various materials to assist persons in working with children of substance abusers.

Bradley (1988) encourages counselors to provide children the opportunity to participate in a group that focuses on substance abuse so that they can receive the education and support that is necessary in acquiring healthy coping skills and breaking the family pattern of chemical dependency.

Preventing the Abuse of Children

Millions of elementary children are abused physically, sexually, and psychologically every year. Many of them are never reported, perhaps not even noticed by others and very few appropriately treated.

Psychological damage is almost always an outcome of the sexual and physical abuse of children. Cooney (1991) describes the emotional effects of sexual abuse as the following:

1. The loss of childhood *Children who are abused have been introduced to the adult world of sexuality .... Victims of sexual abuse are worried about whether "it" will happen again tonight and may have trouble fitting in with other children.*
2. Guilt *Children who are abused often feel that they are somehow responsible for the abuse .... they feel that they are bad because of what they were forced to do. The truth is that children do not control adults. Nothing that a child says or does or wears causes him or her to be abused .... The child is a victim and is no more responsible than is the victim of a hit-and-run driver.*
3. Low self-esteem *Because sexual abuse involves sexual activity that children eventually realize is inappropriate, victims often feel that they are bad. They wrongly believe that they are not as good as their peers or as deserving of praise or recognition. If something good happens to them or someone acknowledges their accomplishments, victims are inclined to believe that they do not deserve recognition....*
4. Many kinds of fear are associated with sexual abuse *Some victims have a constant fear of physical abuse.... Separate from concerns about physical harm are the fears of what will happen if the sexual abuse were discovered. The abuser may tell the child that if anyone finds out about what has been going on the child*

will be put in jail or in a detention center or taken away from the family. There may also be threats about other family members: "Your mother will have a heart attack". . . . These are very real possibilities to children who are terrified that they might be responsible for the death or the dissolution of the family. . . . Victims of sexual abuse may be in a constant state of fear and anxiety about the next incident of molestation. They may lie awake at night waiting and wondering if something is going to happen.

5. Confusion *The popular image of an adult, particularly a parent, is of one who would only do good things. When a child is molested , he or she feels real confusion about right and wrong but cannot accept the possibility that Dad or Grandpa would ever do wrong. The confusion about right and wrong may cause the child to doubt his or her own judgment. Instead of concluding that the abuser is doing wrong the child often concludes that there must be something wrong with him or her for feeling uneasy or frightened about the abuse . . . .*
6. Depression *Children who are abused carry a heavy emotional burden. . . . They are carrying a secret that they are not supposed to share. The adults on whom they should be able to depend have let them down. The loneliness and guilt associated with sexual abuse may seem overwhelming. Depression may be linked to suicide attempts, drug and alcohol abuse, running away and self-abusive behavior. Eating disorders like anorexia nervosa and bulimia have been linked with the depression resulting from sexual victimization.*
7. Anger *It is a normal reaction to become angry when someone mistreats us . . . . Victims of sexual abuse are mistreated over a long period of time. They may be angry with themselves for not being able to escape the abuse. They may be angry with their father or mother who didn't notice what was happening or who didn't believe them when they tried to talk about the abuse.*
8. Inability to trust others *Sexual abuse represents a betrayal of trust. The person who was most trusted by the child has betrayed that trust . . . .*
9. Helplessness *A victim of sexual abuse feels powerless against the abuser. The abuser is in charge and controls the victim . . . . It is not unusual for the victim of sexual abuse to be victimized by others in the family or the neighborhood . . . .*
10. Attitudes toward sexuality *Adult sexuality involves mutual sharing, concern for the needs of both partners, and an aspect of respect and trust. All of these factors are absent when an adult engages in sexual activity with a minor. No matter how gentle the abuser may appear, there is no question that he is in charge. The most basic need of a child to be treated as a child is violated. Only the needs of the adult are considered in sexual abuse. Premature sexual activity has lasting effects on the victim. The victim may feel like "damaged goods."(p. 67-72)*

The International Conference on the Psychological Abuse of Children and Youth (1983), whose primary tasks were to consolidate information and provide directions for future research in the field, supported the following generic definition (cited in Hart, Germain & Brassard, 1987):

> *Psychological maltreatment of children and youth consists of acts of omission and commission which are judged on the basis of a combination of community standards and professional expertise to be psychologically damaging. Such acts are committed by individuals, singly or collectively, who by their characteristics (e.g., age, status, knowledge, organizational form) are in a position of differential power that renders a child vulnerable. Such acts damage immediately or ultimately the behavioral, cognitive, affective, or physical functioning of the child. Examples of psychological maltreatment include acts of rejecting, terrorizing, isolating, exploiting, and missocializing. (p. 6, p. 194)*

Neese (1989) states that

> *because children spend a large portion of their developmental period in the school system, promoting health and personal and social growth becomes a function of that system. Psychological maltreatment affects children in ways that can be damaging to their development and learning. Counselors are often perceived as the human relations specialists in the schools and may need to intercede on behalf of children who are being abused or neglected psychologically either by educators or peers. (p. 200)*

On the other hand, prevention programs in this area appear to be in the early development stages. One of the reasons for rather belated efforts in this arena is the involvement of the school in what in the past has been a "hush-hush" area and, secondly, invading what many consider to be the inner sanctum of the family. The latter is especially true in instances of suspected child neglect and physical and/or psychological abuse (which some parents may dismiss as appropriate disciplinary measures). Too, in the instance of sexual abuse especially, some community groups will resist any school effort to engage in what they broadly label "sex education." Thus, the mounting of successful child abuse prevention programs requires a great deal of careful planning on the part of the counseling team involved. Some suggestions for this planning include:

1. Parents must be involved. They must be assisted through educational/informational means to be prepared for their responsibilities in any successful preventive effort.
2. The support of significant community groups, individuals, and the media must be actively solicited.
3. Coordination and joint planning with school social workers, health personnel, local mental health agencies, and others as appropriate is essential.
4. Careful attention must be paid to "labeling." The use of inflammatory terminology should be avoided.
5. As in other prevention programs, at-risk children should be identified to the extent possible (for example, children whose parents were abused as children are at greater risk for abuse themselves).
6. Support groups and individual counseling must be available for at-risk pupils and for parents as well.

7. Counselors should also serve where necessary as linkage agents putting the pupil in touch with social workers and other appropriate helping professionals.

8. Every individual pupil must be known well enough by at least one educational professional, usually the classroom teacher, to be able to detect behavior changes, mood changes, failure to eat, sudden fear of being with a particular individual, extensive bruises, burns or welts, changes in appearance, and unexplained irregular attendance.

9. All school personnel must be aware of their legal responsibility for reporting (all states have laws requiring the reporting of child abuse).

Parent education programs are needed also to deal with child abuse problems. One parent abuse program called "Hugs 'n Kids," was implemented with abusive parents as well as parents who were considered at-risk of abusing their children (Golub, Espinosa, Damon and Card, 1987). The program incorporated videotapes of episodes which are typical between parents and their children. Such a program could be effective with parents of elementary school children who are being abused. The videotapes can be used to stimulate discussion and to encourage parents to bring up concerns regarding their abusive behavior.

Kraizer (1985) emphasizes that an essential component to any preventative program is educating the children regarding who to tell and where to go for help. Anxiety is often reduced for the child who has resources at hand; however, the child should also understand that if one adult does not listen, they need to keep telling until someone will listen and take action (Vernon and Hay, 1988).

Vernon and Hay (1988) suggest the following activities which can be used to inform children about various aspects of child abuse. "Express It" (Vernon and Hay, 1988, p. 309) involves the counselor/teacher reading about hypothetical situations in which abuse might be occurring. Students are asked to describe how they would feel if the situation happened to them and how they might express their feelings. Discussion can focus on how feelings are or are not expressed and how the same experience might bring different reactions from various people.

"I Can Do It" (Vernon and Hay, 1988, p. 310) involves students being broken into groups and role-playing the following situation according to how their favorite television, comic book, or movie hero would handle it. They are asked to pretend that they are walking in the park when someone they don't know very well asks them to go for a ride. When they are trying to decide, their favorite hero arrives on the scene and helps them handle the situation. Discussion should focus on how the hero handled the situation, how this might be different than how the children would handle it, and the fact that in real life a superhero will not appear to take over the problem.

In "It's Me" (Vernon and Hay, 1988, p. 310), students are given an outline of a child's body and are requested to fill in their outline, including eyes, ears, hair, and nose. Next they are asked to put a swimsuit (appropriate for their sex) on this person. Discussion then follows which focuses on private body parts that people do not see and touch and parts of the body that are not private and that are okay for others to touch if they are given permission to by the child.

By participating in these activities, children learn to identify issues related to abuse and can discuss ways to prevent abusive situations as well as reporting abuse when it does occur.

A special issue of the *Journal of Elementary School Guidance and Counseling* (1988) is devoted to child abuse. Included in this issue, along with articles related to the topic of abuse with children is a column containing reviews of books and media materials regarding abuse awareness and prevention.

School Dropouts

One of the most persistent problems facing U.S. educators throughout the years of this century has been the school dropout. While the numbers dropping out in the elementary school years are relatively small, it is being increasingly recognized that school dropout prevention begins during the elementary years. As in other prevention programs, those experiencing success in dropout prevention seem to share some procedures in common as follows.

The first step is, as previously noted, one of profiling the typical dropout of the school system. This involves assuming the traits, experiences, and backgrounds of previous dropouts, including an examination of their elementary school years.

A second important ingredient in dropout prevention, lies in maximizing school successes and minimizing failures during these years. It is especially important that the basic skills of reading, writing, math, and spelling be mastered to provide a basis for success in high school. It is also equally important that children "learn to love learning," that they enjoy school, its challenges and opportunities. A positive psychological environment in the elementary school, democratically effective classrooms, and planned programs of classroom guidance are other important ingredients in dropout prevention.

Of course, all efforts must be under the umbrella of a schoolwide plan. Such a plan can and should be the responsibility of the counseling staff. Such a plan should, of course, be coordinated with all other ongoing prevention efforts in the school and school system.

Ruben (1989) suggests that a beneficial dropout prevention strategy would involve offering workshops which are geared toward boosting teachers, and counselors' self-esteem so that they can in turn have a positive impact on raising the self-esteem of students.

AIDS

Acquired immune deficiency syndrome (AIDS) is a fatal viral disease which suppresses the body's immune system causing increasing vulnerability to many other infections. This disease has effected all socioeconomic and educational levels of the population and the epidemic is rapidly spreading. The only known anecdote is prevention. The key factor in prevention programs is education and obviously such programs must be initiated in the elementary schools. Counselors in elementary schools must therefore assume a leading role in the planning and implementation of such programs. Counselors must also consider how they may support students with AIDS themselves or affected family members. In all of these educational and supportive efforts, close cooperation with the medical community is obviously vital.

The duty of the counselor is to be informed and to inform others about AIDS-related issues. There have been nearly 196,000 cases of AIDS in the United States and nearly 65 percent of the cases have been fatal (Leerhsen, 1991). While researchers are baffled by the disease and are continuing to work toward discovering a cure, adults as well as children experience fear and confusion regarding the causes and consequences of contracting the disease. Children must have the opportunity to discuss their concerns and anxiety related to AIDS while they also should be educated regarding preventative steps to take in avoiding the disease. School counselors are in an optimal position to encourage this discussion and must become involved in educating students about the issue. Counselors can help by

- Listening sympathetically to the childrens' concerns and feelings about AIDS
- Being prepared to counter any misinformation that the children have heard about AIDS and how it is and is not transmitted
- Explaining the facts about AIDS
- Allowing children to discuss their feelings about famous people they know (such as pro-basketball player Irvin "Magic" Johnson) who have contracted the disease. These people may serve as heroes or rolemodels to the children and it will likely be traumatic for the children to realize that their "hero" has been infected with AIDS

Other Prevention Concerns

The many major social ills of today's society which can be ameliorated by effective prevention programs in the elementary school are nearly endless. In some school districts, some of these and indeed, some not even mentioned, will be of the highest priority. These could include such critical concerns as other sexually transmitted diseases, teen pregnancies, eating disorders, teen suicides, youth crime, and youth unemployment. All can be worthy of and assisted by well planned prevention efforts in the elementary school.

Summary

Preventive programs in elementary schools seek to assist elementary pupils in avoiding undesirable behaviors and their consequences. They represent a planned and systematic effort to prevent that which is undesirable. Too, elementary school counselors are often the only helping professionals in the school setting who are: (1) skilled in prevention techniques; and (2) working with populations as well as individuals. Studies indicate that elementary schools are responding to the preventive needs of their populations and that positive outcomes are occurring as a result.

Key preventive initiatives include the building of self-esteem and the development of coping skills in children. Health and wellness are also important, including the development of stress management skills. These and other preventive techniques are aimed at such major social concerns as the prevention of substance abuse, child abuse, early school leaving, AIDS, youth crime, and unemployment.

Chapter 9

Consultation

Helping relationships are a basic category of all human relationships, and we must not only be better at managing such relationships when we are in the formal roles of helpers and consultants, but we must teach effective helping to parents, managers, and all others who are involved with other people.
—EDGAR SCHEIN (1989)

Introduction

The label of "consultant" is a popular one on the U.S. economic scene today. Business consultants are available to help with corporate organizing, international sales, or development of marketing strategies. On a more personal level, we may call upon consultants to assist us in preparing our tax returns, investing in the stock market, and so on. In fact, the title of consultant has become so commonly a recognized label for professional expertise that we now hear of used car sales consultant, hair stylist consultant, travel consultant, lawn care consultant, but to name a few. In practice, the label has been so freely applied that some have, with tongue in cheek we hope, defined a consultant as "anyone fifty miles from home with a briefcase!"

In a more serious vein, a consultant is usually viewed as one who shares his or her special knowledge, insights, and/or skills with others for the purpose of providing them or their clients with improvements, reinforcement, and/or special knowledge. Consultation itself may be viewed as a process for sharing the consultant's "expertise" with a client or clients for the purpose of benefitting the latter or a third party being served by the consultants' client. It should be noted that in most counseling and psychological literature consultation is viewed as a triadic structure in which a consultant assists a consultee to more effectively serve a third party.

Of course, the education profession has its share of consultants, commonly active in such areas as school law, finances, taxation, and architecture. In another sense, many could, of course, lay claim to having the special knowledge necessary to claim the title of consultant in their specialty fields. In the case of the elementary school counselor, however, it should be noted that "consultation" is an expectancy of role and function. It is an anticipated and major activity of the counselor in the elementary school setting. In fact, since its earliest inception and authoritarian writings, consultation has been deemed an important and emphasized responsibility of the elementary school counselor in contrast to its relatively recent emphasis in secondary school programs. This role is exemplified, as will be noted later in this chapter, in the many opportunities the elementary school counselor will have to consult with teachers, parents, administrators and others regarding concerns they may have or needs that need to be served for their pupils/children.

The Practices and Process of Consultation

The counselor-consultant recognizes that there are certain assumptions underlying the consultation process. These can be briefly stated in an elementary school context as follows:

1. A need or problem exists that cannot be adequately met by the primary care giver (teacher, parent, and so on.).
2. The counselor possesses special expertise or knowledge which will enable him or her, as a consultant, to aid the consultee more effectively and assist his or her primary client(s).
3. The consultee is motivated and capable of implementing the counselor-consultant's suggestions.
4. The consultant is conscious of the framework of the organization or system such as school or family, involved and its potential influences for those involved.

An unwritten assumption that the counselor must keep in mind is that consultation, even though it involves many of the same skills, is not counseling. Blocher (1987) notes that

> *Consultation is not the same as counseling in that the consultant does not assume full professional and ethical responsibility for the final outcome with the ultimate client. The consultant is careful not to infringe on the relationship between mediator and client. This distinction is very important. A consultant is not in a supervisory role to the mediator or consultee. Instead, the consultant's role is to enhance the work of the consultee. For example, when a counselor works in a consulting relationship with a teacher, the counselor respects the teacher's professional competence and expertise and also respects the professional role and responsibility of the teacher in regard to the student.*

TABLE 9–1 Individual Counseling and Consultation

Counseling	Consultation
1. Establish rapport by listening and communicating understanding and respect.	1. Establish rapport by listening and communicating understanding and respect.
2. Identify the problem. "What are you doing?"	2. Identify the problem. "What do you see as Jenny's main problem?"
3. Identify consequences. "How does this help (or hurt) you in reaching your goal of _____?"	3. Identify consequences. "What happens when Jenny does this?"
4. Evaluate past solutions "What have you tried to solve this?"	4. Evaluate past solutions. "What have you (or Jenny) tried to solve this?"
5. List alternatives. "What could you be doing?"	5. List alternatives. "Can you think of other things that might help?"
6. Contract—make a plan. "Which alternative will you choose, and when will you do this?"	6. Contract—make a plan. "Which alternative will you choose, and when will you do this?"
7. Follow up to evaluate results of plan.	7. Follow up to evaluate results of plan.

From Counseling Children (p. 238) by C. L. Thompson and L. B. Rudolph, 1983, Monterey, CA: Brooks/Cole. Reprinted by permission.

It is also important for the consultant to remember that his or her relationship with the consultee is not primarily therapeutic in nature. Consultees typically do not come to the consultant for personal counseling. They come for specific help with fairly well-defined professional problems (p. 265). Thompson and Rudolph (1983) contrast individual counseling and consultation as noted in Table 9–1.

The process of consultation is usually, though not always, initiated by the party needing assistance—the consultee—in relationship to a third party. In the interaction that follows between the consultant and consultee, an approach is developed for the consultee's application, evaluation, and if needed (with the consultant's aid) modification. Myrick (1987) illustrated the process as follows:

> *Using Figure 9–1 the process can be illustrated. Let's assume a student has become increasingly disruptive in a teacher's classroom and causes the teacher some concern (No. 1). Eventually the teacher experiences enough discomfort to seek some help from a school counselor (No. 2). The counselor-consultant and teacher share information, explore ideas, and arrive at a plan of action (No. 3).*

The teacher, or consultee, then puts the plan into action with the student (No. 4). (pp. 334-335)

Models for Consultation

As the practice of consultation has increased in popularity, simultaneous increases in consultative theory and research and various models and systems for their classification have begun to emerge. Four consultation models identified by Kurpius (1978) indicated that a counselor functioning as a consultant can: (1) provide direct service to a client identified by a third party; (2) prescribe a solution to a specific problem identified by a consultee; (3) assist others in developing plans for solving a problem; or (4) take direct responsibility for defining the problem and proposing a solution.

Blocher (1987) identifies seven models of consultation as follows:

1. *Triadic consultation*—three distinct roles characterize this model. They are the consultant who provides the expertise, the mediator who applies what he or she receives from the consultant and the client who is the object or recipient of the service.

2. *Technical consultation*—a more narrow and focused intervention in which a consultant's expertise is sought in relation to a specific situation or problem.

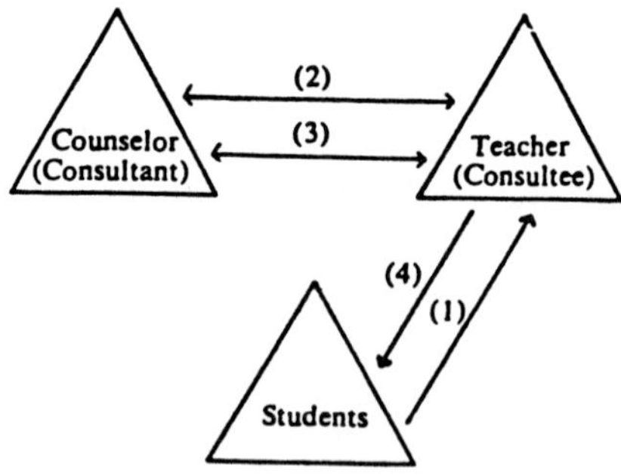

FIGURE 9–1 The Consultation Process

From *Developmental Guidance and Counseling: A Practical Approach* (p. 335) by R. D. Myrick, 1987 (Minneapolis, MN: Educational Media Corporation). Copyright 1987 by the Educational Media Corporation. Reprinted by permission.

3. *Collaborative consultation*—suggests a cooperative relationship in which information and resources are pooled and the consultant and consultee work together as equal partners in the process.

4. *Facilitative consultation*—the consultant facilitates the consultee's access to a variety of new resources. In this model both parties recognize the consultant's legitimate interest in the broad aspects of the functioning of the consultee system.

5. *Mental Health Consultation*—the consultant assists a consultee (therapist) gain a better understanding of one's interaction with a client through such means as analyzing the treatment approach, consideration of their (consultee's) responses to their client and in general, providing support to the consultee.

6. *Behavioral consultation*—focused on the use of behavioral management techniques as suggested or taught by the consultant to a consultee in order to influence or shape the behavior of the consultee's clients in a systematic way.

7. *Process consultation*—the consultant delivers services to an organization in order to increase the effectiveness of a work group in reaching its goals. This consultation addresses the interactions among groups of individuals who work with each other in face-to-face relationships.

Bundy and Poppen (1986) reviewed 21 studies of school counselors' effectiveness as consultants with 86 percent showing significantly positive results. The predominant models used in the 18 studies reviewed were categorized as Adlerian (7 of 18 studies) and Behavioral (6 of 18). Other reported models included parent effectiveness training and multimodal approaches.

Another view of consultation models is presented by Medway and Updyke (1985) who conducted a meta-analysis of 54 studies of consultation interventions. They classified the consultation interventions using the following three consultation model descriptions:

- Mental health consultation stresses intrapsychic causes and changing feelings, attitudes, and perceptions in the consultee in order to improve work-related interactions with present or future clients. Consultant interventions include instructing, modeling, questioning, supporting, and relationship building.
- Behavioral consultation applies social learning theory principles to understanding how certain environmental contingencies influence consultee and client behavior. It involves specifying consultee problems, devising and implementing a behavior change, plan to solve them, and monitoring and evaluating plan effectiveness.
- Organizational development applies principles of group dynamics and social psychology to understanding organizational problems and to assisting members of the organization to make needed change at a systems level. Among its purposes are the improvement of communication, decision-making, climate, and fit between individual goals and system needs.

Consultation Activities

Consulting with Teachers

Classroom teachers are the keys to the successful implementation of any elementary school programs. The primary role of the school is to prepare the pupil for living as a positive and contributing member of society through learning. Teacher-pupil interaction provides the core of this learning. Schools do not exist for administrators to administer or counselors to counsel. They exist for teachers to teach and pupils to learn. The role of administrators, counselors, social workers, school psychologists, and so on, is to, in some way, contribute to and enhance the effectiveness of this teaching-learning process.

We believe, and empirical evidence supports our viewpoint, that elementary school counselors can and do make significant and vital contributions to the teaching-learning process in the elementary school. One of the many ways in which these contributions are made is through the process of consultation with the classroom teacher. The goals of such consultation are to increase the effectiveness of the teacher's teaching and the pupils' learning; it seeks to enhance the vital learning process; to contribute to teachers loving to teach and pupils loving to learn! There are numerous ways in which counselors in consultation with teachers can make such contributions.

The alert and effective elementary school counselor can find numerous occasions and ways to assist their elementary teacher colleagues through consultation. Some examples would include helping teachers become more group conscious and group skilled; assisting the classroom teacher in helping pupils learn the basic interpersonal relationship skills so essential to school and societal adjustment and personal happiness; and working with teachers to remedy maladaptive pupil behavior.

All schools are group oriented and nearly all instruction takes place in groups. Yet, most elementary school teachers have little, if any, exposure to even the basic skills of group leadership, group processes, and group dynamics that are common in counselor preparation programs and later on-the-job practice. The elementary counselor can, through in-service and consultation, assist the classroom teacher in the learning and application of these skills for more effective classroom interaction and management.

There are also a wide range of other consulting opportunities. For example, elementary school counselors consult with teachers in an effort to remedy, through a team approach, maladaptive student behaviors. These maladaptive behaviors typically occur in the classroom in one of two forms—apathy or disruptive behavior. Both behaviors interfere with successful learning experiences in the school environment. Often a maladaptive student's behavior influences the atmosphere of the entire classroom. Consultation is one means, in addition to counseling, by which elementary school counselors can assist children and teachers.

First, let's consider the apathetic child. He or she is the student who could likely go unnoticed for the whole school year. This child prefers to remain "invisible." Possibly feelings of inadequacy or some other issue related to self-concept could produce this reaction from a child. Participating in classroom activities, including classwork, are not options chosen by this student. This is generally the existing condition which sends up the red flag to the teacher. Otherwise, the child may be considered shy.

The teacher who has in her class a child whose behavior is disruptive to the class can benefit from consultation with the counselor. Of course, these children are easy to discover, not only in the classroom, but also in the library, the cafeteria, and on the playground. The child's behavior indicates that he or she needs assistance.

Consultation addressing both types of situations begins with the teacher describing her previous attempts at either motivating the student or modifying the child's behavior. Secondly, the counselor inquires about the personal history of the child and takes note if recent changes have occurred within the family. If the information is not volunteered by the teacher, inquiry is made into the child's past school behavior patterns. Unfortunately, a child's behavior typically precedes his or her entrance into the next grade level. Therefore, the necessary information will be available from the teacher.

Having received this information, the counselor is prepared to give the teacher feedback on what has likely occurred, and possibly why, up to this point. The counselor will be able to evaluate whether this child is experiencing self-concept problems, such as feelings of inadequacy, anxiety related to family concerns, or perhaps the classwork level of difficulty exceeds the cognitive developmental level of the child. Depending on the issue, the counselor offers different approaches that the teacher may try. These are discussed and explained, and often the counselor is able to share with the teacher what behavior changes can be expected in the child. Some recommended strategies include: contracts, earning free time, use of a timer, providing assignments that guarantee student success, giving children leadership responsibilities, assigning children as classroom helpers, and issuing an abundance of TLC (tender loving care). It is often helpful to reiterate to teachers that "children do not really care how much they know, rather they need to know how much they care." When applicable, counselors remind teachers of physical, emotional, social, and cognitive developmental aspects of children which may be helpful in determining appropriate intervention strategies. Before the end of the consultation, a follow-up date and time are scheduled for the near future.

Consultation with Administrators

Consultation by the elementary school counselor facilitates positive and helpful relationships with administrators by keeping them informed about student and teacher concerns and assisting them in working with schoolwide concerns. Often, through consultation, counselors provide valuable input to administrators regarding the well-being of students and faculty.

School counselors consult with administrators on such student issues as placement, curriculum, and current legal information regarding child abuse. At times consultation may involve administrators, teachers, and/or parents. An example of a consultation which includes all significant others in a child's life would be to work together on a plan that integrates consistent changes both at school and at home. Whenever counselors intervene regarding a child's behavior, it is important to state that a child's behavior will not change unless the people with whom he or she interacts change their behavior.

Another issue of consultation with administrators is to "educate" them about the counselor's role in implementing schoolwide programs that have a potential for positive impact on the school's psychological environment. Schoolwide activities such as *Warm Fuzzy Week* and *IALAC DAY* can enhance feelings of unity and cooperation among administrators, teachers, and children. Activities such as *Secret Pals* among teachers are effective in boosting morale especially in the long winter months.

There may be times when teachers come to the counselor with faculty concerns that create stress and tension in the work environment. In these situations, the counselor acts as a liaison to the administration, offering an objective view of issues along with strategies that may reduce tension and alleviate problem situations. When counselors are in a consultation role with any team member, it is wise to remain objective and to be prepared with creative alternative solutions.

Consultation with Parents

Typically, after counselors have consulted with teachers about a student concern, as stated above, the parent is invited in to provide more information and to receive input on the situation at school. The counselor may choose to consult with parents in the teacher's presence or not, depending on the circumstances and available times for appointments. There will be occasions when counselors consult with parents regarding other issues such as test interpretation, placement, and planning for next year. In those cases, consultation provides information, explanation, and guidance.

When consulting with parents regarding maladaptive behavior, first and foremost the counselor must communicate concern for the child and for his or her success in school. It is critically important that the counselor and teacher both communicate explicitly to the parents that they are not blaming them or their child-raising techniques for any problem behaviors their child may be exhibiting. Simply stating an awareness of the presence of difficulties and that they are interfering with the child's success in school may be sufficient. At this point the counselor may go on to inform parents of specific behaviors or attitudes that may be thwarting their child's success. Parents are usually aware that a problem exists prior to their coming in for the consultation process. With encouragement and a positive attitude from the counselor, parents typically contribute background knowledge and are helpful.

After gathering information from the parent(s), the counselor may proceed with the strategies previously discussed with the teacher. During consultation the counselor remains objective and never accusatory. Keep in mind that parents generally want to be helpful to their children. Suggestions are given so that school and home actions and consequences are consistent. At the appropriate time, parents can be informed of their roles in the execution of a plan to redirect their child's energies to more productive outcomes. Parents show they care by attending parent conferences. Likewise show your sensitivity by conveying appreciation for their attendance. At the end of consultation, set a date or time for a follow-up meeting.

Consultation with Community Agencies

School counselors consult with community agencies such as mental health agencies, the department of social services, and medical centers which conduct detailed psychological evaluations. Often when more extensive and/or in-depth counseling is required for a child, a community mental health referral may be made. The counselor's role is generally to consult with the attending counselor from that agency by informing them of historical data which led to the referral. Of course, if test results or other confidential materials are transferred from the school, a written *Release of Information Form* must be signed by the parents prior to any release of records. Agency counselors typically inform school counselors of the role they prefer them to assume after the transfer. These roles vary from asking that the school counselor have no contact with the child because of possible confusion resulting from two styles of counseling to supporting and maintaining contact with the child at school and with the agency counselor.

The department of social services includes child protective services to which school counselors report abuse and neglect cases. Consultation involves relaying information to social workers and requires a written account of the incident. Often, the counselor is requested to be present with the child when the social worker comes to interview them regarding the charges. (This is the preferred practice among school counselors.)

Consultation with the department of social services may also involve discussion with social workers on the impending placement of foster children in the school. Confidentiality is, of course, in all the above cases, critical.

Community or major medical centers in a state, such as a teaching research hospital, often provide extensive psychological evaluations of school children. The counselor acts as a referring agent and liaison between the agency and the school. Consultation involves providing information initially through the school psychologist that indicates the request of an evaluation. When results are compiled, the counselor, teacher, and school psychologist may attend the reading and explanation of results. Recommendations for placement and/or strategies are heard at that time.

Consultation with Other Helping Professionals

Other helping professionals include other school counselors, school psychologists, psychologists, and private psychiatrists. Reasons for consulting with other school counselors include the transfer of a client to another school in which you believe continued counseling services are needed; for the exchange of counseling and guidance strategies; and to coordinate opportunities for professional growth at conferences and workshops.

Consultation with the school psychologist will likely be in regard to children who have been referred for special education. These services include: learning disabilities classes, emotionally handicapped classes, classes for children who have below-average intelligence, and children who are hearing, sight, or otherwise physically impaired. As might be anticipated, the inevitable paperwork must be completed before testing of any kind can proceed. The counselor may or may not be responsible for coordinating this paperwork.

Consultation with the school psychologist before and after testing should be anticipated when, as is frequently the case, the counselor is the liaison between the school and the school psychologist. In each situation, initial information will be provided by the elementary school counselor regarding the child's circumstance and need for attention. Should psychological assessment be conducted, the counselor should anticipate consulting again with the school psychologist regarding results and appropriate follow-up. Finally, parents, the sending teacher (provided another placement is recommended), the receiving teacher, an administrator, the school psychologist, and the counselor, consult regarding the best placement for a child. This may be referred to as a case staffing meeting.

At times children are referred for therapy to a private psychologist or psychiatrist. Consultation with these professionals is to provide historical data regarding behavior and school circumstances. After therapy is in progress, consultation includes updates on the child's progress at school. This requires that the counselor continue to observe the child and maintain contact for feedback from teachers.

The Counselor-Consultant and the Elementary School Environment

In recent years, elementary schools have been experiencing the effects of the "accountability" and "excellence in education" movements. A major thrust of these movements has been the improvement of academic performance and the monitoring of this progress through various state and national standardized testing programs. In the quest for higher academic accomplishments, we must not lose sight of the importance of the environment for learning—the environment of the school and the classroom which promotes learning. This environment frequently referred to as the school climate, may be defined as how people feel about the qualities of a school and the people in that school. "Climate" includes the total physical and psychological environment to which people respond. Climate further reflects how students, teachers, administrators, and the community feel about their school.

Schools with positive climates are affectively healthy places where people care, respect, and trust each other. These are people-centered systems in which beliefs, values, procedures, rules, regulations, and policies show respect for the students, faculty, and staff who work there. People in such schools feel a high degree of pride and ownership which comes from having the opportunity to make decisions and choices about their lives in the school. Furthermore, positive school climates change as the needs of people within the schools change, reshaping to meet new needs (Kaplan and Geoffrey, 1990, p. 8).

As Krumboltz (1987) noted,

> *Schools could be happy places—places where young people learned new ideas and skills enthusiastically under the tutelage of creative teachers and supportive administrators. Indeed, for some youngsters schools are just such places. However, for all too many others, schools are places where fear and failure pervade the atmosphere. (p. 1)*

Elementary school counselors are in a key position to promote the kind of environment or climate which will facilitate "learning to love learning." Characteristics of the environment for effective counseling—trust, respect, caring, attending, facilitating, and so on, are also the bases for a positive school and classroom environment.

> *Counselors serve in a capacity which enables them to integrate the contributions of teachers, administrators, parents, educational specialists and the students themselves to create a school environment where children can learn and achieve successfully. (Krumboltz, 1988, pp. 1-2)*

Counselors must be consultants in an advocacy role to facilitate the development of such an environment. In creating this positive school environment, the elementary school counselor must not lose sight of the preventive, developmental, and enhancement emphasis desired in elementary school counseling programs. Finally, much of how the elementary school pupil will anticipate their future schooling will be determined by their attitudes towards the school. Their attitudes will be shaped by their elementary school experiences as influenced by the school's environment in which they occur.

Summary

Consultation is a major activity of the elementary school counselor. In this activity, the counselor shares his or her special skills and/or knowledge with others (teachers, parents, administrators) to enable them to work more effectively with elementary children—and to create an environment conducive to "learning to love learning." It is important to keep in mind that the consultation process is different from the counseling process even though basic elements, rapport establishment, problem identification, and so on, may be present in both. A variety of consultation models (Kurpius, 1978; Blocher, 1987; Medway and Updyke, 1985) have emerged for classifying consultation interventions.

Chapter 10

Assessment for Child Guidance

All things are engaged in writing their history. The planet, the pebble, goes attended by its shadow. The rolling rock leaves its scratches on the mountain; the river, its channel in the soil; the animal, its holes in the stratum; the fern and leaf, their modest epitaph in the coal. The falling drop makes its sculpture in the sand or the stone. Every act of man inscribes itself in memories, manners and face. Every object is covered with hints which speak to the intelligent.
-RALPH WALDO EMERSON

Introduction: Roles and Objectives of Assessment

A song from the musical "The King and I", sings about "getting to know you, getting to know all about you." This song from this popular production, with its major focus on children, would seem appropriate to introduce this chapter on assessment in a book with its major focus on children. Certainly, in any program of child guidance, assessment will play a major role. The emphasis on this role is noted in a study by Morse and Russell (1989) who surveyed elementary school counselors and found the five highest ideal roles include the following:

1. *Helping the teacher better understand individual students' needs by discussing students' behaviors, attitudes, and progress*
2. *Working with students in groups to help them learn appropriate social skills*
3. *Working with students in groups to enhance self-concepts*
4. *Working with students in groups to help them understand their feelings*

5. *Working with students in groups to help them develop problem-solving skills (p. 58)*

While number one directly emphasizes the role of assessment, all of these ideal roles suggest learning about—knowing/assessing pupils. The importance of assessment for pupil understanding of self in addition to teacher and counselor understanding is also highlighted by the results of this study. Rotter (1990) notes that the Council for the Accreditation of Counseling and Related Educational Programs (CACREP) standards for counselors who work in K-12 settings state that

> *School Counseling (sic) is designed to facilitate self-understanding and self-development through individual and small-group activities. Counseling denotes a professional relationship that involves a trained school counselor, a student, and significant others in the student's life. The focus of such relationships is on personal development and decision-making (sic) based on self-understanding and knowledge of the environment. (Rotter, 1990, p. 183)*

A number of other role and function studies, as well as introductory texts underline the importance of pupil assessment as a basic elementary school counselor responsibility in any school program of counseling and guidance. The objectives of the assessment function are:

1. To help the elementary school counselor better understand the pupils they serve

2. To assist the elementary school teacher in better understanding the pupils they teach

3. To assist the elementary school children to better understand themselves; their behaviors, feelings, strengths, and weaknesses

4. To assist parents in gaining additional insights into the behaviors, feelings, strengths, and weaknesses of their elementary school sons and daughters

5. To assist the elementary school principal and other appropriate professionals in better understanding individual pupils and the pupil population in general

6. To assist elementary school teachers, administrators, and counselors in the assessment of the academic progress of student groups

In the paragraphs which follow, pupil assessment will be discussed from the standpoint of both standardized techniques and non-standardized approaches.

Standardized Assessment

Standardized assessment is largely embodied in the process of standardized testing. The label "standardized" is derived from the application of the label "standards" to:

1. the uniform procedures and conditions prescribed for the ad scoring, and interpretation of the instrument

2. the standards of performance measured by the instrument t the creation of "norms" (normal patterns of performance by a specified population)

In many school systems, all standardized assessment or testing will be a primary responsibility of a school psychologist. In others, the school psychologist may have responsibility for administering individual and special psychological measures while the school counselor is responsible for group administered achievement testing programs. In any event, due to both the popularity and sensitivity of standardized testing, it is important that elementary school counselors be aware of the basic criteria for the selection of standardized tests as well as the common methods of reporting standardized test results. The following paragraphs present brief introductions to these topics but are not intended to substitute for desired coursework in standardized testing and measurement.

Guidelines for Test Selection

Basic criteria for determining the appropriateness of a standardized test include its validity, reliability, norms, and practicality.

Validity

Validity is the ability of a test or other analytical tool to assess that which it purports to assess. To describe validity in more functional terms and to show that it is related to the suitability of a certain instrument for a certain situation, validity is the degree to which an instrument or technique assesses that which it is being used to assess. In keeping with this concept of validity, a person who is to conduct standardized testing must determine the desired analytical objectives and the ability of a particular tool to fulfill them. The degree to which the tool succeeds is its validity. The instrument selected must measure what one wants measured and who one wants to measure!

For an instrument to be valid, it must also meet different kinds of conditions. For example, if one desired to predict future success or behavior from the results of present measurement or evaluation, one would need to know the predictive validity of the instrument being used as a basis for the prediction. In practice, a counselor may attempt to predict a student's success in the future on the basis of current performance as measured by test results. The degree to which it predicts successfully constitutes its predictive validity.

Standardized test items must also be representative of the content areas or behavioral patterns being assessed and must be appropriate for the individual under study and for the given circumstances. When an instrument meets these conditions, it is said to have content validity. It involves a process of logical analysis in which the following professional judgments should be made in terms of the relationship of the test items to course objectives and instruction (Hopkins, Stanley, and Hopkins, 1990).

1. *Does the test content parallel the curricular objectives in content and process?*
2. *Are the tests and curricular emphasis in proper balance?*
3. *Is the test free from prerequisites that are irrelevant or incidental to the present measurement task? (For example, are the reading and vocabulary levels of the science test appropriate for the examinees? (Hopkins, Stanley, and Hopkins, 1990, p. 77)*

When alternate measures are available, the degree to which the alternate instrument obtains the same data as the first is referred to as the second instrument's concurrent validity.

A fourth type of validity is construct validity. Construct validity pertains to the adequacy of the theory or concept underlying a specific instrument. In other words, it involves logically ascertaining the psychological attributes that account for variations in the test scores or other derived data. Construct validity is reported in terms of the kinds of responses the test should elicit, and the ways in which those responses should be interpreted on the basis of logical inferences about the behavior the test is designed to appraise.

Reliability

The second essential criterion to be considered in the selection of standardized analytical instruments is reliability. Reliability reflects the consistency with which an instrument can elicit the same responses from an individual on more than one occasion. It should be noted that in attempting to determine an instrument's reliability through successive administrations, the conditions under which the instrument is administered (directions, time allotted, and so forth) must be identical. The elapsed time between administrations cannot be too long, lest growth or decline occur in the information or other variable being assessed. An approach frequently employed to overcome this difficulty is to report a test's internal consistency, which is found by comparing the consistency of each student's responses to a test's odd-numbered questions with the consistency of the student's responses to its even-numbered items.

Norms

The population from which the norms for a standardized test were established is important in determining the appropriateness of an instrument to assess an individual or group outside the norm group. Counselors therefore need to be aware of the makeup of the norm group on which the test was established and its similarity to those for which the test is being considered.

Practicality

The third major category of criteria for selection includes those factors that determine how practical a certain instrument or technique would be for attaining desired objectives in a given situation. Practicality includes the cost of the instrument or requisite materials; the time needed for the utilization of the tool or technique; the personnel needed to administer the technique, in terms of number of persons and levels of training required; the difficulty of scoring or compiling the obtained data; and the difficulty of interpreting and applying the data.

Test Interpretation

Another form of validity which we might put forward could be labeled "interpretative validity." This could be defined as the degree to which the results of a standardized measuring instrument are accurately interpreted. This suggests that no standardized tests should be used in the elementary school that cannot be accurately interpreted and reported by those responsible for the process. Certain guidelines for this process are suggested as follows:

1. Be thoroughly familiar with the test manual and technical manual of the test.

2. Take, score, and interpret the test yourself. This provides you insights you will not obtain by simply giving the tests to others.

3. Determine if the test is appropriate to the need for which it would be designed to serve.

4. Determine that the instrument is within your capacity and training to administer, score, and interpret.

In elaborating on item four above, a good working knowledge of elementary statistical concepts is important to the accurate interpretation of standardized measures. A few of the commonly used statistical terms associated with standardized testing are those used to describe averages, variations from the average, relationships, and test results.

Averages are known as measures of central tendency. The three common measures are the mean, median, and mode. The mean indicates the mathematical average of a group of scores. The median designates the mid-point of a set of scores with 50 percent of the scores being above and 50 percent below that point. The mode represents the most frequent score of a group of scores.

Variations from the average are referred to in statistical terms as measures of variability. Two common such measures are the range and standard deviation. The range is, at its simplest, determined by the spread from the lowest to the highest score. The standard deviation is a statistical process that enables test interpreters to determine the exact distance of a score from the mean.

It is frequently desirable to examine the relationship between a test score and some other meaningful variable (for example, standardized math achievement test score and grade in mathematics class). The statistical process for comparing relationships between two variables is to compute correlation coefficients.

The results of standardized tests can be reported in a variety of ways. Since the raw score of a test in itself is meaningless, it must be converted into a score that enables the individual taking the test to be compared with others. There are several common methods for converting raw scores into a more meaningful result. The frequently used method of percentile indicates the relative rank the individual would have in the norm group. It is indicative of the percentage of individuals in the sample who would fall below a specific raw score. A standard score denotes an individual's distance from the mean in terms of the standardized deviation of the distribution. Test scores may also be reported by age norms and grade norms. These scores are based on the average scores achieved by pupils at a designated age or grade.

The foregoing has introduced you to some of the terminology of test interpretation only. We have not discussed the statistical processes involved since counselors anticipating the use of standardized tests will want in-depth experiences provided through appropriate coursework in such areas as measurement and/or statistics.

Areas of Standardized Testing

Standardized tests may be catalogued according to those assessing intelligence, aptitude, achievement, interest, and personality. In most elementary schools, achievement testing is far and away the most popular, followed by aptitude and intelligence. Interest testing is sometimes conducted in the highest elementary grade and personality testing is usually confined to a limited number of individuals, if utilized at all. Tests and testing programs are designed to be administered to groups of pupils, often the entire school population. Again, on rare occasions, intelligence or personality tests may be administered individually, usually by a school psychologist since special training is necessary to qualify for the administering, scoring and interpreting of individually administered tests. General coursework in the areas of group testing should be anticipated for elementary school counselors to use such instruments for assessment purposes.

Intelligence Testing

Intelligence testing is the oldest area of standardized testing with its origins generally attributed to Alfred Binet, a French psychologist, and his associate, Theodore Simon in 1908. Since then, intelligence tests have proliferated in numbers and controversies. Individually administered, as well as many group-administered I.Q. tests are available to the qualified helping professional.

Although commonalities exist regarding the nature of intelligence, there are as many definitions as there are psychologists who define it. Binet and Simon (1916) contributed "... judgment, otherwise called good sense, practical sense, initiative, the faculty of adapting one's self to circumstances. To judge well, to comprehend well, to reason well, these are the essential activities of intelligence" (cited in Sattler, 1992, p. 45). David Wechsler (1958) states that intelligence is "The aggregate or global capacity of the individual to act purposefully, to think rationally and to deal effectively with his environment" (cited in Sattler, 1988, p. 45). Intelligence tests are thus designed to measure the concurrent human abilities reflected in definitions such as to adapt and adjust to the environment, to learn, and to perform abstract thinking.

> *The items on intelligence tests represent attempts to assess individual differences in the effects of experiences common to nearly everyone in the culture. It is assumed that, given equality of experiences, people of higher intelligence will benefit more from those experiences than people of lesser intelligence. Consequently, to the extent that the test makers are successful, differences among individuals' scores on intelligence tests should be more a matter of variations in basic ability than variations in experience. (Aiken, 1988, pp. 154–155)*

Individually administered intelligence tests may be used for assessing neurological functioning, diagnosing learning disabilities, and intelligence levels of nonreaders. Group tests have frequently been used to measure academic promise. Of course, school counselors and others involved in their use, must be aware of the many variables that will influence the validity of intelligence testing. While I.Q. tests may measure intelligence in view of how the developers have defined intelligence, these definitions do not include such factors as creativity, motivation, or social skills among others. Further, the speed factor on the traditional group test is now being challenged by some.

Aptitude Testing

An aptitude is generally defined as one's ability to either perform or to learn to perform or acquire a particular skill or knowledge. An individual's aptitudes are often suggested as reflected in a pattern of traits. This has resulted in a trait and factor approach to aptitude testing. Thus, an individual's aptitudes may be measured through standardized psychological measures, traditionally referred to as aptitude tests, which can be profiled to indicate the test taker's potential.

Aptitude tests have been very popular for facilitating career decision-making so, as a result, have found limited use in elementary schools. This is especially true of the popular aptitude batteries which have been normed on post-elementary school age groups. Some individual aptitude tests may be appropriate for upper elementary school children in such areas as music and art, for example, but these usually require special training to administer, score, and interpret.

Achievement Testing

Achievement testing is by far the most popular area of standardized testing in U.S. education. It has become an integral part of the "rites of passage" through our school systems beginning in the elementary school. While earlier in their history, achievement tests were utilized to assess academic outcomes of individual pupils and on occasion, even classroom groups, in recent years, their utilization has been broadened to evaluate whole grades, teacher effectiveness, and even schools. As the label implies, achievement tests measure what has been achieved in the way of learning. Achievement tests may measure how much is learned over a period of time, how rapidly one is learning, what one is learning, and the level of learning. Drummond (1988) identifies the various types of achievement tests as follows:

1. Survey achievement batteries *Partially norm-referenced and partially criterion-referenced tests that measure knowledge and skill in reading, mathematics, language arts, social studies, and science*
2. Subject area tests *Achievement tests in a single subject area, such as math or spelling*
3. Criterion-referenced tests *Tests that measure knowledge and comprehension of a specific skill or competency, for example, the ability to draw specified inferences from pictorial or written content or the ability to read a metric scale and give the weight of an object in metric and English units of weight*
4. Minimum level skills tests *Tests that measure objectives or skills identified as the minimum skills to be achieved in order to pass from one level or grade to another*
5. Individual achievement tests *Tests that are administered individually across a wide age or grade range to measure achievement*
6. Diagnostic tests *Tests that are used to assess the strengths and weaknesses of individuals in a given subject area by measuring a limited number of skills thoroughly (Drummond, 1988, p. 117)*

If achievement tests are to be accurate measures of pupil learning, there are several considerations to keep in mind as follows:

1. Does the test measure what the pupils have had an opportunity to learn over the period being tested?
2. Are the test items and reading level of the test appropriate to the pupils being examined?
3. Is the formatting of the test (method of examining and type of questions) one with which the pupils have reasonable familiarity?
4. Do the subject items on the test represent approximately the proportion of time spent on those items in classroom instruction and textbook readings?
5. Are the tests judged to be reasonable measures of pupil learning by the classroom teachers who have taught the subject material to the pupils being tested?
6. If a norm-referenced test, is the population on which the test was normed similar to your pupil population?

A final broader question might also be asked: Are pupils learning how to think, learn, and solve problems and enjoying the experience—or simply achieving a rote learning experience designed to respond to subject-matters boxed in by externally decreed testing programs? This question is not meant to deny the value or utilization of such useful assessment instruments as achievement tests, but represents a plea to use them wisely and in the best interests of the learner.

Interest Tests

Interest tests are primarily used to assess interests in relation to possible career areas and/or levels of career development and maturity. As such, the more popular interest inventories are normed for high school and older populations. As such, they are popular in high school testing programs, college career centers and various community agencies providing career counseling or advisement. Despite their popularity, interest tests have limited predictability for success in either school subjects or specific careers. Since there does seem to be some evidence linking scores on interest inventories to career choice, as well as career fields to be avoided, counselors may assume that interest tests are more indicative of what a client will not do than what they can do.

Of course, the interests of elementary school children are in a fantasy or developmental stage. Thus, the more popular interest inventories would not be appropriate. While elementary school pupils have not reached the level of development to make mature and realistic decisions, there are some interest inventories designed to introduce and familiarize elementary school pupils with a wide-range of school and non-school activities and occupations.

> *Illustrative of such instruments are the* Career Awareness Inventory *(by L. M. Fadale) and the* Individual Career Exploration *(by A. Miller-Tiedman), both available from Scholastic Testing Service. The two forms of the* Career Awareness Inventory (Elementary, *for grades 3-6, and* Advanced, *for grades 7-12) take 60-90 minutes to complete. Designed to help students assess how much they know about careers and their career choices, it tests seven areas of career knowledge and is used as a basis for class lectures or discussions. The* Individual Career Exploration, *which takes about two hours to complete, consists of a picture form for grades 3-7 and a verbal form for grades 8-12. Based on Roe and Klos's (1969) theory of occupational choice, it is designed to help students focus on future occupations in relation to their current interests, experiences, abilities, and ambitions. (Aiken, 1988, pp. 297-298)*

Personality Testing

Personality tests are designed to assess and describe a wide range of traits and characteristics that comprise the variables of an individual's personality. These variables will differ according to the theoretical viewpoints of the test developers and also the purpose for which the instrument has been designed. Some personality tests may measure personality across a number of categories while others may focus on a single component such as self-esteem. Personality tests have lower validity and reliability than achievement and ability tests. Thus, much of their usefulness lies in the skills and understandings of the counselor, psychologist or other qualified professional utilizing such instruments.

While standardized personality testing is not very common in elementary school counseling programs, there are some recognized instruments available. We would note that some of these instruments utilize unusual techniques—a visual stimuli presented to the child who then gives a verbal response. Such instruments as the Rorschach, various draw "something" tests, and the Bender *Visual Motor Gestalt* require highly specialized training. Most group paper and pencil personality tests normed for elementary school-aged children are based on the factor analysis statistical method. "Factor analysis helps us see how many distinguishable individual differences can be identified in a set of scores and how significant the influence of each dimension is" (Cronbach, 1984, p. 283).

> *Cattell and his associates have developed a series of personality tests based on the factor analytic method. The* Early School Personality Questionnaire *(ESPQ) is read or presented by tape to children aged 6 to 8. A special answer sheet uses pictures to guide the children in marking their answers. The* Children's Personality Questionnaire *(CPQ) is used with children aged 8 to 12. (Aiken, 1988, p. 159)*
>
> The Eysenck Personality Questionnaire *(EPQ) is a 90-item pencil-and-paper inventory measuring extroversion-introversion, neuroticism-stability, and tough mindedness or psychotism. It also has a Lie scale and can be given to individuals 7 and older. (Aiken, 1988, p. 159)*

There are also several popular single dimension personality tests, such as self-concept scales and anxiety tests, that are normed for children. Additionally, there are also problem checklists and inventories appropriate for elementary school pupils. We would conclude by cautioning that personality testing is seeking to measure the ever-changing personality of the elementary school pupil, that personality measures themselves are of limited validity and reliability and that the assessing of personality is another very sensitive area that must be approached with both tact and the necessary skills and knowledge. Standardized testing programs in the elementary school and the thrust toward "excellence in education" has served as an impetus for many states to devise programs that assess students on a statewide basis in basic skills. For example, several states test all students in grades one, two, three, six, eight, and eleven. A cautionary note, however, is in order since the younger children may not follow standardized directions well, are not "test-conditioned" and will not sit still for extended periods of time. Elementary schools commonly test in the subject areas of reading, math, science, and writing. Results are interpreted as determining whether pupils have mastered the minimum amount of information in the basic skill subject areas for a specific time period. Results may also determine whether remediation programs are needed.

Another type of assessment program in elementary schools is to administer nationally-normed achievement tests. These test scores provide rankings of individual students and the entire school population with the nation's average. Elementary school counselors may function as coordinators for the testing process in schools. Responsibilities include in-servicing teachers regarding administration of the test; scheduling test times; emphasizing test security with teachers; dissemination of test materials; collection of test materials after testing; the resubmission of completed test forms; and paperwork at the end of testing.

Although duties of this nature decrease the counselor's counseling and guidance time with children, there are reasons that counselors are chosen for this task. One of the most common is that counselors do often have some specialized training in standardized assessment, are usually school-based (whereas school psychologists are system-based), and that counselors assist teachers with often accompanies the interpretation of results. Too, pupils will feel more comfortable, less shy or stubborn, if the test givers are familiar to the children.

When schoolwide testing programs are implemented in elementary schools, it is advisable that testing occurs simultaneously in all classrooms. (Otherwise, the noise level in the halls and on the playground could be a distraction to those who are testing.) Teachers should also be reminded to place "Testing. Please do not disturb." signs on their doors to prevent other interruptions.

Preparation for testing generally begins several weeks prior to testing. During the days of actual test administration, a disruption to the regular school day schedule is obviously created. A counselor's organizational skills and planning strategies can facilitate a school's movement through this sometimes stressful period. Since a counselor is aware of the feelings of others and can anticipate them, counseling skills can be utilized with both professional colleagues and pupils in this coordination and implementation process.

One elementary school counselor suggests that teachers will appreciate receiving a special note in their boxes during test times. Several elementary counselors mentioned distributing special stickers to teachers to wear during testing such as "Kids are special people." Testing time can be a stressful time, challenging the creativity and human relations skills of the elementary school counselor to transform various stressful tasks into pleasant experiences for all.

Non-Standardized Techniques for Pupil Assessment

In addition to standardized tests for assessing aspects of the elementary school child's development, a number of non-standardized techniques are available to assist counselors, teachers, and other professionals in the school setting, and, of course, parents, more accurately understand the behavior and development of the individual child.

These include observation and observation reports and such pupil participation techniques as questionnaires, autobiographies, and so on. The paragraphs which follow briefly discuss these techniques.

Observation Techniques and Observation Reports

Observation is a technique that almost everyone has employed at one time or another. Often upon meeting a person for the first time, we begin to analyze her or him on the basis of what we see. Occasionally, we even do this when observing strangers riding beside us on a bus or sitting next to us at a ball game. In the same way, we watch entertainers in movies, on the stage, or on our television screen and draw conclusions, albeit often inaccurate ones, about the type of person we think he or she is. Indeed, it would seem that if "practice makes perfect," we would only need to use the technique of observation for any planned program of child study.

The effectiveness of casual observation, however, must be tempered with caution. Because observing "comes naturally" to all of us, and because we are constantly absorbing visual impressions, we tend to overestimate the accuracy of random or unsystematic observations. For instance, the playback of films has given us proof in recent years that even highly trained observers such as baseball umpires, football officials, and racing judges, conscious of the need for accuracy in their observations and viewing the scene from a vantage point, do sometimes err in their observations. Frequently, examples also may be found in the conflicting versions that witnesses to the same event or incident will, in all sincerity, report. Perhaps we can offer convincing proof by asking that the reader identify

1. Whose pictures appear on $5, $10, and $20 bills?
2. What are the colors of the top and bottom stripes in the United States flag?

The accuracy and completeness of our recall of observations usually tends to depreciate rapidly with the passage of time. Secondly, it is difficult to compare or verify undirected observations because individuals are seldom making their observation within the same frame of reference. Also, we frequently look for only those things in our observations of others that reinforce a bias or preconceived concept we have toward a given individual or object. Finally, even in the same setting, two observers may take note of or have different values; hence, reach conflicting views of the same situation.

The limitations of observation procedures as a means of studying behavior are not intended to suggest the downgrading of this technique. In fact, observation is very important in understanding young children. None of the previously described techniques can help one understand the elementary child and his or her behavior like observation. The focus of observation is the behavior of the child. We have simply pointed out the need for guidelines and for instruments which will increase the accuracy and objectivity of this important technique of observation for learning more about the behavior of children.

Pupil: Jane Whiz **Observer:** Gilda Sharp

Where Observed: 5th Grade History Period
When: October 2, 10:15 a.m.

Anecdote
I returned the first of my monthly quizzes to my American history class this morning. I told the class that I was well satisfied with their performance as a group, but I did not indicate high students or low students or a distribution of my grades, since I find this always provokes endless discussion from some students in the attempt to gain the one or two points necessary for the next-higher grade. Jane, one of my better students, approached me after class and asked, "Mr. Haseley, did I make the highest grade in the class?" I replied, "Jane, you made a good grade. I could tell you studied for the exam." Jane then repeated her question. I told her that while she had not been the highest in the class, she still had made the highest letter grade possible—an A. She then said, "Mr. Haseley, it is important for me to know where I stand in the class." I am afraid that I became a bit curt at this point when I said, "Jane, you were third highest. Stop worrying about it."

Observer's Comments
I do not understand what Jane thought she was going to accomplish by her behavior and questions. She has never acted this way before, but I honestly felt she was anti-teacher today.

FIGURE 10–1 Anecdotal Report Form

Observing the Elementary School Child

The preparation and use of observation instruments must take into consideration what we want to know or observe about the child. The answer is, of course, all aspects of the child's development: for example, physical, emotional, intellectual, and social.

Physically, we note the growth of the child as measured by height and weight. We also observe for muscular development and coordination, as well as how they use and care for their body. We observe their emotional development to see how they display, control, and direct their emotions; how they handle frustrations and develop and exhibit attachments.

We observe their intellectual characteristics by noting their use of vocabulary, length of sentences, curiosity, creativity, and problem-solving. Opportunities to observe the many aspects of the child's social development include how the child relates to his or her peers and adults; how they function in groups; how they behave alone; and what do they do with their free time. The following paragraphs will describe some of the techniques for recording these observations.

Observation Reports

One of the most popular forms for reporting observations in the school setting has, for a number of years, been the anecdotal record. Anecdotal report forms provide for identifying information, spaces to report the observed incident and record comments of the observer. By providing guidelines for recording and reporting observations, this technique encourages objectivity and exact descriptions. Examples of anecdotal record forms may be noted in Figure 10–1.

An anecdotal record is an objective description of an event or episode that a teacher or counselor has observed and feels significant enough to record in writing. These recorded events or episodes are called anecdotes or behavior descriptions.

In writing anecdotal reports, it is important to record objectively the behavior description of the event. While interpretations and recommendations for action are important and give meaning to the factual description of behavior, they should be distinctly separate from the event being recorded. Remember, all episodes do not justify an interpretation, and many are simply indicative of trends in the growth and development of the individual. It is a series of anecdotal reports that is likely to provide meaningful behavioral clues and insights. A final suggestion—due consideration must be given to the background or setting of the incident or the record is not complete and cannot be interpreted correctly.

Rating Scales and Observation Checklists

Rating scales and observation checklists are instruments designed to record systematic and objective appraisal of pupils through the technique of directed observation. Such instruments can be easily prepared by elementary school counselors to elicit the kinds of information desired. In doing so, the items for observation should be clear and concise and easily understood. Like items should be grouped together and items should be avoided that may prejudice the observer or his or her replies. Such instruments should also be limited in length. Well designed instruments will focus on specifics and provide objective and comparable data.

In their simplest form, a rating scale might consist of a series of items representing pupil traits with an easy-to-use scale for recording their judgments. See Figure 10–2 for an example of one item of a rating scale summary.

These scales attempt to provide an approach to obtaining comparable data from several sources both by directing attention to designated items for observation and by providing a scale for recording the response. Rating scales and observation checklists should be used along with other assessment techniques in seeking the most accurate and complete picture possible of the individual pupil.

Increasing the number of qualified raters observing a given student increases the validity of the rating results. A single rating report on a student could be seriously misleading.

The Observation Checklist

The observation checklist presents personality traits and characteristics that the teacher and others may observe for in pupils. After the observer has made the

ITEM Personality	SCALE: XXX				XXX
	(1)	(2)	(3)	(4)	(5)
Ability to relate to others, friendliness, cooperation, social attitudes, behavior traits	uncooperative shows limited development of positive personality traits, poor attitudes				Very likable and popular, cooperative, possesses desirable personality traits

FIGURE 10–2 Rating Scale Summary Report

necessary judgments, the observer checks those items she or he feels are characteristic of the pupil.

This instrument has certain advantages; it is easy to administer and simple to fill out. However, it does not provide for the substantiating and descriptive details of the anecdotal record, nor does it provide, as the rating scale does, for an indication of the degree to which the subject possesses a given trait.

Figure 10–3 is an example of a common form of observation checklist.

Pupil Participating Techniques

Values of Pupil Participating Techniques

Some of the most useful techniques for individual analysis are those that call for the active participation of the pupil. The information they yield can serve as a key resource for teachers, administrators, and counselors in schools at any level, for they may suggest insights into pupil behavior and feelings. Pupil participating techniques are also valuable to the pupils themselves as they directly engage them in guided self-assessment, a process that can lead to self-understanding. In this way these techniques help to fulfill an important purpose of the school counseling program—assisting students toward fuller self-knowledge. Figure 10–4 is an example of a pupil participation sheet must can be used in the classroom to assess pupil participation.

The aim of pupil participation goes beyond the providing of insights into current behavior: It is also meant to demonstrate to the pupil that the school is actively concerned with her or him as an individual. Furthermore, it is important that a student's strengths, weaknesses, and unique personal characteristics are understood and accepted by both the student and the school, and that mutual understanding is clearly communicated. Pupil-participating techniques can play a strategic role in facilitating such communication.

The most important techniques (the pupil personnel questionnaire; the autobiography, essay, and other subjectively written pupil reports; and the individual interview) will be taken up separately in the sections that follow.

Observation Checklist

Personal characteristics of ____________________
(name of student)

Observed by (name or code) ____________________

Periods (dates of observation): from __________ to __________

Conditions under which student was observed: ____________________

Instructions: Place a check mark in the blank to the left of the following traits you believe to be characteristic of the student.

Positive Traits		Negative Traits	
_____	1. Neat in appearance	_____	16. Unreliable
_____	2. Enjoys good health	_____	17. Uncooperative
_____	3. Regular in attendance	_____	18. Domineering
_____	4. Courteous	_____	19. Self-centered
_____	5. Concern for others	_____	20. Rude
_____	6. Popular with other students	_____	21. Sarcastic
_____	7. Displays leadership ability	_____	22. Boastful
_____	8. Has a sense of humor	_____	23. Dishonest
_____	9. Shows initiative	_____	24. Resents authority
_____	10. Industrious	_____	25. A bully
_____	11. Has a pleasant disposition	_____	26. Overly aggressive
_____	12. Mature	_____	27. Shy and withdrawn
_____	13. Respects property of others	_____	28. Cries easily
_____	14. Nearly always does his/her best	_____	29. Deceitful
_____	15. Adjusts easily to different situations	_____	30. Oversolicitous

Comments: ____________________

FIGURE 10–3 Observation Checklist

From *Introduction to Counseling and Guidance* (3rd ed.), (p. 272) by R. L. Gibson and M. H. Mitchell, 1990, (New York: Macmillan). Copyright 1990 by Macmillan. Reprinted by permission.

Pupil Questionnaire

The questionnaire is one of the most popular pupil participating techniques of all. It consists of a series of questions that may be designed to elicit from the pupil either general information or specific kinds of data for special purposes. The well-designed questionnaire is easy to administer and offers the school counselor, teacher, and administrator a technique for securing a maximum of useful information with a minimum expenditure of time and money.

To what extent does the pupil participate in class discussions?

____ 1 ____________ 2 ____________ 3 ____________ 4 ____________ 5

No participation	Occasional Participation	Frequent Participation

FIGURE 10–4 Participation Sheet

Uses The questionnaire can be useful as follows:

1. The collection of basic information for individual counseling office record folders.

2. The collection of supplementary information for improved understanding of pupils. Questionnaires can be designed to collect information of special value in pupil understanding. For example, subject-matter teachers, college advisers, and group sponsors may find it helpful to use specially designed questionnaires to collect information of particular value in their special fields.

3. Securing responses for use in validating information collected through other techniques. As a representative student response, the questionnaire offers a chance to validate by means of comparison the information received from other sources.

4. Sampling pupil opinions and attitudes. Questionnaires designed for a student-opinion sampling can vary widely, ranging from a series of items covering a single subject to coverage of a wide range of topics.

5. Making evaluations. Pupil viewpoints can add a worthwhile dimension to surveys and evaluations of various school programs, including the counseling program. Such evaluations are useful in planning improvements and in planning activities and the curriculum.

Designing the Questionnaire Much of the usefulness of any questionnaire depends on the adequacy of its design. Hence the following steps are recommended in developing a questionnaire: (1) determining the purpose or purposes of the questionnaire; (2) determining the types of information needed to serve these purposes; and (3) designing questions to secure the information that is appropriate to the grade and reading level of the pupil and their maturity and experiences.

There are also some specific criteria that should be kept in mind. For example, the age level of the pupils responding may determine the kinds of questions to be asked and the way they should be stated. If questions are easily answered, pupils will be inclined to complete the form accurately and honestly. (Many questionnaires require the respondent only to check one of several possible answers to each question. Such an instrument, which may appropriately be called a checklist, obviously entails very little writing effort and ensures the relative objectivity and specificity of the student's responses.)

It is also important for the questions to be the kind that pupils feel they can truthfully answer with a minimum of personal threat. Even one threatening question—for instance, "Do you ever cheat in your schoolwork?"—can arouse anxieties and doubts that may bias the responses to every item. In the occasional instances where it becomes desirable to secure pupil opinions of a controversial or confidential nature, unsigned questionnaires can be permitted. The results of an unsigned questionnaire are usually more reliable, but at the same time they are limited in regard to interpretation and analysis. The anonymity of the unsigned questionnaire makes it useful in terms of group results, useless in the analysis of individual respondents.

Limitations of the Questionnaire The limitations of the questionnaire are, for the most part, the results of improper construction and administration. Weaknesses of wording, length, and kinds of questions result in inaccurate or incomplete responses. Certain questions, such as those dealing with the economic status of the family, the parent-child relationship, and the general home environment, may arouse parental resentment and suspicion. The very manner in which the questionnaire is presented can deter a pupil from responding willingly and accurately and can lead to misunderstanding, which the pupil may convey to the parent.

Even under the most favorable conditions, it must be expected that some pupils will give inaccurate data that could prove misleading to the unwary. Thus again, interpreting the data gained through one technique against the background of all other pupil data must be emphasized as a very important step.

The Autobiography

The autobiography, which, in simplest terms, can be defined as one's life story written by oneself, is a literary instrument with which both the great and the humble throughout history have furnished insights into the events of their lives. Although the autobiography has often served to illuminate a period of history, its special contribution lies in the picture it gives of distinctive personalities, their perspective on life, and the ideas and activities of the writers.

For the same reasons, the pupil autobiography is a popular counseling technique for learning more about pupils. It is distinguished among the many methods used in collecting student information by the direct access it affords to the student's ideas and to the facts of his or her personal history; in the hands of a trained counselor, it can be an extremely valuable document. Of course, the writing skill and ability to express oneself may limit its utilization in the elementary school to pupils in upper grade levels.

Other Self-Report Techniques

In addition to the autobiography, several other self-report techniques are worthy of consideration. The pupil papers they produce are seldom as long, detailed, and informative as the autobiography, but they serve useful purposes of their own. This group includes essays on topics of current interest or personal concern, the "write a problem" technique, and diaries and daily schedules.

Essays

The writing of essays on topics of current interest or personal concern offers many of the values of the autobiography, especially in its ability to provide illuminating insights into a pupil's problems and viewpoints. And like the autobiography, it moves the student to self-examination and provides a safe outlet for release of tensions. However, the limits of the elementary school pupil in both self-expression, self-insight, and writing skills must be considered.

The "Write a Problem" Technique

Similar to the essay, but even less structured, is the "write a problem" technique. This may or may not be presented as a formal classroom assignment. When it is assigned in a class, the pupil is called upon to write about one or more topics or problems that concern her or him. The results provide a comprehensive view of pupil problems. By determining which topics are chosen most often and written about with the strongest feeling, teachers and counselors can gain perspective on the matters of greatest concern to pupils as a group.

Diaries and Daily Schedules

An indication of the pupil's daily activities can be obtained through the use of schedule or diary techniques. The chief difference between the two is that, in the former, the pupil presents an hour-by-hour accounting of daily activities, whereas, in the latter, he or she presents them in summarized form. These techniques are helpful in organizing information and, thereby, revealing how pupils actually spend their time. Pupils and the counselors and teachers assisting them find both schedules and diaries a useful basis for more effective study planning, wiser use of leisure, and better budgeting of time.

Recording for Pupil Assessment

Since the first recording of data on stone tablets through the present computer era, it is safe to say, recordkeeping has been universally regarded as a necessary evil. This consensus, of course, does not make the prospect of recordkeeping any more palatable to today's teacher, counselor, or school administrator, whose attitudes are typically expressed in such remarks as these: "If all the school records that the classroom teacher is required to keep were laid end to end, and all the school administrators that require teachers to keep these records were placed in a similar position, we could begin the celebration immediately." "When the stack of records becomes as high as the pupil, the pupil is ready for graduation." "Who cares if Johnny can't read; the main thing is—is that fact on his record?"

Thus, while no one will deny the importance of client/pupil recordkeeping, the counselor must be fully aware of the problems and legal responsibilities that may confront him or her as she or he approaches record development and record utilization for pupil analysis.

A number of significant changes have affected pupil recordkeeping in recent generations. Computers and other technological developments have altered methods of storing, displaying and utilizing data. Too, increased attention is now being paid to student records which, as Hummel and Humes (1984) note is

> *one of the dramatic developments in recent decades was the attention paid to student records. As class action suits developed during the 1960s, there was concern on the part of parents with regard to the use and misuse of pupil records and interpretation. This resulted in legislation in several of the state jurisdictions and culminated in the passage of federal legislation, namely, the Family Rights and Privacy Act (commonly referred to as the Buckley Amendment). Almost immediately the schools had to change their way of doing business. With the passage of this legislation, not only were parents permitted full access to pupil records and the privilege of denying access to them, but they now had the right to challenge the content of the pupil's record. Accordingly, cumulative records were purged and federal, state, and local guidelines were established for subsequent collection and use.*
>
> *The new approach to recordkeeping posed many problems for pupil services. School psychologists, social workers, and school counselors had traditionally been prime contributors to the cumulative record through psychological reports, social case histories, and counselor notations. They now not only had to review the records for appropriateness, but also had to change ways of reporting results and contacts. Perhaps hardest hit were school psychologists who had been accustomed to writing clinical reports designed only for professional view and scrutiny. Reports now had to be written that could be also shared with parents and, at age eighteen, with students. There developed much "tooth gnashing" over watered-down reports that would contribute but little to the presenting problem. This difficulty was finally resolved through the medium of detailed oral reports, usually at team meetings, to be followed by more general written reports. (pp. 358-359)*

Elementary school counselors must be very aware of the key responsibilities they have regarding pupil records under the previously mentioned Family Educational Rights and Privacy Act of 1974. Flygare (1975) pointed out the following key statements:

- A student (or the student's parents) must be given access to the pupil's records within 45 days from the time a request is made.
- A student (or the student's parents) must be granted a hearing by the institution upon request to determine the validity of any document in the student's file.

- Confidential letters or statements placed in the file prior to January 1, 1975, need not be disclosed under the law.
- A student may waive his/her right of access to confidential letters regarding admissions, honors, or employment.
- An educational institution cannot, with certain exceptions, release personally identifiable information about students.
- Educational institutions must notify students and parents of their rights under the law. (Flygare, 1975, p. 15)

Counselors must also be aware of and avoid sex-role stereotyping or discrimination in any form such as boy-girl test norms, career exploration activities, etc. Unverified statements of an uncomplimentary or libelous nature, statements with negative implications even the factual, opinions regarding home or family life are but a few examples of those which would place a counselor legally "at risk." Counselors must also be aware that they have limited legal guarantee to protect the confidentiality of school counseling records and the right of privileged communication.

Summary

Elementary school counselors who are truly effective are those who really know the children in their elementary school. They care enough to know enough. In order to know the individual child as accurately as possible, a number of techniques are utilized. Standardized testing, popular in most elementary schools for achievement measurement, provides objective assessments of certain pupil traits, including academic attainment. Counselors must be aware of criteria for test selection as well as procedures for administration and guidelines for interpretation.

Observation is an important subjective technique for understanding the child's behavior. Anecdotal reports, rating scales, and observation checklists can promote direction and accuracy in observations. Other instruments such as questionnaires, autobiographies, essays and diaries can provide useful insights into the life of children. Recordkeeping insures that important pupil data are noted or filed and organized for future consultation.

Chapter 11

Developing Programs of Counseling and Guidance in Elementary Schools

I believe the children
are our future;
teach them well and
let them lead the way.
Show them all the beauty
they possess inside.
Give them a sense of pride
To make it easier.
Let the children's laughter
remind us how we used to be . . . *
—WHITNEY HOUSTON (1985)

Introduction

During the 1980s, there was increased public interest in how effectively and efficiently service organizations served their publics in all arenas including educational and community agencies. For educational organizations, an inflationary economy resulted in efforts to ensure that educational expenditures resulted in "good values." Excellence in education became a universal goal and the national wellness movement with its emphasis on prevention reached down into the schools. Additionally, schools were called upon to respond to such major societal concerns as substance abuse, child abuse, AIDS, teen pregnancies, school dropouts, and so on. An outcome of the merging of these variables was renewed

*By Linda Creed and Michael Masser.

FIGURE 11–1 Sequence of Procedures for Developing an Accountable Program of Counseling and Guidance

Step 1	Step 2	Step 3	Step 4	Step 5	Step 6
Assessment of Needs through Data Collection	Interpretation of Data	Priority Needs	Program Objectives	Program Procedures (Activities developed based on program resources available)	Planning for Program Improvement (Based on evaluation of outcomes and procedures)

and insistent calls for educational organizations, and their subunits, to be more accountable. While the term "accountability" initially came into prominence in educational circles in the 1970s, the demand for accountability continued throughout the 1980s and will clearly be with us through the 1990s. The application of the concept of accountability has direct and significant implications for the organization and development of programs of counseling and guidance in elementary schools. As applied to organizations, including educational ones, the term accountability suggested an accounting for one's investments or a responsibility for one's actions. It requires evidence of accomplishments or gains in relationship to the mission of the organization. For education, it is expected that some factual evidence of pupil accomplishments will be provided in return for public fiscal support for education. Programs must justify their existence through factual evidence of achievements relevant to the purposes for which taxpayers or other payers established the programs. Accountability goes on to also expect that the program's accomplishments will be achieved efficiently and economically.

For counseling programs in elementary schools to be accountable, they must identify the needs they should be serving, how best to meet these needs and how to prove that they have successfully (hopefully) served these needs. These are the basic ingredients of an accountability model, which translates into organizational development steps as noted in Figure 11–1.

Accountable programs are designed to optimize the potential of the professional staff for the effective delivery of needed services and to ensure the continuous responsiveness of the program to the on-going needs of its clientele. The next section describes basic considerations in accountable program development.

Basic Considerations in Program Development

Needs

Counseling programs are responsible for responding to two kinds of needs: (1) those mandated by law or local policy (for instance, reporting incidents of child abuse); and (2) those determined by some form of needs assessment. These form

Type of Data	Source or Locale	Now Collected	Who Collects	By When	Comments
I. Environment					
Population	Census-Courthouse	Personal visit with data collection form	Ima Petty	Oct. 10	
Geographic	State Survey-Box 811 State Capital	Letter of Request	Will Reed	Oct. 15	
Economic	Major business and Chamber of Commerce Census	Personal data collection, visit, and interview	"Luckey" Bucks	Oct. 10	Mrs. Money will answer ques-tions at C of C
Sociopersonal	Census	As Indicated	Lotta Smiley	Oct. 20	
	Local Government Employment Office	Personal visit with data collection form as indicated	Will Reed	Oct. 20	
	Community Mental Health Center				
	Boy/Girl Scouts Offices	Personal visit with data collection form as indicated	Will Reed	Oct. 20	
	Children's Recreational Agencies				
		Personal visit and interview with data collection forms	Will Reed	Oct. 20	
	Churches		Ima Petty	Oct. 25	
	Civic Clubs		Ima Petty	Oct. 25	
	Family Services		Ima Petty	Oct. 25	
Political	Census	As indicated	Ima Petty	Oct. 10	May also want to interview local party heads.
Media	Local newspapers—offices of the Snowdeep Times	Personal visit Review selected issues over a five-year period	Will Reed	Oct. 10	Especially note front, editorial, plus educational column on Friday
II. Organization					
Annual school report	Principal's office	Personal visit	Ima Petty	Nov. 8	
Miscellaneous school reports	Principal's office	Personal visit	Ima Petty	Nov. 8	

FIGURE 11–2 Data Collection Plan for Counseling Development Program Snowdeep Elementary School

Type of Data	Source or Locale	How Collected	Who Collects	By When	Comments
II. Organization					
Board of Education minutes	Principal's office	Personal visit	Ima Petty	Nov. 8	
School Principal	Principal's office	Individual interview	Lotta Smiley	Nov. 8	
Teachers	(Use Room 110)	Individual interviews	"Luckey" Bucks	Nov. 8	
III. Target Population					
Pupils	School	Questionnaires mailed to total sample	Ima Petty	Nov. 20	Time limit 45 minutes (one class period)
Teachers	School	Questionnaires to total sample	"Luckey" Bucks	Nov. 20	
Parents	Various addresses	Questionnaires mailed to representative sample	Will Reed	Dec. 1	
School administrators	County education offices	Qustionnaires mailed to total sample	Lotta Smiley	Dec. 1	
Community leaders	Various addresses	Questionnaires mailed to representative sample	Lotta Smiley	Dec. 1	

FIGURE 11–2 *continued*

a factual basis for a program "doing what they should be doing." In the latter (needs assessment) activity, factual data are collected from those sources which are germane to the target population the program is designed to serve. In elementary schools, the target population is obviously the pupil enrollment in the school. With elementary school populations, counselors keep in mind that data gathering is for the purpose of identifying preventive, developmental and remediation or treatment needs. Much factual data needed may already be available and recorded in existing school records, community agency documents, census reports, and the like. Other data for substantiated needs may be collected through a variety of techniques such as questionnaires, interviews, checklists, and rating scales. In planning this phase of a program's development, it is important to prepare a data gathering plan, in writing, to ensure the collection of significant data by specific timelines with assigned responsibilities for each task. Figure 11–2 presents an example of such a plan.

Once the assessment data have been collected, it should be summarized and interpreted with a view to identifying those priority prevention, development, or remediation needs for the pupils served by the elementary school's counseling and guidance program.

Program Objectives

From the previously identified factually based priority needs, plus any additionally mandated activities, appropriate program objectives can now be stated. Accountability requires that these objectives be stated in measurable terms. In addition, they should be stated clearly and concisely and in a manner that ensures they will be easily understood by the various concerned publics, such as pupils, teachers, parents, and the community. Program objectives must, of course, reflect pupil needs but also be relevant to staff expertise and interests and resources available. The public's expectations may be an influence as well. Of course, no objectives should be proposed that are not attainable.

Program Planning (Procedures, Resources, and Evaluation)

Need identification and setting objectives represent the program base while the program's activities, utilization of resources, and evaluation of outcomes may be viewed as the program's core. As a part of a program's written plan, the planners must identify a set of procedures (activities) which not only promise to achieve the program's objectives, but promise to do so efficiently and economically. All procedural activities must be linked to one or more specific objectives and conversely, each program objective should be linked to one or more procedures. Important to this whole phase of program planning is the application of available or allocated resources. Of primary concern are professional staff; but support staff, supplies, equipment, and facilities are all important in determining what a program can reasonably hope to achieve. Included in any accountable program's

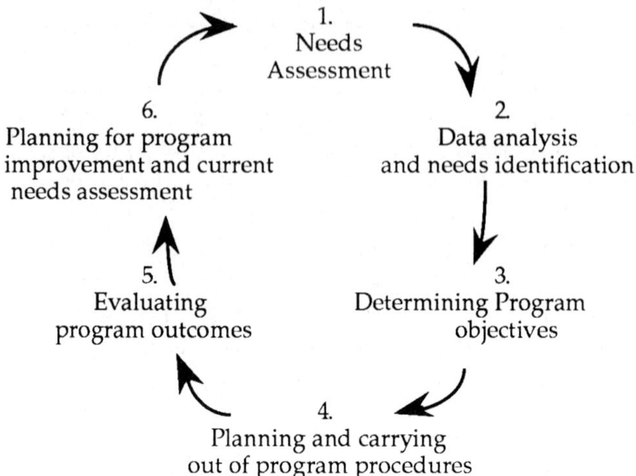

Figure 11–3 The Cycle of Program Planning and Functioning

procedures must be provisions for collecting proof of the program's accomplishments. The reason program objectives are stated in measurable terms is to enable factual evaluation of their outcomes. This evaluation activity is also critical to continued program development and improvement. Figure 11–3 indicates how evaluation feeds continuously into program improvement and development.

While the counseling staff should provide leadership and direction for program improvement, other personnel must also be committed to this improvement and the changes inherent in improvement. The Wisconsin Department of Public Instruction (1986, p. 32) noted these responsibilities as follows:

- *The school administration must commit to guidance program improvement and be*
  - *ready to participate in planning,*
  - *ready to assume key roles in planning for the developmental guidance program, and*
  - *ready to support abandonment of current activities that do not support new priorities.*
- *Counselors must commit to guidance program improvement and be*
  - *ready to become personally involved,*
  - *ready to assume key roles in planning for the developmental guidance program, and*
  - *ready to assume managerial responsibilities for the developmental guidance program.*
- *The school board must commit to guidance program improvements and be*

- *ready to adopt policy statements,*
- *ready to support planning time,*
- *ready to participate in the planning process, and*
- *ready to lend fiscal support.*

- *School staff must commit to guidance program improvement and be*
    - *ready to contemplate new ideas and change and*
    - *ready to become personally involved.*

(Wisconsin Department of Public Instruction, 1986, p. 32)

Staff Development

Consistent with and essential to program development and improvement is the ongoing professional development of the counseling staff. A "hallmark" of any true profession is the continuous updating and upgrading of its membership. We expect our physicians, dentists, and lawyers, for example, to be "up on the latest." (None of us would choose as a family doctor one who stopped learning when he graduated from medical school twenty years ago!) Our clients have the right to expect the same. Further, changing times demand new knowledge and skills. Thirty years ago substance abuse was scarcely noted in schools, computers were a rarity and dual career families were not the norm. Counselors and their programs must be responsive to changing times. Staff development enhances that responsiveness. Additionally, staff development responds to the basic need of individuals to self-actualize, to develop their potential. Staff development then is responsive to both the assessed needs of a target population and the assessed interests of the professional staff.

Most school districts have access to a variety of staff development resources. The Georgia Department of Education (1983) suggested the following examples:

- *Workshops by local staff*
- *University courses*
- *University sponsored workshops*
- *Send an individual or team away to a source (workshop) to bring back information and skills to share with others*
- *Send individual or team to observe model projects*
- *Create a consortium of local school districts to use each others' expertise*
- *Use outside consultant over period of time*
- *State department workshops*
- *Self-instructional packages*
- *Instructional television. (p. 32)*

They also noted the importance of not just learning new skills, but also having the need/opportunity to apply them. For example, to learn a new skill/technique, activities need to be constructed to first make an individual aware and then to allow some experimentation in trying out the skill/technique so that the individual can become competent in that skill/technique. It is important that staff development activities include all the elements described (knowledge to be learned, skill/technique needed, attitudes/values required, and application stages) and attend to the appropriate learning phases to be effective. Dwelling only on knowledge to be learned without providing staff with the skills/techniques to apply the knowledge, the impact of the activities will be lessened considerably. (p. 76)

Professionalization

Complimentary to staff development and vice versa, is the professionalization of the elementary school counselor. Professionalization, of course, requires becoming the very best practicing counselor one can become, but it also goes beyond. This also assumes that active and labeled members of the profession qualify themselves for the appropriate certification or licensure. Such a procedure is necessary to protect both the public and the profession. Currently, all states have specific criteria for certification of school counselors.

Professionalization also anticipates the active participation in and advancement of one's chosen profession. This participation includes an active membership in appropriate professional organizations, sharing one's experiences through attendance at, and participation, in professional conferences and programs, and advancing the profession through research and the search for new knowledge, and professional writing. Remember to inform your school principal of new ideas you are implementing as a result of your conference or workshop attendance. It is important that others recognize the benefits of your active participation in professional activities even though they may require your absence from school on occasion.

A prime professional organization for elementary school counselors is the American Counseling Association (ACA) and its school counselors division, the American School Counselors Association (ASCA). In addition, ACA has 56 state branches and four regional branch assemblies. Among the activities which ASCA sponsors is an annual summer conference for school counselors. ACA notes other benefits of membership as follows:

- An annual subscription to the *Journal of Counseling and Development*
- Eighteen issues of the *Guidepost*, ACA's official newspaper
- Information access to the latest books, films, videotapes, and other materials
- Library bibliographic search services
- Eligibility for professional liability insurance programs
- Legal defense services
- Professional development through workshops, conferences, and conventions
- Network opportunities

A final index of professionalization is "public service." Service in this sense might be defined as voluntary contributions to the public well-being above and beyond one's assigned duties. It is through such service that a profession demonstrates to the public its active concern for the well-being of society. It is an important activity in gaining that all important public trust.

Communications: Public and Professional

Counselors are trained to be skilled communicators in the counseling relationship; however, there is an abundance of evidence that indicates our frequent shortcomings in communicating with our various interested and important publics. We cannot expect blind support for counseling programs in our elementary schools. (Remember, our parents did not have elementary school counselors.) There is no historical background which contributes to the general public's understanding of what elementary school counselors do and why it is important that they do it. It is, therefore, important that elementary school counselors become "public relations activists." A high priority must be given to communicating the goals, activities, and accomplishments to all the appropriate publics. These publics include: those within the school setting—teachers, pupils, and administrators; important external groups—parents, board of education members, Chamber of Commerce, civic and religious groups; and the general public.

To insure appropriate and ongoing communications to all served or potentially supporting publics, programs should develop a written communications plan which targets specific populations to receive certain information by the most appropriate media by certain dates. (This becomes your "marketing plan.") Figure 11–4 illustrates one such plan for our imagined Lockjaw Elementary School.

In this marketing or communication plan keep in mind that you are communicating not only to inform but to influence as well. Communicating influentially is facilitated by factual data related to program needs and outcomes expressed in a manner that influences positive responses, support, and/or acceptance. Finally, communication is not only sending, it is also receiving! Listening and being responsive to others is important if you expect others to listen to you and, of course, hearing others is important in maintaining program relevancy also.

Professional Research

Professional research is an essential and critical technique that a profession uses for advancement of the profession. Professional research recognizes the need for increased knowledge, continuous improvement and refining of the profession; all important in laying claim to and maintaining of the public's trust. In the early generations of the profession, much of the professional research affecting counseling theory and practice was carried out in institutions of higher education and/or through government offices, resulting in the erroneous assumption that local or practitioners' research was unworthy, not needed or not sophisticated enough. Goldman (1978) addressed some of these concerns in his introduction to *Research Methods for Counselors* when he wrote:

What Audience	What Information	What Purpose	How Communicated	By Whom	When
Pupils	General information on program and counselors	Orientation to services and staff	Classroom visits	All Counselors	Beginning of each semester
			Bulletin board display Poster	Artie Guy	First of each month
					As needed
	Special activities and services	Inform special need pupils of opportunities	School announcements Poster	Artie Guy	
			Classroom visits	All Counselors	
Teachers	Presentation of classroom guidance materials	Selection of materials and coordinate planning of classroom guidance visits	Teacher-counselor conferences	Ima Goody grades 1–2 Carla Rogers grades 3–4 Artie Guy grades 5–6	Beginning of each semester
	Consultation services available	Orientation to and use of services	Teacher-counselor conferences	(as above)	First week of every month
	Special activities and programs	Orientation	Faculty meetings and announcements	Ima Goody	To be determined
	Evaluative feedback	Faculty evaluation of counseling services	Questionnaire to	Designed and distributed by Carla Rogers	Dec. 1 and May 1
School Principal	General information on program planning, activities, accomplishments and concerns	To inform, receive feedback and suggestions and gain support	Invited to attend one counseling staff meeting each month by personal invitation and follow-up memo	Carla Rogers (Chair)	Monthly

continued

FIGURE 11–4 Communications Plan for the Lockjaw Elementary School Program

What Audience	What Information	What Purpose	How Communicated	By Whom	When
Parents	General information on program, its services and the counseling staff	Orientation to services and staff and gain support for use of programs services	Participation in P.T.A. meetings newsletter	All Counselors	First meeting of each semester
Community	General information on program, services and staff	Orientation of general public and gaining support for programs	Press releases to local newspaper (The Lockjaw "Goff and Gab"), local radio station	Artie Guy	Monthly (1st week) plus special releases
			Presentations to civic organizations	All counselors	Upon invitation
			Invitations to a community form on issues related to the needs of our children	Carla Rogers	Mid-October and Mid-February

FIGURE 11–4 *continued*

> *From 1969 to 1975 I was editor of the* Personnel and Guidance Journal. *I resolved from the beginning that we would publish only those articles that had something to say to counseling practitioners, that we were a reader's not a writer's journal. We found almost no research manuscripts during those years that satisfied that criterion; quite a few research reports were received, especially in the earlier years, but almost every one of them either was so technical that it could not be truly understood except by very research-sophisticated people, or was so limited in its implications that it really had nothing to offer the practicing counselor . . . I came to the realization that the problem was not "research" as a general idea but rather the kinds of research that have predominated in our field. I became convinced that the kinds of research methods and the kinds of research studies that prevail in the field are largely inappropriate or inadequate for most of the kinds of knowledge and insight counselors require in their daily work. (Goldman, 1978, pp. 4-5)*

Stockton and Hulse (1983) appropriately called attention to the fact that "Counseling is an applied discipline with an emphasis on practice; yet, if the profession does not assume responsibility for intellectual inquiry which might provide answers to basic questions concerning effective practice, the field cannot advance" (p. 303). In joining those calling for more "usable" research in our field, we would emphasize that research: (1) can provide positive outcomes; (2) can be carried out by even beginning practitioners within a simple framework of research procedures; and (3) can be interesting (Gibson & Mitchell, 1990, p. 438).

In recent years, the calls have continued, increasingly calling for more practitioners to engage in research at their local levels and certainly, nowhere is this need more evident than in the field of elementary school counseling. In further encouraging this viewpoint, we note that research can be both meaningful to the profession as well as motivational to the professionals involved in investigations related to their interests and needs. Too, there are various recognized kinds of research that professionals can choose to engage in as follows:

Basic Research In educational settings, basic research is conducted for the purpose of developing theory or for establishing some general principles. This in turn can lead to implications for the solving of problems.

Applied Research The applying or evaluating of a theory through the collection of data appropriate to the testing of the theory.

Action Research Action research is designed to solve problems through the application of scientific method. It provides a systematic framework for problem solving. It can also be a model for program or practice evaluation.

Historical Research can involve the interpretation of documents, comparing and cross-checking differing pieces of data or information and the study of chronological events.

Descriptive Research has a focus on answering questions pertaining to the present. Descriptive studies are frequently based on surveys, comparative studies or case studies.

Experimental Research Experimental research seeks to develop predictions of what will happen in the future given certain specific circumstances. These circumstances or variables are established through an experimental process that leads to their identification.

In conducting research, certain procedural expectancies provide direction for the researcher and increase the credibility of the results. In broad general terms these procedures, in sequence, are as follows:

1. Recognition of the need for information (identification of the problem—what you need to know). What question(s) do you want answered?
2. Survey of the relevant literature. Are the answers already "out there"? What's been done? What approaches show promise? This procedure provides an increased depth of understanding of the problem.
3. Formulation of the specific research problem—what exactly do we need to know (refining number 1. above).
4. Identification of the type of specific information needed to respond to number 3. above.
5. Development of procedures for collecting the appropriate data as identified in number 4. above.
6. Utilization of data analysis (How will the data be analyzed and treated in order to maximize interpretation and validity of findings?).
7. Interpretation and reporting of conclusions (What do the analyzed results mean in terms of the research questions asked? What can be concluded from the results? What are the implications? How shall the study be communicated and to whom?)

Blocher (1987) identifies the following questions which readers of research reports should ask when dealing with experimental results: (Reprinted with the permission of Macmillan Publishing from *The Professional Counselor*, by D. H. Blocher. Copyright © 1987 by Macmillan Publishing Company.)

- *Is the problem clearly described?*
- *Did the study test a specific set of hypotheses?*
- *Is the source of these hypotheses clearly indicated?*
- *Have the hypotheses been logically derived from an underlying theory or body of previous research?*
- *How has the investigator operationally defined crucial constructs so that results really are relevant to hypotheses?*
- *How have the measuring instruments and techniques been chosen?*
- *Have the instruments been validated and their reliability established?*
- *Is the method of the experiment reported clearly and completely enough for the study to be replicated?*
- *How were the subjects selected?*
- *Are there biases built into the selection process that will limit the general value of the results?*

- *Is the rationale for the setting and the size of the sample presented adequately?*
- *What kind of control procedures are used and what factors are actually controlled?*
- *Are the experimental and control conditions randomly assigned to subjects?*
- *Are the experimental and control treatments described clearly and fully?*
- *Is the rationale for the statistical analysis explained?*
- *Are the results printed clearly, completely, and logically?*
- *Do the authors distinguish between the statistical significance and the practical meaning of the results?*
- *Are the limitations of the study clearly and completely spelled out?*
- *Do the conclusions and interpretations of the authors follow logically and directly from the results or are they somewhat speculative?*
- *How do the results from this study compare with those from previous research on the topic?*
- *Do these results tend to support, modify, or refute important parts of the underlying theory?*
- *What are the implications of this study for professional practice?*
- *What further research is needed to support the implications of this study for professional practice?*
- *How will I utilize these findings as a professional counselor? (p. 386)*

It will be helpful for you when reviewing the counseling research literature to refer to these questions. However, it is important to keep in mind that some of the questions might deal with areas that you have not yet become knowledgeable about, such as statistical significance, control procedures, statistical analysis, and so on. More information regarding these concepts can be gained through courses in research design and statistics.

Finally, we would note the importance of becoming familiar with those professional journals which present articles reporting research studies of interest to the counseling profession. These would especially include those published by the American Counseling Association and the American Psychological Association. Two such journals which focus specifically on school counselors are published by ACA. They are the *Journal of Elementary School Guidance and Counseling* which is published four times per year, and the *School Counselor,* which is published five times per year.

Summary

The success of the elementary school counseling program will be largely dependent on how successful the program is in identifying the real needs of its pupil population and then organizing its resources and selecting the appropriate activities to meet these needs. In this process, public as well as professional communications are important. The professional elementary school counselor recognizes the importance of research in advancing the effectiveness of counseling in the elementary school.

Chapter 12

Legal and Ethical Guidelines for Counselors

It costs so much to be a full human being
that there are very few who have
the enlightenment or the courage
to pay the price . . . One has to abandon
altogether the search for security,
and reach out to the risk of living
with both arms.
One has to embrace the world
like a lover.
—MORRIS L. WEST (1989)
The Shoes of the Fisherman

Introduction

As true public service professions emerge, they assume certain responsibilities aimed at protecting and enhancing their service to the public and at the same time protecting and enhancing the profession itself. Ethical and legal guidelines are clearly central to deserving the public trust for any profession. It is especially important to an emerging and relatively unknown profession such as counseling. Additionally, the developing of these guidelines are also important in helping the profession view and define itself. The criteria for measuring a profession's professionalization are generally agreed upon (Dunlop, 1968; McCully, 1953). "These criteria stipulate that the profession's group and its members: (1) can clearly define their role; (2) offer unique services; (3) possess special skills and knowledge; (4) have an explicit code of ethics; (5) have the legal right to offer the service as the profession describes it; and (6) have the ability to monitor the practice of their profession (Nugent, 1981)." (Hummel, Talbutt, and Alexander 1985, p. 5).

Too, the rapid growth of the counseling profession has brought it into a broader range of employment settings over the past decades. Not only are counselors functioning in a broader range of employment environments, but they are also functioning in a much more complex legal environment. This is attested to by the fact that counselors are, with increasing frequency, being seen in court and in related ethical disputes. For example, elementary school counselors are frequently involved in court proceedings resulting from reports of suspicion of child abuse. School counselors are also called upon to testify on occasion in child custody hearings.

Remley (1985) suggests that a counselor follow these guidelines in testifying on behalf of a child.

1. *Avoid discussing the case in casual conversations. Do not offer opinions regarding the merits of the case. Words spoken informally without careful consideration can be used against counselors during cross-examination.*
2. *Before the court date, attempt to speak either with the attorney representing the side that will be helped by your testimony or to the prosecutor who will be conducting the direct examination. Ask the attorney to review anticipated questions in advance and to predict questions that might be asked during cross-examination by the opposing attorney.*
3. *When testifying, be as objective as possible. Relate facts without personal interpretations. If asked an opinion, you should state it freely but be prepared to give the reasoning behind the opinion. Try to relax. All the counselor must do in these situations is tell the truth in an objective manner.*
4. *If asked to disclose information you consider confidential, turn to the presiding judge and request that you not be ordered to answer the question. Clearly state that the reason for your request is the importance of confidentiality in counseling relationships and the expectation of privacy the client had at the time the interaction took place. If ordered by the judge to answer the question posed, you should do so; otherwise you can be held in contempt of court and fined or jailed. If you believe that answering such a question would breach an ethical obligation to a client, ask the judge for an opportunity to consult with an attorney. (pp. 185-186)*

It is important that the functioning counselor develop an awareness of the ethical guidelines, legal privileges, and restraints affecting his or her profession. The practicing counselor must become attuned to thinking and acting in an ethical and legal manner at all times and must be aware of the related issues and concerns as well. Ferris and Linville (1985) point out that:

Many of the ethical dilemmas a counselor confronts are associated with when and how to report child abuse, the use and reporting of test scores, and informal communications within the school community. Concern and caring for the student is not enough. Professional organization standards and public law, integrated with the counselor's beliefs concerning the welfare of the student and the family, are essential to the process of ethical resolution of the dilemmas counselors face in schools. (p. 175)

Legal, Ethical Issues and Concerns

Privileged Communication (Confidentiality)

Few issues have so consistently plagued the profession as the status of privileged communication or client right to confidentiality. Privileged communication is a legal right that exists by state statute and protects pupil clients from having their confidential communications disclosed in court without their permission (Sheely and Herlihy, 1987, p. 268). The issue of confidentiality continues to be a paramount legal, as well as ethical, issue confronting the counseling profession. Sheely and Herlihy indicate that in a survey of existing privileged communication statutes and rules of evidence in the 50 states and the District of Columbia, it was noted that counselors in schools were granted the right to privileged communication (although often limited) in 20 states. Four criteria that are generally accepted by modern law scholars as evidence of the appropriate test for what qualifies as privileged communication are cited by Fischer and Sorenson (1991). They in turn, are citing Wigmore, a leading authority on Anglo-American law of evidence, as indicated in the following:

1. *The communications must originate in confidence that they will not be disclosed.*
2. *The confidentiality must be essential to full and satisfactory maintenance of the relationship between the parties.*
3. *The relationship must be one which, in the opinion of the community, should be seriously fostered.*
4. *The injury to that relation, caused by disclosure, would be greater than the benefit gained to the process of litigation. (Fischer & Sorenson, 1991, p. 12)*

Counselors, of course, should not misinterpret situations where these criteria are met as being legal guarantees of their right to the privileged communication of their clients in those states which do not have statutes extending this protection. However, following these guidelines will at least enhance the possibility should legal issues arise. Of course, privileged communication is a client's right and if the client chooses to waive this right the counselor clearly has no grounds for withholding the information. In discussing guidelines for confidentiality, Remley (1985) suggests that counselors take the following steps in regard to fulfilling their confidentiality responsibilities with children.

1. *Always inform the child before another person is consulted regarding the child's problem. The child's consent is desirable but not always necessary.*

2. *Try to involve the child in the decision-making process once adults are contacted. Avoid taking actions that may create for the child a feeling of betrayal by the counselor or other involved adults.*
3. *Keep the child informed of decisions as they are made. (p. 183)*

Remley (1985) further emphasizes that:

Counselors in elementary and middle schools often must involve adults in the problems of their clients who are minors. As a result, the child's expectation of privacy sometimes is outweighed by the need to inform parents, guardians, or other adults. On the other hand, school counselors should keep as confidential as possible details of interactions with their clients who are minors. They should also recognize that some adults involved in a child's problem have expectations of privacy identical to those of the client. Although the child's rights are the primary concern, it is important for counselors to make sure that no person's right to confidentiality is totally disregarded. In fact, because situations requiring disclosure of confidential information are rare, it is essential that the child's consent to disclose be secured whenever possible. (p. 195)

Concern for the welfare of the child must always be considered in regards to issues of confidentiality. The answers are not simple. Elementary school counselors must put much thought and caring into making decisions related to confidentiality issues. In the *American Counselor* (1992), Remley insists that counselors who do not understand their legal obligations are in no way excused if the legal rights of others are violated by them. He suggests that counselors take the following steps in seeking clarification regarding legal issues:

1. *Read all rules and regulations that apply to your place of employment.*
2. *When you are unsure of your legal obligations, consult with your supervisor and follow his or her advice.*
3. *Attend seminars and read professional literature related to topics that concern you.*
4. *Purchase individual professional liability insurance.*

Licensure

Professional licensure is a process of legal recognition by a state pertaining to the exclusive right of those trained in meeting the profession's qualifications for practice and entitling them in turn to practice and use the title of the profession. To date, 37 states have licensure laws recognizing professional counselors. Licensure has been in the decade of the 1980s, and will continue to be in the 1990s, a major issue and concern of the counseling profession as a whole. Much of this focuses on the rights of counselors in private practice seeking third party payments. Licensure also represents the degree of recognition that the profession has publicly achieved. For school counselors certification is more significant.

Certification indicates that a counselor has reached the level of training specified by the individual state to qualify them for employment and practice in the school as a counselor. Certification standards generally are a part of the total teacher education certification standards of a state. At this time, all 50 states have specified certification standards for school counselors. In some instances, however, they are somewhat vague regarding elementary school counselors. In other instances, they simply appear to apply the former secondary school certification standards to the elementary school's certification process with the usual addition of experience as an elementary school teacher or an internship in an elementary school setting.

Standards of Training

A third issue that is becoming an increasingly important one and does relate to both licensure and certification, is the issue of standards of training. In an effort to upgrade and standardize training standards in the counselor education profession, the American Counseling Association has recognized a separate, independent accreditation body known as the Council for the Accreditation of Counseling and Related Educational Programs (CACREP) with attending standards and procedures for programs to be accredited. CACREP standards are currently represented in counselor training programs in 78 institutions.

Libel/Slander

The defamation of an individual's reputation or character through libelous or slanderous statements has become increasingly the subject of legal and ethical actions against counselors. In the elementary school setting, the counselor may be called upon to make and report judgments, to complete recommendations, and to record observations. All of these provide potential situations in which libel suits or charges of slander could emerge. Many such actions have been stimulated since the passage in 1974 of the Family Educational Rights and Privacy Act as it is titled (or the Buckley Amendment as it is commonly referred to). This act stipulated that parents have the right to inspect and review any and all official school records, files, and data directly related to their children. As Aiello & Humes (1987) indicate, in *Mattie T.* v. *Johnston* (1976), it was pointed out by the court that the FERPA

> *does not prevent the release of records to parents, but is aimed at preventing release of records to unauthorized individuals or organizations without the consent of the student or the parent. Thus, it is clear that either parent of a student has access to the records of that student, in the absence of a court order or other official instrument prohibiting that access. (p. 179)*

This includes all material that is incorporated into each student's cumulative record folder and intended for school use or to be available to parties outside the school or school system. This also covers identifying data, academic coursework

TABLE 12–1 Analysis of Statements in School Records and Suggestions for Change

Inappropriate statement	Analysis	More appropriate statement
"Insecure"	Ambiguous, inferential Does not describe behavior	"Has difficulty accepting responsibility" or other behaviorally descriptive statements
"Does not reach potential"	No way of really assessing potential	"X's behavior would indicate greater capabilities in ______, but she has not been able to demonstrate this in a school situation."
"Often tardy—has weak excuses."	Implies that child is lying	"Often tardy in (a.m. or p.m.)"
"Pushy"	Does not describe student's behavior	Delete
"Conference appointment was made; mother did not appear."	Negative overtones Implies careless attitude	"Close cooperation with parents is very desirable."
"Has to be reprimanded frequently."	Does not describe behavior or conditions under which it occurs	Delete or include description of student's behavior.

Reprinted with permission of the American Counseling Association from "Ethical and Legal Dilemmas of Working with Students with Special Needs" (p. 209) by D. E. Jenkins in *Elementary School Guidance and Counseling, 19,* 1985. Adapted form "Telling It IS Improving School Records," by C. C. Wilhelm and M. Case in the *School Counselor, 23,* 1975. Reprinted with permission.

and levels of achievement, attendance data, standardized test scores, health data, family background information, and teacher or counselor ratings and observations and verified reports of recurrent behavior patterns.

To safeguard against libel or slanderous acts, counselors must ensure that any statements they make regarding their elementary pupils/clients are truthful, can be verified and do not ridicule, disgrace or harm the reputation of the individual. Jenkins (1985) provides examples of inappropriate comments in school records, analysis of these comments, and suggestions for change. Table 12–1 illustrates these examples.

Counselors must also guard against passing on confidential information to third parties through casual conversations, giving such information out over the telephone and leaving records unattended where others can read them.

Avoiding Liability

The elementary school counselor should not assume that they are immune to malpractice lawsuits. In recent generations, we have seen a gradual increase in the amount of litigation targeting counselors in a wide range of settings. There are two important protective steps which the elementary school counselor should take.

1. Professional associations have excellent malpractice insurance at very economical rates. This is a must even though the counselor does not anticipate engaging in activities or practicing in a way that would make her or him legally vulnerable.

2. Expert legal advice is available. Most school corporations retain a legal adviser or law firm possessing expertise in school law and other legal matters of which schools must be aware. School counselors should have individual conferences or a representative of a law firm address them at least once a year to keep them up to date on legal matters relevant to their role and function.

By way of example, counselors should certainly be familiar with the provisions of Title IX and the Educational Amendment (1972), which took effect in July, 1975 which provides that "no person shall, on the basis of sex, be excluded from participation in, be denied the benefits of, or be subject to discrimination under any education program receiving financial assistance. Another example is the previously mentioned the Family Educational Rights and Privacy Act of 1974 (referred to as the Buckley Amendment) which gives parents the right of access to school records regarding their child, including counseling records.

Another important legislative act for school counselors is the Education for all Handicapped Children Act (Public Law 94-142 of November, 1975 which gives all children the right, regardless of their handicap, to a free, appropriate education. This law implies significant participation by certified counselors in the education of the handicapped. Jenkins (1985) specifies skills within the counselor's role of mainstreaming students with special needs as follows:

1. *Working with nonhandicapped elementary school children to encourage acceptance of individual's differences.*
2. *Helping handicapped children understand their strengths and weaknesses and make use of existing skills to function in an environment not equipped for handicapped persons.*
3. *Developing counseling activities for all elementary school children, including those with special needs.*
4. *Developing activities to assist the development of a positive self-concept in the child with special needs.*
5. *Formulating teacher, parent, and administrator counseling groups to discuss attitudes and feelings toward the student with special needs. (p. 203)*

Counselors should also be aware of the legal implications of the dispensing of any kind of medication, the provisions of sexual information, illegal search and seizures, invasion of privacy, and any type of discriminatory activity.

It is also expected that counselors will function within the limits of their professional expertise. As a legal precaution, as well as an ethical responsibility,

Fischer and Sorenson (1991) point out that the legal principles governing such cases are as follows:

> *One who undertakes gratuitously or for consideration to render services to another which he/she should recognize as necessary for the protection of the other person or things, is subject to liability for the other, for physical harm resulting from his/her failure to exercise reasonable care to perform his/her undertaking, if (a) his/her failure to exercise such care increases the risk or harm or (b) the harm is suffered because of the others' reliance upon the undertaking. (p. 35)*

Professional counselors, including those in schools, can be held legally responsible where malpractice or negligence is alleged to have occurred. Hopkins & Anderson (1990) note that there are several principal situations in which malpractice has generally been found as follows:

1. *The procedure followed was not within the realm of accepted professional practice;*
2. *The technique used was one the counselor was not trained to use (lack of professional competence);*
3. *The counselor failed to follow a procedure that would have been more helpful;*
4. *The counselor failed to warn and protect others from a violent client;*
5. *Informed consent was not obtained; or*
6. *The counselor failed to explain the possible consequences of the treatment. (p. 25)*

Remley (1985) suggests preventative measures which school counselors can take in avoiding malpractice suits. They include:

1. *Knowing their job descriptions and not deviating significantly from them in their daily work; revising a job description if it does not reflect current responsibilities or practices.*
2. *Knowing the ACA and ASCA ethical standards and practicing according to those standards.*
3. *Consulting with other professionals before acting when difficult legal or ethical situations arise.*
4. *Attending workshops and conferences to stay informed of current developments in the counseling field. (p. 187)*

Professional Values and Codes of Ethics

When the professional values of a profession are translated into standards of conduct for the members of that profession, they are usually titled "codes of ethics." Such codes provide guidelines for the membership of the profession to follow in their practice. They also indicate to the public what they may anticipate in their utilization of the services of the profession and its membership. There are two basic statements of ethical practice and behavior that apply to work in the counseling profession: ethical standards of the American Counseling Association; and Ethical Principles for Psychologists. These codes are expected to serve as guidelines to be followed by the members of these associations in their professional practices. Failure to do so may result in a member being expelled. Types of items to be found in most codes are as follows:

1. *The specific duties or rights that differ from ordinary ethical requirements*
2. *The specific duties or rights that may be the application of general ethical principles in a particular professional area*
3. *A reiteration of certain ordinary ethical requirements that need emphasis for some reason*
4. *Aims or general goals that the professional should aspire to realize*
5. *Requirements that relate to coordinating or protecting the interests of the members of the profession*
6. *A statement of the responsibilities of members of the profession for reporting code violations or other violations. (Mabe & Rollin, 1986, p. 294)*

Ethical guidelines appropriate for the elementary school counselor are contained in Appendix B.

Personal and Professional Development

You have been informed of the counselor's responsibilities to protect the service provided and the counseling profession itself. Prior to this, however, counselor education programs must prepare students to fulfill their roles as counselors through the development of personal and professional skills. The content of many courses will focus on the dynamics of human behavior and how the personal qualities you bring to counseling influence the growth of your clients.

Although enrolling in a counselor training program is a singular task, it unlocks the door to numerous multi-leveled internal and external human experiences for which some students may be unprepared. At some level, you have decided to undergo a significant change in your life and will subsequently discover that while learning academically, you concurrently grow and develop personally. Your education will, at times, evoke the intense examination, and often renegotiation, of the self and the self in relationship with others.

While learning counseling theories and skills, you will simultaneously rearrange personal characteristics of yourself into a new and more meaningful whole: one that is consistent with your emerging beliefs about human nature, human potential, and the human capacity to change.

The rudimentary phase in becoming a counselor involves the personal encounter with yourself in which you reach deep inside to discover and express who you are; how you became who you are; and who you will become. In a sense you become your own first client. Learning to facilitate change in others begins with the powerful evolution of yourself.

The fact that you are reading this text is evidence that professional growth and development has begun. Whether you are just beginning your course of study, or increasing your current level of functioning, a growthful change is occurring. Further, living more fully becomes a way of life for those who strive to maintain the richness derived from stretching their internal limits.

Professional Organizations

Characteristics of our society continue to metamorphose, thus altering the nature of forces that influence the development of young lives. Increased drug availability and AIDS are but two negative factors that have transpired to endanger the lives of our children. Advanced computer technology and its impending influence on existence and future careers is a positive factor, yet one that requires attention.

In order to keep pace with the innovations and minimize, or prevent, negative consequences to our children, counselors have the option to become members of professional organizations. The national organization for all counseling professionals in schools and related settings is the American Counseling Association (ACA) which currently has nearly 60,000 members. The American School Counselor Association (ASCA), an affiliate of ACA, currently has over 12,000 members who receive support through journals, conferences, and networking systems. State and local divisions of these national organizations also inform members of current trends in counseling.

Presentations at workshops and conferences update and revitalize counselors and their programs. Exhibitors at these conferences display materials such as books, games, videos, and puppets for perusal and purchase. Also, counselors have opportunities to share their own accomplishments and techniques by presenting at conferences. Another professional growth opportunity is service on committees with other counselors.

Although attendance at these meetings requires counselors to take professional leave from children at school, the knowledge received benefits all students.

The confluence of all these systems: those responsible for increasing your knowledge, skill, cognitions, and psychological awareness, integrate to enhance your functioning as a whole person at work. In *Jonathan Livingston Seagull*, Richard Bach (1973) explains the objective of growth and development which is endemic to counselor education programs:

> *There's a reason to life! We can lift ourselves out of ignorance, we can find ourselves as creatures of excellence, and intelligence, and skill . . . The most important thing in living is to reach out and touch perfection in that which you most love to do . . . You have to practice and see the real gulls, the good in every one of*

> *them, and to help them see it in themselves . . . You need to keep finding yourself, a little more each day.* (pp. 30, 60, 123, 124)

Summary

In summary, this chapter contains legal and ethical guidelines to be adopted as the requisite credo by all professional counselors. That is, all counseling activities must be implemented within the framework of high legal and ethical professional standards.

Issues discussed were privileged communication, licensure, standards of training, libel and slander, avoiding liability, and professional development. We concluded this chapter, as well as this text, with a description of the imminent personal evolution that is likely to occur as one becomes a helping professional. Participation in programs of professional development, such as counselor education programs, permits the individual to reach higher levels of human functioning. This in turn enables the professional counselor to transfer those gifts to the populations he or she serves while rendering counseling and guidance services in the elementary school and beyond.

Appendix A

Research of Interest to Elementary School Counselors

Research of Interest

Allan, J., & Bardsley, P. (1983). "Transient children in the elementary school: A group counseling approach," *Journal of Elementary School Guidance and Counseling, 17*, 162-169.

Abstract

Examined the effects of a school counselor led group designed to provide an opportunity for six transient third grade students to share thoughts and feelings regarding moving. Positive benefits resulting from the group experience were reported by the students, their teachers and the principal of the school.

Allred, G. B., & Dobson, J. E. (1987). "Remotivation group interaction: Increasing children's contact with the elderly," *Journal ofElementary School Guidance and Counseling*, 21, 216-220.

Abstract

Describes the procedures and results of a study involving 15 sixth grade students in a remotivation program with 15 elderly nursing home residents. Conclusions indicated that planned interactions between children and older adults can help to meet the needs of both generations for more meaningful social roles, while helping children to develop more positive images of aging.

Baker, S. B., Swisher, J. D., Nadenichek, P. E., & Popowicz, C. L. (1984). "Measured effects of primary prevention strategies," *Personnel and Guidance Journal, 62*, 459-464.

Abstract

Conducted a meta-analysis of over 40 primary prevention studies to investigate the measured effects of primary prevention strategies. Studies selected were those that were controlled experiments with empirical comparisons between treatment and controlled conditions and studies in which treatment conditions had goals and involved participants. This allowed the studies to be classified as primary prevention. Fifteen of the studies utilized or included elementary school populations. It was concluded that considering the difficulties that limit opportunities to conduct successful primary prevention programs in the school, the results are encouraging.

Bertoia, J., & Allan, J. (1988). "Counseling seriously ill children: Use of spontaneous drawings," *Journal of Elementary School Guidance and Counseling*, 22, 206-221.

Abstract

Discussed the process and results of an elementary school counselor's use of spontaneous drawings in counseling a terminally ill child. Conclusions referred to the benefits of using spontaneous drawings in the counseling process and suggested that the same procedures be used also in other times of crisis.

Bleck, R. T., & Bleck, B. I. (1982). The Disruptive Child's Play Group. *Journal of Elementary School Guidance and Counseling*, 17, 137-141.

Abstract

Reported on the effects of the Disruptive Child's Play Group that was offered by elementary school counselors for third grade students in 13 schools. Conclusions showed that counselors using structured play can have positive effects on the attitudes of disruptive children and the DCPG provides a means of dealing with disruptive children that is familiar and acceptable to many elementary schools.

Boser, J. A., Poppen, W. A., & Thompson, C. L. (1988). "Elementary school guidance program evaluation: A reflection of student counselor ratio," School Counselor, 36, 125-135.

Abstract

This study examined the perceived effectiveness of guidance programs in Tennessee public schools representing the following three distinct student-to-counselor ratios: (a) one school, one counselor, fewer than 600 students; (b) one school, one counselor, 750-1000 students; and, (c) three to four schools, one counselor, 1000 to more than 2000 students per counselor. It was found that as the student to counselor ratios increase, the number of students who cannot be adequately served by the counselor also increases, thus reducing the overall effectiveness of the counselor as perceived by students, parents and school staff members.

Bowker, M. A. (1982). "Children and divorce: Being in between," *Journal of Elementary School Guidance and Counseling*, 17, 126-130.

Abstract

Describes the use of a filmstrip project in an in-school support group for fifth grade students who have been involved in a family breakup. All involved pointed out that the positive effects of using the filmstrip project with group counseling exceeded their expectations. This model of counseling is highly recommended for use in support groups which focus on divorce.

Bowman, R., & Myrick, R. (1987). "Effects of a peer facilitator program on children with behavior problems," *School Counselor*, 34, 369-378.

Abstract

Evaluated whether a peer helper program would impact the attitudes and self-concepts of 54 fifth grade students trained by school counselors as peer facilitators and whether peer facilitators would be effective in helping 54 second and third grade students improve their classroom behaviors and school attitudes. Results showed that elementary school peer facilitators from upper grades experienced several benefits from participating in the program and that they can be effective in improving classroom behaviors and school attitudes of second and third graders with behavior problems.

Bruckner, S. T., & Thompson, C. L. (1987). "Guidance program evaluation," *Journal of Elementary School Guidance and Counseling*, 21, 193-196.

Abstract

Research completed over a four year period for elementary school developmental group guidance meetings is presented. Conclusions were that the meetings were well received by the students and that data for the four year period covered in the study provide the direction for changes in the group guidance program.

Bundy, M. L., & Boser, J. (1987). "Helping latchkey children: A group guidance approach," *School Counselor*, 35, 58-65.

Abstract

This study developed a curriculum to give latchkey children more comprehensive instruction in survival skills. Field tests were conducted to determine the effectiveness of the program with 15 participants. It was found that children who participated in the program became more knowledgeable about the procedures they should use when home alone.

Bundy, M. L., & Poppen, W. A. (1986). "School counselors' effectiveness as consultants: A research review," *Journal of Elementary School Guidance and Counseling*, 20, 215-222.

Abstract

Thirteen studies were examined to determine how effective elementary school counselors are in consulting with teachers. Evidence from this literature review indicates that counselors should trust the efficacy of their consulting role and seek to enlarge the range of services within that role.

Burt, M. A., & Myrick, R. D. (1980). "Developmental Play: What's it all about?" *Journal of Elementary School Guidance and Counseling*, 15, 14-19.

Abstract

Discusses Developmental Play (DP) as an intervention to use with dysfunctioning children and examines the reactions of 19 first, second and third graders who participated in a DP program. Results indicated that DP is a relatively new strategy for working with children who have special guidance needs and it seems to offer promise to teachers and counselors who work with dysfunctioning children.

Carter, S. R. (1987). Use of puppets to treat traumatic grief: A case study. *Journal of Elementary School Guidance and Counseling*, 21, 210-215.

Abstract

Describes the outcome of using puppet play therapy with a 10 year-old fifth grader who had witnessed his father's murder. Involvement in the therapy allowed the student a safe outlet for expressing and finally experiencing his anger and grief. Conclusions specified the strength of this method as allowing the child the freedom to progress at a comfortable pace, control over issues, and a deep feeling of safety.

Cobb, H. C., and Richards, H. C. (1983). "Efficacy of counseling services in decreasing behavior problems of elementary school children," *Journal of Elementary School Guidance and Counseling*, 17, 180-187.

Abstract

Assessed the effectiveness of an elementary school counseling program that involved 90 fourth and fifth grade students in guidance activities and was intended to improve classroom climate and conduct. Results supported the belief that counselor-consultation interventions can be successful in reducing the behavioral problems of elementary school children and that a combination of group guidance, small group counseling, and teacher consultation appears as a very effective method of intervention.

Conroy, E. H. (1987). "Primary prevention for gifted students: A parent education group," *Journal of Elementary School Guidance and Counseling*, 22, 110-116.

Abstract

Describes a parent education group led by an elementary school counselor with the purpose of facilitating the 23 parent participants in developing a better understanding of their children and increasing their comfort in raising their gifted children. Conclusions indicated that offering a parent education group is one effective way for counselors to begin a partnership with parents and because parents are ultimately responsible for the education and mental health of their children, they need information to make good decisions.

Downing, J., Jenkins, S., & Fisher, G. (1988). "A comparison of psychodynamic and reinforcement treatment with sexually abused children," *Journal of Elementary School Guidance and Counseling*, 22, 291-298.

Abstract

Examines the outcome of two divergent counseling intervention strategies with families of 22 elementary school children who have been sexually abused. Conclusions support a treatment blending the positive aspects of both orientations in treating sexually abused children and their parents.

Gerler, E. R. (1985). "Elementary school counseling research and the classroom learning environment," *Journal of Elementary School Guidance and Counseling*, 20, 39-48.

Abstract

This review explores research evidence of elementary school counselors' effectiveness in helping children to improve classroom behavior, to explore feelings, to improve socially, and to enhance sensory awareness and mental imagery. It was concluded that counselors should be able to use this evidence for demonstrating the importance of their work to school policy makers.

Gerler, E. R. (1988). "Recent research on child abuse: A brief review," *Journal of Elementary School Guidance and Counseling*, 22, 325-327.

Abstract

This article reviews recent studies showing the harmful effect of child abuse as well as the beneficial effects of educational programs designed to deal with abuse. Conclusions confirm that preventative programs are much needed.

Gerler, E. R., & Anderson, R. F. (1986). "The effects of classroom guidance on childrens' success in school," *Journal of Counseling and Development*, 65, 78-81.

Abstract

The effects of classroom guidance on childrens' classroom behavior, attitudes toward school, and achievement in language art and mathematics were investigated. The study involved 896 children from 18 different schools in North Carolina. The results of this study show that elementary school counselors can use classroom guidance to influence childrens' classroom behavior positively.

Gianotti, T. J., & Doyle, R. E. (1982). "The effectiveness of parental training on learning disabled children and their parents," *Journal of Elementary School Guidance and Counseling*, 17, 131-136.

Abstract

Determined whether employing a Parent Effectiveness Training Program for 92 parents of 46 children with learning disabilities would encourage positive changes in the self-concepts of the learning disabled elementary school children. It was concluded that a training program for parents, such as PET, has much to offer the active school counselor whereby it can make a significant impact on parents, children, and classroom teachers as well as on the relationships between and among these three groups.

Goodman, R. W., & Kjoonas, D. 1984). "Elementary school family counseling: A pilot project," *Journal of Counseling and Development*, 63, 255-257.

Abstract

The authors present a pilot project in elementary school family counseling that describes a model of counseling intervention using a consultant and a counselor team. Treatment outcomes and implications are discussed.

Gumaer, J. (1984). "Developmental play in small group counseling with disturbed children," *School Counselor*, 31, 445-453.

Abstract

Evaluates the effectiveness of a small group approach that is based on the theoretical concepts of a developmental play program in counseling eight emotionally disturbed children. Conclusions emphasized that developmental play in small group counseling may be one way for counselors to intervene and provide some comfort for disturbed children and their teachers.

Guyton, J. M., & Fielstein, L. L. (1989). "Student led parent conferences: A model for teaching responsibility," *Journal of Elementary School Guidance and Counseling*, 24, 169-172.

Abstract

Discussed the consequences of an elementary school student-led parent conference. Results from faculty, parents, and students demonstrated that the student conferences were successful, that students appeared to develop a sense of accountability and that parents seemed to have gained a better understanding of their child's progress.

Hadley, H. (1988). "Improving reading scores through a self-esteem intervention program," *Journal of Elementary School Guidance and Counseling*, 22, 248-252.

Abstract

Identified the impact that a 12-week affective education program had on the academic growth of 165 second grade students along with the results of a replication of this study with two other second grade classrooms of students. Indications of a significant positive impact on academic growth were reported from both programs.

Hitchcock, R. A., & Young, D. (1986). "Prevention of sexual assault: A curriculum for elementary school counselors," *Journal of Elementary School Guidance and Counseling*, 20, 201-207.

Abstract

Emphasizes the unique position elementary school counselors are in to develop and provide programs regarding the prevention of sexual assault of children. Also discusses such a program that was implemented with 3,500 school children during the 1984-85 school year. Counselor responses to the program were reported as positive while parental support of the program was described as substantial.

Kameen, M. C., Robinson, E. H., & Rotter, J. C. (1985). "Coordination activities: A study of perceptions of elementary and middle school counselors," *Journal of Elementary School Guidance and Counseling*, 20, 97-104.

Abstract

Examined 193 counselors' perceptions of their coordination activities. Results indicated that counselors spend a majority of time in information dissemination and maintenance, testing, and placement coordination. They felt more time should be spent in guidance, in-service, and community activities.

Miller, G. M. (1988). "Counselor functions in excellent schools: Elementary through secondary," *School Counselor*, 36, 88-93.

Abstract

Discusses an effort to determine what functions counselors perform in schools that have been recognized as excellent and to determine which functions were perceived by elementary, middle, and high school counselors as significantly different for each school level. The results of the study are suggested as helpful to counselors who wish to examine the functions which they are performing in their schools and to compare them with what counselors in outstanding schools are doing.

Miller, M. J. (1988). "Student as Worker: A simple yet effective career education activity," *Journal of Elementary School Guidance and Counseling*, 22, 246-252.

Abstract

Discusses a group activity with 15 elementary school students that involved comparing being at school to being at work. Results suggested that elementary school counselors would do well to harness the openness, enthusiasm, and curiosity of students by continually being on the alert for situations that would provide youngsters with profitable career-related experiences.

Morse, L. A. (1987). "Working with young procrastinators: Elementary students who do not complete school assignments," *Journal of Elementary School Guidance and Counseling*, 21, 221-228.

Abstract

Described a multimodal group counseling intervention intended to assist 31 procrastinating students in grades 3-6 in the completion of their school tasks. Positive change in the homework completion rate of the students in the study suggests that a multimodal approach, although time consuming, may prove successful in working with this type of student.

Navin, S. L. & Bates, G. W. (1987). "Improving attitudes and achievement of remedial readers: A parent counseling approach," *Journal of Elementary School Guidance and Counseling*, 21, 203-209.

Abstract

Investigated the impact of a parents' counseling group on the reading attitudes and achievement of seven students. Results suggest that group counseling for parents can have positive effects on remedial readers and that elementary school counselors should consider developing counseling groups for parents as part of all remedial reading programs.

Oldfield, D., & Petosa, R. (1986). "Increasing student on-task behaviors through relaxation strategies," *Journal of Elementary School Guidance and Counseling*, 20, 180-186.

Abstract

The purpose of this study was to assess the impact of psychophysiological relaxation strategies on the on-task behavior of elementary school children. The findings support the hypothesis that the acquisition of relaxation skills positively influences the ability of children to be attentive to instructional events in a school setting.

Olson, M. J., & Dilley, J. S. (1988). "A new look at stress and the school counselor," *School Counselor*, 35, 194-198.

Abstract

Reviews research on school counselors' stress. Concludes that stress is not so much a function of conflict between roles that are differently endorsed by different publics as it is of the sheer number of roles that are strongly endorsed. Claims that mental health and quality of work of counselors is adversely affected by the stress of not always being able to meet all the demands required.

Omizo, M. & Omizo, S. A. (1987). "Group counseling with children of divorce: New findings," *Journal of Elementary School Guidance and Counseling*, 22, 46-52.

Abstract

This article presented a group intervention strategy to assist children of divorce and to determine the efficacy of the intervention on the childrens' self-concept and locus of control. Participation in these group sessions enhanced some areas of self-concept and internal locus of control among elementary school children whose parents were divorced.

Omizo, M. & Omizo, S. A. (1988). "Group counseling's effects on self-concept and social behavior among children with learning disabilities," *Journal of Humanistic Education and Development*, 26, 109-117.

Abstract

Examined the efficacy of 10 weekly group counseling sessions on the self-concept and social behavior among 62 fourth, fifth and sixth grade children with learning disabilities who were from various ethnic backgrounds. Participation in the group sessions was found to be beneficial to the self-concept and specific areas of social behavior among the children with learning disabilities. The need for the study to be replicated with other populations who are having similar difficulties and for a long-term efficacy of the intervention strategy to be done was recommended.

Post-Kramer, P. (1988). "Effectiveness of Parents' Anonymous in reducing child abuse," *School Counselor*, 35, 337-342.

Abstract

Recommendations were made to school counselors regarding whether participation in the Parents' Anonymous self-help group impacted parents' self-concept, understanding of children and abusive behaviors. Conclusions indicated that school counselors and counselors in community agencies must coordinate their efforts to reduce the abuse of children. Program evaluation and greater articulation between counselors working with parents and their children can help achieve this goal.

Robinson, E. H., & Wilson, E. S. (1987). "Counselor-led human relations training as a consultation strategy," *Journal of Elementary School Guidance and Counseling*, 22, 124-131.

Abstract

Examined the degree to which 92 teachers in 13 schools could increase their level of human relation skills when trained by highly functioning counselors, the degree to which student achievement is influenced by teachers with high levels of facilitation skills, and the degree to which student self-concept is affected by teachers with high levels of facilitation skills. Results support the notion that trained counselors performing a consultative role with teachers can have an impact on student achievement and that interventions with teachers using human relationship development training has the potential to help the counselor meet the goals of education in general.

Sharples, M. R. (1987). "Guidance Shorts: The creative use of little time. *Journal of Elementary School Guidance and Counseling*, 21, 198-202.

Abstract

Reviews the effects of a "guidance shorts" program developed and implemented by an elementary school counselor in four schools with approximately 2,000 students. Conclusions point to various benefits of the program and counselors are encouraged to use the program format in order to meet specific needs in their schools.

Tedder, S., Scherman, A., & Wantz, R. (1987). "Effectiveness of a support group for children of divorce," *Journal of Elementary School Guidance and Counseling*, 22, 102-109.

Abstract

Reports the effectiveness of a group for 17 fourth and fifth grade children who were impacted by divorce. Concluded that children's divorce groups encouraged positive results and that children usually have easier access to their school counselors than they do to any other trained professional. Suggested that school counselors be aware of the issues, theories, and possible interventions available in order to work with children in these situations.

Thompson, C. L., Cole, D., Krammer, P. P., & Barker, R. (1984). "Support groups for children of divorced parents," *Journal of Elementary School Guidance and Counseling*, 19, 88-94.

Abstract

The purpose of this column is to exchange ideas about implementing and developing guidance programs in elementary schools. An eight week counseling group designed to help children cope with divorce is described.

Vernon, A., & Hay, J. (1988). "A preventative approach to child sexual abuse," *Journal of Elementary School Guidance and Counseling*, 22, 306-312.

Abstract

Describes a sexual abuse prevention program that was implemented in a second, fourth and sixth grade class by an elementary school counselor. Positive responsiveness from student participants, school staff and parents was reported. The significant role of the counselor in prevention abuse programs was also indicated.

Wilgus, W., & Shelley, V. (1988). "The role of the elementary school counselor: Teacher perceptions, expectations and actual functions," *School Counselor*, 35, 259-266.

Abstract

School counselors from seven elementary school participated in an analysis of the role of the school counselor. Results indicated that what is needed are counselors who are action oriented, not reactive; creative not complacent; aggressive not passive; and energetic, not lethargic.

Wilson, N. S. (1986). "Counselor interventions with low-achieving and under achieving elementary , middle and high school students: A review of the literature," *Journal of Counseling and Development*, 64, 628-634.

Abstract

The author reviews experimental studies and evaluates the effects of counselor interventions on the grade point average of underachieving of low-achieving students in elementary, middle and high schools. Programs with characteristics related to improved achievement are included.

Appendix B

TABLE 1 States That Mandate Elementary School Counselors

	Elementary Counselor Mandate		Source of Mandate			Counselor—Student Mandated Ratio	Funding Source		Is State Considering A Mandate	
State	Yes	No	Legis-lature	State Dept	State Board	Ratio	State	Local	Yes	No
Alabama	x			x		1400	x	x		
Alaska		x								x
Arizona		x								x
Arkansas	x		x			1450		x		
California		x								x
Colorado		x								x
Connecticut		x								x
Delaware		x							x	
District of Columbia		x								x
Florida		x								
Georgia		x							x	
Hawaii	x		x	x		none	x			
Idaho		x								x
Illinois		x								x
Indiana		x								x
Iowa	x		x	x	x	none	x			
Kansas		x								x
Kentucky		x							x	
Louisiana		x								x
Maine	x		x			none		x		
Maryland		x								x
Massachusetts		x							x	
Michigan		x								x
Minnesota		x								x
Mississippi		x							x	

TABLE 1 *continued*

	Elementary Counselor Mandate		**Source of Mandate**			**Counselor—Student Mandated Ratio**	**Funding Source**		**Is State Considering A Mandate**	
State	Yes	No	Legis-lature	State Dept	State Board	Ratio	State	Local	Yes	No
Missouri		x								x
Montana	x				x	1400	x	x		
Nebraska		x								x
Nevada		x							x	
New Hampshire	x				x	1500		x		
New Jersey		x								x
New Mexico		x								x
New York		x								x
North Carolina	x		x	x	x	1400	x	x		
North Dakota		x								x
Ohio		x								x
Oklahoma		x								x
Oregon		x							x	
Pennsylvania		x								x
Rhode Island		x							x	
South Carolina	x		x	x	x	Flexible	x			x
South Dakota		x							x	
Tennessee		x							x	
Texas		x							x	
Utah		x								x
Vermont	x			x		1400		x		
Virginia	x		x		x	1500	x			
Washington		x							x	
West Virginia	x		x			1500		x		
Wisconsin		x								x
Wyoming		x								x

From *Children Achiving Potential: An Introduction to Elementary School Counseling and State Level Policies* (p. 31) by H. L. Glosoff and C. L. Koprowicz, 1990 (Washington, DC: National Conference of State Legislators and Alexandria, VA: American Counseling Assocation.

Appendix C

The Practice of Guidance and Counseling by School Counselors

ASCA Role Statement

The following role statement is an incorporation and revision of four role statements prepared separately in the 70s. "The Unique Role of the Elementary School Counselor" was originally published in *Elementary School Guidance and Counseling*, Volume 8, No. 3, March 1974. It was revised and the revision, approved in August 1977 by the ASCA Governing Board, was printed in *Elementary School Guidance and Counseling*, Volume 12, No. 3, February 1978. "The Role of the Middle Junior High School Counselor" was circulated separately in photocopy form by ASCA. "The Role of the Secondary School Counselor" first appeared in School Counselor, Volume 21, No. 5, May 1974; the revision, formulated by the 1976-77 ASCA Governing Board, was printed in the March 1977 *School Counselor* (Volume 24, No. 4). "The Role and Function of Postsecondary Counseling" first appeared in *School Counselor*, Volume 21, No. 5, May 1974.

The present version, incorporating all four role statements, was prepared in October 1980 by G. Dean Miller upon invitation from ASCA officers J. Thompson, H. Washburn, and J. Terrill, The role statement as it appears below was approved by the 1980-81 ASCA Governing Board in January 1981.

Professional Rationale

The national association believes that the professional identity of the school counselor is derived from a unique preparation, grounded in the behavioral sciences, with training in clinical skills adapted to the school setting. This statement attempts to identify and clarify the role of the school counselor who functions at various educational levels in United States society. The different educational levels (elementary, middle or junior high, secondary, and postsecondary) approximates the different steps of developmental growth from childhood through adolescence to adulthood. Therefore, the focus of school counselors serving different school levels is differentiated by the developmental tasks necessary for the different stages of growth the students confront going through school. This statement also commits to public records certain professional responsibilities of school counselors and identifies a set of philosophic assumptions about the conditions under which important psychological growth occurs in the practice of guidance and counseling.

It is understood that schools in all societies are concerned with transmission of cultural heritage and socialization of the youth. Career socialization is recognized as a very important aspect of this process. In the Unites States, schools are concerned about the individual student, and it is through the concept of guidance that efforts are directed toward personalizing the school experience in a developmental way.

Counselors as developmental facilitators function as school-based members of student support-services teams that include staff members from other helping professions such as school psychology, social work, and nursing. These staff, depending upon their student-staff ratios and service orientation, may also function in a specialized remedial way to assist with problem areas and—beginning with the very young—join counselors to intervene in a developmental way to foster psychological growth and thereby attempt collectively to prevent the costly, hard-to-change negative behavior characteristics that often begin to take form and retard growth by the middle elementary school grades.

Counselors believe that students achieve and grow in positive ways when competencies develop and the home and school strive both separately and together to establish supportive interpersonal relationships and maintain healthy environments. Counseling and guidance is an integral function in the school that is maximized when counselors provide consultation and in service programs for staff regarding the incorporation of developmental psychology into the curriculum. They also provide parents with additional understanding of child and adolescent development in order to strengthen the role of parents in the promotion of growth in children. Individual and small group counseling is provided to complement indirect helping through parents and teachers. Important direct interaction with students, however, is provided through a developmentally oriented guidance curriculum. Counselor interventions, regardless of their conceptual origin, aim to serve the needs of students who are expected to function in school settings in the various educational, vocational, and personal-social domains. As the student progresses through the different school levels, assistance with processing information, problem solving, and decision making is increased in proportion to the developmental demands made upon students and their ability to conceptualize and assume responsibility for the consequences of their behavior.

The validation of new knowledge from the behavioral sciences along with social and economic changes in society impact the role of the counselor and other members of the school staff. Through study and retraining, the effective practicing counselor—regardless of the educational level of the students service—continues to be informed and competently, skilled throughout the professional career.

The Nature of the Helping Process

To accommodate students at different educational levels, the organizing and specifying of various guidance programs across the life span calls for an awareness of the developmental needs identified in the psychology of children, adolescents, and adults. The clinical skills and knowledge base of the counselor is most effectively used if effort is directed in an organized way toward making the school, the teachers, and the curriculum sensitive to those aspects of personal development most associated with life success. Because of its association with life success the cognitive-developmental stages of psychological maturity deserve highest recognition in conceptualizing the major thrust of guidance interventions for the different educational levels. Such interventions aim to do more than inform students about problems they will face: The purpose is to promote through education important life success qualities (development of competencies, ego maturity, moral reasoning, and so forth). Counselors performing under this theoretical orientation will tend to emphasize certain interventions, no matter what the level of the educational setting—elementary, middle or junior high, secondary, or postsecondary. Major functions performed by such school counselors include the following:

- Structured developmental guidance experiences presented systematically through groups (including classrooms) to promote growth of psychological aspects of human development (e.g., ego, career, emotional, moral, and social development). Such interventions can logically become an integral part of such curriculum areas as social studies, language arts, health, or home economics. Individual or small group counseling is provided when the needs deserve more attention or privacy.
- Consultation with and in-service training for teachers to increase their communication skills, improve the quality of their interaction with all students, and make them more sensitive to the need for matching the curriculum to developmental needs of students.

- Consultation and life-skills education for parents to assist them to understand developmental psychology, to improve family communication skills, and to develop strategies for encouraging learning in their children.

As noted above, counselors serving different school populations function differently, due primarily to the variations in the developmental stages of the students and the organization of the school. Some of the major level differences in functions include the following.

Elementary School Counselors

- Provide in-service training to teachers to assist them with planning and implementing guidance interventions for young children (preschool to 3rd grade) in order to maximize developmental benefits (self-esteem, personal relationships, positive school attitude, sex-fair choices, and so forth) in the hope of preventing serious problems or minimizing the size of such problems, if and when they do occur.
- Provide consultations for teachers who need understanding and assistance with incorporating developmental concepts in teaching content as well as support for building a healthy classroom environment.
- Accommodate parents who need assistance with understanding normal child growth and development; improving family communication skills; or understanding their role in encouraging their child to learn.
- Cooperate with other school staff in the early identification, remediation, or referral of children with developmental deficiencies or handicaps.
- As children reach the upper elementary grades, effort is directed through the curriculum toward increasing student awareness of the relationship between school and work, especially the impact of educational choices on one's lifestyle and career development.

Middle or Junior High Counselors

- Concentrate efforts (through group guidance, peer facilitators, and teacher in-service training) to smooth the transition for students from the more confining environment of the lower school to the middle or junior high school where students are expected to assume greater responsibility for their own learning and personal development.
- Identify, encourage, and support teachers (through in-service training, consultation, and co-teaching) who are interested in incorporating developmental units in such curriculum areas as English, Social Studies, Health, and Home Economics.
- Organize and implement a career guidance program for students that includes an assessment of their career maturity and career-planning status; easy access to relevant career information; and assistance with processing data for personal use in school-work related decision making.

Secondary Counselors

- Organize and implement through interested teachers guidance curricula interventions that focus upon important developmental concerns of adolescents (identity, career choice and planning, social relationships, and so forth).
- Organize and make available comprehensive information systems (print, computer-based, audio-visual) necessary for educational-vocational planning and decision making.
- Assist students with assessment of personal characteristics (e.g., competencies, interests, aptitudes, needs, career maturity) for personal use in such areas as course selection, post-high-school planning, and career choices.
- Provide remedial interventions or alternative programs for those students showing in-school adjustment problems, vocational immaturity, or general negative attitudes toward personal growth.

Postsecondary Counselors

- Participate in a comprehensive program of student support services to facilitate the meeting of transitional needs throughout adulthood (orientation activities; academic, personal, and career counseling; financial aids; independent living; job placement, career development; geriatric concerns; and so forth).
- Through individual and cooperative efforts with other staff, offer students the opportunity to participate in deliberate psychological education that fosters maturity in such areas as ego development, moral reasoning, career development, and emotional aspects of personal relationships.
- To accommodate students with varying maturity and ability levels, provide differential assistance to help students identify and use school and community-based opportunities (internships, independent study, and travel) in order to crystallize vocational choice and career plans (e.g., choice of major, choice of vocation, lifestyle, and work values).

Professional Commitment of School Counselors

The counselor, as a school-based practitioner, is bound in relationship with others to certain practices. These counseling and guidance relationships are based on the following principles:

- It is the counselor's obligation to respect the integrity of the individual and promote the growth and development (or adjustment) of the student receiving assistance.
- Before entering any counseling relationship, the individual should be informed of the conditions under which assistance may be provided.

- The counseling relationship and information resulting from it must be kept confidential in accordance with the rights of the individual and the obligations of the counselor as a professional.
- Counselors reserve the right to consult with other competent professionals about the individual. Should the individual's condition endanger the health, welfare, or safety of self or others, the counselor is expected, in such instances, to refer the counselee to another appropriate professional person.
- Counselors shall decline to initiate or shall terminate a counseling relationship when other services could best meet the client's needs. Counselors shall refer the client to such services.

Commitment to Students

- The counselor recognizes that each student has basic human rights and is entitled to just treatment regardless of race, sex, religious preference, handicapping condition, or cultural differences.
- The counselor is available to all to provide assistance with personal understanding and use of opportunities, especially those available in the school setting.
- The counselor assumes that both cognition and perception influence behavior and the valuation process.
- The counselor in the helping relationship creates an atmosphere in which mutual respect, understanding, and confidence prevails in the hope that growth occurs and concerns are resolved.

Commitment to Parents

- The counselor recognizes that parents are the first teachers of their children and in this regard have a profound influence upon human development.
- Parents are entitled to basic human rights and their facilitative-supportive relationship to learning is recognized in the educational partnership that embraces the home and school.
- To capitalize upon the influence of parents in the educational process, the counselor involves them at strategic periods and events in order to maximize the student's response to opportunities provided by the school.

Commitment to Teachers

- The counselor acknowledges that teachers, in creating positive, interactive relationships with students, provide the primary basis for intellectual, emotional, and social growth in the school.
- The counselor, in the consulting relationship, endeavors to acquaint teachers with applications of various theories of learning and human growth in order that a good match occurs between curriculum intervention and student developmental needs.

- The counselor recognizes that teachers need support and assistance in dealing with the normal problems of student growth and adjustment, especially during the period of adolescence.

Commitment to Administrators

- The counselor acknowledges that the school administrator plays the major role in providing the support necessary for implementing and maintaining an organized team approach to guidance in the school. The counselor depends upon the school administration to support the elimination of unnecessary clerical work and other activities that detract from program delivery and counseling.
- The counselor, in recognizing the importance of the administrator's contribution, develops a close working relationship with the administrator and provides technical assistance so that appropriate assessment, planning, implementation, and evaluation occur relative to the guidance needs of the students.
- In identifying the counselor's responsibility in implementing an organized guidance program, legislative mandates and professional ethics must be taken into consideration in matters dealing with confidentiality and privileged communication as well as what duties constitute good professional practice.

Commitment to Others in the Community

- The counselor is aware that others in the community play a significant role in the overall development of children and youth.
- To capitalize upon the above contributions, the counselor maintains an ongoing set of liaison relationships with various individuals and agencies in an effort to coordinate programs and services on behalf of students in the school and those in transition status between school and some other institution.
- Ongoing relationships are formed on the premise that cooperative efforts are in the best interest of the individuals concerned when personal information is treated in an ethical manner.

The Counselor's Responsibility to the Profession

To assure good practice and continued growth in knowledge and skills for the benefit of students, parents, and teachers, as well as the profession, the counselor:

- Has an understanding of his or her own personal characteristics and their effect on counseling-consulting relationships.
- Is aware of his or her level of professional competence and represents it accurately to others.

- Is well informed on current theories and research that have impact-potential upon professional practice.
- Uses time and skills in an organized systematic way to help students and resists any effort aimed at unreasonable use of time for nonguidance activities.
- Continues to develop professional competence and maintains an awareness of contemporary trends in the field as well as influences from the world at large.
- Fosters the development and improvement of the profession by assisting with appropriate research and participating in professional association activities at local, state, and national levels.
- Discusses with professional associates (teachers, administrators, and other support staff) practices that may be implemented to strengthen and improve standards or the conditions for helping.
- Maintains constant efforts to adhere to strict confidentiality of information concerning individuals and releases such information only with the signature of the student, parent, or guardian.
- Is guided by sound ethical practices for professional counselors as embodied in the Ethical Standards of the American Personnel and Guidance Association—American School Counselor Association.
- Becomes an active member of American School Counselor Association and state and local counselor associations in order to enhance personal and professional growth.

Appendix D

Ethical Standards

American Counseling Association

Preamble

The Association is an educational, scientific, and professional organization whose members are dedicated to the enhancement of the worth, dignity, potential, and uniqueness of each individual and thus to the service of society.

The Association recognizes that the role definitions and work settings of its members include a wide variety of academic disciplines, levels of academic preparation, and agency services. This diversity reflects the breadth of the Associations's interest and influence. It also poses challenging complexities in efforts to set standards for the performance of members, desired requisite preparation or practice, and supporting social, legal, and ethical controls.

The specification of ethical standards enables the Association to clarify to present and future members and to those served by members the nature of ethical responsibilities held in common by its members.

The existence of such standards serves to stimulate greater concern by members for their own professional functioning and for the conduct of fellow professionals such as counselors, guidance and student personnel workers, and others in the helping professions. As the ethical code of the Association, this document establishes principles that define the ethical behavior of Association members. Additional ethical guidelines developed by the Association's Divisions for their specialty areas may further define a member's ethical behavior.

As revised by ACA Governing Council, March 1988.

Section A: General

1. The member influences the development of the profession by continuous efforts to improve professional practices, teaching, services, and research. Professional growth is continuous throughout the member's career and is exemplified by the development of a philosophy that explains why and how a member functions in the helping relationship. Members must gather data on their effectiveness and be guided by the findings. Members recognize the need for continuing education to ensure competent service.

2. The member has a responsibility both to the individual who is served and to the institution within which the service is performed to maintain high standards of professional conduct. The member strives to maintain the highest levels of professional services offered to the individuals to be served. The member also strives to assist the agency, organization, or institution in providing the highest caliber of professional services. The acceptance of employment in an institution implies that the member is in agreement with the general policies and principles of the institution. Therefore the professional activities of the member are also in accord with the objectives of the institution. If, despite concerted efforts, the member cannot reach agreement with the employer as to acceptable standards of conduct that allow for changes in institutional policy conducive to the positive growth and development of clients, then terminating the affiliation should be seriously considered.

3. Ethical behavior among professional associates, both members and nonmembers, must be expected at all times. When information is possessed that raises doubt as to the ethical behavior of professional colleagues, whether Association members or not, the member must take action to attempt to rectify such a condition. Such action shall use the institution's channels first and then use procedures established by the Association.

4. The member neither claims nor implies professional qualifications exceeding those possessed and is responsible for correcting any misrepresentations of these qualifications by others.

5. In establishing fees for professional counseling services, members must consider the financial status of clients and locality. In the event that the established fee structure is inappropriate for a client, assistance must be provided in finding comparable services of acceptable cost.

6. When members provide information to the public or to subordinates, peers, or supervisors, they have a responsibility to ensure that the content is general, unidentified client information that is accurate, unbiased, and consists of objective, factual data.

7. Members recognize their boundaries of competence and provide only those services and use only those techniques for which they are qualified by training or experience. Members should only accept those positions for which they are professionally qualified.

8. In the counseling relationship, the counselor is aware of the intimacy of the relationship and maintains respect for the client and avoids engaging in activities that seek to meet the counselor's personal needs at the expense of that client.

9. Members do not condone or engage in sexual harassment which is defined as deliberate or repeated comments, gestures, or physical contacts of a sexual nature.

10. The member avoids bringing personal issues into the counseling relationship, especially if the potential for harm is present. Through awareness of the negative impact of both racial and sexual stereotyping and discrimination, the counselor guards the individual rights and personal dignity of the client in the counseling relationship.

11. Products or services provided by the member by means of classroom instruction, public lectures, demonstrations, written articles, radio or television programs, or other types of media must meet the criteria cited in these standards.

Section B: Counseling Relationship

This section refers to practices and procedures of individual and/or group counseling relationships.

The member must recognize the need for client freedom of choice. Under those circumstances where this is not possible, the member must appraise clients of restrictions that may limit their freedom of choice.

1. The member's primary obligation is to respect the integrity and promote the welfare of the client(s), whether the client(s) is (are) assisted individually or in a group relationship. In a group setting, the member is also responsible for taking reasonable precautions to protect individuals from physical and/or psychological trauma resulting from interaction within the group.

2. Members make provisions for maintaining confidentiality in the storage and disposal of records and follow an established record retention and disposition policy. The counseling relationship and information resulting therefrom must be kept confidential, consistent with the obligations of the member as a professional person. In a group counseling setting, the counselor must set a norm of confidentiality regarding all group participants' disclosures.

3. If an individual is already in a counseling relationship with another professional person, the member does not enter into a counseling relationship without first contacting and receiving the approval of that other professional. If the member discovers that the client is in another counseling relationship after the counseling relationship begins, the member must gain the consent of the other professional or terminate the relationship, unless the client elects to terminate the other relationship.

4. When the client's condition indicates that there is clear and imminent danger to the client or others, the member must take reasonable personal action or inform responsible authorities. Consultation with other professionals must be used where possible. The assumption of responsibility for the client's(s') behavior must be taken only after careful deliberation. The client must be involved in the resumption of responsibility as quickly as possible.

5. Records of the counseling relationship, including interview notes, test data, correspondence, tape recordings, electronic data storage, and other documents are to be considered professional information for use in counseling, and they should not be considered a part of the records of the institution or agency in which the counselor is employed unless specified by state statute or regulation. Revelation to others of counseling material must occur only upon the expressed consent of the client.

6. In view of the extensive data storage and processing capacities of the computer, the member must ensure that data maintained on a computer is: (a) limited to information that is appropriate and necessary for the services being provided; (b) destroyed after it is determined that the information is no longer of any value in providing services; and (c) restricted in terms of access to appropriate staff members involved in the provision of services by using the best computer security methods available.

7. Use of data derived from a counseling relationship for purposes of counselor training or research shall be confined to content that can be disguised to ensure full protection of the identity of the subject client.

8. The member must inform the client of the purposes, goals, techniques, rules of procedure, and limitations that may affect the relationship at or before the time that the counseling relationship is entered. When working with minors or persons who are unable to give consent, the member protects these clients' best interests.

9. In view of common misconceptions related to the perceived inherent validity of computer-generated data and narrative reports, the member must ensure that the client is provided with information as part of the counseling relationship that adequately explains the limitations of computer technology.

10. The member must screen prospective group participants, especially when the emphasis is on self-understanding and growth through self-disclosure. The member must maintain an awareness of the group participants' compatibility throughout the life of the group.

11. The member may choose to consult with any other professionally competent person about a client. In choosing a consultant, the member must avoid placing the consultant in a conflict of interest situation that would preclude the consultant's being a proper party to the member's efforts to help the client.

12. If the member determines an inability to be of professional assistance to the client, the member must either avoid initiating the counseling relationship or immediately terminate that relationship. In either event, the member must suggest appropriate alternatives. (The member must be knowledgeable about referral resources so that a satisfactory referral can be initiated.) In the event the client declines the suggested referral, the member is not obligated to continue the relationship.

13. When the member has other relationships, particularly of an administrative, supervisory, and/or evaluative nature with an individual seeking counseling services, the member must not serve as the counselor but should refer the individual to another professional. Only in instances where such an alternative is unavailable and where the individual's situation warrants counseling intervention should the member enter into and/or maintain a counseling relationship. Dual relationships with clients that might impair the member's objectivity and professional judgement (e.g., as with close friends or relatives) must be avoided and/or the counseling relationship terminated through referral to another competent professional.

14. The member will avoid any type of sexual intimacies with clients. Sexual relationships with clients are unethical.

15. All experimental methods of treatment must be clearly indicated to prospective recipients, and safety precautions are to be adhered to by the member.

16. When computer applications are used as a component of counseling services, the member must ensure that: (a) the client is intellectually, emotionally, and physically capable of using the computer application; (b) the computer application is appropriate for the needs of the client; (c) the client understands the purpose and operation of the computer application; and (d) a followup of client use of a computer application is provided to both correct possible problems (misconceptions or inappropriate use) and assess subsequent needs.

17. When the member is engaged in short-term group treatment/training programs (e.g., marathons and other encounter-type or growth groups), the member ensures that there is professional assistance available during and following the group experience.

18. Should the member be engaged in a work setting that calls for any variation from the above statements, the member is obligated to consult with other professionals whenever possible to consider justifiable alternatives.

19. The member must ensure that members of various ethnic, racial, religious, disability, and socioeconomic groups have equal access to computer applications used to support counseling services and that the content of available computer applications does not discriminate against the groups described above.

20. When computer applications are developed by the member for use by the general public as self-help/stand-alone computer software, the member must ensure that: (a) self-help computer applications are designed from the beginning to function in a stand alone manner, as opposed to modifying software that was originally designed to require support from a counselor; (b) self-help computer applications will include within the program statements regarding intended user outcomes, suggestions for using the software, a description of the conditions under which self-help computer applications might not be appropriate, and a description of when and how counseling services might be beneficial; and (c) the manual for such applications will include the qualifications of the developer, the development process, validation data, and operating procedures.

Section C: Measurement and Evaluation

The primary purpose of educational and psychological testing is to provide descriptive measures that are objective and interpretable in either comparative or absolute terms. The member must recognize the need to interpret the statements that follow as applying to the whole range of appraisal techniques including test and nontest data. Test results constitute only one of a variety of pertinent sources of information for personnel, guidance, and counseling decisions.

1. The member must provide specific orientation or information to the examinee(s) prior to and following the test administration so that the results of testing may be placed in proper perspective with other relevant factors. In so doing, the member must recognize the effects of socioeconomic, ethnic, and cultural factors on test scores. It is the member's professional responsibility to use additional unvalidated information carefully in modifying interpretation of the test results.

2. In selecting tests for use in a given situation or with a particular client, the member must consider carefully the specific validity, reliability, and appropriateness of the test(s). General validity, reliability, and related issues may be questioned legally as well as ethically when tests are used for vocational and educational selection, placement, or counseling.

3. When making any statements to the public about tests and testing, the member must give accurate information and avoid false claims or misconceptions. Special efforts are often required to avoid unwarranted connotations of such terms as IQ and grade equivalent scores.

4. Different tests demand different levels of competence for administration, scoring, and interpretation. Members must recognize the limits of their competence and perform only those functions for which they are prepared. In particular, members using computer-based test interpretations must be trained in the construct being measured and the specific instrument being used prior to using this type of computer application.

5. In situations where a computer is used for test administration and scoring, the member is responsible for ensuring that administration and scoring programs function properly to provide clients with accurate test results.

6. Tests must be administered under the same conditions that were established in their standardization. When tests are not administered under standard conditions or when unusual behavior or irregularities occur during the testing session, those conditions must be noted and the results designated as invalid or of questionable validity. Unsupervised or inadequately supervised test-taking, such as the use of tests through the mails, is considered unethical. On the other hand, the use of instruments that are so designed or standardized to be self-administered and self-scored, such as interest inventories, is to be encouraged.

7. The meaningfulness of test results used in personnel, guidance, and counseling functions generally depends on the examinee's unfamiliarity with the specific items on the test. Any prior coaching or dissemination of the test materials can invalidate test results. Therefore, test security is one of the professional obligations of the member. Conditions that produce most favorable test results must be made known to the examinee.

8. The purpose of testing and the explicit use of the results must be made known to the examinee prior to testing. The counselor must ensure that instrument limitations are not exceeded and that periodic review and/or retesting are made to prevent client stereotyping.

9. The examinee's welfare and explicit prior understanding must be the criteria for determining the recipients of the test results. The member must see that specific interpretation accompanies any release of individual or group test data. The interpretation of test data must be related to the examinee's particular concerns.

10. Members responsible for making decisions based on test results have an understanding of educational and psychological measurement, validation criteria, and test research.

11. The member must be cautious when interpreting the results of research instruments possessing insufficient technical data. The specific purposes for the use of such instruments must be stated explicitly to examinees.

12. The member must proceed with caution when attempting to evaluate and interpret the performance of minority group members or other persons who are not represented in the norm group on which the instrument was standardized.

13. When computer-based test interpretations are developed by the member to support the assessment process, the member must ensure that the validity of such interpretations is established prior to the commercial distribution of such a computer application.

14. The member recognizes that test results may become obsolete. The member will avoid and prevent the misuse of obsolete test results.

15. The member must guard against the appropriation, reproduction, or modification of published tests or parts thereof without acknowledgement and permission from the previous publisher.

16. Regarding the preparation, publication, and distribution of tests, reference should be made to:

a. Standards for Educational and Psychological Testing, revised edition, 1985, published by the American Psychological Association on behalf of itself, the American Educational Research Association and the National Council of Measurement in Education.

b. The Responsible Use of Tests: A Position Paper of AMEG, APGA, and NCME. Measurement and Evaluation in Guidance, 1972, 5, 385–388.

c. Responsibilities of Users of Standardized Tests, APGA, Guidepost, October 5, 1978, pp. 5–8.

Section D: Research and Publication

1. Guidelines on research with human subjects shall be adhered to, such as:

a. Ethical Principles in the Conduct of Research with Human Participants, Washington, D.C.: American Psychological Association, Inc., 1982.
b. Code of Federal Regulation, Title 45, Subtitle A, Part 46, as currently issued.
c. Ethical Principles of psychologists, American Psychological Association, Principle #9: Research with Human Participants.
d. Family Educational Rights and Privacy Act (the Buckley Amendment).
e. Current federal regulations and various state rights privacy acts.

2. In planning any research activity dealing with human subjects, the member must be aware of and responsive to all pertinent ethical principles and ensure that the research problem, design, and execution are in full compliance with them.

3. Responsibility for ethical research practice lies with the principal researcher, while others involved in the research activities share ethical obligation and full responsibility for their own actions.

4. In research with human subjects, researchers are responsible for the subjects' welfare throughout the experiment, and they must take all responsible precautions to avoid causing injurious psychological, physical, or social effects on their subjects.

5. All research subjects must be informed of the purpose of the study except when withholding information or providing misinformation to them is essential to the investigation. In such research the member must be responsible for corrective action as soon as possible following completion of the research.

6. Participation in research must be voluntary. Involuntary participation is appropriate only when it can be demonstrated that participation will have no harmful effects on subjects and is essential to the investigation.

7. When reporting research results, explicit mention must be made of all variables and conditions known to the investigator that might affect the outcome of the investigation or the interpretation of the data.

8. The member must be responsible for conducting and reporting investigations in a manner that minimizes the possibility that results will be misleading.

9. The member has an obligation to make available sufficient original research data to qualified others who may wish to replicate the study.

10. When supplying data, aiding in the research of another person, reporting research results, or making original data available, due care must be taken to disguise the identity of the subjects in the absence of specific authorization from such subjects to do otherwise.

11. When conducting and reporting research, the member must be familiar with and give recognition to previous work on the topic, as well as to observe all copyright laws and follow the principles of giving full credit to all to whom credit is due.

12. The member must give due credit through joint authorship, acknowledgement, footnote statements, or other appropriate means to those who have contributed significantly to the research and/or publication, in accordance with such contributions.

13. The member must communicate to other members the results of any research judged to be of professional or scientific value. Results reflecting unfavorably on institutions, programs, services, or vested interests must not be withheld for such reasons.

14. If members agree to cooperate with another individual in research and/or publication, they incur an obligation to cooperate as promised in terms of punctuality of performance and with full regard to the completeness and accuracy of the information required.

15. Ethical practice requires that authors not submit the same manuscript or one essentially similar in content for simultaneous publication consideration by two or more journals. In addition, manuscripts published in whole or in substantial part in another journal or published work should not be submitted for publication without acknowledgement and permission from the previous publication.

Section E: Consulting

Consultation refers to a voluntary relationship between a professional helper and help-needing individual, group, or social unit in which the consultant is providing help to the client(s) in defining and solving a work-related problem or potential problem with a client or client system.

1. The member acting as consultant must have a high degree of self-awareness of his/her own values, knowledge, skills, limitations, and needs in entering a helping relationship that involves human and/or organizational change and that the focus of the relationship be on the issues to be resolved and not on the person(s) presenting the problem.

2. There must be understanding and agreement between member and client for the problem definition, change of goals, and prediction of consequences of interventions selected.

3. The member must be reasonably certain that she/he or the organization represented has the necessary competencies and resources for giving the kind of help that is needed now or may be needed later and that appropriate referral resources are available to the consultant.

4. The consulting relationship must be one in which client adaptability and growth toward self-direction are encouraged and cultivated. The member must maintain this role consistently and not become a decision maker for the client or create a future dependency on the consultant.

5. When announcing consultant availability for services, the member conscientiously adheres to the Association's Ethical Standards.

6. The member must refuse a private fee or other remuneration for consultation with persons who are entitled to these services through the member's employing institution or agency. The policies of a particular agency may make explicit provisions for private practice with agency clients by members of its staff. In such instances, the clients must be apprised of other options open to them should they seek private counseling services.

Section F: Private Practice

1. The member should assist the profession by facilitating the availability of counseling services in private as well as public settings.

2. In advertising services as a private practitioner, the member must advertise the services in a manner that accurately informs the public of professional services, expertise, and techniques of counseling available. A member who assumes an executive leadership role in the organization shall not permit his/her name to be used in professional notices during periods when he/she is not actively engaged in the private practice of counseling.

3. The member may list the following: highest relevant degree, type and level of certification and/or license, address, telephone number, office hours, type and/or description of services, and other relevant information. Such information must not contain false, inaccurate, misleading, partial, out-of-context, or deceptive material or statements.

4. Members do not present their affiliations with any organization in such a way that would imply inaccurate sponsorship or certification by that organization.

5. Members may join in partnership/corporation with other members and/or other professionals provided that each member of the partnership or corporation makes clear the separate specialties by name in compliance with the regulations of the locality.

6. A member has an obligation to withdraw from a counseling relationship if it is believed that employment will result in violation of the Ethical Standards. If the mental or physical condition of the member renders it difficult to carry out an effective professional relationship or if the member is discharged by, the client because the counseling relationship is no longer productive for the client, then the member is obligated to terminate the counseling relationship.

7. A member must adhere to the regulations for private practice of the locality where the services are offered.

8. It is unethical to use one's institutional affiliation to recruit clients for one's private practice.

Section G: Personnel Administration

It is recognized that most members are employed in public or quasi-public institutions. The functioning of a member within an institution must contribute to the goals of the institution and vice versa if either is to accomplish their respective goals or objectives. It is therefore essential that the member and the institution function in ways to: (a) make the institutional goals specific; and public; (b) make the member's contribution to institutional goals specific; and (e) foster mutual accountability for goal achievement.

To accomplish these objectives, it is recognized that the member and the employer must share responsibilities in the formulation and implementation of personnel policies.

1. Members must define and describe the parameters and levels of their professional competency.

2. Members must establish interpersonal relations and working agreements with supervisors and subordinates regarding counseling or clinical relationships, confidentiality, distinction between public and private material, maintenance and dissemination of recorded information, work load, and accountability. Working agreements in each instance must be specified and make known to those concerned.

3. Members must alert their employers to conditions that may be potentially disruptive or damaging.

4. Members must inform employers of conditions that may limit their effectiveness.

5. Members must submit regularly to professional review and evaluation.

6. Members must be responsible for inservice development of self and/or staff.

7. Members must inform their staff of goals and programs.

8. Members must provide personnel practices that guarantee and enhance the rights and welfare of each recipient of their service.

9. Members must select competent persons and assign responsibilities compatible with their skills and experiences.

10. The member, at the onset of a counseling relationship, will inform the client of the member's intended use of supervisors regarding the disclosure of information concerning this case. The member will clearly inform the client of the limits of confidentiality in the relationship.

11. Members, as either employers or employees, do not engage in or condone practices that are inhumane, illegal, or unjustifiable (such as considerations based on sex, handicap, age, race) in hiring, promotion, or training.

Section H: Preparation Standards

Members who are responsible for training others must be guided by the preparation standards of the Association and relevant Division(s). The member who functions in the capacity of trainer assumes unique ethical responsibilities that frequently go beyond that of the member who does not function in a training capacity. These ethical responsibilities are outlined as follows:

1. Members must orient students to program expectations, basic skills development, and employment prospects prior to admission to the program.

2. Members in charge of learning experiences must establish programs that integrate academic study and supervised practice.

3. Members must establish a program directed toward developing students' skills, knowledge, and self-understanding, stated whenever possible in competency or performance terms.

4. Members must identify the levels of competencies of their students in compliance with relevant Division standards. These competencies must accommodate the paraprofessional as well as the professional.

5. Members, through continual student evaluation and appraisal, must be aware of the personal limitations of the learner that might impede future performance. The instructor must not only assist the learner in securing remedial assistance but also screen from the program those individuals who are unable to provide competent services.

6. Members must provide a program that includes training in research commensurate with levels of role functioning. Paraprofessional and technician-level personnel must be trained as consumers of research. In addition, personnel must learn how to evaluate their own and their program's effectiveness. Graduate training, especially at the doctoral level, would include preparation for original research by the member.

7. Members must make students aware of the ethical responsibilities and standards of the profession.

8. Preparatory programs must encourage students to value the ideals of service to individuals and to society. In this regard, direct financial remuneration of lack thereof must not be allowed to overshadow professional and humanitarian needs.

9. Members responsible for educational programs must be skilled as teachers and practitioners.

10. Members must present thoroughly varied theoretical positions so that students may make comparisons and have the opportunity to select a position.

11. Members must develop clear policies within their educational institutions regarding field placement and the roles of the student and the instructor in such placement.

12. Members must ensure that forms of learning focusing on self-understanding or growth are voluntary, or if required as part of the educational program, are made known to prospective students prior to entering the program. When the educational program offers a growth experience with an emphasis on self-disclosure or other relatively intimate or personal involvement, the member must have no administrative, supervisory, or evaluating authority regarding the participant.

13. The member will at all times provide students with clear and equally acceptable alternatives for self-understanding or growth experiences. The member will assure students that they have a right to accept these alternatives without prejudice or penalty.

14. Members must conduct an educational program in keeping with the current relevant guidelines of the Association.

Appendix E

Protection of the Rights and Privacy of Parents and Students—Family Educational Rights and Privacy Act of 1974

Public Law 93-380

Sec. 513.(a) Part C of the General Education Provisions Act is further amended by adding at the end thereof the following new section:

"Protection Of The Rights And Privacy Of Parents And Students"

"Sec. 438. (a) (1) No funds shall be made available under any applicable program to any State or local educational agency, any institution of higher education, any community college, any school, agency offering a preschool program, or any other educational institution which has a policy of denying, or which effectively prevents, the parents of students attending any school of such agency, or attending such institution of higher education, community college, school, preschool, or other educational institution, the right to inspect and review any and all official records, files, and data directly related to their children, including all material that is incorporated into each students's cumulative record folder, and intended for school use or to be available to parties outside the school or school system, and specifically including. but not necessarily limited to, identifying data, academic work completed, level of achievement (grades, standardized achievement test scores), attendance data, scores on standardized intelligence, aptitude, and psychological tests, interest inventory results, health data, family background information, teacher or counselor ratings and observations, and verified reports of serious or recurrent behavior patterns. Where such records or data include information on more than one student, the parents of any student shall be entitled to receive, or be informed of, that part of such record or data as pertains to their child. Each recipient shall establish appropriate procedures for the granting of a request by parents for access to their child's school records within a reasonable period of time, but in no case more than forty-five days after the request has been made.

"(2) Parents shall have an opportunity for a hearing to challenge the content of their child's school records, to insure that the records are not inaccurate, misleading, or otherwise in violation of the privacy or other rights of students, and to provide an opportunity for the correction or deletion of any such inaccurate, misleading, or otherwise inappropriate data contained therein.

"b(1) No funds shall be made available under any applicable program to any State or local educational agency, any institution of higher education, any community college, any school, agency offering a preschool program, or any other educational institution which has a policy of permitting the release of personally identifiable records or files (or personal information contained therein) of students without the written consent of their parents to any individual, agency, or organization, other than to the following—

"(A) other school officials, including teachers within the educational institution or local educational agency who have legitimate educational interests;

"(B) officials of other schools or school systems in which the student intends to enroll, upon condition that the student's parents be notified of the transfer, receive a copy of the record if desired, and have an opportunity for a hearing to challenge the content of the record;

"(C) authorized representatives of (i) the Comptroller General of the United States, (ii) the Secretary, (iii) an administrative head of an education agency (as defined in section 409 of this Act), or (iv) State educational authorities, under the conditions set forth in paragraph (3) of this subsection; and

"(D) in connection with a student's application for, or receipt of, financial aid.

"(2) No funds shall be made available under any applicable program to any State or local educational agency, any institution of higher education, any community college, any school, agency offering a preschool program, or any other educational institution which has a policy or practice of furnishing, in any form, any personally identifiable information contained in personal school records, to any persons other than those listed in subsection (b)(1) unless—

"(A) there is written consent from the student's parents specifying records to be released, the reasons for such release, and to whom, and with a copy of the records to be released to the student's parents and the student if desired by the parents, or

"(B) such information is furnished in compliance with judicial order, or pursuant to any lawfully issued subpoena, upon condition that parents and the students are notified of all such orders or subpoenas in advance of the compliance therewith by the educational institution or agency.

"(3) Nothing contained in this section shall preclude authorized representatives of (A) the Comptroller General of the United States, (B) the Secretary, (C) an administrative head of an education agency of (D) State educational authorities from having access to student or other records which may, be necessary in connection with the audit and evaluation of Federally supported education program, or in connection with the enforcement of the Federal legal requirements which relate to such programs: *Provided,* That, except when collection of personally identifiable data is specifically authorized by Federal law, any data collected by such officials with respect to individual students shall not include information (including social security numbers) which would permit the personal identification of such students or their parents after the data so obtained has been collected.

"(4) (A) With respect to subsections (c)(1) and (c)(2) and (c)(3), all persons, agencies, or organizations desiring access to the records of a student shall be required to sign a written form which shall be kept permanently, with the file of the student, but only for inspection by the parents or student, indicating specifically the legitimate educational or other interest that each person, agency, or organization has in seeking this information. Such form shall be available to parents and to the school official responsible for record maintenance as a means of auditing the operation of the system.

"(B) With respect to this subsection, personal information shall only be transferred to a third party on the condition that such party will not permit any other party to have access to such information without the written consent of the parents of the student.

"(c) The Secretary shall adopt appropriate regulations to protect the rights of privacy of students and their families in connection with any surveys or data-gathering activities conducted, assisted, or authorized by the Secretary or an administrative head of an education agency. Regulations established under this subsection shall include provisions controlling the use, dissemination, and protection of such data. No survey or data-gathering activities shall be conducted by the Secretary, or an administrative head of an education agency under an applicable program, unless such activities are authorized by law.

"(d) For the purpose of this section, whenever a student has attained eighteen years of age, or is attending an institution of postsecondary education the permission or consent required of and the rights accorded to the parents of the student shall thereafter only be required of and accorded to the student.

"(e) No funds shall be made available under any applicable program unless the recipient of such funds informs the parents of students, or the students, if they are eighteen years of age or older, or are attending an institution of postsecondary education, of the fights accorded them by this section.

"(f) The Secretary, or an administrative head of an education agency, shall take appropriate actions to enforce provisions of this section and to deal with violations of this section, according to the provisions of this Act, except that action to terminate assistance may be taken only if the Secretary finds there has been a failure to comply with the provisions of this section, and he has determined that compliance cannot be secured by voluntary means.

"(g) The Secretary shall establish or designate an office and review board within the Department of Health, Education, and Welfare for the purpose of investigating, processing, reviewing. and adjudicating violations of the provisions of this section and complaints which may be filed concerning alleged violations of this section, according to the procedures contained in sections 434 and 437 of this Act."

(b)(1)(i) The provisions of this section shall become effective ninety days after the date of enactment of section 438 of the General Education Provisions Act.

(2)(i) This section may be cited as the "Family Educational Rights and Privacy Act of 1974."

Protection of Pupil Rights

Sec. 514. (a) Part C of the General Education Provisions Act is further amended by adding after section 438 the following new section:

"Protection of Pupil Rights"

"Sec. 439. All instructional material, including teacher's manuals, films, tapes, or other supplementary instructional material which will be used in connection with any research or experimentation program or project shall be available for inspection by the patents or guardians of the children engaged in such program or project. For the purpose of this section 'research or experimentation program or project' means any program or project in any applicable program designed to explore or develop new or unproven teaching methods or techniques."

(b) The amendment made by subsection (a) shall be effective upon enactment of this Act.

Appendix F

Position Statements of the American School Counselor Association

The School Counselor and Student Rights

(Reviewed & reaffirmed 1982)

The American School Counselor Association (ASCA) supports the constitutional rights of all persons to their individual and collective freedom to express views and feelings which have also been recognized by the courts of this nation.

The United States Congress has enacted into law protection of the rights and privacy of parents and students, particularly relating to the records maintained on each student (PL 93-380).

ASCA is committed to be actively involved in assuring that students be treated as citizens of the U.S.A. with all due rights, privileges and responsibilities.

Counselors are serving as advocates, activists, and catalysts for assuring these rights. Therefore, ASCA further supports and promotes:

1. improved record keeping;
2. law-abiding discrimination in the release of information/data from student records;
3. the recording of positive, meaningful and non-valuative evaluations on student records and documents;
4. positive reinforcements in the learning processes;

5. student orientation to all rights and due processes open to him/her ie., how to get one's rights as a student; what to do if searched, seized or interrogated; reviewing one's school records (or parental review of same); resources of assistance available to students; freedom to express one's views; freedom of the press; disseminating information regarding state statutes on corporal punishment; the right to have a Student Bill of Rights in the school, school system, or state;

6. student orientation and understanding of their responsibilities and their rights under the Constitution and PL 93-380.

ASCA supports legislation and court actions which will insure rights of students as citizens of the U.S.A. ASCA's position is that the counselor is the "student advocate"—supporter, intercessor, pleader, defender, through speaking, writing, and action!

The School Counselor and Confidentiality

(Adopted 1974; reviewed and reaffirmed 1980; revised 1986)

The members of the American School Counselor Association (ASCA) affirm their belief in the worth and dignity of the individual. It is the professional responsibility of school counselors to fully respect the right to privacy of those with whom they enter counseling relationships.

Confidentiality is an ethical term denoting a counseling practice relevant to privacy.

Privileged Communication is a legal term denoting a requirement to protect the privacy between counselor and student.

Counselors must keep abreast of and adhere to all laws, policies and ethical standards pertaining to confidentiality. It is the responsibility of the counselor to provide prior notice to students regarding the possible necessity for consulting with others.

Where confidentiality is provided, ASCA recognizes that a counseling relationship requires an atmosphere of trust and confidence between the student and the counselor. A student has the right to privacy and to expect confidentiality. This confidentiality must not be abridged by the counselor except where there is a clear and present danger to the student and to other persons.

The counselor reserves the right to consult with other professionally competent persons when this is in the interest of the student. Confidentiality assures that disclosures made will not be divulged to others except when authorized by the student. Counseling information used in research and training of counselors should be fully guaranteed the anonymity of the counselee.

In the event of possible judicial proceedings the counselor should initially advise the school administration as well as the counselee if available, and if necessary, consult legal counsel. When reports are required to be produced, every effort should be made to limit demands for information to those matters essential for the purposes of the legal proceedings.

Guidelines

1. The main purpose of confidentiality is to offer counselees a relationship in which they will be able to deal with what concerns them without fear of disclosure. Furthermore, counselors have a similar responsibility in protecting the privileged information received through confidential relationships with teachers and parents.

2. In reality, it is the student who is privileged. It is the student's or students parent or guardian in cases of minors who own information and the student or guardian has the right to say who shall have access to it and who shall not.

3. The counselor and student should be provided with adequate physical facilities that guarantee the confidentiality of the counseling relationship.

4. With the enactment of P.L. 93-380 which speaks to the rights and privacy of parents and students, great care should be taken with recorded information.

5. Counselors must be concerned about individuals who have access to confidential information. Counselors must adhere to P.L. 93-380.

6. All faculty and administrative personnel should receive in-service training concerning the privacy rights of students. Counselors should assume the primary responsibility for educating school personnel in this area.

7. It should be the policy of each school to guarantee secretaries adequate working space so that students and school personnel will not come into contact with confidential information, even inadvertently.

8. Counselors should undertake a periodic review of information requested of their students. Only relevant information should be retained.

9. Counselors will adhere to ethical standards and local policies in relating student information over the telephone.

10. Counselors should be aware that it is much more difficult to guarantee confidentiality in group counseling than in individual counseling.

11. Communications made in good faith concerning may be classified as privileged by the courts and the communicating parties will be protected by law against legal action seeking damages for libel or slander. Generally, it may be said that an occasion of this particular privilege arises when one acts in the bona fide discharge of a public or private duty. This privilege may be abused or lost by malice, improper and unjustified motive, bad faith or excessive publication.

12. When a counselor is in doubt about what to release in a judicial proceeding, the counselor should arrange a conference with the judge to explain the counselor's dilemma and get advice as to how to proceed.

13. Counselors have a responsibility to encourage school administrators to develop written policies concerning the ethical handling of all records in their school system. The development of additional guidelines relevant to the local situation are encouraged.

14. Finally, it is strongly recommended that state and local counselor associations implement these principles and guidelines with appropriate legislation.

With the passage of the Family Educational Rights and Privacy Act, P.L. 93-380 (The Buckley Amendment), great care must be taken with recorded information. It is essential that counselors familiarize themselves with this Law which is a part of the omnibus Education Amendments of 1974 and support its intent to all their publics.

Provisions of this law on parent and student rights and privacy.

1. Deny federal funds to any educational institution that refuses a student's parents access to their child's school record. Parents also have the right to challenge the accuracy of any records.

2. Deny federal funds if records are released to outside groups without parent consent with exception of other school court orders and financial aid applications, with clearance procedures of parents even on the exceptions.

All counselors should have a copy of the complete law.

The School Counselor and Child Abuse/Neglect Prevention

(Adopted 1981; revised 1985)

Introduction:

The incidence of reported child abuse and child neglect has increased significantly, both nationally and statewide, during the past several years. Generally, state laws require people in the helping professions, who have reasonable cause to believe that a child is suffering serious physical or emotional injury, to report this situation to the appropriate authorities. School counselors are mandated reporters and need policies, referral procedures, and information. However, it is not simply a legal issue of reporting child abuse, but also a moral and ethical responsibility of school counselors to help children and adults cope with abusive behavior, facilitate behavioral changes, and prepare for parenting styles and positive interpersonal relationships. Counselors must commit themselves to providing strategies to help break the cycle of child abuse.

Rationale:

There are societal beliefs and values that parents have the right to discipline their children as they choose. The consequence of such beliefs, to some individuals, is physical and/or emotional harm and lowered self-esteem. The cycle of abuse seems to be self-perpetuating. Research shows that a large percentage of abusive parents were abused children. Counselors having an understanding of the dynamics of child abuse can aid in early recognition and detection of families with the potential for child abuse. School counselors are often in a unique position to identity potential and actual cases of abuse/neglect of children. Responsible action by the counselor can be achieved through the recognition and understanding of the problem, knowing the reporting procedures, and participating in available child abuse information programs.

The American School Counselor Association recognizes that it is the absolute responsibility of school counselors to report suspected cases of child abuse/neglect to the proper authorities.

We also recognize that the abuse of children is not limited to the home and that corporal punishment by school authorities might well be considered child abuse. The American School Counselor Association supports any legislation which specifically bans the use of corporal punishment as a disciplinary tool within the schools.

Definitions:

Abuse: The infliction by other than accidental means of physical harm upon the body of a child, continual psychological damage or denial of emotional needs.

Corporal Punishment: Any act of physical force upon a pupil for the purpose of punishing that pupil.

This definition specifically excludes any reasonable force exercised by a school employee which is used in self-defense, in defense of other persons or property or to restrain or remove a pupil who is disrupting school functions and who refuses to comply with a request to stop.

Some examples of child abuse are:

1. Extensive bruises or patterns of bruises.
2. Burns or burn patterns.
3. Lacerations, welts or abrasions.
4. Injuries inconsistent with information offered.
5. Sexual abuse is any act or acts involving sexual molestation or exploitation, including but not limited to rape, carnal knowledge, sodomy, or unnatural sexual practices.
6. Emotional disturbance caused by continuous friction in the home, marital discord, or mentally ill parents.
7. Cruel treatment.

Neglect: the failure to provide necessary food, care, clothing, shelter, supervision, or medical attention for a child.

Examples of child neglect are:

1. Malnourished, ill clad, dirty, without proper shelter or sleeping arrangements, lacking appropriate health care.

2. Unattended, lacking adequate supervision.
3. Ill and lacking essential medical attention.
4. Irregular/illegal absences from school.
5. Exploited, overworked.
6. Lacking essential psychological/emotional nurturance.
7. Abandonment.

Endorsements:

The American School Counselor Association strongly endorses, supports and encourages incorporation into the counselor's role the following:

- The awareness that all state statutes make school counselors immune from both civil and criminal liability when reporting suspected cases of child abuse/neglect cases in good faith. Failure to report may result in legal penalties. Thorough knowledge of local child abuse policy and procedures is essential.
- It is not the responsibility of the school counselor to prove that the child has been abused/neglected, or to determine the cause of suspected abuse/neglect, or to determine whether the child is in need of protection.
- The protection of confidentiality and the child's right to privacy with discussion of the situation limited to school staff members who have a need to know or authorized personnel from appropriate agencies. Counselors should develop their position as a liaison between the school, child, and the appropriate agency.

Counselor Role:

The American School Counselor Association encourages its members to participate in the implementation of the following guidance and counseling activities:

- Coordinate team efforts involving the principal, teacher, counselor, school nurse, protective services worker, and the child.
- Serve as a support to teachers, and other school personnel, especially if the child was abused as a result of a report sent home about the child from school.
- Emphasize the non-punitive role of protective services and allay fears that the child will be removed immediately from the home.
- Facilitate the contact between the child and the social worker. The issue of confidentiality and re-establishing the trust of the child after the report is made is critical to the child-counselor relationship.
- Provide on-going counseling services to the child and/or family after the crisis is over, or refer to an appropriate community agency.
- Provide programs designed to help prevent child abuse. Counselors can help children with coping skills and ways to prevent their own abuse by

improving their self-concepts, being able to recognize stress in their parents, and being sensitive to cues that abuse may occur if their own behavior is not changed.

- Help teachers and administrators in understanding the dynamics of abuse and abusive parents, and in developing a non-judgmental attitude so they can react more appropriately in crisis situations.
- Provide developmental workshops and/or support groups for parents focusing upon alternative methods of discipline, handling anger and frustration, and enhancing parenting skills.

Summary:

School counselors are key people in the child abuse prevention network. The school counselor must be able to guide and help, and provide all appropriate services during a crisis situation. Up-to-date information can sometimes mean a turning point in the life and behavior of an abusive family.

The School Counselor and The Education of the Handicapped Act

(Adopted 1980, revised 1986)

The adoption of public law 94-142, and amended as P.L. 98-199, the education for all handicapped children act, by the federal government has provided the framework for more appropriate educational programming for exceptional students. Such components of the law as due process, individual educational programs and the least restrictive environment offer opportunities to utilize the counselors skills for the benefit of this portion of their clientele. It is particularly important that the role of the counselor in these procedures is clearly defined and understood by all concerned.

The purpose of this position statement is to define those role functions that are and are not reasonably within the scope of P.L. 94-142. The American School Counselor Association (ASCA) believes school counselors, might reasonably be expected to perform the following functions in the implementation of P.L. 94-142.

1. To assist in the identification of students with handicapping conditions, including securing informed parental consent for referral to the committee on the handicapped.

2. To serve as a member of the multi-disciplinary team for the purpose of defining the most appropriate educational planning and placement for children with handicapping conditions,

3. To prepare and present such portions of the student's individual educational programs at the meeting of the committee on the handicapped, as may relate to services to be performed of, coordinated by the school counselor.

4. To provide input to the committee on the handicapped as to a student's present level of functioning, effective needs and the appropriateness of certain programs to meet those needs.

5. To provide supportive counseling for the parents of students with handicapping conditions as it relates to the educational objectives stated in the individual educational plan.

6. To provide guidance and counseling services to students with handicapping conditions consistent with those provided to students without handicapping conditions.

7. To provide educational counseling for students, as mandated by the committee on the handicapped, consistent with the objectives in the student's individual educational plan.

8. To consult with teachers, school psychologists, school social workers and other appropriate personnel on the educational and affective needs of exceptional students.

9. To assist in the development and implementation of professional development activities for staff working with exceptional students in self-contained or mainstreamed environments.

ASCA believes that there are certain responsibilities pertaining to the implementation of P.L. 94-142 that are **NOT PRIMARILY** those of the school counselor, although the counselor may be involved to varying degrees in these duties. It must be noted that while the school counselor has become increasingly involved in meeting the guidance and counseling needs of students with handicapping conditions, adequate staffing needs must be taken into consideration so as not to diminish the quality of guidance and counseling services provided to mainstream students. Practical consideration of local conditions and state regulations must limit the counselor's involvement in the following activities:

1. To serve as the local educational agency's one representative in formal due process procedures related to the placement of or programming for students with handicapping conditions.

2. To prepare individual educational programs for students with handicapping conditions other than those portions related to guidance and counseling services.

3. To act as the only source of information concerning the special educational programs of a district.

4. To make decisions concerning the placement or retention of exceptional students.

5. To serve in any supervisory capacity in relation to implementation of PL. 94-142.

6. To serve as a member of the multi-disciplinary team reviewing placement referrals for students who are not normally a part of the counselors caseload.

The School Counselor and Developmental Guidance

(Adopted, 1978; reviewed and revised 1984)

During recent years a number of counselor educators and school counselors have advanced the proposition that counseling can and should become more proactive and preventative in its focus and more developmental in its content and process. Viewed in the context of an evolving societal emphasis upon personal growth and an expanding professional expertise, developmental guidance has resulted in a potentially dynamic and promising approach to the helping relationship of the school counselor. The concept of developmental guidance has been discussed under various rubrics, such as (deliberate) psychological education, human relations training, and preventative mental health. Developmental guidance is a reaffirmation and actualization of the belief that guidance is for all students and that its purpose is to maximally facilitate personal development.

Definition

Developmental guidance is that component of all guidance efforts which fosters planned intervention within educational and other human development services programs at all points in the human life cycle. It vigorously stimulates and actively facilitates the total development of individuals in all areas—personal, social, emotional, career, moral-ethical, cognitive, aesthetic—and to promote the integration of the several components into an individual life-style.

Endorsement

The American School Counselor Association (ASCA) formally endorses, supports, and encourages the incorporation of developmental guidance in the role and function of the school counselor.

Antecedents

In the past the role of the school counselor has suffered from the restrictions of historical precedent, philosophical tradition, financial support, administrative definition, and counselor selection and preparation. Counselor functions have often been limited to crises management, adjustment coordination, vocational guidance, and clerical and quasi-administrative tasks.

Catalysts

Prompted by cultural change, progressive philosophy, advancement of knowledge and methodological improvement in the behavioral sciences, a climate of open public discourse, pressures of educational accountability, institutional economics, and professional survival, the "traditional" work of the school counselor is in need of well-seasoned revision.

Direction

If counseling is viewed humanistically, holistically, and comprehensively—that is developmentally—then the rationale for developmental guidance is clearly defined: Counseling should be habilitative as well as rehabilitative, proactive as well as reactive, preventative as well as remedial, skill-additive as well as problem-reductive, and characterized by outreach as well as availability. Developmental guidance is the summative terminology which connotes this emphasis.

Specifically, then, developmental guidance refers to the process and content of confluent human development as promoted by planned, purposeful, and sequential intervention.

Content

The content of developmental guidance will vary according to the developmental levels, stages and needs of participants; counselor competence and resources; and other factors. Examples of programs of contemporary interest include the following: human development (theories, stages, tasks, principles); career development (awareness, exploration, selection, employability skills); academic development (achievement motivation, study skills, test preparation, test wiseness); communication skills; interpersonal relations; decision making; values clarification; marriage and family planning; parent education; moral development; affective education; conflict resolution; leadership training; assertion training; relaxation training; human sexuality; drug education; death education; and situational adjustment and self-management (divorce adjustment, depression management, weight control, behavior modification). This list is not exhaustive.

Intervention

Many means and resources for developmental guidance intervention are available, and counselors should select from among these alternatives according to needs identified in his or her work situation. Examples of means of delivery include: mini-courses, academic release time from designated classes for developmental guidance activities, curricular scheduling of guidance activities, extended hours (after school and evening), and classroom guidance. Examples of techniques and resources include: resource centers and libraries; programmed texts and workbooks; co-facilitation and consultation with teachers, paraprofessionals, peer counselors, and others; counseling and educational kits; curricular aids, media, bibliotherapy, cinematherapy; contracting; and experiential education. Examples of strategies include: direct service delivery, consultation, team teaching, peer facilitating, and paraprofessional counseling.

Medium of Delivery

In terms of efficiency, as well as effectiveness, group approaches are the preferred medium of delivery for developmental guidance activities. By definition, "group" refers to a natural or created cluster of individuals, as small in number as two or of unlimited size. The clusters may be identified as families, classrooms and grades, employees, clients, or other composites of persons who come together as a result of shared need or purpose, common attributes, and/or other coincident characteristics.

Competencies

Essential preparation for developmental guidance intervention involves a thorough understanding of human development (descriptive and theoretical); knowledge of counseling theory and practice; competence in counseling techniques and group processes; skill in program development and management; assessment, appraisal, and diagnostic skills based on developmental concepts; practical competence in basic statistics, applied research, and program evaluation methods; and specific knowledge in the area of developmental emphasis. The counselor should be personally effective and comfortable in all areas in which developmental guidance intervention is offered.

Developmental guidance specialists must, at a minimum, be able to effectively deal with questions such as: What are the general characteristics, expectations, tasks, and behaviors of individuals at this state of development? What are this individual's characteristics, expectations, tasks, and behaviors? What can impede the process of development for this individual? What will facilitate the process of development for this individual?

Because the emphasis on developmental guidance is fairly new, counselor educators may need to modify the counselor education curriculum in order to prepare counseling students as proficient developmental interventionists. Because such an approach has often been taught as an ideal rather than as reality, as an attitude instead of a skill, counselor educators may be required to further develop their educative role.

Counseling students should seek to add the skills of developmental guidance intervention to their repertoire—if necessary, through adjuncts and alternatives to the usual counselor education curricula. Practicing counselors whose programs did not include developmental guidance components should seek to acquire the skills of developmental guidance intervention as part of their professional renewal efforts.

The developmental guidance counselor should be involved in a continuing program of professional improvement in developmental guidance expertise and strategies.

Competencies may be acquired, maintained, and improved through a variety of means, for example, graduate study, workshops, institutes and seminars, meetings and programs of professional associations, self-study of journals, contemporary texts and instructional manuals, in-service education, continuing and extended education, internships, and consultation.

Implementation

Many administrators, teachers, other school personnel, students, and parents will be unaccustomed to the concept, intent, and outcome of developmental guidance; therefore, the counselor's competence must be visible; program development and planning thorough; rationale for programs convincing; conduct of procedures professional; and programs measured, evaluated and reported effectively, both formally and informally.

Implementation strategies for the initiation of developmental guidance will require both assertiveness and ingenuity. The entire guidance community, ASCA and its constituent organizations should strive to work in harmony to facilitate the implementation of developmental guidance programs.

The true impact of the developmental guidance concept loses meaning when discussed as a lofty goal, abstract concept or as an isolated piece of rhetoric. For the concept of a sequential and developmental guidance program to be truly meaningful to both the professional staff as well as parents and students, it must be part of a comprehensive K-12 guidance plan. A plan which states its aims in measurable outcomes for all students, specific activities and a built-in evaluation procedure with provisions for necessary annual revisions. There is a necessity for some form of needs assessment which addresses the legitimate needs of the entire school community. The counselor needs to be realistic in evaluating time and fiscal parameters. A curriculum for each grade level or special area is then developed, implemented, assessed and revised annually. In-service education needs to be considered when necessary.

School counselors need to develop their abilities to teach the attitudes necessary to enhance the academic success of their counselees, i.e. for a student to succeed in Geometry, the student needs more than the usual mathematical concepts. In addition, they need to deal with structure, boredom, intimidation and frustration.

The plan should be presented to the appropriate educational agency for adoption. The effects of a written comprehensive K-12 guidance plan helps the consumer to realistically become aware of the goals, objectives and true roles of their local guidance department.

Guidelines

There are several general principles which should help insure quality and effectiveness in the implementation of developmental guidance:

1. The program should be systematic, sequential and comprehensive.

2. The program should be jointly founded upon developmental psychology, educational philosophy and counseling methodology.

3. Both process and product (of the program itself and the individuals in it) should be stressed.

4. All the personal domains—cognitive, affective, behavioral, experiential and environmental—should be emphasized.

5. Programs should emphasize preparation for the future and consolidation of the present.

6. Individualization and transfer of learning should be central to program procedure and method.

7. Evaluation and corrective feedback are essential.

Cross/Multi-Cultural Counseling (Adopted 1988)

The American School Counselor Association recognizes cultural diversifies as important factors deserving increased awareness and understanding on the part of all school personnel, especially the school counselor.

A definition of cross/multi-cultural counseling is the facilitation of human development through the understanding and appreciation of cultural diversities with respect to language, values, ethics, morals, and racial variables.

The American School Counselor Association encourages school counselors to take action to assure students of culturally diverse backgrounds access to appropriate services and opportunities which promote maximum development. Counselors may utilize the following strategies to increase the sensitivity of students and parents to cultural diverse persons and enhance the total school and community environment.

1. Conduct self-examinations of personal values, attitudes and beliefs toward cultural diversity.

2. Maintain awareness of concepts and techniques with a current library of current information.

3. Foster the interest of culturally diverse students in careers which have been traditionally closed.

4. Continue to upgrade materials utilized in the awareness and sensitivity groups.

5. Provide educational awareness workshops for teachers and cultural diverse parents at the local PTO/PTA meetings.

6. Develop a resource list of educational and community support services to meet the socioeconomic and cultural needs of culturally diverse students and their families.

7. Conduct student small groups to enhance self-esteem and cultural awareness.

8. Conduct classroom activities which develop acceptance and appreciation of cultural diversities.

9. Work within the larger community to identify cultural diversities and assist in the development of community-based programs which will propagate

community acceptance of all culturally diverse populations in the larger population.

School counselors can encourage school districts to implement the following strategies to increase awareness of culturally diverse populations.

1. To include culturally diverse parents on curriculum development planning boards, committees and other school projects.
2. Provide awareness workshops for faculty and staff on culturally diverse people.
3. Incorporate culturally diverse faculty resources into the educational process.
4. Develop workshops for culturally diverse parents to educate them on the school system's philosophy of education.
5. Promote schoolwide activities that focus on individual differences and contributions made by the cultural diverse persons.
6. Provide liaison services to facilitate communication between diverse populations in the school and community.
7. Adopt classroom materials that are free of culturally biased information and urge classroom teachers not to utilize any material of that caliber.

School counselors have the responsibility of insuring that the special needs of all students are met. Counselors have the skills necessary to consult with school personnel to identify alienating factors in attitudes and policies that impede the learning process. School counselors need to continue to be aware of and strive to insure that the rights of all students exists so as to maximize their potential in an environment that supports and encourages growth and development of the person.

References

Aiello, H., & Humes, C.W. (1987). Counselor contact of the noncustodial parent: A point of law. *Elementary School Guidance and Counseling*, 21, 177–182.

Aiken, L. R. (1988). *Psychological testing and assessment* (6th ed.). Boston: Allyn and Bacon.

Allan, J., & Bardsley, P. (1983). Transient children in the elementary school: A group counseling approach. *Elementary School Guidance and Counseling, 17*, 162–169.

Allen, G. J. , Chinsky, J. M., Larcen, S. W., Lochman, J. E. , & Selinger, H. V. (1976). *Community Psychology and the Schools.* Hillsdale, NJ: Lawrence Erlbaum.

Allport, G. (1954). *The nature of prejudice.* Cambridge, MA: Addison-Wesley.

Allred, J., & Bardsley, P. (1983). Remotivation group interaction: Increasing children's contact with the elderly. *Elementary School Guidance and Counseling, 21*, 216-220.

Allsopp, A., & Prosen, S. (1988). Teacher reactions to child sexual abuse training program. *Elementary School Guidance and Counseling*, 22, 299–305.

American Psychological Association. (1977). *Standards for Providers of Psychological Services* (rev. ed). Washington, DC: Author.

American Psychological Association Committee on Legislation. (1967). A model for state legislation affecting the practice of psychology. *American Psychologist*, 22, 1095–1103.

American School Counselor Association. (1983). *American School Counselor Association Position Statement: Cross/Multicultural Counseling.* Alexandria, VA: American Counseling Association.

American School Counselor Association (1984). The role of the school counselor in career guidance: Expectations and responsibilities. *The ASCA Counselor, 21*(5), 8–10.

American School Counselor Association (1988). The school counselor and child abuse/neglect prevention. *Elementary School Guidance and Counseling*, 22, 261–263.

American School Counselor Association. (1989). Cross/multicultural counseling. *Elementary School Guidance and Counseling*, 23, 322–323.

Anderson, L. S., & Lemoncelli, R. J. (1982). Meeting the needs of high-risk, difficult-to-reach students: Creative educational approaches. *School Counselor, 29*, 381-387.

Aronson, E. (1978). *The jigsaw classroom.* Beverly Hills, CA: Sage Publications.

Ashabranner, B. (1984). *To live in two worlds: American Indian youth today.* New York: Dodd, Mead, and Company.

Asher, S., & Singleton, L. (1978). Cross-race acceptance in integrated schools. *Integrated Education, 16*(5), 17–20.

Atkinson, D. R., Morten, G., & Sue, D. W. (1989). *Counseling American minorities: A cross cultural perspective* (3rd ed.). Dubuque, IA: William C. Brown.

Attneave, C. L. (1982). American Indians and Alaska native families: Emigrants in their own homeland. In M. McGoldrick, J. Pearce, & J. Giorando (Eds.), *Ethnicity and family therapy* (pp. 55–83). New York: Guilford.

Augoustinos, M. (1987). Developmental effects of child abuse: Recent findings. *Child Abuse and Neglect, 11*, 15–27.

Axline, V.M. (1969). *Play therapy.* New York: Ballantine Books.

Bach, R. (1970). *Jonathan Livingston Seagull: A story.* New York, NY: Avon.

Bachara, G. H. (1976). Empathy in learning disabled children. *Perceptual and Motor Skills, 43,* 541-542.

Baharoglu, B. J. (1989). Developing and upgrading an elementary and middle school guidance program: A case study. *School Counselor, 37,* 23–30.

Bailey, B. A., & Nihlen, A. S. (1989). Elementary school children's perceptions of the world of work. *Elemenatry School Guidance and Counseling, 24,* 135–145.

Baker, S. B., Swisher, J. D., Nadenichek, P. E., & Popowicz, C. L. (1984). Measured effects of primary prevention strategies. *Personnel and Guidance Journal, 62,* 459-464.

Bandura, A. (1969). *Principles of behavior modification.* New York: Holt, Rhinehart, & Winston.

Bandura, A. (1977). *Social learning theory.* Englewood-Cliffs, NJ: Prentice-Hall.

Bandura, A. (1982). The self and mechanisms of agency. In J. Suls (Ed.), *Psychological perspectives on the self.* Hillsdale, NJ: Erlbaum.

Bandura, A. (1986). *Social foundations of thought and action.* Englewood Cliffs, NJ: Prentice-Hall.

Bandura, A. (1989). Human agency in social cognitive theory. *American Psychologist, 44,* 1175-1184.

Barnes, E. J. (1980). The Black community. In Reginald L. Jones (Ed.), *Black psychology* (2nd ed.). pp. 106–130. New York: Harper & Row.

Basile, S. K. (1990). A day in the life of an elementary school counselor. In R. L. Gibson & M. H. Mitchell *Introduction to counseling and guidance* (3rd ed.) (pp. 59-60). New York: Macmillan.

Bauer, C. F. (1981). *My mom travels alot.* New York: Frederick Warner.

Bell, A., Super, D. E, & Dunn, L. B. (1988). Understanding and implementing career theory: A case study approach. *Counseling and Human Development, 20*(8), 1–19.

Bennett, C. (1988). Assessing teachers' abilities for educating multicultural students: The need for conceptual models in teacher education. In C. Heid (Ed.), *Multicultural education: Knowledge and perceptions.* Bloomington, IN. Indiana University.

Berk, R., Bridges, W., & Shih, A. (1981). Does IQ really matter? A study of the use of IQ scores for the tracking of mentally retarded. *American Sociological Review, 46,* 58–71.

Bernard, B., Fafoglia, B., & Perone, J. (1987, February). Knowing what to do—and not to do reinvigorates drug education. *Curriculum Update,* pp. 1-12.

Bertoia, J., & Allan, J. (1988). School management of the bereaved child. *Elementary School Guidance and Counseling, 23,* 30–38.

Bewley, K. (1977). Self-esteem: The alternative to genetic inferiority. *Negro Educational Review, 28,* 95–99.

Binet, A., & Simon, T. (1916). *The development of intelligence in children* (E. S. Kit, trans) Baltimore: Williams & Wilkins.

Black, C. (1979). *My dad loves me, my dad has a disease.* Denver, CO: MAC Publishers.

Black, C. (1981). *It will never happen to me.* Denver, CO: ACT Publishers.

Blackham, G. J. (1977). *Counseling: Theory, process, and practice.* Belmont, CA: Wadsworth.

Blanchard, E., & Mackey, J. (1971). *The American Indian.* (SRS Training Grant 755T70). Washington, DC: National Rehabilitation Association.

Bleck, R. T., & Bleck, B. L. (1982). The disruptive child's play group. *Elementary School Guidance and Counseling, 17,* 137–141.

Blocher, D. H. (1987). *The professional counselor.* New York: Macmillan.

Blotner, R., & Lilly, L. (1986). A comprehensive approach to the delivery of substance abuse prevention services in the New York City School System. *Journal of Drug Addiction, 16,* 83-89.

Bonebrake, L. R., & Borgers, S. B. (1984). Counselor role as perceived by middle school counselors and principals. *Elementary School Guidance and Counseling, 18,* 194–199.

Borke, H. (1971). Interpersonal perception of young children: Egocentrism or empathy? *Developmental Psychology, 55,* 263-269.

Boser, J. A., Poppen, W. A., & Thompson, C. L. (1988). Elementary school guidance program evaluation: A reflection of student counselor ratio. *School Counselor, 36,*125-135.

Bourke, L. (1981). *It's your move: Picking up, packing up, and settling in.* Reading, MA: Addison-Wesley.

Bowker, M. A. (1982). Children and divorce: Being in between. *Elementary School Guidance and Counseling, 17,* 126-130.

Bowlby, J. (1980). *Loss, sadness and depression.* New York: Basic Books.

Bowman, R. P., (1985, February). *The homework song.* Song presented at the South Carolina Association of Counseling and Development Conference, Hilton Head, South Carolina.

Bowman, R. P., & Myrick, R. D. (1987). Effects of an elementary school peer facilitator program on children with behavior problems. *School Counselor, 34,* 369–378.

Boyer, M., & Horne, A. (1989). *Schools and parents: Partners in career equity guidance for young adolescents.* (Equity Career Guidance Project Monograph N0. 2). Terre Haute, IN: Indiana State University, Department of Counseling.

Bradley, D. F. (1988). Alcohol and drug education in the elementary school. *Elementary School Guidance and Counseling, 23,* 99-105.

Brammer, L. M. (1988). *The helping relationship: Process and skills* (4th ed.). Englewood Cliffs, NJ: Prentice-Hall.

Brown, D., & Srebalus, D. J. (1988). *An introduction to the counseling profession.* Englewood Cliffs, NJ: Prentice-Hall.

Bruckner, S. T., & Thompson, C. L. (1987). Guidance program evaluation. *Elementary School Guidance and Counseling, 21,* 193-196.

Bruininks, V. L. (1978). Peer status and personality characteristics of learning disabled and non-disabled students. *Journal of Learning Disabilities, 11,* 484-489.

Bryan, T. H. (1974). Peer popularity of learning disabled children. *Journal of Learning Disabilities ,7,* 31-47.

Bryan, T. H. (1978). Social relationships and verbal interactions of learning disabled children. *Journal of Learning Disabilities, 11,* 107-115.

Bundy, M. L., & Boser, J. (1987). Helping latchkey children: A group guidance approach. *School Counselor, 35,* 58–65.

Bundy, M. L., & Gumaer, J. (1984). Guest editorial: Families in transition: *Elementary School Guidance and Counseling, 19,* 4–8.

Bundy, M. L., & Poppen, W. A. (1986). School counselors'effectiveness as consultants: A research review. *Elementary School Guidance and Counseling, 20,* 215-222.

Bureau of Indian Affairs (1988). *American Indians today.* Washington, DC: Author.

Burke, D. M., & Van de Streek, L. (1989). Children of divorce: An application of Hammond's group counseling for children. *Elementary School Guidance and Counseling, 24,* 112–118.

Burnett, P. C. (1983). A self-concept enhancement program for children in the regular classroom. *Elementary School Guidance and Counseling, 18,* 101-108.

Burt, M. A., & Myrick, R. D. (1980). Developmental play: What's it all about? *Elementary School Guidance and Counseling, 15,* 14-19.

Burton, V. L. (1967). *Katy and the big snow.* Boston: Houghton Mifflin.

Buscaglia, L. (1983). *The fall of Freddie the leaf.* NY: Holt, Rinehart, & Winston.

Canfield, J., & Wells, H. (1976). *One hundred ways to enhance self-concept in the classroom.* Englewood Cliffs, NJ: Prentice-Hall.

Cantrell, R. (1986). Adjustment to divorce: Three components to assist children. *Elementary School Guidance and Counseling, 29,* 163–173.

Carlson, J. (1990). Counseling through physical fitness and exercise. *Elementary School Guidance and Counseling, 24,* 298–302.

Carter, S. R. (1987). Use of puppets to treat traumatic grief: A case study. *Elementary School Guidance and Counseling, 21,* 210-215.

Cartledge, G., & Milburn, J. (1980). *Teaching social skills to children.* New York: Pergamon Press.

Casas, J. M., & Furling, M. J. (in press). Empowering Hispanic parents: Increasing school involvement. In J. Carey and P. Pedersen (Eds.), *Multicultural counseling in schools.* Boston, MA: Allyn & Bacon.

Chandler, C. L., Weissberg, R. P., Cowen, E. L., & Guarez, J. (1984). Long-term effects of school-based secondary prevention program for young maladapting children. *Journal of Consulting and Clinical Psychology, 52,* 165-170.

Childers, J. H., Jr., (1984). Looking at yourself through loving eyes. *Elementary School Guidance and Counseling, 23,* 204-209.

Childers, J. H., Jr., & Basse, D. T. (1980). A Gestalt approach to psychological education. *Elementary School Guidance and Counseling, 15,* 120–126.

Clabaugh, G. (1989). How our schools assimilate minorities: The current struggle. *Educational Horizons, 67,* 107–110.

Clemes, H., & Dean, R. (1981). *Self-esteem, the key to your child's well-being.* New York: Putnam.

Cobb, H. C., & Richards, H. C. (1983). Efficacy of counseling services in decreasing behavior problems of elementary school children. *Elementary School Guidance and Counseling, 17,* 180-187.

Colangelo, N., & Fleuridas, C. (1986). The abdication of childhood. *Journal of Counseling and Development, 64,* 561-563.

Colao, F., & Hosansky, T. (1983). *Your children should know.* New York: Bobbs-Merrill.

Conrad, P. (1984). *I don't live here.* New York: Dutton.

Conroy, E. H. (1987). Primary prevention for gifted students: A parent education group. *Elementary School Guidance and Counseling, 22,* 110–117.

Conyne, R. K. (1987). *Primary Preventive Counseling.* Muncie, IN: Accelerated Development.

Cooney, J. (1991). *Coping with sexual abuse.* New York: Rosen Publishing Group.

Corey, G. (1986). *Theory and practice of counseling and psychotherapy* (3rd ed.). Monteray, CA: Brooks/Cole.

Corey, G. (1990). *Manual for theory and practice of group counseling* (3rd ed.). Pacific Grove, CA: Brooks/Cole.

Corey, G., & Corey, M. (1990). *I never knew I had a choice* (4th ed.). Pacific Grove, CA: Brooks/Cole.

Corey, M. S., & Corey, G. (1987). *Groups: Process and practice* (3rd ed.). Monterey, CA: Brooks/Cole.

Cowen E. L., Pederson, A., Babigian, H., Izzo, L. D., & Trost, M. A. (1973). Long term follow up of early detected vulnerable children. *Journal of Consulting and Clinical Psychology, 41,* 438–446.

Cowen E. L., Trost, M. A., Lorion, R. P., Dorr, D., Izzo, L. D., & Isaacson, R. (1975). *New Ways in School Mental Health: Early Detection and Prevention of School Maladaptation.* New York: Human Sciences Press.

Cox, J. (1986). *Educating able learners: Programs and promising practices.* Austin, TX: University of Texas Press.

Creed, L., & Masser, M. (1977). *Greatest love of all.*(Song).Miami, FL: Gold Horizon Music Corporation and Golden Touch Music Corporation.

Cronbach, L. J. (1984). *Essentials of psychological testing* (4th ed.). New York: Harper & Row.

Culross, R. (1982). Developing the whole child: A developmental approach to guidance with the gifted. *Roeper Review, 5,* 24–26.

Cunningham, B., & Hare, J. (1989). Essential elements of a teacher in-service program on child bereavement. *Elementary School Guidance and Counseling, 23,* 175–182.

Dagley, J. C. (1987). A new look at developmental guidance: The hearthstone of school counseling. *School counselor, 35,* 102–109.

Data file: States that mandate elementary school counselors. (1990, May 11). *Education Daily,* p. 5.

De Saint-Exupery, A. (1971). *The little prince.* New York: Harcourt Brace Jovanovich.

Dettman, D., & Colangelo, N. (1980). A functional model for counseling parents of gifted students. *Gifted Child Quarterly, 24,* 158–161.

Devries, D. L., & Slavin, R. E. (1978). Teams-Games-Tournament (TGT): Review of ten classroom experiments. *Journal of Research and Development in Education, 12,* 28–38.

Dewey, J. (1934). *Art as experience.* New York: Minton.

Dillard, J. M. (1983). *Multicultural Counseling.* Chicago, IL: Nelson-Hall.

Dinkmeyer, D. (1970). *Developing understanding of self and others, kit 2.* Circle Pines, MN: American Guidance Service.

Dodge, K. (1983). Promoting social competence in school children. *Schools and Teaching, 1*(1), 1–4.

Downing, J., Jenkins, S., & Fisher, G. (1988). A comparison of psychodynamic and reinforcement treatment with sexually abused children. *Elementary School Guidance and Counseling, 22,* 291-298.

Downing, C. J. (1982). Parent support groups to prevent child abuse. *Elementary School Guidance and Counseling, 17,* 119–124.

Dreikurs, R., & Soltz, V. (1987). *Children: The challenge* (2nd ed.). New York: Dutton.

Drummond, R. J. (1988). *Appraisal procedures for counselors and helping professionals.* Columbus, OH: Merrill.

Dunlop, R. (1968). *Professional problems in school counseling practice.* Scranton, PA: International Textbook.

Education for all Handicapped Children Act of 1975, 20 U.S.C. 1401 (1977).

Edwards, D. M., & Zander, T. A. (1985). Children of Alcoholics: Background and strategies for the counselor. *Elementary School Guidance and Counseling, 20,* 124–125.

Eicher, M. (1971). *Martin's father.* Chapel Hill, NC: Lollipop Power.

Elkind, D. (1991).Development in early childhood. *Elementary School Guidance and Counseling, 26,* 12-26.

Erikson, E. (1963). *Childhood and society* (2nd ed.). New York: Norton.

Erikson, E. (1968). *Identity, youth, and crisis.* New York: Norton.

Eshleman, J. R., Cashion, B. G., & Basirico, L. A. (1988). *Sociology: An Introduction* (3rd ed.). Boston, MA: Scott Foresman.

Esquivel, G. B., & Keitel, M. A. (1990). Counseling immigrant children in schools. *Elementary School Guidance and Counseling, 24,* 213–221.

Esters, P., & Levant, R. F. (1983). The effects of two parent counseling programs on rural low-achieving children. *School Counselor, 31,* 159-166.

Family Rights and Privacy Act of 1974, 512, 20 U.S.C. 1232g (1974).

Faust, V. (1968). *The Counselor-Consultant in the Elementary School.* Boston, MA: Houghton Mifflin.

Ferris, P.A., & Linville, M. E. (1985). The child's rights: Whose responsibility? *Elementary School Guidance and Counseling, 19,* 172–180.

Feshbach, N. D., & Rose, K. (1968). Empathy in six and seven-year-olds. *Child Development, 39,* 133-145.

Fischer, L. & Sorenson, G.P. (1985). *School law for counselors, psychologists and social workers.* New York: Longman.

Flygare, T. J. (1975). *The legal rights of students.* Bloomington, IN: Phi Delta Kappa Educational Foundation.

Fontana, V. J. (1982). Sexual child abuse. In J. Bulkey, J. Ensminger, V. J. Fontana, & R. Summit (Eds.), *Dealing with sexual child abuse* (pp 1-2). Chicago: National Committee for Prevention of Child Abuse.

Foote, P. (1980). *Girls can be anything they want*. New York: Julian Messner.

Ford-Harris, D., Schuerger, J. M., & Harris III, J. J. (1991). Meeting the psychological needs of gifted black students: A cultural perspective. *Journal of Counseling and Development, 69*, 577–580.

Forman, S. B., & Neal, J. A. (1987). School-based substance abuse prevention programs. *Special Services in-the-School, 3*(3-4), 89-102.

Fournier, M. J. (1977). A self-enhancement activity group for first grade repeaters. *Elementary School Guidance and Counseling, 11*, 267-277

Freed, A. M. (1991). *TA for tots and grown ups too*. Rolling Hills Estates, CA: Jalmar Press.

Freud, S. (1933). *New introductory lectures on psychoanalysis*. New York: W.W. Norton.

Furlong, M. J., Atkinson, D. R., & Janoff, D. S. (1979). Elementary school counselors' perceptions of their actual and ideal roles. *Elementary School Guidance and Counseling, 14*, 4–11.

Furman, E. (1984). Children's patterns in mourning the death of a loved one. In H. Wass & C. Corr (Eds.). *Childhood and death* (pp. 185–202). Washington DC: Hemisphere.

Galyean, B.C. (1985). Guided imagery in education. In A. Sheikh and K.S. Sheikh (Eds.), *Imagery in education: Imagery in the educational process*. Farmingdale, NY: Baywood.

Garbarino, J. (1986). Can we measure success in preventing child abuse? Issues in policy, programming and research. *Child Abuse and Neglect*, 10, 143–156.

Garbarino, J. Stott, F. M., & Faculty of Erickson Institute (1989). *What children can tell us: Eliciting, interpreting, and evaluating information from children*. San Francisco: Jossey-Bass.

George, R. L., & Cristiani, T. S. (1990). *Counseling theory and practice* (3rd ed.). Englewood Cliffs, NJ: Prentice-Hall.

George, R. L., & Dustin, D. (1988). *Group counseling: Theory and practice*. Englewood Cliffs, NJ: Prentice-Hall.

Georgia Department of Education. (1983). *Program Planning Guide: Georgia Comprehensive Guidance*. Atlanta, GA.

Gerler, E. R., Jr. (1982). *Counseling the young learner*. Englewood Cliffs, NJ: Prentice-Hall.

Gerler, E., Jr. (1988). Recent research on child abuse: A brief review. *Elementary School Guidance and Counseling, 22*, 325–327.

Gerler, E. R., Jr. & Anderson, R. F. (1986). The effects of classroom guidance on children's success in school. *Journal of Counseling and Development, 65*, 78-81.

Gerstein, M., & Lichtman, M. (1990). *The best for our kids: Exemplary elementary guidance and counseling programs*. Alexandria, VA: American Counseling Association.

Gianotti, T. J., & Doyle, R. E. (1982). The effectiveness of parental training on disabled children and their parents. *Elementary School Guidance and Counseling, 17*, 131-136.

Gibran, K. (1923). *The prophet*. New York: Alfred A. Knopf.

Gibson, J. T. (1980). *Psychology for the classroom* (2nd ed.). Englewood Cliffs, NJ: Prentice-Hall.

Gibson, J. T., & Chandler, L. A. (1988). *Educational Psychology: Mastering Principles and Applications*. Needham Heights, MA: Allyn & Bacon.

Gibson, R. L. (1972). *Career development in the elementary school*. Columbus, OH: Author.

Gibson, R. L. (1989). Prevention and the elementary school counselor. *Elementary School Guidance and Counseling, 24*, 30-36.

Gibson, R. L., & Mitchell, M. H. (1990). *Introduction to counseling and guidance* (3rd ed.). New York: Macmillan.

Gill, S. J., & Barry, R. A. (1982). Group-focused counseling: Classifying the essential skills. *Personnel & Guidance Journal, 60,* 302-305.

Gilliland, B. E., James, R.K., & Bowman, J. T. (1989). *Theories and strategies in counseling and psychotherapy* (2nd ed.). Englewood Cliffs, NJ: Prentice-Hall.

Ginzberg, E., Ginsburg, S. W., & Axelrad, S., & Herma, J. L. (1951). *Occupational choice: An approach to general theory.* New York: Columbia University Press.

Glasser, W. (1965). *Reality therapy, a new approach to psychiatry.* New York: Harper and Row.

Glasser, W. (1969). *Schools without failure.* New York: Harper and Row.

Glasser, W. (1981). *Stations of the mind: New directions for Reality Therapy.* New York: Harper and Row.

Glossoff, H. L., & Koprowicz, C. L. (1990). *Children achieving potential: An introduction to elementary school counseling and state level policies.* Washington, DC:National Conference of State Legislators and Alexandria, VA: American Counseling Association.

Goble, P. (1978). *The girl who loved wild horses.* Scarsdale, New York: Bradburry Press.

Goldman, L. (Ed.). (1978). *Research methods of counselors.* NY: John Wiley.

Goldsmith, A. (1979). *Discipline, discrimination, disproportionality, and discretion: A legal memorandum.* Reston, VA: National Association of Secondary School Principals.

Golub, J. S., Espinosa, M., Damon, L., & Card, J. (1987). A videotaped parent education program for abusive parents. *Child Abuse and Neglect, 11,* 255–265.

Goodman, R. W., & Kjoonas, D. (1984). Elementary school family counseling: A pilot project. *Journal of Counseling and Development, 63,* 255-257.

Gottfredson, L. S. (1981). Circumscription and compromise: A developmental theory of occupational aspirations. *Journal of Counseling Psychology,* 28, 545–579.

Gowan, J.C. (1978). Incubation, imagery, and creativity, *Journal of Mental Imagery, 2,* 23–32.

Green, B. J. (1978). Helping children of divorce: A multimodal approach. *Elementary School Guidance and Counseling, 13,* 31-45.

Green, V. M. (1981). Blacks in the United /states: the creation of an enduring people? In G. P. Castile & G. Kusher (Eds.), *Persistent peoples: Cultural enclaves in perspective* (pp. 69–77). Tuscon: University of Arizona Press.

Greer, J. G., & Wethered, C. E. (1987). Learned helplessness and the elementary student: Implications for counselors. *Elementary School Guidance and Counseling, 22,* 157-164.

Griffith, A. (1980). Justification for Black career development. *Journal of Non-White Concerns in Personnel and Guidance, 8,* 77–83.

Groening, M. (1991). *Life in Hell.* Santa Monica, CA: ACME Feature Syndicate.

Guild, J. (1984). Project CHARLIE. *Early Years, 15,* 37-39.

Gumaer, J. (1984). Developmental play in small group counseling with disturbed children. *School Counselor, 31,* 445-453.

Gumaer, J., & Voorneveld, R. (1975). Affective education with gifted children. *Elementary School Guidance and Counseling, 10,* 86-94.

Gunnings, B., & Gunnings, T. (1983). A bias review procedure for career counselors. *Journal of Non-White Concerns in Personnel and Guidance, 11,* 78–83.

Guyton, J. M., & Fielstein, L. L. (1989). Student-led parent conferences: A model for teaching responsibility. *Elementary School Guidance and Counseling, 24,* 169–172.

Hadley, H. (1988). Improving reading scores through a self-esteem intervention program. *Journal of Elementary School Guidance and Counseling, 22,* 248-252.

Hadley, R. & Brodwin, M. (1988). Language about people with disabilities. *Journal of Counseling and Development, 67,* 147–149.

Hall, C. S. (1979). *A primer of freudian psychology.* New York: Mentor.

Haney, W. (1987). *An estimation of immigrant and immigrant student populations in the United States as of October, 1986*. Background paper for immigrant student project. Boston, MA: Boston College.

Hannaford, M. (1985). *A Counselor's Task*. Unpublished poem, Dunwoody, GA.

Hansen, J. C., Stevic, R. R., & Warner, R. W., Jr. (1986). *Counseling: Theory and Process* (4th ed.). Newton, MA: Allyn and Bacon.

Harper F. (1977). Developing a curriculum of self-esteem for Black youth. *Journal of Negro Education, 46*, 133–140.

Hart, S. N., Germain, R. B., & Brassard, M. R. (1987). The challenge: To better understand and combat psychological maltreatment of children and youth. In S. N. Hart, M. R. Brassard, & R. B. Germain (Eds.) *Psychological maltreatment of children and youth* (pp. 3-24). New York: Pergamon Press.

Harvath, S. (1990, November). *Expanding your alternatives: MISSION VENUS. Curriculum ideas for elementary school settings*. Paper presented at the 15th Annual National Career Guidance Week, National Vocational Guidance Association, Washington, DC.

Hatcher, B., Pape, D., & Nicosia, R. T. (1988). Group games for global awareness. *Childhood Education, 65*, 8–13.

Havighurst, R. J. (1964). Youth in exploration and man emergent. In H. Borrow (Ed.), *Man in a world at work* (pp. 215–236). Boston, MA: Houghton-Mifflin.

Heid, C. (Ed.). (1988).*Multicultural Education: Knowledge and Perceptions*. Bloomington, IN: Indiana University Center for Urban and Multicultural Education.

Heinrich, R., Corbine, J. L., & Thomas, K. R. (1990). Counseling Native Americans. *Journal of Counseling and Development, 69*, 128–133.

Help your child tame the moving monster. (1986, September). *Parents Magazine*, p. 159.

Henderson, G. (Ed.). (1979). *Understanding and counseling ethnic minorities*. Springfield, IL: Charles C. Thomas.

Herbert, D. (Ed.). (1983). *Counseling youngsters for stress management*. Highlights: An ERIC/CAPS facts sheet. Ann Arbor, MI: Counseling and Personnel Services Clearing House.

Herr, E. L., & Cramer, S. H. (1988). *Career guidance and counseling through the life span: Systematic approaches* (3rd ed.). Glenview, Il: Scott Foresman.

Herring, R. D. (1989). Counseling Native American children: Implications for elementary school counselors. *Elementary School Guidance and Counseling, 23*, 272–281.

Hetherington, E. M., & Parke, R. D. (1986). *Child psychology: A contemporary viewpoint* (3rd ed.). New York: McGraw Hill.

Hickman, M. (1974). *I'm moving*. Nashville: Abingdon.

Hitchcock, R. A., & Young, D. (1986). Prevention of sexual assault: A curriculum for elementary school counselors. *Elementary School Guidance and Counseling, 20*, 201-207.

Hoffman, L.R. & McDaniels, C. (1991). Career development in the elementary schools: A perspective for the 1990s. *Elementary School Guidance and Counseling, 25*, 163–171.

Holland, J.L. (1966). *The psychology of vocational choice*. Lexington, MA: Blaisdell-Ginn.

Holland, J. L. (1973). *Making vocational choices: A theory of careers*. Englewood Cliffs, NJ: Prentice-Hall.

Holland, J. L. (1985a). *Making vocational choices: A theory of careers* (2nd ed.). Englewood Cliffs, NJ: Prentice- Hall.

Holland, J.L. (1985b). *Making vocational choices: A theory of vocational personalities and work environments* (2nd ed.). Englewood Cliffs, NJ: Prentice-Hall.

Holtgraves, M. (1986). Help the victims of sexual abuse help themselves. *Elementary School Guidance and Counseling, 21*, 155–159.

Hopkins, B.R. & Anderson, B.S. (1990). *The counselor and the law* (3rd. ed.). Alexandria, VA: American Association for Counseling and Development.

Hopkins, K. D., Stanley, J. C., & Hopkins, B. R. (1990). *Educational and psychological measurement and evaluation* (7th ed.). Englewood Cliffs, NJ: Prentice-Hall.

Horan, J. J., Kerns, A., & Olson, C. (1988). Perspectives on substance abuse prevention. *Elementary School Guidance and Counseling, 23,* 84-92.

Houston, W. (1985). *Greatest love of all.* New York: EMI Music.

Hughes, S. (1977). *George the babysitter.* Englewood Cliffs, NJ: Prentice-Hall.

Hummel, D. L., & Humes, C. W. (1984). *Pupil services: Development, coordination, administration.* New York: Macmillan.

Hummel, D. L., Talbutt, L., & Alexander, M. D. (1985). *Law and ethics in counseling.* New York: Van Nostrand Reinhold.

Hutchins, D. E., & Cole, C. G. (1986). *Helping relationships and strategies.* Monteray, CA: Wadsworth.

Hyland, C. R. (1989). What we know about the fastest growing minority population Hispanic Americans. *Educational Horizons, 67,* 131–135.

Indiana Department of Education- Indiana School Counselors Association. (1991). *A model for developmental school counseling programs in Indiana.* Indianapolis, IN: Indiana Department of Education.

Isaacson, L. E. (1985). *Basics of career counseling.* Boston: Allyn & Bacon.

Ivey, A. D. , Ivey, M. B., & Simek-Downing, L. (1987). *Counseling and psychotherapy: Integrating skills, theory, and practice* (2nd ed.). Englewood Cliffs, NJ: Prentice-Hall.

Jackson, R. M., Cleveland, J. C., & Merander, P. F. (1975). The longitudinal effects of early identification and counseling of underachievers. *Journal of School Psychology, 13,* 119-128.

Jarolimek, J., & Foster, C. D., Sr. (1989). *Teaching and Learning in the Elementary School.* New York: Macmillan.

Jenkins, D. E. (1985). Ethical and legal dilemmas of working with students with special needs. *Elementary School Guidance and Counseling, 19,* 202–209.

Johnson, R. (1980). School models for career education/development. *Journal of Non-White Concerns in Personnel and Guidance, 8,* 104–118.

Jones, P. (1980). *I'm not moving.* Scarsdale, NY: Bradbury.

Kaeser, S. (1979). Suspensions in school discipline. *Education and Urban Society, 11,* 465–484.

Kameen, M. C., Robinson, E. H., & Rotter, J. C. (1985). Coordination activities: A study of perceptions of elementary and middle school counselors. *Journal of Elementary School Guidance and Counseling, 20,* 97-104.

Kaplan, L. S., & Geoffroy, K. E. (1990). Enhancing the school climate: New opportunities for the counselor. *School Counselor, 38,* 7-12.

Katz, J. H. (1985). The sociopolitical nature of counseling. *Counseling Psychologist, 13,* 615-624.

Katz, M. (1963). *Decisions and values: A rationale for secondary school guidance.* New York: College Entrance Examination Board.

Kazdin, A. E. (1978). *History of behavior modification: Experimental foundations of contemporary research.* Baltimore: University Park Press.

Kempe, R., & Kempe, H. (1978). *Child Abuse.* Cambridge, MA: Harvard University Press.

Kern, R. M., & Carlson, J. (1981). Adlerian family counseling. *Elementary School Guidance and Counseling, 15,* 301–306.

Kirschenbaum, H., & Henderson, V.L. (Eds.). (1989). *The Carl Rogers Reader.* Boston, MA: Houghton Mifflin.

Kohlberg, L. (1963). The development of children's orientations toward moral order: Sequence in the development of moral thought. *Vita Humana, 6,* 11–33.

Kohlberg, L. (1975). The cognitive-developmental approach to moral education. *Phi Delta Kappan, 56*, 670–677.
Kohlberg, L. (1981). *The philosophy of moral development*. New York: Harper and Row.
Kottler, J. A., & Brown, R. W. (1985). *Introduction to therapeutic counseling*. Monteray, CA: Brooks/Cole.
Kraizer, S. K. (1985). *The safe child book*. New York: Dell.
Kraizer, S. K. (1985). The safe child book. New York: Dell.Kutash, I., & Wolf, A. (Eds.), (1986). *Psychotherapist's casebook*. San Francisco, CA: Jossey-Bass.
Krumboltz, J. D. (1987). *The key to achievement: Learning to love learning*. Paper presented at the 20/20 Conference, Arlington, VA.
Krumboltz, J.D., Mitchell, A., & Gellat, H.G. (1975). Applications of social learning theory of career selection. *Focus on guidance, 8*(3), 1–16.
Kubler-Ross, E. (1969). *Death and dying*. New York, NY: Macmillan.
Kurdek, L. A. (1981). An integrative perspective on children's divorce adjustment. *American Psychologist, 36*, 856–866.
Kurdek, L. A., & Siesky, A. E., Jr. (1980). Effects of divorce on children: The relationship between parent and child perspectives. *Journal of Divorce, 4*, 85–89.
Kurpius, D. (1978). Consultation and process: An integrated model. *Personnel and Guidance Counseling, 56*, 335-338.
Larkin, J. (1979). School desegregation and student suspension: A look at one school system. *Education and Urban Society, 11*, 485–495.
Lazarus, P. (1982). Counseling the Native American child: A question of values. *Elementary School Guidance and Counseling, 17*, 83–88.
Lee, C., & Lindsey, C. (1985). Black consciousness development: A group counseling model for Black elementary school students. *Elementary School Guidance and Counseling, 19*, 228–236.
Leershen, C. (1991, November). *Magic's message*. Newsweek, p. 58.
Lerner, R., & Naiditch, B. (1985). *Children are people*. St. Paul, MN: Children are People, Inc.
Levine, E. S., & Padilla, A. M.. (1980). *Crossing cultures in therapy- Pluralistic counseling for the Hispanic*. Monteray, CA: Brooks/Cole.
Levitan, S. A., & Belous, R. S. (1981). Working wives and mothers: What happens to family life? *Monthly Labor Review, 104*, 26–30.
Lewin, K. (1936). *Principles of Topological Psychology*. New York: McGraw-Hill.
Lewis, A. C., & Hayes, S. (1991). Multiculturalism and the school counseling curriculum. *Journal of Counseling and Development, 70*, 119–125.
Lickona, T. (1989-1990). Four strategies for fostering character development in children. *Educational Psychology/Annual Editions*, 47-51.
Lindstrom, R. R., & San Vant, S. (1986). Special issues in working with gifted minority adolescents. *Journal of Counseling and Development, 64*, 583–586.
Locke, D. C. (1989). Fostering the self-esteem of African-American children. *Elementary School Guidance and Counseling, 23*, 254-259.
Lock, R. D. (1988). *Taking charge of your career direction: Career planning guide, book 1*. Pacific Grove, CA: Brooks/Cole.
Long, T., & Long, L. (1984). *The handbook for latchkey children and their parents*. New York: Berkley.
Mabe, A.R., & Rollin, S.A. (1986). The role of a code of ethical standards in counseling. *Journal of Counseling and Development, 64*, 294–297.
MacLeod, J. (1987). *Ain't no makin' it: Leveled aspirations in a low-income neighborhood*. Boulder, CO: Westview Press.
Marshall, H.R., & Hahn, S.C. (1967). Experimental modification of dramatic play. *Journal of Personality and Social Psychology, 5*(1), 119–122.
Maslow, A.H. (1962). *Toward a psychology of being*. Princeton, NJ: Van Nostrand.

Maslow, A.H. (1968). *Toward a psychology of being* (2nd. Ed.). New York: D. Van Nostrand.

Matter, D., & Matter, R. M. (1988). Helping young children cope with the stress of relaxation: Action steps for the counselor. *Elementary School Guidance and Counseling, 23,* 23–29.

Mattie V. Johnson, 74, F.R.D.N.D. (MS 1976).

Maultsby, M. C., Jr. (1982). *Freedom from alcohol and tranquilizers-Booklet 3: The ABC's of Rational Self-Analysis.* Lexington, KY: Rational Self Help Books.

McCully, C. (1963). Professionalization: Symbol or Substance. *Counselor Education and Supervision, 2,* 106-112.

McCully, C. H. (1969). *Challenges for Change in Counselor Education.* Minneapolis, MN: Burgess.

McCurdy, B., Ciucevich, M. T., & Walker, B. A. (1977). Human relations training with seventh grade boys identified as behavior problems. *School Counselor, 24,* 248-252.

McGee, R. (1980). *Sociology: An Introduction* (2nd ed.). New York: Holt, Rinehart & Winston.

McPhail, I. (1979). Test sophistication: An important consideration in judging the standardized test performance of Black students. *Reading World, 18,* 227–235.

McWhirter, M. E. (1970). *Games enjoyed by children around the world.* Middleton, CT: Field Publications.

Medway, F. J., & Updyke, J. F. (1985). Meta-analysis of consultation outcome studies. *American Journal of Community Psychology, 13,* 489-505.

Meichenbaum, D. (1977). *Cognitive-behavior modification: An integrative approach.* New York: Plenum.

Mendoza, G. (1981). *Need a house? Call Mr. Mouse.* New York: Grossett & Dunlap.

Metcalfe, B. (1981). Self-concept and attitude toward school. *British Journal of Educational Psychology, 51,* 66–67.

Miller, G. M. (1988). Counselor functions in excellent schools: Elementary through Secondary. *School Counselor, 36,* 88-93.

Miller, M.J. (1988). Student and worker: A simple yet effective career education activity. *Elementary School Guidance and Counseling, 22,* 246–249.

Miller, M.J. (1989). Career counseling in the elementary school child: Grades K-5. *Journal of Employment Counseling, 26,* 169–177.

Miller, R.M. (1986). Reducing occupational circumscription. *Elementary School Guidance and Counseling, 20,* 250–254.

Mills, J., & Crowley, R. (1986). *Therapeutic metaphors for children and the child within.* New York: Brummer/Magel.

Mitchell, L.K., & Krumboltz, J.D. (1984). Social learning approach to career decision-making: Krumboltz's theory. In D. Brown & L. Brooks (Eds.) *Career choice and development.* San Francisco: Jossey-Bass.

Mitchell, A.M., Jones, G.B., & Krumboltz, J.D. (Eds.) (1979). *Social learning and career decision making.* Cranston, RI: Carroll Press.

Mitchum, M. T. (1989). Increasing self-esteem in Native-American children. *Elementary School Guidance and Counseling, 23,* 266–271.

Morganett, R. S. (1990). *Skills for living: Group counseling activities for young adolescents.* Champaign, IL: Research Press.

Morse, C. L., & Russell, T. (1989). How elementary counselors see their role: An empirical study. *Elementary School Guidance and Counseling, 23,* 54-62.

Morse, L. A. (1987). Working with young procrastinators: Elementary students who do not complete school assignments. *Journal of Elementary School Guidance and Counseling, 21,* 221-228.

Muro, J. J., & Dinkmeyer, D. C. (1977). *Counseling in the elementary and middle schools: A pragmatic approach.* Dubuque, IA: W. C. Brown.

Mussen, P. H., Conger, J. J., Kagan, J., & Huston, A. C. (1984). *Child Development and Personality* (6th ed.). New York: Harper Row.

Myrick, R. D. (1987). *Developmental guidance and counseling: A practical approach.* Minneapolis, MN: Educational Media Corporation.

Myrick, R. D., & Dixon, R. W. (1985). Changing student attitudes and behavior through group counseling. *School Counselor, 32,* 325-330.

Myrick, R. D., Merbell, H., & Swanson, L. (1986). Changing student attitudes through classroom guidance. *School Counselor, 33,* 244-252.

National Center for Health Statistics (1976). *NCHS growth charts.* Washington, DC: National Center For Health Statistics.

National Indian Child Abuse and Neglect Resource Center. (1980). *The social worker and the Indian client.* Tulsa, OK: Author.

National Occupational Information Coordinating Committee (1989). *The national career development guidelines.* Washington, D.C.: National Occupational Information Coordinating Committee. (ERIC Document Reproduction Service No. ED 317 874–880).

Navin, S. L., & Bates, G. W. (1987).Improving attitudes and achievement of remedial readers: A parent counseling approach. *Elementary School Guidance and Counseling, 21,* 203–209.

Neese, L. A. (1989). Psychological maltreatment in schools: Emerging issues for counselors. *Elementary School Guidance and Counseling, 23,* 194-200.

Nickell, P., & Kennedy, M. (1987). Global perspectives through children's games. *How to Do it Series, 5,* 1–8.

North Carolina Association for the Gifted and Talented Task Force. (1986). *What is an appropriate education for a gifted student?* Raleigh, NC: Author.

Nugent, F. (1981). *Professional counseling: An overview.* Monteray, CA: Brooks/Cole.

Oaklander, V. (1988). *Windows to our children.* Highland, NY: Center for Gestalt Development.

Oldfield, D., & Petosa, R. (1986). Increasing student "on-task" behaviors through relaxation strategies. *Elementary School Guidance and Counseling, 20,* 180-186.

Olds, D. L., Chamberlin, R., Jr., & Henderson, C. R., Jr., & Tatelbaum, R. (1986). The prevention of child abuse and neglect: A randomized trial of nurse home visitation. *Pediatrics, 78,* 65–78.

Olson, M. J., & Dilley, J. S. (1988). A new look at stress and the school counselor. *School Counselor, 35,* 194-198.

Omizo, M. M., & Omizo, S. A. (1987). Group counseling with children of divorce: New findings. *Journal of Elementary School Guidance and Counseling, 22,* 46-52.

Omizo, M. M., & Omizo, S. A. (1988). Group counseling's effects on self-concept and social behavior among children with learning disabilities. *Journal of Humanistic Education and Development, 26,* 109-117.

Orlick, T. (1978). *The cooperative sports and games book: Challenge without competition.* New York: Pantheon.

Ostrower, E. G. (1987). A counseling approach to alcohol education in middle schools. *School Counselor, 34,* 209–218.

Otto, L. B., & Call, V. A. (1985). Parental influences on young people's career development. *Journal of Career Development, 9,* 65–69.

Packard, V. (1983). *Our endangered children: Growing up in a changing world.* Boston, MA: Little, Brown and Company.

Padilla, A. M., Ruiz, R. A., and Alvarez, R. (1975). Community Mental Health services for the Spanish-speaking/surnamed population. *American Psychologist, 30,* 892–905.

Parker, W. M., & McDavis, R. J. (1989). A personal development model for black elementary school students. *Elementary School Guidance and Counseling, 23,* 244–252.

Parr, G. D., & Ostrovsky, M. (1991). The role of moral development in deciding how to counsel children and adolescents. *School Counselor, 39,* 14–19.

Pedersen, P. (Ed.). (1985). *Handbook of cross-cultural counseling and therapy.* Westport, CT: Greenwood Press.

Pedersen, P. (1988). *A handbook for developing multicultural awareness.* Alexandria, VA: American Association for Counseling and Development.

Pedersen, P. B., Draguns, J. G., Lonner, W. J., & Trimble, J. E. (Eds.). (1989). *Counseling across cultures* (3rd ed.). Honolulu, HI: University of Hawaii Press.

Petersen, A. C., & Taylor, B. (1980). The biological approach to adolescence. In J. Adelson (Ed.), *Handbook of adolescent psychology.* New York: Wiley.

Peterson, J. (1983). *Counselors for Kids.* Unpublished poem. Moncks Corner, SC: Author.

Peterson, J. V., & Nisenholz, B. (1987). *Orientation to counseling.* Newton, MA: Allyn & Bacon.

Pihl, R. O., & McLarnon, L. D. (1984). Learning disabled children as adolescents. *Journal of Learning Disabilities, 17,* 96-100.

Pogrebin, L. C. (1981). *Stories for free children.* New York: Ms. Foundation.

Polansky, N. A., Chalmers, M. A., Buttenweiser, E., & Williams, D. F. (1981). *An anatomy of child neglect.* Chicago, IL: University of Chicago Press.

Ponterotto, J. G. (1991). The nature of prejudice revisited: Implications for counseling intervention. *Journal of Counseling and Development, 70,* 216–224.

Poppen, W. (1991). *Strategies for dealing with challenges to developmental guidance materials and activities.* University of Tennessee, Department of Educational and Counseling Psychology, Knoxville.

Post-Kamer, P. (1988). Effectiveness of Parents' Anonymous in reducing child abuse. *School Counselor, 35,* 337-342.

Pulaski, M.A.S. (1973). Toys and imaginative play. In J. Singer (Ed.), *The child's world of make-believe.* New York, NY: Academic Press.

Purkey, W. W. (1970). *Self-concept and school achievement.* Englewood Cliffs, NJ: Prentice-Hall.

Reavin, S. (1971). *Hurrah for Captain Jane.* New York: Parents Magazine Press.

Remley, T. P., Jr. (1985). The law and ethical practices in elementary and middle schools. *Elementary School Guidance and Counseling, 19,* 181–189.

Remley, T. P., Jr. (1992, Winter). How can I get my legal questions answered? *American Counselor,* pp. 31-32.

Resnik, H. (1988). Putting it all together: Quest's skills for growing program. *Elementary School Guidance and Counseling, 23,* 93-98.

Reynolds, C. R., Gutkin, T. B., Elliott, S. N., & Witt, J. C. (1984). *School Psychology: Essentials of Theory and Practice.* New York: John Wiley & Sons.

Richardson, E. H. (1981). Cultural and historical perspectives in counseling American Indians. In D. W. Sue (Ed.), *Counseling the culturally different.* New York: Wiley.

Robinson, E. H., & Wilson, E. S. (1987). Counselor-led human relations training as a consultation strategy. *Journal of Elementary School Guidance and Counseling, 22,* 124-131.

Robinson, F.F. (1961). *Effective study.* New York, NY: Harper & Row.

Robinson, V. M. (1983, May). *5,000,000 latchkey children.* PTA Today, pp. 13–15.

Robson, B. A. (1982). A developmental approach to the treatment of divorcing parents. In L. Messinger (Ed.), *Therapy with remarriage families* (pp. 59–78). Rockvile, MD: Aspen Systems.

Roe, A., & Klos, D. (1969). Occupational classification. *Counseling Psychology, 1,* 84-92.

Rogers, C. (1942). *Counseling and psychotherapy.* Boston: Houghton Mifflin.

Rogers, C. (1951). *Client-centered therapy.* Boston: Houghton Mifflin.

Rogers, C. (1961). *On becoming a person.* Boston: Houghton Mifflin.

Rogers, C.R., & Stevens, B. (1967). *Person to person: The problem of being human, a new trend in psychology* (4th Ed.). San Diego, CA: Harcourt Brace Jovanovich.

Rosenberg, B. S., & Gaier, E. L. (1977). The self-concept of the adolescent with learning disabilities. *Adolescence, 12*, 489-498.

Roth, M. R. (1989). The warm fuzzy experiment. *Elementary School Guidance and Counseling, 23*, 234–235.

Roth, P., & Friedman, L. (1987). Alcohol use among youth. *Educational Horizons, 65*, 121–124.

Rotter, J.C. (1990). Elementary school counselor preparation: Past, present, and future. *Elementary School Guidance and Counseling, 24*, 180–188.

Ruben, A. M. (1989). Preventing school dropouts through classroom guidance. *Elementary School Guidance and Counseling, 24*, 21-29.

Rubinstein, R. E. (1991). Telling tales with at-risk students. *Family Life Educator, 9*(4), 4–6..

Sandburg, D. N., Crabbs, S. K., & Crabbs, M. A. (1988). Legal issues in child abuse: Questions and answers for counselors. *Elementary School Guidance and Counseling, 22*, 268–274.

Sattler, J. (1992). *Assessment of children* (3rd ed.). San Diego, CA: Jerome M. Sattler.

Schein, E. H. (1989). Process consultation as a general model of helping. *Consulting Psychology Bulletin*, 3-15.

Schmolling, P., Jr., Youkeles, M., & Burger, W. R. (1989). *Human services in contemporary America* (2nd ed.). Belmont, CA: Brooks/Cole.

Schrader, L. A., & Remer, P. (1980). Statue building: Helping children sculpture their feelings. *Elementary School Guidance and Counseling, 15*, 127–135.

Schulman, J., Ford, B., & Bush, P. (1973). A classroomprogram to improve self-concept. *Psychology in the schools, 10*, 481-487.

Schultz, D.P., & Schultz, S.E. (1987). *A history of modern psychology* (4th Ed.). San Diego, CA: Harcourt Brace Jovanovich.

Scofield, R. T., & Page, A. C. (1983). After school care and the public schools. *Tennessee Education, 13*, 40–47.

Seligman, L. (1980). *Assessment in developmental career counseling*. Cranston, RI: Carroll Press.

Selman R. L., & Selman, A. P. (1979). Children's ideas about friendship: A new theory. *Psychology Today*, pp. 13, 71–72, 74, 79–80, 114.

Sharples, M. R. (1987). Guidance shorts: The creative use of little time. *Elementary School Guidance and Counseling, 21*, 198-202.

Sheehy, G. (1987). *Celebrating human potential: The spirit of survival.* Keynote address at the annual meeting of the American Association for Counseling and Development, New Orleans, LA.

Sheeley, V. L., & Herlihy, B. (1987). Privileged communication in school counseling: Status update. *School Counselor, 34*, 268-272.

Sheikh, A., & Sheikh, K.S. (Eds.). (1985). *Imagery in education: Imagery in the educational process.* Farmingdale, NY: Baywood.

Sherman, A. (1989). Physical fitness as a mode of intervention with children. *School Counselor, 35*, 328-332.

Shertzer, B., & Stone, S. C. (1980). *Fundamentals of Counseling* (3rd ed.). Boston: Houghton Mifflin.

Siegel, B.S. (1986). *Love, medicine, and miracles.* New York: W.W. Norton.

Silverstein, S. (1964). *The giving tree.* NY: Harper & Row.

Simmons, R., Brown, L., Bush, D., & Blyth, D. (1978). Self-esteem and achievement of Black and White adolescents. *Social Problems, 26*, 86–96.

Singer, J.L. (1973). *The child's world of make-believe.* New York: Academic Press.

Singer, J.L. (1977). Imaganation and make-believe play in early childhood: Some educational implications. *Journal of mental imagery, 1*, 127–144.

Singer, J.L., & Singer, D.G. (1976). Imagination play and pretending in early childhood: Some experimental approaches. In A. Davids (Ed.), *Child personality and psychopathology*. New York: Wiley.
Slavin, R. E. (1978). Student teams and achievement divisions. *Journal of Research and Development in Education, 12*, 39–49.
Slavin, R. E. (1981). Cooperative learning and desegregation. *Journal of Educational Equity and Leadership, 1*, 145–149.
Slavin, R. E. (1991). *Educational psychology* (3rd ed.). Englewood Cliffs, NJ: Prentice Hall.
Smilansky, S. (1968). *The effects of socio-dramatic play on disadvantaged preschool children*. New York: Wiley.
Sonnenshein-Schneider, M., & Baird, K. L. (1980). Group counseling children of divorce in the elementary schools: Understanding process and technique. *Personnel and Guidance Journal, 59*, 88–91.
Srebalus, D.J., Marinelli, R.P., & Messing, J.K. (1982). *Career development: Concepts and procedures*. Belmont, CA: Wadsworth.
Staley, N.K., & Mangiesi, J.N. (1984). Using books to enhance career awareness. *Elementary School Guidance & Counseling, 18*, 200–208.
Steiner, C. (1977). *The original warm fuzzy tale: A fairytale*. Sacramento: Jalmar Press.
Stephan, W., & Rosenfield, D. (1979). Black self-rejection: Another look. *Journal of Educational Psychology, 71*, 708–716.
Stock, L. (1987). Native Americans: A brief profile. *Journal of Visual Impairment and Blindness, 81*, 152.
Stockton, R., & Hulse, D. (1983). The use of research teams to enhance competence in counseling research. *Counselor Education and Supervision, 22*, 303-310.
Straus, U. A., & Gelles, R. S. (1986). Societal change and change in family violence from 1975 to 1985 as revealed by two national surveys. *Journal of Marriage and Family Therapy, 48*, 465–479.
Strother, D. B. (1984). Latchkey children: The fastest growing special interest group in the schools. *Phi Delta Kappan, 66*, 290–293.
Sue, S. (1977). Community mental health services to minority groups: Some optimism, some pessimism. *American Psychologist, 32*, 616–624.
Sue, D. W. (1981). Counseling the culturally different: *Theory and practice*. New York: Wiley.
Sue, D. W., & Sue, D. (1977). Barriers to effective cross-cultural counseling. *Journal of Counseling Psychology, 24*, 420–429.
Sue, D. W., & Sue, D. (1990). *Counseling the culturally different: Theory and practice* (2nd ed.). New York: Wiley.
Super, D.E. (1955). Dimensions and measurement of vocational maturity. *Teachers college record, 57*, 151–163.
Super, D.E. (1963). *Career development: Self-concept theory*. New York: College Entrance Examination Board.
Super, D. E. (1975). *The psychology of careers*. New York: Harper & Row.
Super, D.E. (1984). Career and life development. In D.L. Brown & L. Brooks (Eds.), *Career choice and development* (pp. 192–234). San Francisco: Jossey-Bass.
Super, D.E., Crites, J.O., Hummel, R.C., Moser, H.P., Overstreet, P.L. & Warnath, C.F. (1957). *Vocational development: A framework for research*. New York: Teachers College Press.
Super, D.E., & Kidd, J.M. (1979). Vocational maturity in adulthood:Toward turning a model into a measure. *Journal of Vocational Behavior, 14*, 255–270.
Super, D.E., Kowalski, R.S., & Gotkin, E.H. (1967). *Floundering and trial after high school*. (Report No. 1393). New York: Teachers College, Columbia University.
Super, D.E., & Thompson, A.S. (1979). A six-scale, two factor measure of adolescent career or vocational maturity. *Vocational Guidance Quarterly, 27*, 6–15.
Tanner, J. M. (1978). *Foetus into man*. Cambridge, MA: Harvard University Press.

Tedder, S., Scherman, A., & Wantz, R. (1987). Effectiveness of a support group for children of divorce. *Elementary School Guidance and Counseling, 22,* 102-109.

Thomas, E.L., & Robinson, H.A.(1972). *Improving reading in every class: A source-book for teachers.* Boston: Allyn & Bacon.

Thomas, M. (1974). *Free to be you and me.* NY: Bantam Books.

Thomason, T. (1991). Counseling Native Americans: An introduction to non-Native-American Counselors. *Journal of counseling and Development, 69,* 321–327.

Thompson, C. L., Cole, D., Krammer, P. P., & Barker, R. (1984). Support groups for children of divorced parents. *Journal of Elementary School Guidance and Counseling, 19,* 88-94.

Thompson, C. L., & Rudolph, L. B. (1983). *Counseling children.* Monterey, CA: Brooks/Cole.

Tobias, T. (1976). *Moving day.* Westminister, MD: Knopf.

Tolbert, E. L. (1982). *An introduction to guidance: The professional counselor.* Boston, MA: Little, Brown and Company.

Tomlinson, P.R. (1991). A guidance lesson for elementary school classes: I'm curious about your spots. *Elementary School Guidance and Counseling, 25,* 233–235.

Toomin, M. (1982, June). *Biofeedback and imagery in the schools: Summary of several research projects in education.* Paper presented at the Brain/Mind Revolution Conference. Upland, CA.

Trimble, J. E. (1981). Value differentials and their importance in counseling American Indians. In P. Pedersen, J. Draguns, W. Conner & J. Trimble (Eds.), *Counseling across cultures* (pp. 203–226). Honolulu, HI: University Press of Hawaii.

Trotzer, J. P. (1980). Develop your own guidance group: A structural framework for planning a practice. *School Counselor, 27,* 341-349.

Tuckman, B. W., & Hinkle, J. S. (1986, May). Running kids 'r' fit. *The Runner,* p. 34.

Tyler, S. L. (1964). *Indian affairs: A study of the changes in policy of the United States toward Indians.* Provo, UT: Brigham Young University.

Udwin, O., & Shmukler, D. (1981). The influence of sociocultural, economic and home background factors on children's ability to engage in imaginitive play. *Developmental Psychology, 17,* 66-72.

Vacc, N. A., & Wittmer, J. P. (1980). *Let me be me: Special populations and the helping profession.* Muncie, IN: Accelerated Development Corporation.

Vanderkolk, C. J. (1985). *Introduction to group counseling and psychotherapy.* Columbus, OH: Charles E. Merrill.

Vaughn, F., & Walsh, R. (Eds.). (1986). *A gift of peace: Selections from a course in miracles.* Los Angeles, CA: Tarcher.

Vernon, A., & Hay, J. (1988). A preventive approach to child sexual abuse. *Elementary School Guidance and Counseling, 22,* 306-312.

Vinturella, L., & James, R. (1987). Sand play: A therapeutic medium with children. *Elementary School Guidance and Counseling, 21,* 229–238.

Viorst, J. (1988). *The tenth good thing about Barney.* NY: Macmillan/Atheneum.

Wadsworth, B. J. (1989). *Piaget's theory of cognitive and affective development* (4th ed.). New York: Longman.

Waldman, E. (1983, December). Labor force statistics from a family perspective. *Monthly Labor Review,* pp. 16–19.

Wallace, W. A. (1986). *Theories of counseling and psychotherapy: A basic issues approach.* Newton, MA: Allyn & Bacon.

Walton, F. X., & Powers, R. L. (1978). *Winning children over: A manual for teachers, counselors, principals and parents.* Chicago, IL: Practical Psychology Associates.

Watkins, C. E., Jr. (1983). Rational self-analysis for children. *Elementary School Guidance and Counseling, 17,* 304–307.

Watson, W. (1978). *Moving.* New York: Crowell.

Watson, D. L., & Tharp, R. G. (1981). *Self-directed behavior: Self modification for personal adjustment* (3rd ed.). Monteray, CA: Brooks/Cole.

Wechsler, D. (1958). *The measurement and appraisal of adult intelligence* (4th ed.). Baltimore: Williams and Wilkins.

Weis L. (1985). *Between two worlds: Black students in an urban community college.* New York: Routledge & Kegan Paul.

Whitson, S.C. (1989). Using family systems theory in career counseling: A group for parents. *The School Counselor, 36,* 343–347.

Wickers, F. (1988). The misbehavior reaction checklist. *Elementary School Guidance and Counseling, 23,* 70–73.

Wiggins, J. D. (1987). Self-esteem, earned grades, and television viewing habits of students. *School Counselor, 35,* 128-133.

Wilgus, W., & Shelley, V. (1988). The role of the elementary school counselor: Teacher perceptions, expectations and actual functions. *School Counselor, 35,* 259-266.

Wilhelm, C.D., & Case, M. (1975). Telling it is improving school records. *School Counselor, 23,* 84–90.

Williams, J. (1973). *Pentronella.* New York: Parents Magazine Press.

Williams, W. C., & Lair, G. S (1991). Using a person-centered approach with children who have a disability. *Elementary School Guidance and Counseling, 25,* 194–203.

Wilson, N. S. (1986). Counselor interventions with low-achievers and underachieving elementary, middle, and high school students. A review of the literature. *Journal of Counseling and Development, 64,* 628-634.

Wisconsin Department of Public Instruction (1986). *School counseling programs: A resource and planning guide.* Madison, WI: Author.

Wolde, G. (1972). *Tommy goes to the doctor.* Boston, MA: Houghton Mifflin.

Woolfolk, A. E. (1990). *Educational psychology* (4th ed.). Englewood Cliffs, NJ: Prentice-Hall.

Worchel, S., & Cooper, J. (1983). *Understanding Social Psychology (3rd ed.).* Homewood, IL: Dorsey Press.

Wulff, K. R. (1987). International students in the classroom. *How To Do It Series,* 6(1), 415–421. Washington, DC: National Council for the Social Studies.

Yalom, I. D. (1985). *The theory and practice of group psychotherapy* (3rd ed.). New York: Basic Books.

Youngman, G., & Sadongei, M. (1974). Counseling the American Indian child. *Elementary School Guidance and Counseling, 9,* 273–277.

Zaichkowsky, L. B., Zaichkowsky, L. D., & Yeager, J. (1986). Biofeedback-assisted relaxation training in the elementary classroom. *Elementary School Guidance and Counseling, 20,* 261-267.

Zastrow, C., & Kirst-Ashman, K. (1987). *Understanding human behavior and the social environment.* Chicago: Nelson

Zill, N. (1983). *American children: Happy, healthy and insecure.* New York: Doubleday-Anchor.

Name Index

Subject Index